naked money

also by Charles Wheelan

naked money

A Revealing Look at Our Financial System

CHARLES WHEELAN

W. W. Norton & Company
Independent Publishers Since 1923
New York | London

For information about permission to reproduce selections from this book,
write to Permissions, W. W. Norton & Company, Inc., 500 Fifth Avenue,
New York, NY 10110

For information about special discounts for bulk purchases, please contact
W. W. Norton Special Sales at specialsales@wwnorton.com or 800-233-4830

Manufacturing by LSC Communications, Harrisonburg, VA
Production manager: Anna Oler

The Library of Congress has cataloged the hardcover edition as follows:

Names: Wheelan, Charles J., author.
Title: Naked money : a revealing look at what it is and why it matters /
Charles Wheelan.
Description: First edition. | New York : W. W. Norton & Company, [2016] |
    Includes bibliographical references and index.
Identifiers: LCCN 2016001662 | ISBN 9780393069020 (hardcover)
Subjects: LCSH: Money—History. | Finance—History. | Banks and banking—History.
Classification: LCC HG256 .W44 2016 | DDC 332.4—dc23
LC record available at http://lccn.loc.gov/2016001662

ISBN 978-0-393-35373-0 pbk.

W. W. Norton & Company, Inc.
500 Fifth Avenue, New York, N.Y. 10110
www.wwnorton.com

W. W. Norton & Company Ltd.
15 Carlisle Street, London W1D 3BS

1 2 3 4 5 6 7 8 9 0

For CJ

Contents

PART II:
WHY IT MATTERS

Acknowledgments

This was a hard book to write. One does not just sit down at the computer and begin typing interesting thoughts about monetary policy. The substance is hard. So is the task of making it accessible and interesting. I had help at every stage, beginning with the crucial task of background research. Jack Pinto was a terrific research assistant, digging up many of the amusing anecdotes in the book. When Jack graduated, Zachary Hardwick stepped into his huge shoes. Jeffrey Lang was there at the end of the project, when I needed essential details, often on ridiculously short notice.

My Dartmouth colleagues helped in big ways and small. Jim Feyrer was a steady sounding board on all kinds of macroeconomic questions. Wandering into his office to ask random questions is always enjoyable and usually helpful. I admire his diverse intellectual interests.

David "Danny" Blanchflower was both a great resource for the book and a fun golf companion—often at the same time. On several occasions I took a digital recorder in the golf cart so I could record his stories. I am indebted to Doug Irwin, both for his intriguing academic work on the gold standard and for his helpful feedback on the manuscript.

Andrew Samwick has created a wonderful intellectual home for me at Dartmouth's Rockefeller Center. It is a privilege to work every day with such talented, altruistic faculty, staff, and students. Most people don't get up each morning thinking about how they can make undergraduate education better, but at "Rocky" they really do.

Two former Federal Reserve chairmen took time out of their busy lives to speak to me about monetary policy: Paul Volcker and Ben Bernanke. I admire both of their commitments to public service. Volcker—

a.k.a. the superhero "Inflation Fighter Man" in Chapter 5—had the temerity to face down the inflation that plagued the U.S. throughout the 1970s. Bernanke steered the world through the worst financial crisis since the Great Depression. Each of them took a public political beating for their efforts.

The dynamic duo at W. W. Norton, Jeff Shreve and Drake McFeely, do a remarkable job of applying all the tools necessary to turn good ideas into great books. Tina Bennett helps to launch those projects in the first place. I appreciate her longstanding and steadfast advocacy.

Last, but not least, Leah, Katrina, Sophia, and CJ provide just the right balance of chaos, adventure, and support. Thank you for the joy that you bring to our home. Katrina, ever skeptical of the life of a college professor, is fond of asking, "What work do you really do?" At least now I can say, "I wrote this book."

naked money

Introduction

Take a $20 bill out of your wallet and look at it closely. It's nice paper—a high-fiber content so it can go through the wash and come out okay—but still just paper. The engraving is nice, but nothing that approaches fine art. Perhaps most important, there is nothing on that bill promising you something in return—no gold, no silver, nothing. It is a piece of paper with no intrinsic value. If you took it to the Federal Reserve, the institution responsible for issuing American currency (which is then printed by the Treasury), the officials there would offer you nothing. Some of the Federal Reserve Banks, such as Chicago, have a nice little museum, but if you wave your $20 (or even a $100) around in the lobby and demand something tangible in return, you will get a strange look and maybe an escort out of the building.

So what is it worth? Not nothing. *It's worth about $20.* That's not a silly statement, or at least not as silly as it seems. If you take a $20 to a sandwich shop, you'll get a nice lunch for two. At a grocery store, you'll get three pounds of chicken breast or a good bottle of pinot noir. Nearly everyone in the United States, and many people elsewhere in the world, have a very refined sense of what that piece of paper is worth. They would be only too happy to pick up your $20 should it fall out of your pocket—which is not something you can say about every small piece of paper blowing down the street.

This is a book about money—about how those pieces of paper in your pocket have acquired such value, and how a bizarre convention, swapping seemingly useless pieces of paper for real goods, is so fundamental to a modern economy. Of course, while we're at it, we'll look at the even more bizarre notion that you can write a check, wave a phone, or hand someone a rectangular piece of plastic and walk away with new furniture, office supplies, or even a car.

In fact, you can use someone else's money to do all of that. Money is not just about the bills in your wallet. Our whole financial system is built around a simple but powerful idea: credit. Banks, and the many institutions that function like banks, are intermediaries that match lenders and borrowers (taking a fee, of course, for the service). In that lending process, something remarkable happens: financial institutions create credit, which expands the supply of money. Think about this simple example:

1. I have $10,000. You have nothing.
2. I deposit my $10,000 in a bank, and that bank loans you $9,000.
3. I still own my $10,000 while it is deposited in the bank (and can write checks on it), and you now have $9,000.
4. The money supply—money that can be spent right now on goods and services—has gone from $10,000 to $19,000.

Wow. That is the power of credit. Of course, the fact that you are spending money that technically still belongs to me is a source of both economic strength and instability. The good news: credit is what allows students to attend college, families to buy homes, and entrepreneurs to launch new businesses. The banking sector makes it possible for us to make productive use of other people's capital.

The bad news: when credit goes wrong (as in 2008), the results can be devastating for the whole economy. We have a problem when I suddenly want my money and you are not in a position to pay it back, perhaps because you have used it to buy a house or a car or a restaurant.

The history of finance is also a history of financial panics. If lenders want their money back, and borrowers cannot readily produce it, the institution brokering the deal can fail. And when financial institutions are at risk of failing, more lenders rush to get their money—virtually ensuring that failure. We learned in 2008 that some very fancy-sounding components of the financial sector (the repurchase market, the commercial paper market, et cetera) are vulnerable to runs when people get nervous, just like banks were during the Great Depression.

When the system works well, money and credit lubricate it and empower human ingenuity. When the system breaks down, as it did in 2008, the financial edifice implodes at huge human cost. This is a book about that, too.

A central bank, whether it is the U.S. Federal Reserve or the Bank of England or the European Central Bank, is the institution with primary responsibility for managing all this. Central banks are charged with maintaining the value of the currency and protecting the stability of the financial system. (In the United States, the Federal Reserve has the added mandate of using its powers to promote full employment.) These institutions are vested with remarkable powers, including the exclusive right to create new money.

Yes, the U.S. Federal Reserve can just make new money. And yes, that is a power that requires enormous discretion. Since 2008, central bankers have taken on oversized importance. More Americans can probably name the recent Fed chairs (Yellen, Bernanke, Greenspan, and Volcker) than the most recent four chief justices of the Supreme Court (Roberts, Rehnquist, Burger, and Warren).

Ever since the financial crisis, there has been a political battle in the United States over whether the Federal Reserve is doing too little to help the economy recover, or too much. Low interest rates help to put more Americans back to work and raise the wages of others. On the other hand, low interest rates punish savers and can, if they are too low for too long, cause inflation. During the 2012 presidential election, Republican candidate Rick Perry described Fed Chair Ben Bernanke's aggressive response to the financial crisis as treasonous. (For the record, this was an absurd and inappropriate statement, but it certainly gives one a sense of the politics.)

There is nothing new about that, by the way. Perhaps you remember from history class William Jennings Bryan and his famous 1896 "Cross of Gold" speech at the Democratic National Convention. The Federal

Reserve had not yet been created at that point, but Bryan argued that high interest rates were punishing indebted American farmers and the solution was more money (specifically, money backed by silver in addition to gold).

To connect the dots, Rick Perry wanted less new money. William Jennings Bryan wanted more. I don't think they would have liked each other. To the larger point, this is a book that explains what the Fed does, how it does it, and why it matters.

America is not alone in any of this. Other countries also have small pieces of paper you can use to buy things. The money in those places causes political battles, too. Across the Atlantic, the Germans and the Greeks have been bickering for years like a seventy-year-old couple trapped in a loveless marriage. These two countries, along with seventeen others in the European Union (and a handful outside it), have adopted a common currency, the euro. The single currency was launched nearly two decades ago with high expectations for bringing the nations of the continent together, politically and economically. The luster has been fading from that grand experiment. Under the euro, some of the least productive economies on the continent—Greece, but also Italy, Spain, and Portugal—have struggled. Specifically, they have lost some of the most important macroeconomic tools that come with having one's own national currency rather than sharing one with an economic powerhouse like Germany (e.g., setting interest rates and managing the value of the currency). The future of the euro is still in question.

Yes, this is a book about all of that, too.

Across the Pacific, the Chinese government has been managing its currency, the yuan, the same way it manages everything else in the economy: with a lot of government oversight. For more than a decade many observers, ranging from members of Congress to officials at the International Monetary Fund, have accused the Chinese government of deliberately undervaluing the yuan. The effect of this alleged nefarious activity is to make Chinese goods cheaper in the United States and elsewhere, thereby bolstering Chinese exports and keeping workers employed. When Beijing depreciated the yuan by 2 percent in the summer of 2015 in response to a plunge in the Chinese stock market,

U.S. politicians from both political parties blasted the move as an unfair trade practice and "further proof China cannot be trusted on currency policy."[1]

There are a couple of strange things about this. First, lawmakers are condemning China for selling goods to us more cheaply than they should—not a common complaint in capitalist countries. And second, the foregoing presents a conundrum:

When countries share a currency (as with the euro), the result has been currency-related friction.

And when countries have their own currencies (such as the dollar and the yuan), the result has been currency-related friction.

This is a book about currencies, exchange rates, and the frictions that arise when different countries use different pieces of paper as money— and the separate set of challenges that arise when countries try to share money.

But it gets weirder. In Japan, Prime Minister Shinzo Abe was elected, and then reelected, on a promise to create inflation. Yes, you read that correctly. After more than twenty years of falling prices (deflation) and economic malaise, Japan's leader has vowed to end deflation as one tool toward restoring the economy to health. For any reader who lived through America's inflation in the 1970s, or has read about that stretch, it must be ironic that a responsible government has promised more inflation (and has been judged harshly for failing to deliver!). This is a book about inflation, deflation, and whatever the heck has been happening in Japan for two decades.

Back in the United States, when members of Congress are not criticizing China for selling us things too cheaply, they have been crafting new regulations for banks and other financial institutions in response to the 2008 financial crisis. The public is still angry about bailouts, the catch-all term that has come to characterize the response to the crisis. The government made money on many of its interventions, but that is a detail lost on voters who are rightfully angry about spending tax money to fix the mistakes of reckless lenders and borrowers. The lingering question is whether regulators have made the financial system safer or merely laid the groundwork for a different kind of financial panic next time around. Plenty of smart people are worried about the latter.

This is a book about financial crises, including those of 1929 and 2008. (Spoiler alert: I will argue that we did a lot of things right this time that prevented another Great Depression.)

All the while, one of the most intriguing monetary developments has been unfolding on the Internet, with very little oversight from Congress or any other government: the creation of "cryptocurrencies" like bitcoin. Just when you thought nothing could get stranger than paper money—pieces of paper with no intrinsic value issued by governments—along comes money *without even the paper or the government*! Bitcoins are "mined" by computer users who solve complex algorithms and are awarded bitcoins for doing so. Remarkably, those bitcoins can be used to buy real goods and services. Stranger still, the bitcoin computer program was written by a mysterious man (or woman, or group of programmers working under a pseudonym) who has never stepped forward to take credit for his creation. This book will explain bitcoin, to the extent it makes any sense at all.

What do the phenomena I have described have in common? Money. Or more broadly: money, banking, and central banking—three interlinked institutions at the core of the modern economy. Money is a tool that we use to conduct transactions: bags of salt in Roman times; pouches of mackerel in prison; bitcoins when buying illegal drugs or weapons on the Internet; and, of course, dollars, euros, yen, and other government currencies for just about everything else.

To be clear, this is a book about *money*, not *wealth*. They are not the same. Warren Buffett has a lot more wealth than I do; he may or may not have more money. As the book will discuss, money typically refers to assets that can be used immediately to make purchases. Cash is money. So are deposits held in checking accounts or other accounts with check-writing privileges because you can use them to buy things *now*. On the other hand, a fancy car and a big house are not considered "money"; both have great value and are therefore sources of wealth, but neither is frequently used to conduct commerce.

Spanish gold coins held in your safety deposit box might have been money in a different era, but they would not currently be defined as such. Even stocks and bonds are not money. They are assets that one sells for money, which can then be used to buy things. Thus, all money is wealth, but not all wealth is money. This is how I can safely assert that Warren Buffett may not have more money than I do. Sure, he has billions in stocks and bonds, plus a plane and maybe some hotels. But does he keep more money in his wallet and checking account than I do? Maybe, maybe not.

In the same vein, now is a good time to make an important distinction between "currency" and "money." Currency technically comprises the paper notes and coins that circulate—the dollars in your wallet, the coins on your dresser, and so on. Money is a broader concept that includes currency but also other assets that can be used to make purchases or quickly converted to currency, such as checking account deposits. All currency is money, but not all money is currency.

That said, a nation's currency, such as the Japanese yen or the Chinese yuan, typically refers to *all its money*, not just the bills and coins. The language in this regard has evolved in a sloppy way, but context usually makes it clearer.

Finally, "cash" is usually synonymous with currency—but not always. When we say that drug dealers conduct transactions in cash, we really do mean wads of currency. But when a newspaper reports that investors have sold stocks and are holding cash, the story is not suggesting that investors have suitcases full of $100 bills. Instead, the point is that they are holding lots of "liquid" assets, such as deposits in a money market account. Liquidity, a term that will come up throughout the book, is a measure of how quickly an asset can be turned into cash at a predictable price. Treasury bonds are highly liquid; Vincent van Gogh paintings are not.

The nomenclature should not get in the way of the big picture. Money and banking (broadly construed) make a modern economy work. They underlie every important transaction we make. In turn, central banks make money and banking work.

When all of this is functioning well, nobody takes particular notice.

Most of us don't spend much time inspecting the twenties in our wallets. They're just pieces of paper with Andrew Jackson on the front—but pieces of paper that empower a modern economy in an almost miraculous way. When the system breaks down—when "money" goes bad—the results can be disastrous.

Obviously everyone prefers the former to the latter. This is a book about why monetary policy is so hard, and why getting it right matters so much.

what it is

CHAPTER 1

What Is Money?

What is the nature of those little disks or documents, which in themselves seem to serve no useful purpose, and which nevertheless, in contradiction to the rest of experience, pass from one hand to another in exchange for the most useful commodities, nay, for which every one is so eagerly bent on surrendering his wares.

—Carl Menger, founder of the Austrian School of economics, 1892[1]

I n 2009, North Korea did something unusual, even by North Korean standards. The nation issued a new currency that lopped two zeroes off all the bills. Thus one won of the new currency was declared equivalent to 100 won of the old currency.[2] This is not a particularly new trick; assorted countries in the past have issued new currencies with fewer zeroes as a tool for fighting inflation. In 1994, Brazil created an entirely new currency, the real, to replace the inflation-battered cruzeiro real. The government announced that each shiny new real would be worth 2750 cruzeiro reais. (Reais is the plural of real.)

None of this is inherently good or bad for consumers, as long as the old currency can be freely swapped for the new currency. Imagine if the United States had no dollar bill but instead priced everything in pennies. One day the government announced that pennies would no longer be accepted as legal tender. Instead, one hundred pennies could be swapped for a new currency, the dollar, after which all prices would be quoted in dollars. A product that used to cost two hundred would now cost two. In terms of purchasing power, nothing would change. People who had lots of pennies before would now have lots of dollars. Bank accounts would be even easier to convert; every account would just lose two digits. Prices would look lower (hence the tool for fighting inflation), but in terms of accumulated wealth, rich people would still be rich and poor people would still be poor, only in dollars rather than pennies.

Anyone over the age of six recognizes that five dollars is no different than five hundred pennies. (And even the six-year-olds can only be fooled a few times.) We would all just have to carry fewer coins in our pockets. Stores would no longer accept pennies, but if you happened to discover three hundred of them under the cushions of your couch, you could always take them to a bank and swap them for dollars. Brazilians had nearly a year to convert their old cruzeiro reais for the new reais. Some European nations, such as Germany, have said that they will forever exchange old coins and notes (the deutsche mark) for euros, even though the country gave up the deutsche mark for the euro more than a decade and a half ago.

But North Korea is not like other countries. When North Korea engineered its currency reform, the government announced that only a limited amount of the old currency could be swapped for the new currency—about $690 at the official exchange rate (and only $35 at the black market rate).* Anyone holding large amounts of old currency would see much of their accumulated wealth destroyed. That was exactly the point. The North Korean government had become increasingly intolerant of black market activities outside of the country's official ration-based

---

* The official government exchange rate does not always reflect the market value of a currency, particularly in a place like North Korea. Because the North Korean won is essentially worthless outside the country, the rest of the world is not exactly clamoring to accumulate them. As a result, anyone looking to swap won for a more useful international currency, such as dollars or Chinese yuan, is going to find that the won is worth much less than the government says it is. For example, the official exchange rate between the dollar and the won near the end of 2013 was 96 won to the dollar. The black market rate—the rate at which traders will voluntarily give up dollars for won—was 8,000 won to the dollar.

James Pearson, "Black Market Gets Some Respect in North Korea," *New York Times*, November 4, 2013.

economy. Black market traders were sitting on large stashes of cash. With the stroke of a government pen (or whatever Korea's Supreme Leader does to promulgate legislation), the government confiscated most of that illicitly accumulated wealth.

Of course, many ordinary North Koreans hoping to avoid starvation during the winter and spring had also accumulated stocks of cash. After the announcement of the currency reform, the sparse news that leaked out of North Korea made reference to "chaos in markets and rail stations" as savers rushed home to swap old money for new.[3] North Koreans had only twenty-four hours to convert their allotted quota of old currency to new currency. A defector told Barbara Demick, a writer for *The New Yorker*, "In one day, all your money was lost. People were taken to the hospital in shock."[4]

The North Korean government had taken money with value and rendered it worthless. This is a curious power.

It is even more curious when juxtaposed against what was happening in the United States at exactly the same time. In response to the 2008 financial crisis, the Federal Reserve was aggressively "injecting liquidity" into the financial system. The concept of liquidity will be explored in greater depth later in the book. For now, the basic point is that the Federal Reserve was doing everything in its power to lower interest rates so that struggling banks, businesses, and consumers would have easier access to credit after the real estate bust. Here is the part that is almost North Korean in its weirdness: the Federal Reserve accomplished its task by creating new money. From nowhere. There is a windowless room at the Federal Reserve Bank of New York where traders literally created new electronic money and used it to buy billions of dollars of financial assets. Between January 2008 and January 2014, the Fed injected roughly $3 trillion of new money into the American economy.[5]

One minute the money did not exist; the next minute a trader acting at the behest of the Fed bought bonds belonging to assorted private financial institutions and paid for those securities by transferring electronic funds to the accounts of the selling firms. New money. Money that did not exist just seconds earlier. *Click.* That is the sound of a guy sitting at his computer in the New York Fed creating a billion dollars and using it to buy assets from Citibank. *Click, click.* That's $2 billion more.

While North Korea's Supreme Leader was taking money with value and rendering it useless, the Fed was doing the opposite: creating money out of nothing. Neither the North Korean won nor the United States dollar has any intrinsic value. One cannot take either currency to the government that issued it and demand something tangible in return, such as gold or rice or cooking oil (although at least in the United States, you would not be sent to a labor camp for asking). North Korea could wipe out money, and the United States could create it, because money in both countries is just paper, or increasingly bits and bytes on a computer screen.

And that brings us to the third wacky thing going on at roughly the same time that North Korea was destroying money and the United States was creating it: American prisoners were conducting many of their transactions using pouches of mackerel. Yes, the oily fish.

Prison inmates in the United States are not allowed to possess cash. Instead, they typically have accounts at a commissary where small items can be purchased. With no cash circulating, the goods sold in the commissary can be used as currency: books of stamps, PowerBars, and so on. As has been the case throughout history, this kind of commerce becomes easier when there is informal agreement on a single unit of account, such as cigarettes in prisoner-of-war camps during World War II. The item that has emerged as the gold standard for trade in American prisons since the federal smoking ban in 2004 is the pouch of mackerel, or "the mack."[6] (It comes in a pouch rather than a can so that prisoners will not sharpen the container and use it to stab one another.) The mackerel pouches are portable and storable. Curiously, mackerel has little appeal outside of prison, even at discount retailers. But behind bars, mackerel outsells tuna, crab, chicken, and oysters—in part because a pouch of mackerel happens to sell for roughly a dollar in the canteen, so it's relatively easy to think in terms of dollars while using macks. Unlike the dollar or the won, the mackerel does have some intrinsic value. You can always eat it.

In fact, if the North Korean or American economies ran on mackerel, neither the Supreme Leader nor the Federal Reserve could have done what they did. The Supreme Leader cannot go on television and declare that all mackerel is now worthless. It's still mackerel. You might get arrested if you try to trade it for a winter coat, but you can always keep it in the basement and eat it for dinner during the periodic famines. One cannot pronounce something worthless that has worth. True, the government could try to confiscate all the mackerel, but that's a different and much more difficult task.

Similarly, the U.S. Federal Reserve cannot instantaneously generate millions of pouches of mackerel where none previously existed. No one in a windowless room at the Fed can push a button and have pouches of mackerel show up at Citibank. *Click, click, click.* That is the sound of no mackerel being created.

How did money get so weird? The first and most important insight is that money is not synonymous with wealth. A house is wealth. You can live in it or rent it out. A bag of rice is also wealth. You can trade it, eat it, plant it, or store it to do any of those things later. However, a bag of rice—unlike a house—is a relatively uniform commodity, which gives it potential value as a medium of exchange. You might accept a bag of rice as payment from someone even if you don't particularly like rice, just as inmates who don't like oily fish are willing to settle up with pouches of mackerel. Why? Because lots of other people like rice (or mackerel). Rice has value to me in part because rice has value to other people. This is a key feature of all commodities that have served as mediums of exchange across cultures and throughout history: salt, gold, cigarettes, dolphin teeth, wampum, animal pelts.

Now let's expand the example slightly and say that you have ten fifty-pound bags of rice in your basement. You would prefer not to carry them around while conducting commerce. So you create ten elegant paper certificates, each with your signature and a pledge to redeem said paper certificate for one fifty-pound bag of rice. You give one certificate to the golf pro who gives you a putting lesson. You explain to him that he, or anyone else bearing the certificate, can come and claim a bag of rice from the basement anytime. You have now created paper money, albeit paper money backed by a commodity (bags of rice).

And when the golf pro uses the rice certificate to pay the woman who walks his dog, you've created a paper currency that circulates. Anyone holding a certificate who decides they need rice will redeem it. Otherwise, the bags of rice may sit in your basement for quite some time as people use the paper certificates for commerce. Here is the irony: as long as the people using the rice certificates are confident they can redeem them at any time, most will feel no urgency to do so. But it's also true that if there is even a whiff of doubt about the value of those rice certificates—whether it is justified or not—you are going to have a mob of certificate-wielding people banging on your door and demanding rice. This turns out to be a potentially destabilizing feature not just of commodity-based money but of the broader financial system. Even the most complex financial systems can thrive or fail depending on whether people believe they will thrive or fail.

Second, modern money depends on confidence. Consider the curious case of Indian rupees. According to the Reserve Bank of India, any soiled or torn rupee note is legal tender as long as it has two intact serial numbers (as is policy for U.S. currency).* If you present a crumpled, dirty, or torn note at an Indian bank, the law states that the disfigured bill must be replaced with a nice crisp one. Yet on the streets of Mumbai, you will find it very difficult to get anyone to accept a torn or overly worn rupee note, even if the serial numbers are clearly visible and intact. Not shopkeepers, not taxi drivers, not street vendors—and therefore no one who expects to do business with shopkeepers, taxi drivers, or street vendors. No one wants to be the sucker who has to schlep the soiled bill to a bank for exchange. *Of course, if people just accepted the soiled notes, no one would have to schlep them to the bank.* In the United States, I've accepted torn dollar bills, crumpled dollar bills, dollar bills with pictures and phone numbers on them, bills taped together, and even a dollar bill with George Washington's face cut out. If it's got two serial numbers when

---

* Any money declared legal tender by a government must be accepted within that country for all public and private debts. The $20 in your wallet may have no intrinsic worth, but it is legal tender in the United States.

the guy at Starbucks hands it to me, I'll take it. And so will everyone else (which is why I'll take it).

Not in India. No one will accept torn rupees because no one will accept torn rupees. Of course, when I travel to India, I refuse to accept rupees in bad condition—thereby perpetuating the whole phenomenon.

In Somalia in the early 2000s, curiously, the opposite was happening: money with no legal value was thriving. The currency of choice for small transactions was the Somali shilling, which was not legal tender. (Dollars were typically used for large transactions.) Due to a long-running civil war, the Central Bank of Somalia had shut down. A transitional Federal Government was supposedly responsible for monetary policy, but that entity's authority barely extended past the capital of Mogadishu. From a legal standpoint at the time, the Somali shilling had roughly the same legitimacy as Monopoly money. The notes in circulation had been issued two decades earlier by a government that no longer existed. As the *Economist* noted, "Use of paper currency is normally taken to be an expression of faith in the government that issues it."[7] In the Somali case for several decades,* there was effectively no government. Yet the currency—just pieces of paper—marched steadily on. Why?

The short answer is that people accepted Somali shillings because people accepted Somali shillings. If you poke a little harder, there were several reasons for this. First, the shillings were useful as a medium of exchange for small transactions. Just as prison inmates are accustomed to pricing and conducting small transactions in macks, the Somalis were used to buying tea and bread with shillings. Everyone had a pretty good idea how many shillings a small bar of soap ought to cost. Second, Somalia has a strong clan and kinship system. In the absence of a government, this system functioned as the strong social glue that undergirded the faith in the currency. There was an expectation among members of these networks that others in the network would accept shillings. As the *Economist* explained at the time, "Paper currencies always need tacit con-

---

* The transitional government ended in 2012 and the Central Bank of Somalia was reopened.

sent from their users that they will exchange bills for actual stuff. But in Somalia this pact is rather stronger: an individual who flouts the system risks jeopardising trust in both himself and his clan."[8]

Finally, the total absence of a functioning government was a good thing for the value of paper money in this case. The supply of shillings was more or less fixed because there was no government to print more of them. In contrast, quasi-functioning governments often recklessly print currency as they struggle to stay in power. (Take the Belarussian ruble, which was introduced in the 1990s and became known as the bunny, partly because of the hare engraved on the note but also for the currency's remarkable ability to propagate.) The only growth in the supply of Somali shillings during the civil war came from counterfeiters, and even the number of high-quality fakes was limited because of the specialized talent, equipment, and materials needed to make them. For this reason, businesses and even Somali banks sometimes accepted high-quality counterfeit bills, which created a certain mind-bending logic, as explained in one contemporaneous news account: "An imitation of a thing which is already of notional value turns out to be worth something."[9] It's like a bank willing to accept counterfeit Monopoly money—not just fake money, but fake fake money.

But what is fake in this context anyway? The torn Indian rupees are real money, yet you can't use them to buy a cup of tea. The Somali shillings—and certainly the counterfeit Somali shillings—were not real money, in the absence of a government to declare them legal tender, except that you *could* use them to buy a cup of tea. Here, the simple becomes the profound: If you can swap something easily and predictably for goods and services, it's money. If you can't, it's not. There is even a continuum in between. Moneychangers across Africa offer better rates for new American bills than for older ones. A $100 bill signed by a current Treasury secretary gets a better rate than a $100 signed by John Snow (Bush administration) or Robert Rubin (Clinton administration). Clean, crisp bills get a better rate than old, dirty bills. And a single $100 bill is more valuable than five $20s.[10]

None of this makes sense to people who use dollars in the United States, but there is logic to the differential values in Africa. The *Wall*

Street Journal explains, "Some moneychangers and banks worry that big U.S. notes are counterfeit. Some can't be bothered to deal with small bills. Some don't want to take the risk that they won't be able to pass old or damaged bills onto the next person. And some just don't like the looks of them."[11] As always with money, how people behave affects how people behave. The employees of an international cruise ship with multiple ports of call in Africa began to complain to their employers that they were being paid with too many old bills—too many Robert Rubin $100s and not enough Henry Paulsons (Treasury secretary at the time of their compensation revolt).

Let's back up for a moment. All money—from dollars to pouches of mackerel—should ideally serve three purposes. First, money serves as a *unit of account*. People think in terms of a particular monetary unit when placing a value on things. Suppose you interview for an entry-level job and the firm tells you that the starting salary is six cattle and eleven crates of oranges a month. Is that a good salary? At first glance, you would have no idea. To figure it out, you would convert cattle and oranges into dollars, at which point the salary would have some meaning. The unit of account—whether it is dollars, yen, or dolphin teeth—is like a universal translator. No one has to figure out how many carrots a wool sweater ought to cost, or whether a Toyota Corolla with a sticker price of twenty-seven flat-screen TVs is a better value than a Honda Civic that costs three thousand introductory economics textbooks. We convert everything to dollars and then compare. Even as physical money disappears, we will always need some unit of account for pricing transactions. I can swipe a card at Starbucks instead of paying with cash, but I still think in terms of dollars and cents when the card gets debited for a large coffee.

Second, money is a *store of value*. It gives us a way of accepting payment for something now and using that purchasing power later. The prison barber might not have anything he particularly wants at the moment, so when he gives haircuts, he can just stack the macks in his cell. Anyone who accepts dollars as payment can be reasonably certain that they will hold their value in the near future. The same would be true of bags of rice or Forever stamps (which can be used to mail one standard-size letter anywhere in the United States at any point in the future, provided the U.S. Postal Service still exists). Throughout history, commodities that have served as money have typically been nonperishable items like salt, tobacco, and animal pelts, rather than apples, flowers, or fresh fish—for obvious reasons. A prison barber who stacked fresh mackerel in his shop would quickly lose most of his wealth (and probably most of his customers, too).

Of course, this is exactly what made North Korea's monetary machinations so insidious. By limiting the quantity of old won that could be converted to new won, the government wiped out something that citizens assumed would be a store of wealth for the future. The stacks of won hidden in the back of the closet represented future claims on food, clothes, electronics, and other things of value. Once the Great Leader made his proclamation, those stacks of won were reduced to scrap paper, best suited for starting fires or taking to the outhouse.* Something similar happened in American prisons in 2004. Up to that point, cigarettes had been the currency of choice behind bars, not mackerel. Once jails and prisons went smoke-free, however, anyone sitting on a large cache of cigarettes probably felt like a black market trader in North Korea: out of luck.

---

* The outhouse reference is not a glib throwaway. At the peak of Zimbabwe's hyperinflation in the 1990s, the Zimbabwe 1,000 dollar note had less value than a single piece of toilet paper, prompting businesses in neighboring South Africa to post signs warning customers not to throw Zim dollars down the toilet.
Photo by Eugene Baron.

Finally, money is used as a *medium of exchange*, meaning that it can be used to conduct transactions with relative ease. Paper currencies obviously work well in this respect. A stack of $100 bills will fit neatly in your wallet and can be swapped for just about anything you might desire, legal or illegal, in the United States and often beyond. Gold, silver, and other precious metals have been used as mediums of exchange across many different cultures. Prepaid mobile phone minutes are used as money across Africa. Mobile airtime can be transferred to other phones, swapped for cash, or used in shops.[12] The mobile minutes have intrinsic value. The $100s in your purse or wallet do not. The important point is that money need not have intrinsic value in order to be valuable; it need only facilitate exchange.

Modern economies thrive because we can specialize in the production of certain goods or services and then trade with others who specialize in producing different goods and services. Money—in whatever form it might take—makes that easier. The *Economist* encapsulated this fundamental principle: "Were an extraterrestrial to be shown a room full of gold ingots, a stack of twenty dollar bills or a row of numbers on a computer screen, he might be puzzled as to their function. Our reverence for these objects might seem as bizarre to him as the behavior of the male bowerbird (which decorates its nest with shiny objects to attract a mate) seems to us."[13] Money is a means to an end; it facilitates specialization and trade, which make us more productive and therefore richer.

Once we appreciate the basic role of money, then it's not hard to understand the kinds of money that have evolved. Money tends to be portable, meaning that you can carry it around while conducting commerce. Bags of rice do poorly on the portability front, as twenty dollars of rice could easily weight ten pounds or more. It turns out that the rice in the basement example is not as fanciful as it may have seemed a few pages back; issuing paper certificates against a commodity solves the portability problem. In 2010, after Haiti was recovering from the horrible earthquake, the United Nations was working to distribute food aid to the starving population. The distribution system was dangerous and chaotic, in part because workers tossing bags of food from the backs of trucks invited mayhem. Instead, the UN went to a system of coupons—a variation of the rice certificate example. Each coupon could be redeemed for a fifty-five-pound bag of rice. Consumers could store the coupons more safely than the rice; aid agencies could distribute the coupons broadly while storing rice at a smaller number of supervised distribution points. The coupons also became a currency that could be traded for other scarce items.[14]

Money needs to be durable. You'd hate to have your retirement savings die, melt, rot, rust, get eaten by rats, or otherwise disappear. Money also works best when it is divisible, so that one can easily make change or conduct transactions of different sizes. The $100s are nice for commerce; the $1s are handy, too. Gold turns out to be too valuable for many small transactions; at present prices, a pack of gum would cost about one twentieth of a gram of gold, which is smaller than a grain of sand. Societies often come up with clever fixes for a lack of small change. Zimbabwe eventually abandoned its own currency and adopted the U.S. dollar as the currency of choice; U.S. bills circulate but there are few coins. Vendors in Zimbabwe will sometimes take dollars and give change in candy, matches, or even condoms.[15]

Most important, money needs to be scarce in a predictable way. Precious metals have been desirable as money across the millennia not only because they have intrinsic beauty but also because they exist in fixed quantities. Gold and silver enter society at the rate at which they are discovered and mined; additional precious metals cannot be produced, at least not cheaply. Commodities like rice and tobacco can be grown, but that still takes time and resources. A dictator like Zimbabwe's Robert Mugabe could not order the government to produce 100 trillion tons of rice. He was able to produce and distribute trillions of new Zimbabwe dollars, which is why they eventually became more valuable as toilet paper than currency. At its peak in November 2008, the monthly rate of inflation in Zimbabwe was reckoned to be somewhere on the order of 80 billion percent.[16]

So we reach a paradox: modern money—the currencies used in the United States, Canada, Europe, Japan, China, and every other developed country or region—can be produced in unlimited quantities. They are "fiat currencies," meaning that they have value because the governments that issue them declare them to be legal tender. A century ago, those same countries used commodity money—gold, silver, or some combination of the two. How is it that in the name of progress, all of the world's most economically vibrant nations have moved from money with intrinsic value and finite supply to money with no intrinsic value that can be produced in unlimited supply? We don't even need quality paper and specialized ink anymore, just a few keystrokes on a computer. Have we made progress since commerce was conducted using animal pelts and tobacco, or regressed?

I will argue in the balance of this book that fiat currencies promote prosperity and stability. We are better off than we would be with a currency backed by gold, silver, or any other commodity. The vast majority of economists agree. The Booth School of Business at the University of Chicago periodically surveys an ideologically diverse group of prominent economists on policy issues of the day. In 2012, the Booth School asked its panel of roughly forty economists if the average American would be better off, as measured by price stability and employment, if the United States replaced its current fiat currency with a dollar defined as a fixed quantity of gold—in other words, a return to the gold standard. How many of the experts answered that this would be a good idea for the United States? None. Zero.[17] For the record, in all the years that I have been following the Chicago Booth economic surveys (called the IGM Forum), there has never been unanimous agreement on any other question posed.

In short, economists believe (with abundant evidence) that a currency with no intrinsic value is far preferable in a modern economy to a currency pegged to a fixed quantity of any commodity. This is a profoundly counterintuitive idea, given that one crucial attribute of money is scarcity. Fiat money has led to disastrous hyperinflations. Haven't we all seen those photos of Germans pushing around wheelbarrows full of currency during the Weimar Republic just to buy staple goods? In contrast, there is no documented case of a hyperinflation with commodity-based money, for obvious reasons. No one, not even Robert Mugabe, can make the supply of rice, oil, or gold increase by a million percent in a matter of months.

To make sense of this seeming intellectual contradiction, let's take a brief theoretical detour. If we could design the perfect money from scratch, what would it look like? Obviously it would have to serve the three functions described earlier: unit of account, store of value, and medium of exchange. To that end, we would look for a commodity that is portable, durable, divisible, and predictably scarce. Gold (the small change problem notwithstanding) performs admirably by all of those measures. But gold has its drawbacks, too. Gold may make for great jewelry, but it has limited other uses. When an asteroid strikes earth and you are stuck in the basement with your accumulated life savings in gold, you will not feel particularly rich. By comparison, the guy with the bottled water and the cans of refried beans will look like Bill Gates.

Asteroids aside, the supply of gold will not necessarily increase at the same rate as the overall economy. If melting ice in the Arctic exposed new gold deposits, there would be a spike in the quantity of gold relative to other goods, leading to inflation. If the supply of new gold lagged behind the rate of economic growth, there would be deflation. Even if the supply were to increase by just the right amount—at the same rate as economic growth, creating stable prices under normal circumstances— a high proportion of the world's known gold reserves are in China and Russia. If we were designing an optimal currency, we would not entrust control of the money supply to foreign powers whose interests do not always align with our own. So gold has some issues.

We might instead opt for a different commodity, such as bags of rice or wheat. These are nicely divisible and not controlled by Russia or China. We could fix the portability problem; one could imagine a commodity bank that stored bags of rice or wheat and issued paper currency against those assets. We could all conduct transactions using this handy paper currency or its electronic equivalent, but unlike our current dollars, each certificate would be redeemable at the commodity bank for something with intrinsic value. That would give us a portable currency, a predictable unit of account, a reasonable store of value (presuming that the bank can protect the rice from rats), and no risk of hyperinflation.

But do you really want all of your wealth tied up in rice or wheat? These crops are a less predictable store of value than you might think. Suppose a farmer invents a new technology that trebles or quadruples rice yields (as has happened in recent history). Your life savings are now devalued by the fact that the supply of rice has increased dramatically. Or, conversely, there may be some rice scourge that wipes out the accumulated stores of rice. And even under normal circumstances, we have no reason to believe that the supply of the chosen commodity will increase at the same rate as economic growth, meaning that prices will rise or fall depending on its quantity relative to other goods. Would you want to write a long-term contract denominated in rice if you were not sure how valuable rice would be relative to other goods ten, twenty, or thirty years from now?

Fortunately, there is an easy fix for the uncertainty surrounding the supply of any single commodity: a currency backed by a basket of commodities. Suppose each "commodity dollar" could be exchanged for a kilo of rice, a gallon of gasoline, a quart of milk, six songs on iTunes, and so on. The accounting would become a little more difficult, but consumers would grow accustomed to the system as long as the value of the currency remained stable. The holders of these commodity dollars would be insulated against a sudden increase or decrease in the supply of any single commodity. The currency would have real, well-defined purchasing power. The broader the basket of commodities against which the currency is backed, the more stable the value of that currency will be and the more highly correlated it will be with growth in the economy overall.

Remember, this is a theoretical exercise, so let's dream a little. Imagine a currency that could be taken to some dank back room and exchanged for predictable quantities of food, energy, electronics, cars, bicycles. The money would not just be backed by gold or rice; it would be backed by a sample of all the goods and services you regularly consume. Better yet, the purchasing power of this fancy new money vis-à-vis this diverse basket of goods would not fluctuate by more than a few percent a year. You would have a very good idea of what your money would buy in terms of goods and services today, and also well into the future. This cool hypothetical money would deliver all the benefits of money backed by a single commodity, but without the drawbacks. Each unit of money would be redeemable for a broad basket of goods at a predictable rate over a long period of time.

Okay, now for the mind-bending part of this exercise: what I have just described is the dollar, the euro, the yen, and many other fiat currencies. Yes, they are just paper (or bits and bytes), but when the governments issuing those currencies do their jobs properly, those pieces of paper (and bits and bytes) have a predictable value relative to a broad basket of goods and services, even into the distant future.

Therein lies the challenge of modern monetary policy. Central banks can create money from nothing; they can also make money go away. *Click, click, click.* That is the sound of central bankers growing the money supply, or shrinking it. Responsible central bankers can manipulate a fiat currency in ways that stem financial panics and promote stable economic growth. Irresponsible policymakers can use the same awesome power to create money so recklessly that the bills become worth less than toilet paper.

History has seen some of each.

CHAPTER 2

Inflation and Deflation

Inflation or deflation, tell me if you can: Will we become Zimbabwe or will we be Japan?"[1]

—Merle Hazard, self-described "first and only country artist to sing about central banking, mortgage-backed securities, and physics"

During World War II, Nazi Germany mounted an insidious campaign to destabilize the British government. The plot did not involve rockets or guns or any other traditional armaments; rather, the weapon was counterfeit money. Prisoners were enlisted to forge pound notes (and later dollar notes).* The goal was to flood Britain with counterfeit bills, thereby undermining confidence in the British pound and the broader economy. The plot, which ended up saving the lives of some skilled Jewish engravers, was documented in the book *Krueger's Men* and later the Oscar-winning 2007 film *The Counter-*

---

* According to recently declassified CIA documents, an underwater salvage operation in 2000 by Oceaneering Technologies, the same outfit that located the *Titanic*, discovered wooden crates full of counterfeit British pounds and American dollars on the bottom of Lake Toplitz in the Alps of western Austria. The bills, perfectly preserved in the cold, oxygen-free depths, were sunk by the Nazis as the Allies approached in 1945.

David Kohn, "Hitler's Lake," *60 Minutes*, November 21, 2000, http://www.cbsnews.com/news/hitlers-lake-21-11-2000/.

feiters. By 1945, roughly twelve percent of pound notes in circulation (as measured by face value) were counterfeit.

Obviously the counterfeiting scheme did not work in the end, but there was nothing wrong with the theory. Roughly fifty years later, a similar scheme was executed flawlessly in Zimbabwe. Currency flooded the country until it had so little value that merchants began weighing bundles of notes rather than counting them. On July 4, 2008, near the height of the hyperinflation, a beer at a bar in Harare, the capital, cost 100 billion Zimbabwean dollars. An hour later, the same beer in the same bar cost 150 billion dollars. At one point, the reckless printing of new money was interrupted by a shortage of high-quality paper on which to print new bills.[2] The Zimbabwe hyperinflation sped the nation toward economic ruin, proving that the Nazi counterfeiting plot was not entirely crazy as a weapon of economic destruction.

But there is one curious fact about Zimbabwe's devastating hyperinflation. This was not a plot perpetrated by a foreign enemy. Zimbabwe used the hyperinflation weapon on itself, which, to stick with the World War II example, would be like the British government bombing London. The quasi-dictatorial government of Robert Mugabe created so much new money that at one point it produced the largest bill ever recorded: a $100 trillion note. I have one sitting on my desk that I bought on eBay for about $10 (US); most of that value comes from its novelty, not its purchasing power.

Most of the world's money is no longer tethered to any commodity. Zimbabwe could print prodigious quantities of bills until the high-quality paper and ink started to run out; even then, the government could add more zeroes to each bill. In more advanced economies, money is increasingly electronic. You may have only a few bills in your wallet but tens of thousands of dollars in a checking account; those funds on deposit at the bank show up only as an electronic record, yet they have the same purchasing power as a stack of $100s. One central banker with a laptop, an Internet connection, and a pot of strong coffee can create far more new money than Robert Mugabe's overworked printing presses. This can be an inflation disaster—or a very important policy tool. Fiat currencies provide policy flexibility in ways that commodity money cannot. Remember the $3 trillion that the Fed created to fight the 2008 financial crisis?

The goal, therefore, is to get money "right." As the end of the last chapter suggested, money works best—as a unit of account, a store of value, and a medium of exchange—when it has a predictable value over time relative to a broad basket of goods and services. So how do we make that happen? It turns out that getting money right presents some curious challenges. Yes, inflation is bad. Prices are rising steadily, or, as economists tend to think about it, money is losing value. Who among us wouldn't be frustrated if the price of a beer went up by $50 billion between the first and second rounds?

But deflation can be worse; even modest deflation can set in motion a cascade of adverse economic responses. Sure, it may seem great that the price of a beer is *falling* between rounds. If that were the case, your income would probably be falling, too. No tragedy yet—your income is falling and so are the prices of the things you typically buy. But now imagine that your debts are *not falling*. The bank still expects the same mortgage payment every month, even as your paycheck shrinks steadily. Welcome to the Great Depression.

The inflation-deflation conundrum frames the fundamental tradeoff with regard to monetary policy. Commodity money solves the hyper-inflation problem. No government can produce huge new quantities of gold, silver, or mackerel. (Commodity money is still prone to more modest inflation, as will be explained shortly.) Yet the inflexible and uncontrollable supply of commodity money creates problems of its own, namely that the government cannot manipulate the money supply in ways that may be economically advantageous, particularly during economic downturns. During the depths of the 2008 financial crisis, Ben Bernanke, chair of the Federal Reserve at the time, could not have flooded the United States (and the rest of the world) with new cans of mackerel to resuscitate an economy in crisis; however, he was able to create new dollars. In short, the flexibility that enabled Ben Bernanke to fight the Great Recession is also the flexibility that enabled Robert Mugabe in Zimbabwe to create a $100 trillion bill.

As is the case in so many other aspects of life, Goldilocks offers the best insight into effective monetary policy: not too hot (inflation) or too cold (deflation). The value of any money, including commodity money, depends on its supply relative to the supply of other goods. Imagine that you are invited to play poker with some buddies. Your host digs out some old plastic poker chips from the back of a musty closet. They have no intrinsic value, other than a few cents in recycling value for the plastic. But at the start of the poker game, each player buys $100 worth of chips and puts them on the table. The cash used to buy in gets stuck away in a shoebox, along with the extra chips that were not purchased by any players (and therefore still have no more value than the recycling value of the plastic). Meanwhile, the chips on the table have value—because they can be exchanged at the end of the game for the cash in the shoebox.

Now think about three scenarios. In the first, the players gamble all night, with some of the players winning big and others losing everything. But no chips leave the table, and no new chips are introduced. The chips merely move around into different players' piles over the course of the evening. When it comes time to cash out at the end of the evening, the chips will be worth the same amount as when the players bought in at the beginning of the game. If every chip was worth $1, then a player holding 342 chips can expect to swap them for $342 in the cash box. Some players will be unhappy, but that's because they lost money playing poker, not because their chips were worth less than expected at the end of the night. The chips have no intrinsic value, but they did what they were supposed to do. They facilitated a poker game.

Now imagine scenario two. Your host is not as upstanding as you thought. As he lost hand after hand all night, he surreptitiously reached into the cardboard box and helped himself to new chips without depositing any new cash. At the end of the evening, the players are confounded by what happens. When they divide the money in the shoebox by the number of chips on the table, each chip is worth less than it was at the beginning of the evening. Suppose your host stole 250 chips to replenish his stocks over the course of the game. When it comes time to cash in, there are 1,250 chips on the table and still only $1,000 in the shoebox. If no one knows who the culprit is, the logical course of action is to make each chip worth $.80 ($1,000/1250). Obviously putting more poker chips on the table did not make the group richer (though it did work to the advantage of the host, which I will come back to in the next chapter). You can't increase collective wealth without increasing the stock of things with true value, which in this case is the shoebox of cash. The extra chips are just plastic that diminish the purchasing power of the chips already on the table.

Now imagine the final scenario. Suppose that during a break in the game, the host's dog approaches the table and eats some of the players' neatly stacked chips because they smell vaguely of pizza and pretzels. No one notices the missing chips until the end of the game, at which point there are fewer chips than there were when the players bought in. Every remaining chip now has a larger claim on the wealth in the shoebox. If the dog ate 200 chips (again, not an unrealistic estimate based on the behavior of my Labrador retrievers), there would be only 800 remaining chips and $1,000 in the shoebox. If the cash gets allocated across chips equally, each chip will be worth $1.25.

For now, the key insight is that changing the number of chips on the table does not change the value of what's in the shoebox, which is all anyone cares about at the end of the night. When we take our poker parable and apply it to real life, the chips are fiat money and the cash in the shoebox represents goods and services in the economy. What people care about are cars, food, washing machines, college tuition, and other things that have real value. Money is what we redeem to get those things. If the amount of money rises relative to the quantity of goods and services—because of a Nazi counterfeiting plot, or an autocrat printing $100 trillion bills, or for any other reason—we have to exchange more money to get the same quantity of real stuff.

It is most intuitive to think of inflation not as rising prices (though that is clearly happening) but as a fall in the purchasing power of money. If a broad array of goods and services cost twice as much as they did last year, then it must also be true that a dollar buys half as much. In fact, inflation is not limited exclusively to money. Consider the case of frequent flier miles, which are currently undergoing the equivalent of inflation. Beginning in the 1990s, U.S. airlines began awarding lots and lots of frequent flier miles for doing lots and lots of things, a marketing prac- tice that has continued to the present. You can receive miles for flying, but also for renting a car, staying in a hotel, applying for a credit card, using a credit card, and so on. The airlines have been printing frequent flier miles the same way Zimbabwe printed currency. By 2001, custom- ers were accumulating miles four times as fast as they were redeeming them.[3] (And most miles do not expire, subject to minimal flight activity.) The *Economist* warned way back in 2002, when miles outstanding were increasing at 20 percent a year, "Central bankers would suffer sleepless nights at such reckless monetary expansion were it not for the fact that they are usually up in first class collecting double or triple miles. The plain truth is that airlines have been printing too much of their currency. They are issuing more miles than they can ever supply in free seats. . . . As any first-year economics student knows, excessive monetary growth can lead to hyperinflation or devaluation."[4]

Frequent flier miles have no intrinsic value (except for those folks who like to brag about how far they fly). Instead, they represent a claim on something that does have value: a free flight, or an upgrade to a class of service in which your knees don't hit the seat in front of you and the flight attendants smile more. There are three possible outcomes as the number of miles in circulation climbs steadily. First, the airlines can increase the number of free seats on offer. (I'm trying not to laugh out loud as I present this possibility.) If the number of free seats available were to grow at roughly the same rate as the number of frequent flier miles in circulation, the "price" and availability of free seats would be largely unchanged. Fliers could expect to convert miles for free seats in 2015 as they did in 1990—the same number of miles for a free ticket with the same general availability. In the broader economy, this would be the equivalent of a country's money supply growing at the same rate as the production of goods and services. (The latter is typically measured by the gross domestic product, or GDP.) If a country's GDP grows 3 per- cent annually, and the money supply also grows at 3 percent, then the quantity of money relative to goods and services would be unchanged. Under normal circumstances, that would leave prices stable—no infla- tion, no deflation.

Realistically, though, airline companies are not going to cut into their profits by giving away ever more free tickets. That leaves two other options. The airlines can raise the number of miles required for a free ticket, which is classic inflation. The price of a ticket in miles goes up, which simultaneously means that each frequent flier mile is worth less. Alternatively, the airlines could leave frequent flier prices unchanged and ration the available free seats. If it requires only fifteen thousand miles for a free trip to Hawaii, and the typical flier has amassed 57 million frequent flier miles, lots of people are going to want to take a free trip to Hawaii—unless United Airlines makes available only six free seats per month. The seats are still cheap (in miles) when listed on the website, but few people can get them.

This, too, approximates reality in terms of monetary policy. When countries print money recklessly, prices go up—unless the same irresponsible government tries to curb those rising prices by law. In 2012, Venezuela had one of the highest inflation rates in the world—nearly thirty percent a year—for the usual reasons. The populist president Hugo Chavez sought to remedy this problem by combining irresponsible monetary policy with one more idea from the bad government handbook: price controls. The Chavez government imposed price caps on a range of goods, particularly staples for the poor, meaning that prices were not allowed to rise for popular items, as they usually do when demand exceeds supply. Instead, those items sold out. In fact, since the restricted prices were often lower than the cost of production, many firms *reduced* production. Basics like milk, meat, and toilet paper became hard to find, "turning grocery shopping into a hit or miss proposition," according to the *New York Times*.[5] Hugo Chavez transformed powdered milk into something like a free seat on United: a great deal if you happen to be lucky enough to get it at the artificially low price.

All of this explains the most famous aphorism in monetary policy, Milton Friedman's observation "Inflation is always and everywhere a monetary phenomenon."[6] Friedman, winner of the 1976 Nobel Prize in Economics, spent much of his career documenting the relationship between money supply and prices. In a book called *Money Mischief*, he summarized his findings from studying countries throughout modern history: "Inflation occurs when the quantity of money rises appreciably more rapidly than output, and the more rapid the rise in the quantity of money per unit of output, the greater the rate of inflation. There is probably no other proposition in economics that is as well established as this one."[7]

This phenomenon applies to all forms of money, not just paper. Commodity money is prone to bouts of inflation or deflation for the same basic reasons: the supply of a particular commodity does not necessarily rise or fall in sync with the output of other goods and services. Let's think mackerel again. Assume that a special humanitarian shipment arrives and every prisoner in a particular institution gets fifty additional pouches of mackerel. It's not hard to see why the price of haircuts in macks would go up; there are now more pouches of mackerel and the same number of barbers. This is essentially what happened when the Europeans discovered gold and silver in the New World. Beginning around 1500, the Spanish and Portuguese imported roughly 150 tons of silver from the Americas, spending it on the same basic quantity of goods in Europe. The result was a sixfold increase in prices over the next century and a half.[8]

For any given level of output in an economy, prices will rise and fall in proportion to the money supply—with one crucial caveat. (Yes, there is always a caveat.) The relationship between the money supply and prices is also affected by the speed with which money circulates in the economy, or the "velocity" of money. Velocity is prone to be higher—a single dollar will circulate quickly through the economy—when consumers and firms have less need or desire to hang on to cash (and assets that approximate cash, such as checking account deposits).

To make this more intuitive, let's revisit our prison mackerel example, just after the Red Cross has lavished fifty new pouches of mackerel on each inmate. We have no reason to believe that the velocity of mackerel would change appreciably. Suppose each prisoner typically keeps two pouches under the bed to satiate any midnight craving for oily fish and uses the rest for trade. We would expect prison prices in macks to rise roughly in proportion to the increase in the supply of mackerel induced by the humanitarian shipment. But what if there have been several stabbings with shanks made out of sharpened toothbrushes and the warden is threatening a lockdown? As a precaution against losing access to the canteen, many of the prisoners might decide to keep more mackerel under their beds. The speed at which macks circulated for trades would slow down as pouches piled up under bunks. A doubling of the supply of macks in the prison would not lead to a doubling of prices, since many of the new macks would be out of circulation rather than chasing prison goods.

Velocity is the crucial link between money supply and prices. Anything that causes individuals and institutions to hang on to money will slow velocity. For example, economic uncertainty prompts banks, firms, and consumers to stockpile cash (and other liquid assets*) because they fear less access to credit in the future. On the other hand, financial innovations that make it easier to convert assets to cash, such as home equity loans, speed up velocity because they enable households to hold less money for a rainy day (or, more accurately, a hurricane that blows off the roof). For all that, short-term fluctuations in velocity can still be puzzling. As one prominent macroeconomist recently conceded to me as we chatted about velocity while watching our daughters compete in a cross-country race, "Yeah, we don't really understand velocity."† This turns out to be more than an idle observation; changes in velocity make it hard to predict precisely how increases or decreases in the money supply will affect prices, at least in the short term.

The discussion so far might suggest that money has no significant impact on the "real economy." Velocity complicates things, but prices generally adjust to the money supply and people generally adjust to changing prices. Nobody wants hyperinflation, but what's the big deal with 10 or 20 per-

---

* Liquidity is a measure of how quickly an asset can be converted to cash at a predictable price. A Treasury bond is more liquid than a Rembrandt painting, regardless of their respective values, because it can be sold to a willing buyer at a predictable price on a moment's notice. The Rembrandt painting may take months or years to sell at an appropriate price because the market is small and specialized.

† Sadly, economists do talk about these kinds of things in social settings.

cent inflation (or deflation) if we can all buy and sell the stuff that really matters, albeit at prices that go up and down? No harm, no foul, right?

Up to a point, yes. If you knew that prices would rise 10 percent annually, or even 100 percent, you could plan accordingly. You would expect your employer to pay you 10 percent more every year to compensate for rising prices. Any real raise, reflective of merit, would be on top of that. If you borrowed money from a bank, and the bank demanded 4 percent as the "rental rate" for that capital, the interest rate would be 14 percent: 4 percent "real" interest as the price of the loan, plus 10 percent to compensate for the fact that the dollars you would be paying back a year later would have 10 percent less purchasing power than the dollars you borrowed. (Economists use the term "rental rate" because borrowing money from a financial institution is like borrowing a car from Avis or power tools from Home Depot; you pay for the privilege of using something that belongs to someone else, even if you eventually give it back.)

Now is a good time for a short detour to reinforce the crucial distinction between "nominal" figures, which are not adjusted to account for inflation, and "real" figures, which are. In the above example, the nominal interest rate (the price advertised in the bank window) would be 14 percent; the real rate (the true cost of renting someone else's capital) would be 4 percent. Any comparison between prices over time ought to be adjusted for inflation. Hollywood studios routinely ignore this elementary lesson. What are the top five highest-grossing (domestic) films of all time?[9]

Star Wars: The Force Awakens (2015)
Avatar (1997)
Titanic (1997)
Jurassic World (2015)
The Avengers (2012)

You may feel that list looks a little suspicious. These are successful films—but *The Avengers*? Was that really a greater commercial success than *Gone with the Wind*? *The Godfather*? *Jaws*? No, no, and no. Hollywood likes to make each blockbuster look bigger and more successful than the last. One way to do that would be to quote box office receipts in Zimbabwe dollars, which would inspire headlines such as the following: "Hunger Games Breaks Box Office Record with Weekend Receipts of $57 Million Trillion!" But even the most dim-witted moviegoers would be suspicious of figures quoted in a hyperinflated currency. Instead, Hollywood studios (and the journalists who report on them) use nominal figures, which makes recent movies look successful largely because ticket prices are higher now than they were ten, twenty, or fifty years ago. (When *Gone with the Wind* was released in 1939, tickets cost around 50 cents.) The true measure of commercial success is box office receipts adjusted for inflation. Earning $100 million in 1939 is a lot more impressive than earning $100 million in 2015. So what are the top-grossing films in the United States of all time, *adjusted for inflation?*[10]

> *Gone with the Wind (1939)*
> *Star Wars (1977)*
> *The Sound of Music (1965)*
> *E.T. (1982)*
> *Titanic (1997)*

In real terms, *Avatar* is number 14; *The Avengers* falls all the way to 29.

Similarly, programs that spend or collect money over time should be adjusted, or "indexed," to take inflation into account. The federal minimum wage was 25 cents when it was established in 1938. Obviously getting paid a quarter an hour is not going to take you very far in 2015, yet the minimum wage is not automatically adjusted for inflation. Instead, Congress must change it by law to account for rising prices. As a result, there have been long stretches in which the minimum wage stayed constant while prices were rising (meaning that the minimum wage was falling in real terms). The graph below, from the U.S. Department of Labor, shows the difference between the nominal minimum wage over time and the real purchasing power of that wage (measured in 2015 dollars).[11] The real value of the minimum wage was actually higher in 1968 ($10.97 when converted to 2015 dollars) than it is today ($7.25).

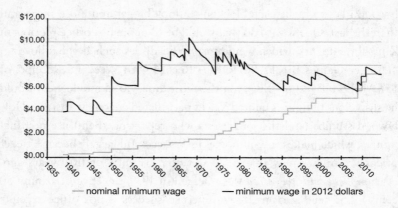

Source: U.S. Department of Labor, Wage & Hour Division, www.dol.gov/whd/min wage/chart.htm.

Still, rising and falling prices do not appear to be a plague of epic proportions. We can always tweak the numbers on the check so that everything comes out okay. If prices quintuple, we'll just pay you five times as much in nominal terms. The economic impact should not be any different than swapping a $5 bill for five singles. Falling prices should be the opposite. Your salary gets cut in half? No problem—as long as prices fall by half, too. Who cares how many zeros are on the paycheck? Why are there twelve more chapters in this book?

Let's start with three crucial wrinkles in the aforementioned logic. First, inflation is never entirely predictable, meaning that rising prices have the potential to complicate and confuse everything they touch (which is the opposite of what money is supposed to do). Second, deflation creates all the problems of inflation—and then some. Falling prices can cause individuals and firms to do things that are bad for the broader economy, which makes prices fall further, which induces more economically destructive behavior . . . and so on. If economists made horror movies, hyperinflation and deflation would each be their own subgenre. Last, it turns out that manipulating the supply of money—just giving or loaning people more pieces of paper—*can* affect the real economy, big time. Passing out more chips at the poker game, even if no more money goes in the shoebox, can affect how players bet at the table, which in turn affects the outcome of the game.

Let's take those complications in order. At a minimum, inflation is a nuisance, as it requires firms and consumers to adapt to changing prices. The faster prices are rising, the more disruptive this will be. If Bert's Big Beef finds that its sandwiches are selling more briskly than usual, presumably it is because consumers have taken a liking to the special sauce and the artisan toasted buns. The logical economic response is to ramp up production and raise prices to earn higher profits. Bert begins construction on a second drive-up window and creates a new 96-ounce rib-eye sandwich, with extra bacon.

But wait a minute. What if consumers are demanding more Italian beef sandwiches because the incompetent government is recklessly print-ing trillion-dollar bills? Consumers are pushing around wheelbarrows of new cash, which makes them feel (temporarily) richer. They want more of everything, and it has nothing to do with the special sauce or the artisan buns at Bert's Big Beef. Prices start to rise throughout the economy. Bert's employees begin to demand higher wages; his suppliers raise prices for bacon, buns, and beef. With the cost of inputs rising, neither the new drive-up window nor the 96-ounce rib-eye sandwich is likely to be profitable. Bert confused a burst of new spending caused by growth in the money supply with an increase in demand for his products. That's the larger point. Prices are supposed to transmit information in a market economy; inflation obscures that mechanism.

Consider the semi-related plague of "panflation," identified by the British newspaper the *Economist*. The U.S. dollar isn't the only thing that has lost value since the 1970s. Apparently we are also suffering from an epidemic of size inflation, whereby clothes labeled any particular size have steadily expanded over time. A pair of size fourteen women's pants is now, on average, four inches wider than they were in the 1970s. Yes, a size fourteen is really what used to be an eighteen; a ten is a fourteen.*

---

* These are British sizes, but American clothes have undergone a similar sizing phenomenon.

No, you do not have the same figure as you did in high school; your pants are just getting bigger, even as the size stays the same. But why? According to the crack investigative team at the *Economist*: "Fashion firms seem to think women are more likely to spend if they can happily squeeze into a smaller label size."[12]

Grade inflation is a different flavor of the same basic problem. An academic performance that earned a C three decades ago now typically gets a B+ or better. According to the *Harvard Crimson*, the median grade at Harvard is an A-; the most frequently awarded grade is an A.[13] Across all American universities, one study found that 45 percent of students get the highest possible grade, compared to 15 percent in 1960. If average students are increasingly getting the highest possible grade, how can employers and graduate schools identify the truly exceptional? Again, a mechanism that is supposed to transmit information has been dulled. As the *Economist* notes, "Inflation of all kinds devalues everything it infects. It obscures information and so distorts behaviour."[14]

Inflation does not merely sow confusion, it can create winners and losers. In the case of grade inflation, the best students get As at Harvard, but so do the mediocre students who would have received Cs in 1960. This is unfair to the truly exceptional students. Monetary inflation is arguably worse—it steals purchasing power from anyone holding cash, particularly low-income people who have fewer opportunities than the rich to park their wealth in assets that appreciate with inflation (like jewelry or real estate). Anyone holding $1,000 during a period of 10 percent inflation will have only $900 of purchasing power at the end of the year. Sure, there are still ten $100 bills tucked under the mattress, but the net effect is no different than if the government came along and stole one of them.

Meanwhile inflation, when unanticipated, is good for borrowers and bad for lenders. Suppose a bank loans you $100,000 in an environment when there is no expected inflation; the real interest rate, or the true "rental rate" on that capital, is 4 percent. What happens if there is a burst of 10 percent inflation over that period? True to the loan agreement, you pay the bank $104,000 after one year—but each of those dollars has lost 10 percent of its purchasing power. In real terms, the bank has given you

$100,000 and is receiving only $93,600 back in return. For many years, it was nearly impossible to get a credit card throughout Latin America, let alone a fixed-rate mortgage, because of the history of inflation and hyperinflation. No sane creditor is going to make a thirty-year loan (or even a one-month credit card loan) if there is uncertainty about the purchasing power of what will get paid back.

Once inflation emerges, it can be hard to tame for the simple reason that people who expect prices to rise will do things that make prices rise. If I expect prices to go up 10 percent next year, I will demand a contract that pays me 10 percent more. My employer will in turn raise prices by 10 percent. And so on. Inflationary expectations create a cycle that is hard to break. China's premier Wen Jiabao compared inflation to a tiger: once unleashed, it is very hard to cage again. Karl Otto Pöhl, a former president of Deutsche Bundesbank, the German central bank, described fighting inflation like trying to put toothpaste back in the tube.[15] You can choose your metaphor—tigers or toothpaste—but dealing with inflation is like many other life challenges: better to avoid the problem in the first place.

So let's just stipulate: modest inflation is an inconvenience; massive inflation distorts the economy massively. If we were to put that on a bumper sticker, it would read MEAN PEOPLE SUCK. SO DOES INFLATION. But here is where monetary policy defies the normal logic of the universe and we reach our second curious wrinkle: inflation may be bad, but deflation is worse. Everyone can understand why having the price of a beer go up by $50 billion between rounds would be a real pain. But what if the price of beer were falling steadily? Isn't that good news? Not necessarily. If the price of beer is falling because of a general decrease in the price level, your salary is probably falling, too. Falling incomes and falling prices would be fine—just like rising incomes and rising prices—but for one crucial detail: our debts are typically fixed (e.g., your monthly mortgage payment of $2,153.21). So let me interrupt your reverie about falling beer prices to allow you to contemplate a less attractive chain of events. You are making less money, your house is worth less, your other assets are depreciating—and you still owe the same amount to the bank every month.

In fact, the real value of your debt is climbing because the dollars that you will have to pay back are worth more than the dollars you borrowed. That's a recipe for a financial train wreck. When enough households are in financial distress because they cannot pay their mortgages, banks get in trouble and have less capacity to loan to healthy businesses, making those businesses less healthy. Everyone is selling assets to make ends meet—driving the price of those assets down (as with housing during the 2008 financial crisis) and spreading the economic conflagration to more households, businesses, and financial institutions. By then, falling beer prices would be small consolation. In fact, falling beer prices would contribute to the problem. If the price of a pint were tumbling, you might encourage your mates to go out for a drink next week, not tonight. The bar owner, seeing a decline in business, would cut beer prices more steeply, thereby contributing to the broader deflation. Beginning in 1989, Japan suffered a deflation-induced economic malaise that became known as the "lost decade"—until it stretched on long enough to become the lost decades.

In a famous 1933 essay, economist Irving Fisher described the phenomenon of a "debt-deflation spiral" based on his observations during the Great Depression. (Prices in the United States fell 30 percent between 1930 and 1932.[16]) Fisher warned of a vicious cycle in which financial distress begets financial distress, turning a modest economic downturn into a depression. He observed, "The more the economic boat tips, the more it tends to tip." A summary of the symptoms associated with Fisher's debt-deflation spiral reads like Stephen King tried his hand at economics writing: "Distress-selling, falling asset prices, rising real interest rates, more distress-selling, falling velocity, declining net worth, rising bankruptcies, bank runs, curtailment of credit, dumping of assets by banks, growing distrust and hoarding."[17] All that's missing is a zombie with a chain saw.

In particular, falling prices can short-circuit the medicine that usually solves routine economic slumps. In a weak economy, interest rates typically fall because there is less demand for credit; struggling businesses and households are less inclined to borrow for an expansion or a bigger house. However, falling interest rates create a natural antidote for modest economic downturns. As credit gets cheaper, households are induced to buy more big-ticket items—cars and washing machines and even homes. Meanwhile, businesses find it cheaper to expand and invest. These new investments and purchases help restore the economy to health.

Deflation renders this natural antidote impotent by raising the true cost of borrowing—the real interest rate. If the bank is advertising loans for 1 percent in the window while prices are *falling* by 5 percent a year, the real interest rate is 6 percent. The bank may only be charging you 1 percent to rent capital for a year, but every dollar you pay back will have 5 percent more purchasing power than the dollars you borrowed. That's an expensive loan in real terms, especially at a time when the broader economy is in distress.

But why can't the banks simply adjust nominal rates to take falling prices into account, as they do with inflation? Couldn't the bank advertise an interest rate of negative 4 percent in the window? Due to deflation, the money paid back would still have more purchasing power than the money loaned out, creating a profit in real terms. And you've just suffered through a long explanation of why real figures are all that matter. You can just see the sign in the bank window: ASK ABOUT OUR NEGATIVE INTEREST RATE LOANS!

Alas, there is a problem: nominal interest rates are almost never negative. To illustrate this phenomenon, let's imagine that you are an eager young banker proposing the seemingly clever idea of negative nominal interest rates to your boss, the senior loan officer at JP Morgan.*

> YOU: It's true that prices are falling at 5 percent a year, but if we make nominal rates negative 4 percent, the real rate will only be 1 percent and some of our customers might start borrowing again.
> BOSS: Who are you?

---

* In the aftermath of the 2008 financial crisis, there were instances of nominal interest rates turning negative. In particular, some banks began charging a small fee for holding large deposits. Thus depositors were getting back less than they deposited—a negative nominal interest rate. In practice, this was akin to a storage fee since large depositors had few other options for safely storing large amounts of money during the post-2008 economic disruption and uncertainty.

YOU: I sit in the cubicle right outside your office.

BOSS: You're telling me that we should loan someone a million dollars at an interest rate of negative 4 percent? They are going to pay us back less than we loaned them?

YOU: Yes! But due to the current deflation, the money they pay back will have gained 5 percent in purchasing power! We'll still earn a positive return on the loan in real terms!

BOSS: So you're telling me that we should loan someone $1 million and ask them to repay only $960,000 a year later?

YOU: Yes! In real terms, we still come out ahead.

BOSS: Okay, Einstein, wouldn't it be better just to leave the $1 million in the vault? Then at the end of the year, we'd have $1 million, not $960,000.

YOU: . . . True.

BOSS: Is $1 million more than $960,000?

YOU: Yes, it is.

BOSS: So what kind of dumbass loans money to people and asks them to pay back less than they borrowed when we can make more money by doing nothing?

The conversation might go on, but it would devolve to topics like cleaning out your cubicle and meeting with human resources for your exit interview.

The effect of deflation on real interest rates presents a related challenge for monetary policy. When an economy is operating below capacity, a central bank like the U.S. Federal Reserve can push on the economic gas pedal by manipulating the money supply to lower interest rates. However, central banks face the same dilemma as commercial banks with regard to falling prices: nominal rates can't go negative. In central banking parlance, this is referred to as the "zero bound." If deflation is running at 4 percent a year, even a nominal rate of zero would result in a real interest rate of 4 percent, which can be a steep cost for borrowing during a time of economic distress. Deflation limits how far the central bank can push on the accelerator—often when the economy needs the most gas.

Now for the last monetary wrinkle: passing out pieces of paper with no intrinsic value can change real economic activity in profound ways. Can we make everyone richer in the long run by adding a zero to every denomination of currency in the United States? Of course not. But in the short run, things are more interesting—beginning with an insight from a famous babysitting experiment. In 1977, the *Journal of Money, Credit, and Banking* published a paper describing a Washington, DC, babysitting co-op in which members exchanged babysitting time with one another by exchanging scrip.[18] Each unit of scrip was worth a half hour of babysitting; the scrip had no other worth. (As far as I know, they were just fancy pieces of paper.) For technical reasons explained in the journal article, the quantity of scrip in the co-op began to shrink. (The money supply was falling.) More important, families began to conserve their scrip because they worried that they would not have enough for future important babysitting needs. (Velocity was falling, too.) This exacerbated the problem.

As economist Paul Krugman later explained in an essay for *Slate*, members were hoarding in anticipation of future needs.[19] But not everyone can hoard at the same time. (Whose kids would they sit for, if everyone else is hoarding?) Krugman explains, "As a result, most couples were anxious to add to their reserves by baby-sitting, reluctant to run them down by going out. But one couple's decision to go out was another's chance to baby-sit; so it became difficult to earn coupons. Knowing this, couples became even more reluctant to use their reserves except on special occasions, reducing baby-sitting opportunities still further." The babysitting co-op was experiencing the equivalent of a recession. In the broader economy, one family's rational response to a weak economy (fewer dinners out, no new car this year) merely exacerbates the economic problem as restaurants and car dealers lay off workers, who then spend less and spread the economic malaise. As in the babysitting co-op, one person's thrift lowers another person's income—a phenomenon popularized by the twentieth-century economist John Maynard Keynes as the "paradox of thrift."

The Washington, DC, babysitting co-op attracted attention because of the simple fix: give out more scrip. According to Krugman, "More coupons were issued, couples became more willing to go out, opportunities to baby-sit multiplied, and everyone was happy." Remember those clicks on the keyboard at the New York Fed creating money that previously did not exist? For all intents and purposes, that was the Fed solving a problem similar to the babysitting co-op recession. The Fed does not give out money; America's central bank uses monetary policy to lower interest rates and inject liquidity into the system, all of which will be explained in chapter 5. Still, this should strike you as a bizarre phenomenon: making paper with no intrinsic value more readily available changes behavior—whether it is scrip for a babysitting co-op or dollars for the world's largest economy.

And so we conclude with the curious tension that characterizes modern money. The American dollar is arguably the worst form of money one might conceive. It has no intrinsic value or inherent scarcity. There is no physical limit on the speed or degree to which the currency can be debased. History is replete with examples of governments acting badly when given the opportunity to do so by paper currencies, beginning in the American case with George Washington and the Continental Congress. (During the American Revolution, the rebellious colonies printed their own paper currency, the continental. The currency depreciated to the point that the expression "not worth a continental" entered the lexicon.) Even the Washington babysitting co-op went on to suffer a bout of inflation; a surfeit of scrip created a situation in which too many people wanted to go out and not enough wanted to babysit.[20]

At the same time, the U.S. dollar is the best form of currency one might conceive. It is widely accepted and has a predictable purchasing power against a broad basket of goods. In that respect, the dollar is better than gold or silver (or mackerel) because it is less prone to swings in value, particularly deflation. A responsible central bank can grow the money supply at whatever rate produces stable prices. In times of economic distress, the right number of clicks on a keyboard at the right time can save jobs and raise incomes.

Of course, there is a stunning complexity associated with determining the right number of clicks and the right time. Fiat money has the potential to be much better than commodity money, or much worse. In the timeless economic classic *Goldilocks and the Three Central Bankers*,

Zimbabwe creates money recklessly and ruins the economy with run-away inflation. Japan allows prices to drift downward for two decades and suffers economic malaise. Goldilocks searches for a central banker who can deliver prices that are just right.

It turns out that nearly everything related to getting prices just right is far harder than it would appear.

CHAPTER 3

The Science, Art, Politics, and Psychology of Prices

A nickel ain't worth a dime anymore.

—Yogi Berra

Dan Dugan is a government agent. He toils in the shadows to make our democratic institutions work better. Few Americans know his job exists. The data he collects are secret; his sources are anonymous. When the *Boston Globe* did an investigative piece on Dugan's shadowy network, it described him as "a government agent with a thick black computer tucked under his arm and a veil of secrecy surrounding his work."[1] Yet that work—and the work of his hundreds of equally anonymous colleagues—makes possible many of the day-to-day activities that we take for granted in our market economy. In 2012, Dugan's cover was nearly blown. The details are still sketchy, but according to the *Globe* investigation, private security guards at an "undisclosed" retail store somewhere in the Boston area confronted Dugan as he studied women's lingerie, an important part of his work. The guards became suspicious after watching him "handle too many skimpy undergarments for a little too long."

Wait a minute. He was doing *what*?

Dan Dugan is an economic assistant for the Bureau of Labor Statistics (BLS), the government agency that compiles and publishes the Consumer Price Index (CPI), America's best-known measure of inflation.[2] To measure inflation, the BLS needs to know how prices are changing.

And to know how prices are changing—for everything from emergency pet care to pilsner beer—the government relies on hundreds of economic assistants like Dugan. And yes, he does have to inspect the lingerie carefully. As another economic assistant explained, "You have to turn the clothes inside out. . . . Is it woven or knit? If it's 20 percent cotton one week and 30 percent the next week, it needs to be right." The economic assistants record prices for roughly 80,000 items each month, collecting price data on a specific good or service that was precisely defined during an earlier visit.[3] Sugar? "There's organic white, organic granulated, powdered, baker's, caster, coarse, liquid, organic liquid." When it comes to comparing prices over time, even apples-to-apples is not good enough. It has to be organic Fuji apples to organic Fuji apples.[4] The seemingly simple concept of "price" can be tricky, too. What if an item has a special price on "Wicked Low Price Wednesday" or can be purchased more cheaply anytime by rewards card members? One BLS price checker recalls chasing a food truck through the streets of Washington, DC, to clarify whether the $6 price for a particular sandwich included vegetables or not.[5]

The best way to quantify inflation (or deflation) is by measuring changes in price over some period of time for some relevant basket of goods. Consider the PNC Bank Christmas Price Index, which measures the annual change in price for all the gifts described in "The Twelve Days of Christmas" (a partridge in a pear tree, two turtledoves, three French hens, and so on).[6] In December 2014, for example, the price for the full complement of 364 gifts (each item multiplied by the quantity specified in the carol) grew by a meager 1 percent from the same time in 2013. Not all goods and services in the Christmas Price Index went up in price by 1 percent. The price of six geese a-laying rose a whopping 71 percent. Turtledoves, calling birds, and gold rings were unchanged, as were all the services (the maids a-milking, lords a-leaping, and the rest). The point is that if you bought your true love the whole package in 2014, it would have cost you 1 percent more than it did the year before, reflecting modest inflation.

Most of us are not buying swans a-swimming or lords a-leaping. The PNC Index was designed to be a tongue-in-cheek variation on the Consumer Price Index, which does the same basic thing for goods and services American households are more apt to buy. Each month the Bureau of Labor Statistics measures prices for 80,000 goods and services; to my knowledge, lords a-leaping are not among them. But that raises a different question: If the CPI aims to measure with a single number how changing prices affect a typical household, which prices matter? The temptation is to say all prices matter, but that could be entirely misleading. A rise in the price of milk affects most American consumers more than a rise in the price of caviar or curling stones. I don't buy cigarettes or cat food or bowling balls; on the other hand, I do buy more golf balls than the average person, particularly when I'm playing badly. What to do?

The key to making the Consumer Price Index relevant and accurate is identifying the basket of goods most relevant for most American households.[7] In this respect, the Bureau of Labor Statistics really is like the CIA. Field agents send raw data back to headquarters where it is analyzed to find meaningful patterns. Specifically, BLS statisticians use expenditure data for a representative sample of families to determine the most appropriate basket of goods for the typical American household. At present, that basket consists of more than two hundred categories of goods and services in eight broad groups: food and beverages, housing, apparel, recreation, and so on.

When calculating the CPI, each item is weighted based on its share in the basket of goods. If the typical household spends three times as much on fresh chicken as it does on Parmesan cheese, then any change in the price of chicken will affect the CPI three times as much as a change in the price of Parmesan cheese. (In the Christmas Price Index, the annual change in the price of lords a-leaping is weighted ten times as heavily as the price of a partridge in a pear tree, since your true love sends you ten lords a-leaping and only one partridge in a pear tree.) The end product is the most commonly cited inflation measure in the United States: the Consumer Price Index for All Urban Consumers (CPI-U), which captures the spending patterns of about 88 percent of the American population.[8] (A related index, the CPI-W, covers Urban Wage Earners and Clerical Workers, which represent 32 percent of the population.) As both names would suggest, this still leaves out rural households, whose basket of goods and shopping options are appreciably different from those of households in metropolitan areas. Nor does it measure regional variations in consumption patterns and prices. The Bureau of Labor Statistics warns, "The CPI frequently is called a cost-of-living index, but it differs in important ways from a complete cost-of-living measure."

This is not a trivial point. One reason we measure inflation as precisely as possible is to update contracts and other kinds of programs to compensate for changes in prices. For example, if our goal with the Social Security program is to deliver benefits to retirees that have constant purchasing power over time, the numbers on those monthly checks have to be adjusted when prices are rising or falling at the Shuffleboard Superstore. The shuffleboard reference is not entirely gratuitous. If we seek to measure changing prices using a representative basket of goods, we must acknowledge that different kinds of consumers have different bundles of goods. The Older Americans Act of 1987 (yes, that's really what it was called) directed the Bureau of Labor Statistics to develop an experimental index, the CPI-E, that might better reflect consumption patterns for Americans sixty-two and older.[9] Senior citizens get discounts on products ranging from movies to airline tickets. On the other hand, older people typically spend more on out-of-pocket medical expenses. (A BLS economist was not able to say for certain if shuffleboard equipment is included in either the CPI or the CPI-E.[10]) From 1982 to 2011, prices rose in the CPI-E at an average rate of 3.1 percent compared to the CPI-U's 2.9 percent, in large part because health care prices rose at roughly double the rate of other goods and services over that period.[11]

For all that, the CPI-U (hereafter referred to as the CPI) is a reasonable approximation of the change in price for the things we tend to buy. As our consumption patterns evolve, the basket of goods used to calculate the CPI changes, too. Outdated items are dropped and new items are added. Automobiles were added in 1935; air conditioners in 1964; cell phones in 1998.[12] Meanwhile, typewriters were gradually phased out as their share of the typical consumer's consumption bundle dwindled and eventually disappeared. Yet any mention of cell phones (or televisions, computers, or automobiles) opens the door to yet another methodological challenge: yes, the prices are changing, but these products are also getting better, faster, smaller, and safer. My iPhone allows me to watch Netflix on Wi-Fi; the phone I had a decade ago was five times larger and did nothing other than make and receive calls (with relatively lousy reception). On the other hand, the phone I had while growing up offered near perfect sound quality; I went twenty-five years without ever saying, "Can you hear me now?" Unfortunately that phone was tethered to the wall by a cord. As the *Economist* has noted, "Your cotton shirts are wrinkle proof. Your clothes dryer is clever enough to shut off automatically when it senses that your socks are dry, and your television may allow you to watch two different channels at once. All of this innovation surely makes life better—but just how much?"[13]

Here we come to the part where measuring changes in price is as much art as science. We know that a television in 2015 is not the same as a television in 2005, nor is a Toyota Camry. The relevant question for any price index is how much of any price increase should be offset by improvements in quality. In theory, if a car is 7 percent more expensive and also 7 percent "better" (safer or more dependable or more comfortable), the price has not gone up. How exactly does one quantify how much better a car is because it now has antilock brakes and audio controls on the steering wheel? In what the *Wall Street Journal* has described as "a warren of beige-walled cubicles at the Bureau of Labor Statistics," some forty commodity specialists make these determinations.

The analysts use a process called "hedonics" to break down the price of a good into its component parts: memory, speed, functionality, durability, et cetera.[14] If a new model of toaster is deemed 20 percent better as evaluated by this process, and it costs 20 percent more than the old toaster, there is no price increase for purposes of measuring inflation. The improved toaster is essentially treated as a new product at a new price rather than the old product at a higher price. For example, BLS analysts determined that the value of quality changes for a sample of new 2015 domestically produced automobiles was $45.78—not $43 or $51, but $45.78. These 2015 cars are $45.78 better than the comparable 2014 models. Dealers are allowed a small markup on this quality improvement, so for purposes of measuring inflation, $48.39 can be subtracted from any model's yearly price increase when calculating inflation.[15]

Hedonics, like any statistical process, can confuse precision for accuracy. Statisticians are doing their best to account for quality changes when measuring prices, but at the end of the day sensible judgment matters as much as good math. Bureaucrats must measure not only whether the lords a-leaping cost more than last year but also whether they have become better dancers. Still the basic methodology behind measuring inflation should make sense. A modern economy depends on sound money, and sound money depends on measuring changes in prices as accurately as possible.

Sounds easy? Consider a seemingly arcane question that turns out to have huge political and fiscal implications: How do consumers change their basket of goods in response to changing prices? An example will help make the point. Suppose the price of citrus fruit rises sharply because of frost in southern Florida. The price of orange juice and related products would obviously go up. But something else just as significant would happen: most of us would consume less orange juice (and other citrus products) in response to the higher prices. How should that be reflected as we measure inflation?

If our goal is to measure changes in the cost of living, obviously we have to measure changes in prices—but also changes in consumption patterns induced by those higher or lower prices. Yes, my Social Security check ought to get bigger if the stuff I typically buy gets more expensive; however, that bigger check ought to be offset somewhat if I buy less of the stuff that is getting more expensive—fewer oranges and more bananas. Failure to take this behavioral change into account will overstate the true rise in the cost of living. Perhaps you have heard people at dinner parties or sporting events complaining about this phenomenon, the dreaded "consumer substitution bias." Okay, maybe not. (And if so, you might want to explore new social options.)

The stats geeks* at the Bureau of Labor Statistics have a fix for consumer substitution bias, too. In 2002, the BLS introduced the Chained

---

* Having written *Naked Statistics*, a book on the power and importance of statistics, I mean this in the very best sense.

CPI for All Urban Consumers (C-CPI-U), described breathlessly as a "new, supplemental measure of inflation." Just as we can sample consumer behavior to derive an appropriate basket of goods, we can also study how consumers substitute across products when prices change. If consumers respond to a price increase by buying less of something, for example, the weight of that item in the basket of goods is reduced accordingly (and the weight of what they buy instead is increased). The specifics approximate rocket science, but the intuition is simple: when the price of apples goes up, people buy fewer apples; this minimizes the inflationary impact of more expensive apples. As one would expect given the methodology, the chained CPI typically produces a lower figure for inflation than the traditional CPI. From 1999 to 2014, the average annual price increase in the traditional CPI was 2.33 percent, while the average increase measured by the chained CPI was 2.08 percent.[16] More important, the chained CPI is designed to more closely approximate changes in the cost of living than the traditional CPI.[17]

This sounds like stuff that policy wonks debate in windowless offices at the Department of Labor. Technically, that's true. But these seemingly academic methodological matters also inspire vitriolic congressional battles. Why? Because hundreds of billions of dollars are at stake. Some of the largest line items in the federal budget are social programs that pay benefits with automatic cost-of-living adjustments. If the government promises to pay Social Security recipients or veterans $1,750 a month, the intent of the program is to keep the purchasing power of that benefit constant over time. If we understate the true rate of inflation, the beneficiaries of government programs will be shortchanged. If we overstate inflation, taxpayers get a bill for programs that grow increasingly generous rather than merely compensating for rising prices.

Something similar happens on the tax side. The United States has a progressive income tax, meaning that people with higher incomes pay a higher tax rate than those who earn less (e.g, 33 percent instead of 28 percent). We can debate the merits of that system another time. For now, we should agree that a household whose income has grown from $100,000 to $110,000 only because of inflation should not pay a higher tax rate. In terms of purchasing power, they are not any richer than they were before; the tax system should not treat them as if they were. As a result, income tax brackets are indexed for inflation to prevent "bracket creep," a phenomenon in which households pay higher tax rates because the numbers on their paychecks are bigger but the real value of those paychecks has not grown. Each year the brackets are adjusted so that when we soak the rich, we don't soak people who just seem rich because of changing prices. In 2013, individuals paid the Internal Revenue Service 39.6 percent on any income over $400,000; in 2014, the tax tables were adjusted for inflation so that individuals had to earn over $406,750 to be taxed at that rate.[18]

Who cares? Well, if we index the brackets in a way that overstates inflation, Kim Kardashian will pay less in income taxes than the law intends. (After boring you to tears with the Bureau of Labor Statistics, and then transitioning to the IRS, I had to work Kim Kardashian into this paragraph.) It's one thing to adjust taxes and government checks for inflation; it's another to do it wrong—and in a way that costs the government staggering sums. Way back in 1995, one year after Justin Bieber was born, the U.S. Senate created a panel of prominent economists to evaluate the accuracy with which the BLS was measuring inflation. The so-called Boskin Commission* concluded that the CPI systematically overstated changes in the cost of living by 1.1 percentage points per year. That may seem like chump change—it's not. The commission pointed out that the upward bias in the CPI was responsible for more government spending than any federal program outside of Social Security, health care, and defense, and if left uncorrected, this seemingly picayune methodological glitch would add $1 trillion to the national debt between 1996 and 2008.

Specifically, the Boskin Commission identified a number of inaccuracies that resulted from static assumptions about where and how consumers shop. The report noted, "The strength of the CPI is in the underlying simplicity of its concept: pricing a fixed (but representative)

---

* Officially known as the U.S. Advisory Committee to Study the Consumer Price Index. Stanford economist Michael Boskin was the chair.

market basket of goods and services over time. Its weakness follows from the same conception: the 'fixed basket' becomes less and less representative over time as consumers respond to price changes and new choices."[19] Consumers typically respond to rising prices in three ways, all of which the CPI failed to capture fully. First, they find cheaper places to buy the same product. (This was a particularly salient point because the Boskin Commission report coincided with the spread of outlets and superstores.) They also substitute across products (bananas for apples). And then they substitute within product categories (Gala apples for Red Delicious). Meanwhile, the CPI was criticized for understating quality improvements (particularly household goods that had become more durable and dependable) and for being too slow to incorporate new products. I mentioned earlier that cell phones were added to the CPI in 1998. What I did not mention is that by then there were already fifty-five million cell phone subscribers, and the cost of a phone and service had fallen by 51 percent over the previous decade.[20] The longer it takes for new products to be adopted into the statistical basket of goods, the less their price drops will be reflected in the broader price index.

The BLS subsequently made numerous methodological changes to address issues raised by the Boskin Commission. (Broader use of hedonics to measure quality changes was one of them.) The BLS also began publishing the chained CPI (C-CPI-U), which more fully accounts for consumer substitution effects, as noted earlier. But the chained CPI has never been adopted for purposes of indexing federal taxes and benefits, a point that has come up in recent budget negotiations. The 2010 Simpson-Bowles deficit reduction commission recommended that the federal government switch to the chained CPI, as did a similar debt reduction task force chaired by former senator Pete Domenici and budget expert Alice Rivlin. Since inception, the chained CPI has grown by an average of 0.3 percent less than the traditional CPI. To paraphrase Everett Dirksen,*

---

* Senator Everett Dirksen is often credited with saying, "A billion here, a billion there, and pretty soon you're talking real money." Apparently there is no record of him actually saying that.

.3 percent here, .3 percent there, pretty soon you're talking real money. Like $220 billion in real money. That is what the Congressional Budget Office estimated would be saved over ten years if the federal government switched to the chained CPI for calculating cost-of-living increases.*[21]

Of course, that is $220 billion in benefits that people will not receive, which has inspired arguments over whether this is a cut in Social Security benefits or not. Both sides have logic on their side. Yes, Social Security checks would grow more slowly if indexed using the chained CPI. That's a cut. But it's a cut that is consistent with the original intent of the program, which was to adjust checks for the real increase in the cost of living. To fiscal hawks, it is as if there was a typographical error in the benefit formula decades ago and everyone has been getting more than they were supposed to get ever since. Changing the cost-of-living adjustment is not a benefit cut, it is a correction. If the subsequent benefits are not sufficient, the programs ought to be reformed directly, rather than by inflating checks through an inaccurate cost-of-living adjustment. Many groups that advocate for adoption of the chained CPI have also called for revisions to federal benefit programs to offset any undue hardship.

Suffice it to say that on America's shuffleboard courts, the nuance of the cost-of-living debate is often lost. A smaller check is a smaller check. As economist Robert Gordon, a member of the Boskin Commission, reports, "The suggestion that the bias had caused excessive growth in Social Security and other benefits evoked a sharp and damning political reaction, as the AARP (American Association of Retired Persons) sent its lobbyists scurrying through the corridors of Congress to throw cold water on those senators and representatives who had initially been sympathetic to reducing the budget deficit by adjusting the indexation formula by some fraction of the Commission's bias estimate."[22]

I have described the CPI as a speedometer for measuring the purchasing power of the dollar. Okay, now we know that there is really no single

---

* The savings grow even larger over time because they compound—smaller increases are calculated on top of smaller increases.

perfect measure of changing prices, so it is more accurate to say there is a dashboard of tools that can be used to measure inflation or deflation, including the various flavors of the CPI. On the one hand, these indices are likely to be highly correlated. Even the wacky PNC Christmas Price Index has done a decent job of tracking the CPI over several decades. Since 1984, when a PNC economist came up with this clever marketing ploy, the Christmas Price Index has climbed by 118 percent; over the same stretch, the CPI has risen 127 percent. The average annual price increase over this period for both indices is 2.8 percent. On the other hand, even a fraction of a percentage point can make a huge difference over time, and we probably don't want to be adjusting veterans benefits using the Christmas Price Index.

Which measure of inflation is best? That typically depends on who is asking and why they care. For example, the Federal Reserve pays particular attention to "underlying inflation" (previously called core inflation), a measure of changing prices that excludes volatile categories of goods, such as food and energy. After all, who needs gas or food? (A snarky headline in the *New York Times* once proclaimed, "If You Don't Eat or Drive, Inflation's No Problem.") But given the Fed's mission of delivering price stability, underlying inflation is a crucial gauge on the dashboard. The food and energy sectors are prone to shocks—such as a bad harvest in the Midwest or Russian president Vladmir Putin shutting down a major natural gas pipeline to Europe—that are not representative of price changes in the broader economy. If the goal is to understand systemic changes in prices across the economy, especially the relationship between interest rates and prices, a jump in petroleum prices caused by Putin's pique could obscure rather than inform the bigger picture. As officials from the Federal Reserve Bank of San Francisco explain, "Although the prices of [food and energy] may frequently increase or decrease at rapid rates, the price disturbances may not be related to a trend change in the economy's overall price level. Instead, changes in food and energy prices often are more linked to temporary factors that may reverse themselves later."[23] Think of it like slamming on your brakes when you pass a police car on the highway; yes, you are going slower, but not in a way that accurately represents how fast you typically drive.*

The *Economist* has created a McFlation Index that uses changes in the price of a Big Mac in different countries as a simple back-of-the-envelope method for capturing changes in the broader price level. The Big Mac is consistent across countries; each one is its own basket of goods: beef (outside of India), wheat, rent, wages, pickles, special sauce, and so on. How does the price of a Big Mac change over time relative to official inflation statistics? That last clause—relative to official inflation statistics—is what makes the McFlation Index more than a humorous curiosity. While the United States is not likely to begin using the price of Big Macs to index Social Security benefits, this simple tool is a good way to detect when other countries are cooking the books—like Argentina, where burger inflation between 2000 and 2010 was 19 percent annually compared to an official inflation rate of just 10 percent.[24] Why fudge the official statistics? Governments often promise various cost-of-living adjustments, or in the case of Argentina, interest rates on government debt that rise with inflation (to ensure investors a fixed real rate of return). One way to minimize these costs is by cheating on the official inflation numbers. The McFlation Index correctly flagged Argentine perfidy. In 2013, the International Monetary Fund officially censured the Argentine government for deliberately reporting inaccurate inflation statistics.[25]

Another useful indicator on the price dashboard is future inflation. After all, investors and businesses and labor unions often care more about price changes next year than they do about last year. The challenge with measuring future price changes is that, well, they have not happened yet. Until the Bureau of Labor Statistics can figure out a way to send economic assistants into the future to fondle lingerie, we would need some kind of crystal ball to figure out what prices will be in 2020.

In a way, we have the crystal ball. The best predictor of what prices

---

* PNC Bank also produces a Core Christmas Price Index that excludes swans, which tend to be the most volatile gift in "The Twelve Days of Christmas."

will be next year is what people think prices will be next year—so-called expected inflation.* Anyone making an agreement that involves payments over time will build in some expectation about future inflation. When the U.S. Treasury sells a bond that pays some annual rate of interest, say 3.2 percent, that interest rate consists of two parts: a real rate of interest (the return one gets for loaning money to the U.S. government) and some added amount to compensate for rising prices over the term of the bond (an inflation premium). But anyone looking at the nominal rate on a ten-year Treasury bond would not be able separate the two. How much of the 3.2 percent is real interest and how much is expected inflation? Maybe the real rate of interest is 3.2 percent and investors expect perfectly stable prices. Or perhaps the real rate of interest is 2 percent and investors expect prices to rise 1.2 percent each year over the next decade. Who knows?

We do, thanks to a simple but powerful kind of security introduced by the U.S. government back in 1996: Treasury Inflation-Protected Securities, or TIPS. Inflation-protected securities pay some fixed rate of interest every six months plus an adjustment for inflation, as measured by the CPI-U. As I sit here writing this chapter, the current annual yield on a ten-year TIP is 0.34 percent, not including the nominal adjustment for inflation. Here is the cool part: we can infer what the market believes about future inflation by comparing the yield on TIPS to the yield on regular Treasury bonds that are not indexed for inflation. The current yield on a regular ten-year Treasury bond is 1.93 percent.[26] That tells us that the market expects the annual inflation rate over the next ten years to be 1.59 percent (1.93 minus 0.34) because investors are indifferent to whether they get a real rate of return of 0.34 percent plus the change in the CPI-U each year or a nominal rate of 1.93 percent. As Taylor Swift's business manager has probably explained to her, the only way those bonds are the same is if our best guess for the increase in the CPI-U each year is 1.59 percent. Inflation or deflation over the next decade will almost certainly turn out to be different than what the markets are pre-

---

* Or sometimes "inflationary expectations."

dicting today, but the spread between regular Treasuries and TIPS still gives us the best snapshot of current expectations.

There are more price indices on the dashboard, but I am going to stop describing them. If you are aware of the inherent methodological challenges in measuring changes in prices—getting the right data for the right goods and adjusting appropriately for quality and consumer behavior—you can figure out the strengths and weaknesses of different indices. For now, we can all agree that measuring changing prices is much harder than it appears. Presumably we can therefore also agree that everybody would be better served by perfectly stable prices—neither rising nor falling for all eternity.

Right?

No, my naïve reader. No, no, no. Just as a tuberculosis epidemic is good for people who sell antibiotics, inflation is good for some people, and deflation is good for others. Let's start with deflation, the most egregious form of changing prices. After I described the Stephen King–type economic horror induced by falling prices in the last chapter, no one can possibly think this is a good thing. Wrong. For individuals living on a fixed nominal income (such as Japanese pensioners), falling prices make every yen go farther. If prices are falling at 10 percent a year, the real value of that check is growing at 10 percent a year. Lenders benefit as well, assuming the deflation was unexpected and borrowers can still afford to pay off the loan. Every dollar or yen that gets paid back is worth more than the dollars or yen that were loaned out. Yes, there is a general consensus among economists that falling prices are bad for the economy overall. There is also agreement that deflation should never have to happen, as every modern economy has a fiat currency that can be printed on demand. Ben Bernanke once famously suggested that falling prices in Japan could be fixed easily by dropping money out of helicopters. (This was a metaphor, not a literal policy suggestion.) Deflation is like a disease that can be cured by eating pizza and ice cream while watching TV on the couch; we would not expect it to afflict the country for a long time. Yet you are going to read a whole chapter on Japan's two-decade battle with deflation. This seeming contradiction can be explained as much by politics as economics. Some powerful groups don't mind falling prices at all.

Other folks are quite keen on inflation. Debtors like rising prices because it erodes the real value of their debts. (Again, this has to be unexpected inflation or else the expected price increases would have been included in the nominal price of the loan.) As you'll see in chapter 8, some of the fiercest battles in U.S. history were essentially battles over rising or falling prices. Perhaps you have a dusty recollection from high school history of the populist presidential candidate William Jennings Bryan. In his 1896 speech at the Democratic National Convention in Chicago, he famously declared to America's monied interests, "You shall not crucify mankind upon a cross of gold."[27] Bryan was arguing for the free coinage of silver to supplement America's gold standard. Metallurgy aside, Bryan was arguing for expanding the money supply to create a burst of inflation. Who wanted that? Farmers in the West, who were drowning in their debts. Who despised such an idea? Bankers in the East, who wanted to be repaid in dollars backed by gold, not in some depreciated silver-backed currency. For as long as there have been creditors and debtors—which is a darn long time—creditors have tried to protect the value of the currency and debtors have sought to devalue it.

Governments tend to be huge borrowers; for that reason, they tend to benefit from inflation, too, assuming their debts are not indexed for rising prices. The United States borrows hundreds of billions from the rest of the world, in dollars. China is one of America's biggest foreign creditors—we owe the Chinese a trillion dollars, give or take some billions. To put a finer point on it, these are the same dollars that the Federal Reserve can create with a few computer clicks. As will be explored in chapter 12, the danger for our Chinese creditors is not that the United States will default on our debt. We would never have to do that. Instead, Congress could order the Federal Reserve to print new dollars to repay our debts, thereby devaluing all existing dollars, creating significant inflation, and honoring our legal obligation to Chinese creditors while really paying them back far less than we borrowed—a default in all but name.

It speaks well of the United States that international creditors are willing to buy U.S. government bonds at extremely low nominal interest rates (implicitly suggesting that the likelihood of the United States inflating away its debts is negligible). Countries like Argentina do not have that luxury. One of the reasons Argentina's debt is indexed for inflation (prompting the bogus inflation statistics referenced earlier) is that the government has a history of irresponsible monetary policy, including hyperinflation. That brings us to the answer to the question that you may have asked in the first couple of chapters: Why would Zimbabwe (and the Weimar Republic in Germany, and Brazil, and Argentina, and many other countries) inflict hyperinflation on themselves?

The answer is that governments have a lot to gain—in the short run—from printing and spending new money, particularly when access to other forms of revenue is limited or nonexistent. Printing new paper money is a surreptitious way to tax citizens—an inflation tax.* Printing more money diminishes the value of the money already in circulation, which is effectively a tax on that currency. Economists refer to this phenomenon as "seignorage," which reflects the difference between the cost of producing money (essentially zero in the modern era) and the value of that new money. Seignorage is like the host of the poker game who reaches into the closet to get more plastic chips for himself without putting any more cash in the shoebox. He gets richer at the expense of everyone else holding chips.

It is no coincidence that countries at war or with particularly dysfunctional governments are most prone to serious inflation. If the army is demanding to be paid, printing new money does not require a functional tax system or willing international lenders—just paper, ink, and some pliant bureaucrats over at the mint. Yes, that describes Zimbabwe in the 1990s and Argentina in the 1980s, but also George Washington and his revolutionary compatriots in the 1770s, who printed those continentals to finance the Revolutionary War. The paper currency allowed the

---

* A government can also devalue commodity-based money, such as gold or silver coins, by reducing the content of the precious metal. If the army was due a fixed payment in gold francs, the king could make those gold francs go farther by putting less gold in each of them. Still, there are physical limits to how much a commodity can be debased. Hyperinflations are uniquely a phenomenon of paper currencies.

Continental Congress to pay for the early years of the war without any appreciable gold reserves or a national tax system. And yes, the inevitable result was serious inflation. These historical examples and many others prove that, to paraphrase Milton Friedman, inflation is everywhere and always a *political* phenomenon.

But wait, money turns out to be psychological, too—and not just the fact that we all want lots of it. Many of us act like small children when it comes to separating out inflation from real changes in the value of money. Just as a three-year-old might prefer five singles to a $5 bill, many adults seem to care about the numbers on the bills more than their real worth. Here is a quick quiz. Which would you prefer: (a) getting no raise when prices are unchanging, or (b) getting a 5 percent annual raise when prices are rising at 5 percent a year? There is no trick math here. The correct answer, at least to an economist, is that we should be indifferent between those two scenarios. In the first case, all the numbers stay the same from year to year; in the other, our check gets bigger but so do the price tags on all the things we typically buy.

In fact, there is a human tendency to prefer getting a raise, even when inflation eats away all the benefit. And we abhor getting a pay cut, even when falling prices might compensate for some or all of the smaller check. Economists describe this tendency to think in nominal terms, rather than real (inflation-adjusted) terms, as "money illusion."

A group of academics—both economists and behavioral psychologists—documented this phenomenon by posing a series of hypothetical questions to a large group of people, including both Princeton undergraduates and random folks at Newark International Airport and in New Jersey shopping malls. (The answers across the groups were not appreciably different.) For example, an interviewer asked a respondent to compare the following scenarios: one person receives a 2 percent raise when there is no inflation and a different person receives a 5 percent raise when there is 4 percent inflation.

Most respondents correctly inferred that the first person is better off financially, but a majority answered that the second person would be happier! Similarly, respondents were asked to compare a hypothetical person, Carl, who bought a house for $200,000 and sold it a year later for

$246,000 at a time when inflation was 25 percent, to Adam, who bought a house for $200,000 and sold it a year later for $154,000 after prices had fallen by 25 percent. That's a lot of numbers, so let's summarize:

Carl makes a 23 percent gain on paper, but prices have gone up 25 percent, so in real terms he has suffered a 2 percent loss.

Adam has lost 23 percent on paper, but prices have fallen 25 percent, so he's made a 2 percent gain when deflation is taken into account.

Yet the most common answer is that Carl got the best deal. Apparently our brains and our wallets are not always in sync.

The authors of the study conclude that "money illusion is a widespread phenomenon in the United States today."[28] They point to several social phenomena that suggest a tendency by all of us to think in nominal rather than in real terms. The first is "sticky prices," which is the tendency of prices to be more rigid in nominal terms than economic conditions warrant. For example, workers are particularly averse to taking nominal pay cuts, even when the job market has gone weak. Reducing wages, even temporarily, can save jobs when a business is struggling, yet that is a surprisingly unusual arrangement.

Second, firms rarely enter into contracts that are indexed for changing prices, even when history suggests that the value of a dollar or euro could change appreciably over the duration of the contract. As one professor, a member of the Stable Money Association, puzzled almost a hundred years ago, "We have standardized every other unit in commerce except the most important and universal unit of all, the unit of purchasing power. What business man would consent for a moment to make a contract in terms of yards of cloth or tons of coal, and leave the size of the yard or the ton to chance?"[29]

Third, much of our common discourse, particularly news reports, confuses nominal and real values. I gave the example of Hollywood box office receipts in the last chapter, but the same is true with CEO compensation, philanthropic gifts, government spending, and athletes' salaries. A baseball player who becomes the highest paid shortstop ever might really be fifteenth when inflation is taken into account.

The psychology is complex. People are not oblivious to changing prices; they often just find it easier to ignore them. The implications of this behavioral quirk are enormous. For example, workers may resist a 3 percent pay cut when prices are stable, as noted above but be willing to accept a 1 percent raise when there is 4 percent inflation. (Both contracts leave workers 3 percent worse off in real terms.) This phenomenon is more than a curious mental illusion; it suggests that labor markets are likely to be more flexible when there is modest inflation than they are when prices are stable or falling. Similarly, consumers follow nominal price cues when making major decisions. A homeowner may resist selling a house for less than he or she paid, regardless of the value of the deal in real terms. Conversely, rising prices might induce an owner to sell "for a profit" even if the deal is a loser when inflation is taken into account. Eldar Shafir, Peter Diamond, and Amos Tversky, the academics who documented our curious mental accounting using the data from the New Jersey survey respondents, write in their study, "The implications of money illusion may be the most important factor to consider when contrasting between zero and other low rates of inflation."[30]

That brings us to an odd place. There are three strong arguments that a little inflation is better than none at all. First, there is the economic lubrication described above: because of money illusion, markets work more smoothly when workers and consumers can take real losses disguised as nominal gains. (A guy who gets a 1 percent pay increase when inflation is 3 percent can still tell his drinking buddies that he got a raise.) Second, a low but positive level of inflation protects against slipping into deflation, particularly during times of economic weakness. And third, modest inflation gives the central bank more room to lower real interest rates before bumping up against the zero bound. (Remember, nominal interest rates cannot go negative, other than in the most extraordinary of circumstances.) In 2013, as the United States was still recovering from the Great Recession, the *New York Times* reported, "Inflation is widely reviled as a kind of tax on modern life, but as Federal Reserve policymakers prepare to meet this week, there is growing concern inside and outside the Fed that inflation is not rising fast enough."[31]

Yes, not enough inflation. So let's recap the first three chapters: Inflation is bad. Deflation is worse. Hyperinflation is worst of all. Yet there are some political actors who benefit from each. Meanwhile, the whole point of money is to facilitate commerce, which is presumably best achieved by prices that don't change at all, except that commerce actually works more smoothly when prices are rising gradually over time. Go figure.

So yes, getting prices just right is a challenge.

And I have not mentioned the bankers yet—you know, the folks who brought you the 2008 financial crisis (with a lot of help from their friends). One of the most important things we can do with money is lend it to other people. Credit is the backbone of a modern economy. When we borrow money to go to college, to buy a car, to start a business, or to speculate in Las Vegas real estate, our lives get steadily better.

As long as we can pay it back. Speculating in Las Vegas real estate—with someone else's money—can turn out badly, as we saw in 2008. Money is a tricky business, even without borrowing and lending. But once the banks get involved (and other institutions that act like banks), things can get really crazy.

CHAPTER 4

Credit and Crashes

Yes, we have been through this before, tragically many times.

—Yale economist Gary Gorton, in testimony before the
U.S. Financial Crisis Inquiry Commission[1]

Sometime in the next five years you may kick yourself for not reading and re-reading Kindleberger's Manias, Panics, and Crashes.

—Nobel laureate Paul Samuelson, in a promotional blurb for the book—
three years before the 2008 global financial crisis

There are a lot of good books on the 2008 financial crisis. You might begin by reading Ben Bernanke's essays on the Great Depression, or his new memoir. Bernanke is a scholar of the Great Depression; his views on that crisis informed his response as chairman of the Federal Reserve while the financial crisis unfolded on his watch. You can read the memoirs of participants like Hank Paulson and Tim Geithner (Treasury secretaries under George W. Bush and Barack Obama, respectively). You might also consult an old classic by Irving Fisher, *Booms & Depressions*, which was originally published in 1932 but has timeless insights into the causes and consequences of financial crises.[2] If you would like a summary of many different views, you could read Andrew Lo's article in the *Journal of Economic Literature*, "Reading about the Financial Crisis: A Twenty-

One-Book Review."[3] Yes, he read all of those books so that you do not have to.

Of course, you should read the final report of the Financial Crisis Inquiry Commission, the ten-member panel appointed by Congress in 2009—while the crisis was still under way—to "examine the causes, domestic and global, of the current financial and economic crisis in the United States."[4] The bad news: the report is 632 pages, including dissenting views and endnotes. The good news: it is available free online. You might also peruse *The Squam Lake Report: Fixing the Financial System*, a report prepared by fifteen of the world's most prominent economists who came together in the fall of 2008 for a retreat (on Squam Lake in New Hampshire) to make recommendations for improving the long-term stability of the financial system.[5]

Or you could just watch *It's a Wonderful Life*. Yes, the film with Jimmy Stewart and Donna Reed. *It's a Wonderful Life* is not just a time-less holiday classic; it is also the most accessible way to understand the inherent vulnerabilities of a modern financial system. If you understand the bank run scene, when depositors are queued up outside the Bailey Bros. Building & Loan demanding their money and George Bailey saves the day by dipping into his honeymoon fund to pay off the anxious depositors, then you can understand the 2008 financial crisis, the Great Depression, the periodic bank panics in the United States in the nine-teenth and twentieth centuries, and the future financial crises that are still likely to happen. The rest is just detail.

Banks—and institutions that act like banks, regardless of what the name says on the door—are the heart of the financial system. Banks (and the like) match savers with borrowers, putting capital in the hands of entre-preneurs, homebuyers, and other parties who can make productive use of someone else's money. People like me, who are saving for the staggering cost of our children's higher education, earn a return on the money we set aside. (In economics equations, the letter that represents the interest rate is r, rather than i, because it represents the rental rate on capital.) People like my former students who need money to start businesses or to attend graduate school can "rent" my savings to do things that will presumably make them better off, even after paying the interest on the loan. I don't loan money directly to students; instead, a bank takes a cut for acting as the intermediary—paying interest to me for my savings and then loaning those funds out at a slightly higher rate to borrowers. When all of this works well, society benefits and financiers earn a tidy profit in the process. A modern economy cannot function without a vibrant and profitable banking sector.

But when things go bad . . . Well, let's go back to George Bailey in Bedford Falls. For those who have never seen *It's a Wonderful Life*, or have not previously thought of it as the greatest teaching tool on financial panics ever made, George Bailey (played by the young, likable Jimmy Stewart) runs the Bailey Bros. Building & Loan Association, a small town bank (in the broad sense of the word) that makes home loans in the town of Bedford Falls. A series of events in the film creates a run on the Building and Loan.* Customers fearing for its solvency are lined up outside the door, trying to get their money out before it's too late. The script describes the scene:

> An iron grill blocks the street entrance to the Building and Loan. It has been locked. A crowd of men and women are waiting around the grill. They are simply-dressed people, to whom their savings are a matter of life and death.[6]

These simply dressed people want their money, which is not an unreasonable request. The finances of the Bailey Building and Loan are ostensibly sound, meaning the bank's assets exceed its liabilities— but that does not mean there is enough cash in the vault to honor the demands of all the depositors *who want their money now*. George Bailey's problem in that moment is timeless and instructive. Financial institutions often "borrow short and lend long," meaning that if a high proportion of

---

* Astute readers have asked why the Federal Deposit Insurance Corporation wouldn't have insured the accounts at the Building & Loan to prevent such a bank run. One reason is that the Building & Loan wasn't technically a bank. Another reason, pointed out by even more astute readers, is that FDIC insurance was created in 1933, and while *It's a Wonderful Life* was released in theaters in 1946 (to initially disappointing results), the bank run portrayed in the film appears to have happened in 1932.

depositors (or other investors) suddenly want their money back, the funds are likely to be tied up in loans or other investments that cannot easily be converted to cash. The funds may be safe in the sense that the bank has not made a bad loan. Still the money is not in the vault, nor can it be retrieved quickly. If enough investors show up demanding payment, they cannot all get it. Worse, when word gets out that an institution cannot fully honor its obligations, others will rush to be paid before it's too late, thereby exacerbating the crisis. It is a classic bank run, and when there is a rush for the exit, even a healthy institution can collapse.

George Bailey implores the customers crowding the teller's window to understand all this. When the first depositor demands all the money in his account, George explains, "You're thinking of this place all wrong. As if I had the money back in a safe. The money's not here. It's in Joe's house . . . right next to yours. And in the Kennedy house, and Mrs. Macklin's house, and a hundred others. Why, you're lending them the money to build, and then, they're going to pay it back to you as best they can. Now what are you going to do? Foreclose on them?"[7]

The inspiring speech is not enough to placate the panicked crowd. In the end, George Bailey quells the incipient bank run with his own money, parceling out cash to any depositor who demands it. Of course, the psychology of a bank run works in reverse, too. Once borrowers are assured they will be paid, they are less prone to demand payment. In the lingo of finance, George Bailey used his honeymoon savings to serve as the "lender of last resort." The emergency capital ends up saving an institution that might otherwise have collapsed and dragged other businesses with it. This, too, is a singular feature of financial institutions. They do not fail quietly alone. Each is like a mountain climber tethered to many others—when one slips, many can fall.

In fact, *It's a Wonderful Life* shows us what would have happened if the Building & Loan had collapsed—the counterfactual, as social scientists call it. The conceit of the film is that an angel allows George Bailey to see what the world would have been like if he had never lived (and therefore had not bailed out the Building & Loan). In that scenario, Bedford Falls is transformed into a den of desperate people, sleazy businesses, and general economic distress, as the script describes:

> The character of the place has completely changed. Where before it was a quiet, orderly small town, it has now become in nature like a frontier village. We see a SERIES OF SHOTS of night clubs, cafes, bars, liquor stores, pool halls and the like, with blaring jazz MUSIC issuing from the majority of them. The motion picture theatre has become a burlesque house. Gower's drugstore is now a pawnbroker's establishment, and so on.

Okay, to get the main point here one does not have to believe in angels, or that one bank failure would destroy Bedford Falls, or even that pawn shops, liquor stores, and pool halls are inherently bad. The important idea is simpler and indisputable: financial panics happen, and when they do, the damage spreads beyond the affected parties. Think of 2008—one did not have to be involved in the housing bubble in any way to feel the impact of its collapse. When things go bad, the rest of us end up with pawnshops and pool halls, figuratively speaking, and government is often called on to clean up the wreckage. As the *Economist* has noted, "The old saw about bankers—that they believe in capitalism when it comes to pocketing the profits and socialism when it comes to paying for the losses—is too true for comfort."[8] The relevant policy question is if and how the government ought to intervene to reduce the likelihood of financial crises and to lessen the damage of those that do happen. Always has been, always will be.

The next chapter will explore the role of central banks (such as the Federal Reserve in the United States), which serve a crucial function at the intersection of government and finance. Before we get there, however, let's first examine the awesome power of credit, the financial equivalent of TNT. The dynamite metaphor is not as random as it might appear. A fractional banking system—where banks make money by lending out funds that belong to someone else—can help us build great things, or it can cause financial panics that harm borrowers, lenders, and lots of innocent parties. To understand the unique promise and pitfalls of credit, let's leave the fictional world of Bedford Falls and enter a place even less tethered to reality: a hypothetical rural society sustained primarily by rice farming. This is a simple, happy place with no shady subprime mortgage brokers or evil investment bankers. No one has ever heard of a credit default swap. There is no central bank and no fiat currency. It's all about the rice. If Frank Capra, writer and director of *It's a Wonderful Life*, were to make a film about an idyllic farming hamlet, this is the kind of place he would portray. Yet this society is every bit as prone to a financial boom and bust as the United States was in 2008, perhaps more so.

Let's start with that rice, which is a very good commodity to serve as money—durable, scarce, and easy to measure and divide. But not perfect. Carrying around bags of rice is a pain, literally and figuratively. For that reason, responsible individuals might seize upon a logical business opportunity: rice storehouses. The proprietor of the rice storehouses would issue receipts for any rice you deposit. These receipts would likely substitute for the rice itself in everyday transactions. Voilà, we have a commodity-based paper currency, or perhaps even several currencies, depending on the number of rice storehouses.

The credibility of such a currency would depend on the credibility of the rice storehouse issuing the receipt. As long as people believe a certificate will be redeemed at face value, they will accept it as payment and use it as such. Other than those folks who actually need rice—to eat or to plant—most of the residents in the hamlet would rather have certificates than fifty-kilo bags of rice. The storehouse can anticipate a small and relatively predictable number of redemptions (e.g., more at planting time or during the wedding season).

The "money supply" in this area is a function of the quantity of rice on deposit, as that is what determines the number of rice certificates in circulation. This money supply will naturally ebb and flow. When the harvest is particularly good, the deposits on account will rise. After a bad harvest, the quantity of rice on deposit will fall. These fluctuations are likely to be quite large; when the rice haul is good, it is likely to be good for everyone, and vice versa. This leads us to the first interesting insight from our hypothetical hamlet: there will be large swings in the money supply, and therefore in prices, even with a commodity-based currency. (This is similar to the price swings caused by the discoveries of gold and silver in the New World that were described in chapter 2.) When rice is abundant, so are rice certificates. If the quantity of other goods that people want (liquor, furniture, firewood) is unchanged, their price as measured in rice will rise. This is just basic supply and demand. When everyone has lots of rice, there will be more of it chasing other goods. This is the basic relationship between the money supply and prices, whether we are talking about gold, paper dollars, or rice certificates.

Meanwhile, even without government or a central bank, the rice storehouse can facilitate checking accounts, or something akin to them. If you have rice on account at the storehouse, and I have rice on account at the storehouse, we do not need to swap rice certificates to conduct commerce. When I buy a case of rice wine from you (our hamlet needs to have some fun), I can simply write a note to the storehouse owner telling him to transfer some of the rice in my account to your account. Now we have checking accounts (typically called "demand deposits" in the finance literature), even without giving our hamlet electricity or running water. The proprietor of the storehouse would debit my account seven bags of rice and credit your account the same.

If you have an account at a different rice depository, my rice "check" can still work in the same way. It is likely that other villagers are also writing checks, some of which are directing rice to be sent from your storehouse to mine. The owners of the rice storehouses need not haul bags of rice back and forth every time one of these requests is made. They can keep a running tally and settle up at the end of the day, or the end of the week. Checks and other electronic transactions are handled this way in a modern financial system. One important if unglamorous role of the Federal Reserve is to facilitate the "plumbing" of the financial system by serving as a clearinghouse for member banks, all of which are required to keep reserves on account with the Federal Reserve. In advanced economies, funds held in checking accounts (demand deposits) are treated as part of the money supply just like currency—as they should be since the funds in your checking account can be used for transactions almost as easily as the cash in your wallet.

So far, so good. Our idyllic hamlet seems well served by a basic rice banking system. How do we end up with pool halls and pawnshops? Let's move on to the element of rice banking that will eventually cause riots in the dusty streets, or at least a lot more consumption of rice wine. The proprietors of the rice storehouses will undoubtedly observe over time that most people with accounts do not show up to demand their rice. Instead, the deposits and withdrawals ebb and flow in a predictable pattern. What a waste! All this potentially productive rice locked away, just attracting rats. So let's introduce an enterprising storehouse owner who realizes that he can make a profit by loaning out bags of rice from the vault while they are sitting there idle.

Yes, our rice loaning entrepreneur is technically loaning out something that does not belong to him, but why not? That's what Jimmy Stewart was doing in *It's a Wonderful Life*, and everybody likes him, particularly during the holidays. After all, these loans have the potential to make all parties better off. New farmers can get started by borrowing rice to plant, which they will repay with interest after the harvest. The borrowers offer collateral, such as the title to their land, so the storehouses will be compensated in the event of default. Meanwhile, families with surplus rice can earn a small sum for keeping their rice in the vault, whereas previously they had to pay a storage fee. The rice banker makes a profit by acting as the intermediary between rice lenders and rice borrowers. Banking really does make our Norman Rockwell–inspired hamlet better off—just as it has everywhere else, for all of history. As the *Economist* has noted, "The rise of banking has often been accompanied by a flowering of civilization."[9]

This is why we love bankers—until we want to kill them with pitchforks. When we last left our bucolic rice-based economy, storehouse owners had reckoned that they could safely loan out some of the rice sitting in their vaults. Assume that the typical storehouse proprietor feels comfortable keeping half the rice in the vault and loaning out the other half (a reserve ratio of 0.5, if one is going to be technical about it). Something really wacky happens when rice bankers start loaning out other people's capital: *money is created*. Some very, very simple math can make a very, very powerful point. Suppose there are ten thousand bags of rice on deposit in various storehouses, each with one paper rice certificate issued against it. The money supply in the hamlet is ten thousand bags of rice. When the storehouse proprietors decide to loan out five thousand bags of rice (half of what is on account), the money supply grows to fifteen thousand bags of rice. This is not magic; it is fractional banking, or at least a simple version of it.

Everyone with rice at a storehouse has a certificate for that deposit; those certificates are circulating for commerce (or checks can be drawn on the deposits). When the bank (storehouse) makes loans, another five thousand bags of rice (or certificates) enter circulation. We are double counting, but that is exactly the point. The money I deposit in the bank counts as my money, and when it gets loaned out, it counts as someone else's money, too.*

Banks generate credit, and credit is new money. Even with a gold standard. Or rice.

For this reason, the banking system plays a crucial role as a link between the Federal Reserve and the money supply, which will be explored in the next chapter. As an aside, any other institution that generates credit can create money, too. In 2009, when California did not have enough cash on hand to pay its bills, the state issued IOUs and used them to pay creditors, including taxpayers who were owed refunds. The IOUs were redeemable for dollars roughly three months after they were issued (or before then, if the state fixed its budget problems) and paid 3.75 percent interest.[10] The same thing happened during the Great Depression, particularly when local banks had failed or were forced to close by the government. Institutions with enough credibility that oth-

---

* This process can continue. Suppose the farmer taking out the loan is not ready to use the borrowed rice (or rice certificates) and deposits them for the time being in her own bank. Half of these funds can be loaned out, too (assuming a reserve ratio of 0.5). *Now we are triple counting.* Half of my rice can be loaned to someone, so that each bag of my rice on deposit creates a half bag of new money when loaned out. And each of those half bags, when deposited in a bank and partially loaned out, can generate another quarter bag of new money. As you might surmise, this process can continue until there is no more incremental rice to loan out. In a fractional banking system, the formula for the expansion of the money supply from new deposits, the money multiplier (m), is the following: m = 1/reserve ratio. If the reserve ratio is 0.5, as in our example, every new bag of rice deposited adds two bags of rice to the money supply. The lower the reserve ratio, the more dramatic the expansion of the money supply. With a reserve ratio of 0.1, every bag of rice (or dollar) on deposit increases the money supply tenfold. You should also appreciate that the money multiplier works in reverse. When banks slow down their lending, or hold more reserves, the money supply will contract sharply.

ers would accept their homemade IOUs issued an estimated $1 billion in scrip. These money substitutes were printed on metal, leather, paper, fish skin, and even old tires.[11] An IOU is a loan (from the party getting the IOU to the party writing it). Any loan is an expansion of credit, and any expansion of credit expands the money supply. As Charles Kindleberger has noted, there are essentially an infinite number of ways in which credit can be expanded on a fixed money base.[12]

For now, we are slowly working our way toward riots and mayhem in our bucolic hamlet. (The use of the phrase "double counting" foreshadows how this might end badly.) The financial system amplifies booms and busts, primarily because of the "procyclical" nature of credit. Banks lend most aggressively when times are good and most cautiously when times are bad—which makes the good times better and the bad times worse. When a party gets going, credit has the effect of turning up the music and adding grain alcohol to the punch. When that party starts to falter—for any reason, real or imagined—credit becomes scarcer, which is like dumping out the punch and turning on the lights. Again, the metaphor is not chosen at random. The quote that best encapsulates the boom leading up to the 2008 financial crisis was from Citigroup CEO Chuck Prince, who told the *Financial Times* in the summer of 2007, "As long as the music is playing, you've got to get up and dance. We're still dancing."[13] It is not coincidence that former Fed vice chair Alan Blinder titled his book on the subsequent crisis *After the Music Stopped*. Suffice it to say, Citigroup stopped dancing, Citi shareholders lost a staggering amount of money, and Chuck Prince stepped down as CEO.

For now, we are still dancing in our hamlet. Let's envision a boom: The harvest is good. Families are awash with rice. Deposits at the rice storehouses climb, enabling more loans. Land values are rising, both because credit is more readily available and because villagers believe future harvests will continue to be bountiful. One feature of booms is a heightened optimism, sometimes bordering on delusion. Sir Isaac Newton, the famous scientist who also happened to have lost a great deal of money in a speculative real estate bubble, concluded, "I can calculate the motions of the heavenly bodies, but not the madness of people."[14] Some prominent economists would dissent here—there is a small cadre in the profession who cling to the belief that there is no such thing as a "bubble" or a "mania." In their highly ideological view of the world, there is always a rational explanation for large swings in asset prices, not just mass hysteria. My sense is that these folks need to read more history, spend more time outdoors, or both.* I would like to live in the world they describe, where humans are always and everywhere rational, I just don't believe we do.

In any event, the interaction between a booming economy and aggressive credit markets can promote reckless behavior that ends in crisis. To recap: The money supply has gone up because of the big harvest. It has gone up even further because banks are lending more aggressively. Land values are rising, both because of higher expectations about future crops and because it has become easier to buy land on credit. (Rising land values facilitate borrowing, and vice versa.) A bank might also lower the proportion of rice deposits held in the vault, say from 0.5 to 0.25, freeing up even more rice to be loaned out. This is not entirely irrational, as farmers are sitting on bountiful harvests and expecting good crops in the future; few will be rushing to the bank to demand their deposits. Robert Solow has written, "Large quantities of liquid capital sloshing around the

---

* If I sound mildly bitter on this point, it's because I am. In graduate school I had a disagreement with my macroeconomics professor—one of the most influential finance experts in the world, who now teaches at one of the most influential universities in the world—over the role that psychology plays in markets. He insisted that psychology does not determine market outcomes, only economic fundamentals. I disagreed, as it seemed asinine to me to overlook human nature, which is prone to euphoria and panic. Time has been kinder to my view of markets than his. (The 2002 Nobel Prize in Economics recognized important work at the intersection of psychology and economics; the subfield of behavioral economics now explores this important area.) Okay, yes, I'm still annoyed that I got a B- in that class, and that is small of me. But when I take a bigger view, I get even angrier. With very few exceptions, the macroeconomic community did not anticipate the collapse of the real estate bubble nor its dire effects on the broader financial system. In fact, the crisis was almost certainly made worse by many precise but inaccurate macroeconomic models that downplayed the global risks and gave false comfort to reckless financiers. Seldom in academe has the ratio of arrogance to excellence been so out of whack in a way that imposed such large human cost.

world should raise the possibility that they will overflow the container."[15] Yes, that is more foreshadowing. If this were a film, we might begin to hear the first strains of ominous music, barely audible.

Some investors, who have little or no interest in growing rice, begin to buy land (using credit) with the expectation of selling later when prices have gone up even further. (If we were to be unkind, we might call these investors "speculators.") On the outskirts of the hamlet, land previously thought to have little productive use has become more valuable. (Hereafter we will refer to this as subprime land.) Meanwhile, political leaders in the village are united in their belief that poor citizens should have greater access to credit to buy subprime land. Conservative rice farmers, who live in the "red" part of the hamlet, consider this to be an important part of their vision for an "ownership society." Over in the "blue" part of the hamlet, rice farmers also believe that poor villagers should be able to buy land. For too long, greedy bankers have shut the door to opportunity on these marginalized citizens! These red and blue politicians may not agree on whether gay rice farmers should be allowed to marry one another, but they are united in the belief that more lending to low-income people—so they can finally afford a paddy of their own—is a good thing.

Asset prices (and debt) are rising. Farmers are feeling richer. Prosperity percolates through the hamlet, contributing to growth in businesses that have nothing to do with rice farming. Everyone is dancing—not the waltz, the jitterbug. As Kindleberger wrote in his book *Manias, Panics, and Crashes*, "During the mania the increases in the prices of real estate or stocks or in one or several commodities contribute to increases in consumption and investment spending that in turn lead to accelerations in the rates of economic growth."[16] Yes, this is how the United States felt in 2005. And East Asia in the early 1990s. And Japan in the 1980s. And the United States in the Roaring Twenties (when there literally was a dance craze, the Charleston). *Because this is the way it always looks before a crash.*

Now is the time to cue the scary music, the kind that makes people want to stop dancing and run to the bank to get their money. Everything I have just described begins to run in reverse. Maybe the dancing stops because there is a bad harvest, or a bad weather forecast, or even a rumor of a bad weather forecast. In any event, the dancing tends to stop abruptly. Something spooks the farmers and the bankers. Greed turns to fear; recklessness becomes paranoia. Land values begin to fall, particularly for subprime land. The banks curtail credit, which further hurts land prices. Some farmers cannot repay their loans, either because the harvest has fallen short of expectations or because they were counting on rising land values to repay their debt. Bad loans create trouble for the rice banks, which prompts villagers to rush to get back whatever rice they can. At this point, a winsome storehouse owner implores depositors not to withdraw all of their rice at once: "You're thinking of this place all wrong. As if I had the rice back in a safe. The rice is not here. It's in Joe's paddy . . . right next to yours. And in the Kennedy paddy, and Mrs. Macklin's paddy, and a hundred others. Why, you're lending them the rice to plant, and then, they're going to pay it back to you as best they can after the harvest. Now what are you going to do? Foreclose on them?"

The rice banks do foreclose, selling off land that was put up as collateral, which drives prices down further. Banks with too many bad loans go bust. Even some healthy banks can be dragged into insolvency when anxious depositors rush to get their rice back. Farmers who wisely realize that this would be a great time to buy land are handicapped by the fact that paranoid bankers have turned off the credit taps. *Every bad thing makes more bad things happen.*

As Kindleberger wrote, "The decline in the prices of some assets leads to the concern that asset prices will decline further and that the financial system will experience 'distress.' The rush to sell these assets before prices decline further becomes self-fulfilling and so precipitous that it becomes a panic. The prices of commodities—houses, buildings, land, stocks, bonds—crash to levels that are 30 to 40 percent of their prices at the peak. Bankruptcies surge, economic activity slows, and unemployment increases."[17] This sounds just like 2008—except that Kindleberger died in 2003. In fact, he was describing America's panics in 1816, 1826, 1837, 1847, 1857, 1866, 1873, 1907, 1921, and 1929. This is not just bad luck. As Yale economist Gary Gorton told the Financial Crisis Inquiry Commission, "There is a fundamental, structural, feature of banking, which if not guarded against leads to such crises."

This is a convenient time to discuss in greater detail the difference between liquidity and solvency (or perhaps more important, the difference between illiquidity and insolvency). In a crisis, the distinction between these concepts is crucial. Liquidity is a measure of the ease and predictability with which an asset can be converted to cash. Cash is the most liquid asset, because it is already cash. (If you read that sentence over and over, it starts to look profound . . .) Aside from actual dollars, which are impractical for holding large sums, U.S. Treasury securities are the world's most liquid asset. Roughly half a trillion dollars' worth of Treasury bonds are bought and sold *every day*.[18] Liquidity is a continuum, with cash on one end and unique assets, such as fine art, on the other. Every Rembrandt painting is unique; the number of potential buyers is small. It takes time to arrange such a sale, and the commission for selling such a work tends to be high. If you need to raise a large amount of cash in the next fifteen minutes, selling Treasuries is a perfectly viable option—selling a Swiss ski chalet or a vintage baseball card collection less so.*

Solvency, on the other hand, is a binary concept. An entity is solvent if its assets exceed its liabilities; it is insolvent (broke, bankrupt) if its liabilities are more than its assets. Even if all the assets can be liquidated quickly and easily, the revenue generated is not sufficient to pay off all the creditors. But here's the thing: assets that are liquid in normal times are not liquid in a crisis because so many people are trying to sell the same thing at the same time. Even if your balance sheet is healthy, assuming that you can sell assets to survive a financial panic is like assuming you can run to the grocery store to get water during a hurricane. It doesn't work if everyone else is rushing to do the same thing.

---

* During the 2008 financial crisis, global investors were so eager to park their money in U.S. Treasury securities that yields briefly turned negative. As opposed to earning interest, panicked investors were willing to pay a small premium to park their capital in highly liquid securities with a very low risk of default.

In a crisis, illiquidity can turn into insolvency. That was Bailey Bros. Building & Loan's problem in *It's a Wonderful Life*. We are led to believe that the institution has sufficient resources to pay off its depositors—*in the long run*. But the depositors are in the lobby demanding their money *now*. A lender of last resort—George Bailey and his honeymoon cash—can prevent illiquidity from turning into insolvency, by meeting short-term liquidity needs, but also by preventing (or ending) the panic itself. Remember, people are less apt to demand their money back if they know they can get their money back. This was the fundamental insight of Walter Bagehot, a nineteenth-century editor of the *Economist* who wrote an influential treatise on finance and central banking, *Lombard Street*, after a financial panic in London in 1866. Bagehot wrote, "The ultimate banking reserve of a country (by whomsoever it is kept) is not kept out of show, but for certain essential purposes, and one of those purposes is the meeting a demand for cash caused by an alarm within the country."[19] Bagehot's admonition remains the mantra of central bankers to this day: *lend freely against all good collateral at a punitive rate.* In other words:

1. Lend as much money as any solvent institution needs to get through a liquidity problem, recognizing that just having access to such borrowing makes the liquidity problem less likely.
2. Demand sufficient collateral to cover the loan if it does not get paid back, recognizing that what's pledged as collateral may be valuable but illiquid (e.g., the bank building).
3. Charge a rate of interest high enough to discourage unnecessary borrowing (and remind the borrower that it would have been better not to have this problem) but not so high as to discourage the borrowing that can avert a panic.

We now rejoin our farming hamlet, where the village council has appointed a Rice Panic Inquest Commission, Elizabeth Warren is running for chief elder, and angry farmers with pitchforks have surrounded the rice storehouses.* We now introduce one more character, Ram, who sold rice cakes in our hamlet before the crash. Ram is young, attractive, and hard-working. During the boom, Ram was smart enough not to speculate in land or to take on excessive debt. But after the crash, his business was devastated, both because the demand for his products collapsed and because he cannot get even a basic, well-collateralized loan to keep his business running. Ram is wiped out; his family is growing hungry and desperate.

Here is why Ram matters: he is the innocent victim. No one likes the bankers or the speculators. Farmers who borrowed too much have themselves to blame. But Ram, well, he's collateral damage. So what to do about Ram? That is the question at the heart of any financial system, simple or complex. There is a compelling case, both economically and morally, that government should let a crisis run its course: a lot of stupid people who did a lot of stupid things will pay an appropriate price for their actions—and perhaps do fewer stupid things in the future. As Treasury Secretary Andrew Mellon supposedly advised President Herbert Hoover during the depths of the Great Depression, "Liquidate labor, liquidate stocks, liquidate the farmers, liquidate real estate. . . . It will purge the rottenness out of the system. . . . Values will be adjusted, and enterprising people will pick up the wrecks from less competent people."[20] In other words, wipe out anyone and anything foolish enough to get swept up in the crisis and start over with what is left.

There is some dispute about what Mellon actually said, since President Herbert Hoover related the comments and we have no video. However, you can watch the YouTube clip of CNBC reporter Rick Santelli's famous 2009 diatribe on the floor of the Chicago Board of Trade in which he rails against bailing out overly indebted U.S. homeowners. He turns to the traders crowding around him and yells, "How many of you people want to pay for your neighbor's mortgage that has an extra

---

* After America's first bank panic in 1792, angry investors surrounded the New York jail holding one of the culpable speculators and pelted it with stones.
"The Slumps that Shaped Modern Finance," *Economist*, April 12, 2014.

bathroom and can't pay their bills?" Someone yells back, "How about we all stop paying our mortgage!"[21] Santelli says he is going to hold a tea party in Chicago on Lake Michigan—the moment that is credited with launching the Tea Party.

Bad grammar aside, Santelli and his supporters have a point. Why should we spend a lot of our time and money fighting a house fire caused by a guy smoking in bed? That's where Ram complicates things. Think of him as the next-door neighbor whose house may also be consumed in the blaze. In fact, as 2008 reminds us, this can be a pretty densely populated neighborhood. Therein lies the dilemma: To protect the neighborhood, we may have to invest public resources in saving the house of the guy who was smoking in bed—who may or may not learn his lesson. Or we may have to impose regulations on homeowners before there is a fire (e.g., sprinklers and smoke detectors) to protect the neighborhood. Both are unpopular. No one likes regulations before a crisis, when they seem intrusive and expensive. And no one likes bailing out bad actors once a crisis unfolds.

It is ironic that Chicago, the place where Rick Santelli launched the Tea Party, was once completely wiped out by fire. A fire that began in a single barn destroyed the modern equivalent of $4 billion in property and left 100,000 people homeless.[22] Even as we lament regulation and government bailouts, we expect government to stop those kinds of conflagrations. The argument in favor of regulating the financial industry (and intervening to dampen a crisis, if necessary) typically comes down to three points:

1. No matter how stupid or reckless the financiers, government should protect the innocents who might otherwise be severely burned in a financial fire.

2. Modest interventions, such as insuring bank deposits or acting as a lender of last resort, can have oversized impact; it is a sensible use of public resources to prevent or stop a barn fire given the potential damage if it were to spread.

3. Government cannot credibly commit to standing idly by in a crisis (no matter what politicians say before it happens), so we might as well try to prevent it.

In every modern economy on the planet, government plays an active role in regulating banks and related financial institutions. I would bet that if we discover intelligent life on other planets, they will have financial crises and regulators, too. I say that not because I have extensive knowledge of extraterrestrial life, but because finance has certain inherent properties that cause events to repeat themselves—over time, across countries, and maybe even in outer space. Each crisis appears unique. After 2008, we were inundated with mind-numbing details about mortgage-backed securities, the repo market, credit default swaps, TARP, Sarbanes-Oxley, and a boatload of acronyms: CDOs, SIVs, M&Ms. (Okay, the last one is just candy.) If we are to understand 2008, these details matter; that's what chapter 9 is for, and the books I mentioned at the outset of this chapter. But if you want to understand banking in general—the things that tie 1792 together with 2008—the lessons are fewer and more basic. I urge you to watch or re-watch *It's a Wonderful Life*. The important concepts are all in there. In the meantime, there are a handful of core concepts related to credit that are just as relevant today (and in the future) as they were in the eighteenth century.

First, and perhaps most important, banks are good. Yes, I will be writing about crashes and bailouts again in a moment, but let us not lose sight of the profound economic benefits that stem from matching lenders with borrowers. I am using "bank" in the broadest sense of the word. For regulatory and legal purposes, a bank is different from a savings and loan, which is different from a hedge fund or the money market or the repurchase agreement market. Finance is steadily evolving (often in response to the regulations imposed after the last financial crisis). The "shadow banking" sector represents a large and growing group of nondepository institutions that borrow and lend, albeit with less regulation than traditional banks and without taking consumer deposits. These institutions have the same advantages and vulnerabilities as George Bailey's Building and Loan. For our purposes here, if it lends like a bank, and it borrows like a bank, then it's a bank.* The *Economist* has described these collective institutions as an "economic time machine, helping savers transport

---

* Technically, a bank has borrowed funds from its depositors.

today's surplus income into the future, or giving borrowers access to future earnings now."[23] In the process, they scour the globe for investment opportunities, moving capital to wherever it can be used most productively. This is right up there with electricity and antibiotics in terms of making our lives better. Really.

Second, any entity using borrowed money is prone to liquidity problems, or outright panic, if lenders fear they cannot get their money when they want it. Traditional bank deposits are now insured up to $250,000 for each depositor. If you read in the newspaper that the bank holding your checking account is on the brink of insolvency, you will likely peruse the article out of curiosity and then turn to the sports section. The shadow banking system has no such protection. If everyone heads for the exits, bad things happen. The Germans even have a word for it: *Torschlusspanik*, which roughly translates to trying to get through the door before it is slammed shut. Anyone reading this book is old enough to have vivid memories of 2008 (or is a very precocious reader).

I sat down with Ben Bernanke in the spring of 2015 to debrief on his role as chair of the Federal Reserve during the financial crisis. He describes the sequence of events that began in 2007 as a "classic financial panic," albeit one without traditional bank runs (because of the deposit insurance) but rather "electronic runs" on other noninsured financial institutions. How bad was it? Bernanke, not a man prone to hyperbole, explains, "The financial system was in great danger of becoming dysfunctional. History suggests, and our experience after Lehman* suggests, that a dysfunctional financial system—a major financial crisis—has massive effects on the economy. We were facing in 2008 probably the worst financial crisis in the history of the United States." For the record, Bernanke is a scholar of the Great Depression, so when he says that the events of 2008 could have led to the worst financial crisis in the history of the United States it's not like he has overlooked the 1930s.

---

* The investment bank Lehman Brothers was a global financial services firm that declared bankruptcy on September 15, 2008, setting in motion a cascade of adverse events that spread and deepened the global financial crisis.

Third, we try to prevent the *Torschlusspanik*, or if we fail at that, to minimize the damage. The system typically benefits from a "lender of last resort." In most countries that is now a crucial role of the central bank (the Federal Reserve in the United States). Historically, consortiums of private investors have also played that role. In the panic of 1907, John Pierpont (J. P.) Morgan, the corporate titan who dominated American finance at the turn of the twentieth century, pledged his personal resources to backstop the banking system and corralled a group of other bankers to do the same. (The Federal Reserve System had not yet been created.) Sometimes entire countries are prone to panic, when investors rush to get their pesos out of Argentina or their lira out of Turkey. In that domain, the International Monetary Fund plays the role of lender of last resort.

Fourth, just to make all of this harder, anything that cushions the pain of the *Torschlusspanik* makes the reckless behavior that caused it all the more likely. This is the concept known as moral hazard. Taxpayers have a right to question why the fire department is rushing to put out a fire in the home of someone who stores gasoline near the furnace. And they are correct that putting out the fire will give that knucklehead one more reason to watch television rather than clean out the furnace room. But when the alternative is letting the neighborhood burn, there are not a lot of easy choices.

Bankers have done something unique: they have unified the world's major religions against them. Jesus expelled the moneychangers from the temple. Muhammad banned usury. The Torah directs that all debts be discharged every seven years. The unifying belief is that moneylending is somehow unjust and unproductive. Economists see it entirely differently. *Moneylending is the good part of banking.* The whole point is to put idle capital into the hands of those who can make productive use of it; anyone who facilitates such a deal is performing a valuable service and should be paid as such. The problem is when moneylending goes wrong—namely when depositors rush the temple and the moneylenders don't have the money. If Jesus were a central banker, that would be his concern.

CHAPTER 5

Central Banking

Our economic system will work best when producers and consumers, employers and employees, can proceed with full confidence that the average level of prices will behave in a known way in the future—preferably that it will be highly stable.

—Milton Friedman[1]

Getting prices right is hard. The financial system is inherently prone to panics. Those financial panics can derail the broader economy. Who are the adults in charge of all this?

We just heard from one, Ben Bernanke, who was chair of the Federal Reserve, America's central bank, during the financial crisis. A central bank, whether it is the U.S. Federal Reserve or the Bank of Canada or the European Central Bank, is the institution with primary responsibility for managing the money supply and protecting the stability of the financial system. In the United States, Congress has also charged the Federal Reserve with using monetary policy to promote full employment.

Central banks have evolved in different countries in different ways. (The European Central Bank, for example, was created to manage monetary policy in all the countries that share the euro.) Central banks are government entities, albeit more like the Supreme Court than Congress. They are created and empowered by national governments. Congress created the Federal Reserve and could, in theory, eliminate it. Yet top central bank officials are typically shielded from direct democratic control (like Supreme Court justices). The senior Federal Reserve Board members, including the chair, are appointed by the president and confirmed by the Senate. Once in office, however, they cannot be removed by the president or Congress for any policy-related decisions.

Why does that matter? Because doing what is best with regard to monetary policy is not always about doing what's popular. In fact, if economics nerds—of which there are many—had a central banking superhero, it might be Inflation Fighter Man. This superhero would have a single power, raising and lowering interest rates, and with that power he could whip rising prices into submission. Inflation Fighter Man would be balding and tall, almost six foot seven, with a slight stoop, a gravelly voice, and a penchant for cheap cigars. With his power over interest rates, Inflation Fighter Man would send a powerful signal throughout the economy that rising prices could not stand.

Unions demanding higher wages? *Boom!* Inflation Fighter Man raises interest rates until the economy slows to the point that workers fear for their jobs. Forget the double-digit raise! Once Inflation Fighter Man tightens the screws on monetary policy, workers are happy just to be employed at whatever wage they made last year. Companies looking to raise prices? *Pow!* Inflation Fighter Man makes it so expensive for consumers to borrow that homebuilders and auto manufacturers and other businesses dependent on consumer credit must hold prices down to stay in business. Doesn't sound like a hero? That's the point. Read on!

Inflation Fighter Man is so feared and respected that when he says he will break the back of inflation, people everywhere know he is willing to do whatever it takes. This credibility becomes a self-fulfilling prophecy. When Inflation Fighter Man makes an utterance about his intentions— usually while enveloped in a haze of smoke from those cheap cigars— markets around the world react. *Wham!* Prices and interest rates change immediately because he says they will change. Yes, Inflation Fighter Man controls interest rates, but his reputation is also a hidden power.

Like any good superhero, Inflation Fighter Man has a dark side. Fighting inflation inflicts pain. Raising interest rates deliberately slows the economy: consumers purchase less, asset prices fall, firms find it more expensive to borrow and invest. Entire industries, such as real estate, fall into distress. This special power—manipulating interest rates—can impose real costs on real lives. Those who suffer blame Inflation Fighter Man; they send him angry letters (or worse) and plead with Congress for relief. But Inflation Fighter Man keeps his eye on the prize. He knows that price stability is what maximizes prosperity in the long run. Inflation Fighter Man is not cowed by personal attacks and emotional stories of economic distress. He knows that society will be better off when the system is rid of inflation—and the expectation of inflation—once and for all. Then households will no longer see the value of their savings eroded by inflation; businesses can make plans knowing what prices will be five, ten, or even thirty years in the future. Sure enough, when the world emerges from an inflationary period, people everywhere say, "Thank you, Inflation Fighter Man."

There is a reason that Inflation Fighter Man is tall, stooped, bald, and keen on cheap cigars. His character is based on the most heroic inflation fighter of all time, Paul Volcker, who was chair of the Federal Reserve, America's central bank, from 1979 to 1987. In 1980, inflation in the United States was running at 14 percent.[2] The economy was also weak, defying expectations that inflation should be good for growth and employment. Inflationary expectations were baked into the cake. Everyone expected price increases, which brought about price increases, which planted inflationary expectations ever more deeply. Something would have to change to break the back of inflation. Not only would that require a drastic dose of higher interest rates, but the public would have to believe that the Fed would tolerate the economic pain associated with a sustained period of high interest rates. Paul Volcker was just the guy. As William Poole, former president of the Federal Reserve Bank of St. Louis, has explained, "The days of 'easy credit' turned into the days of 'very expensive credit.' The prime lending rate exceeded 21 percent. Unemployment reached double digits in some months. . . . Volcker's tough medicine led to not one, but two, recessions before prices finally stabilized."[3] The result of this bitter medicine was three decades of modest inflation and economic stability that came to be known as the Great Moderation.

When Inflation Fighter Man is turned into a blockbuster film, there will be changes to update him from the 1970s. First, the cigar must go. The Federal Reserve is now a smoke-free workplace. Also, Inflation Fighter Man will be a woman. Janet Yellen took over as chair of the Federal Reserve in 2014, the first woman to hold that post. Yellen is neither tall nor balding. Meanwhile, the world has emerged from the financial crisis of 2008 facing a different threat than it did in the 1970s: falling prices. In the United States, Europe, and Japan, monetary policy officials are working hard to ward off deflation. Governments are consistently missing their inflation targets—on the low side. In early 2015, a full seven years after the onset of the financial crisis, the *Economist* declared, "The world is grievously underestimating the danger of deflation."[4]

So, in an acknowledgment of changing times, the blockbuster film will be called *Deflation Fighting Woman*. Nonetheless, feminists will rightfully point out that Angelina Jolie, in the lead role, bears no resemblance to Janet Yellen. And why does the Fed chair need a tight-fitting body suit? Did Alan Greenspan wear curve-hugging spandex? Ben Bernanke? No and no. Still, the diehards will camp out for tickets. Why? Because Deflation Fighting Woman (or Inflation Fighter Man) is the most powerful unelected official in the world. He or she can affect the economic fate of billions of people around the planet. Raising and lowering interest rates in the United States really is a superpower. Like any superpower, it can be used for ill or for good, which makes for an exciting film.

In real life, central banks have become some of the world's most important economic institutions. With currencies backed only by the paper on which they are printed, a responsible central bank is all that stands between stable prices and Zimbabwe-like hyperinflation. (Yes, Zimbabwe had a central bank—just not a good one.) The people who lead central banks have striking amounts of unchecked powers by democratic standards. Ben Bernanke steered the global economy through the financial crisis, drawing on his experience as a scholar of the Great Depression so as not to repeat the monetary mistakes made then. (Chapter 9 will discuss the degree to which he succeeded.) Janet Yellen has had to deal with slowly reversing the extraordinary measures taken post-2008 and the specter of deflation (without a body-hugging spandex suit or X-ray vision). In Europe, Mario Draghi, president of the European Central Bank, is trying to hold the euro together, as countries like Spain, Portugal, Italy, and Greece struggle with the burdens imposed by a single supranational currency. (That's chapter 11.) The degree to which these central bankers succeed or fail affects the fate of the global economy—employment, bankruptcies, wealth, even war and peace. Global monetary policy after World War I spawned the Great Depression and gave rise to many of the economic tensions that helped bring the Nazi Party to power.

Meanwhile, all kinds of people lambaste central bankers for all kinds of reasons (often conflicting). While there is broad consensus in the economics profession on the basic things that any central bank should seek to do (promote stable prices and steady economic growth), there is less agreement on how those goals are best accomplished. John Taylor, one of the most prominent voices in the field of monetary policy and a noted conservative, has accused the Federal Reserve (and the U.S. government) of doing just about everything wrong in the 2000s. The subtitle of his 2009 book is *How Government Actions and Interventions Caused, Prolonged, and Worsened the Financial Crisis*. In general, critics from the political right have criticized the Fed's response to the financial crisis as reckless and inflationary. As an extreme example, Texas governor Rick Perry declared while running for president in 2012 that Ben Bernanke's aggressive actions as Fed chair were "almost treasonous."

On the other political flank, progressives like Paul Krugman, a Nobel Prize winner and no monetary policy slouch, believe that the Fed should have been far more aggressive in lowering interest rates in the aftermath of the financial crisis (and that the Europeans are still being too timid in that regard). Meanwhile, libertarians like Ron Paul would like to eliminate the Fed altogether and return to the gold standard. (Hence his book *End the Fed*.) Conspiracy theorists on both the left and the right see the Federal Reserve at the heart of myriad nefarious global plots. One of the first Fed-related conspiracy theories was that the wealthy banker J. P. Morgan (mentioned earlier for putting together the consortium to stop the Panic of 1907) plotted the construction and sinking of the *Titanic* (1912) to kill off critics of the creation of the Federal Reserve System (1913).* A 1989 book, *Crossfire*, blamed John F. Kennedy's assassination on forces loyal to the Federal Reserve. (Kennedy issued Executive Order 11110, which was supposedly the beginning of an effort to rein in the unchecked power of the Fed; he had to be stopped.) Modern conspiracy theories focus on the Fed as part of a cabal of global bankers intent on enriching themselves at the expense of the rest of us, a view clearly sharpened by the bank bailouts during the financial crisis. If you have an Internet connection and a free afternoon, you can read a lot of wacky theories. *Research Magazine* ran an article in 2010 on the Fed and its enemies, documenting many "baseless, even bizarre beliefs." Some are funny; some are scary; all are creative. But as the author of the piece aptly notes, "That such ideas are outlandish does not make them inconsequential."[5] The reading material in Osama bin Laden's compound included *Secrets of the Federal Reserve*, a book written by a Holocaust denier alleging that the Federal Reserve is a criminal syndicate controlled by elite financiers for their own interests.[6]

The Federal Reserve is an opaque institution, poorly understood. The Fed has compounded that image problem at times by deliberately obscuring its activities. Alan Greenspan's language was so impenetrable during his tenure as chair that the *Motley Fool* radio program created a game show called "What Did the Fed Chief Say?" The hosts would play audiotape of Greenspan's testimony before Congress and invite listeners to call in to the program and summarize what the Fed Chief was trying to say. I was the judge; anyone who could accurately summarize excerpts

---

* J. P. Morgan, a proponent of the Federal Reserve System, helped to create and finance the holding company that owned the White Star Line, the shipping company that built the *Titanic*. He booked passage on the maiden voyage but canceled at the last minute. John Jacob Astor IV, the richest man in the world at the time and a critic of the idea of creating an American central bank, went down with the ship. Morgan's devious plan was supposedly inspired by an 1898 novel, *Wreck of the Titan*, in which an "invincible" ship sinks in the North Atlantic because it is traveling too fast and hits an iceberg. In the book, most of the passengers die for lack of lifeboats. See http://www.reddit.com/r/conspiracy/comments/1xni4f/did_jp_morgan_build_the_titanic_to_kill_off_the/.

from Greenspan's remarks in plain English would win a free hat. We gave away surprisingly few hats.

Part of the motivation for this book is to clear away the mysteries surrounding the Federal Reserve, and central banks in general. The role of a central bank is typically threefold: to manage the money supply; to act as a lender of last resort; and to regulate the financial industry. (The regulatory responsibility is often shared with other arms of government.) In the United States, the Federal Reserve has the added mission of using monetary policy to promote full employment. Every developed nation has an institution similar to the Fed: the Bank of England, the Reserve Bank of India, the European Central Bank (which oversees the entire eurozone), the Bank of Japan, and so on. The responsibilities of these institutions stem directly from phenomena covered in previous chapters. A central bank can prevent panics, smooth economic fluctuations, and protect the value of a fiat currency. Of course, central banks can also commit monetary malpractice. Zimbabwe's central bank wrecked the economy with too much money; in the United States during the 1930s, the relatively young Federal Reserve allowed the money supply to shrink precipitously, turning what might have been a routine economic downturn into the Great Depression. Yes, a doctor can cure cancer; he can also amputate the wrong limb. So it is with central bankers.

Like so many things American, the Federal Reserve System is a quirky combination of centralized and decentralized powers. The Federal Reserve comprises twelve regional Reserve Banks serving districts across the country. A seven-person board of governors oversees the system; each governor is appointed by the president for a single fourteen-year term, subject to confirmation by the Senate. The president also appoints the chair and vice chair (currently Janet Yellen and Stanley Fischer, respectively). As noted earlier, none of the board members can be fired for their policy-related decisions or behavior; like Supreme Court justices, they are appointed by the political process but subsequently insulated from that process. The twelve regional Reserve Banks are quasi-public institutions designed to serve both the public and the member banks in the district. All federally chartered banks are required to be a member of their regional Reserve Bank—and therefore hold stock in that institution. State-chartered banks can opt to be shareholders. The member banks choose the board of directors for each Reserve Bank; the board in turn chooses a president.

This arcane structure, particularly the fact that the regional banks are "owned" on paper by America's private banks, contributes to the myriad conspiracy theories swirling about the Fed. In practice, government officials in Washington make monetary policy with meaningful input from the presidents of the regional Reserve Banks. The Federal Open Market Committee (FOMC) is the entity that raises or lowers interest rates and sets other key policies. The FOMC consists of the seven members of the board of governors, the president of the Federal Reserve Bank of New York, and four other presidents of the regional banks on a rotating basis. (Everybody gets a turn!) So yes, it is true that Deflation Fighting Woman is really just one member of an important committee with just one vote. (The film title *Woman Who Sits on a Powerful Committee* tested badly with focus groups, even with Angelina Jolie in the title role.) The reality is that the Fed chair holds disproportionate sway over monetary decisions. In recent decades, the FOMC has tended to operate by consensus, with the chair responsible for building that consensus. Members do on occasion dissent from committee votes, but those dissenting votes are newsworthy (unlike the Supreme Court, where it is the unanimous decisions that are unusual).

The tools of a central bank follow logically from our discussion of banking in the last chapter. First, the central bank sets the reserve requirement, the quantity of funds that a commercial bank must hold in the vault or on deposit at the Fed in the event that depositors come asking for their money. A reserve requirement of 50 percent means that banks are allowed to loan out half of their funds on deposit; a reserve requirement of 10 percent allows banks to loan significantly more—$9 for every $10 on deposit. The latter expands credit more aggressively but also leaves the system more vulnerable to shocks. As was discussed in the last chapter, a fractional banking system creates new money. If the reserve requirement is 50 percent, every new dollar injected into the banking system expands the money supply by $2, whereas if the reserve requirement is 10 percent, every new dollar in the banking system has the potential to expand the money supply by $10.* All else being equal, lowering the reserve requirement expands the money supply; raising it does the opposite. As noted earlier, banks can hold these reserves on deposit at the Fed as opposed to keeping huge quantities of cash in the vault. A central bank can pay interest on reserves held there, and even interest on reserves held above the legal reserve requirement (excess reserves). Manipulating this interest rate—essentially the rate that banks get for keeping their funds on deposit at the Fed rather than loaning them out—is one more tool the central bank can use to encourage or discourage lending by its member banks.

A central bank can also loan funds directly to the banking system through a mechanism called the "discount window." The Fed is the lender of last resort; as the name would suggest, banks are encouraged to go elsewhere first. The interest rate at which the Fed will loan funds directly to banks, the discount rate, is typically set slightly above the market rate at which banks borrow from one another.† Historically there has been not only a small pecuniary penalty for borrowing from the central bank but also a stigma. Borrowing from the Fed is like borrowing money from your parents once you are over thirty. You can do it, but everyone involved would prefer that you found the funds somewhere else. The Fed's discount lending adheres to Walter Bagehot's admonition that a lender of last resort ought to lend freely at a punitive rate. At the height of the financial crisis, both Morgan Stanley and Goldman Sachs, two of

---

* This relationship is formally known as the money multiplier, which connects the quantity of deposits to the broader money supply. The money multiplier = 1/reserve ratio. For large commercial banks in the United States, the required reserve ratio is 10 percent. Thus, every new dollar of deposits has the potential to expand the money supply by $1/.1, or $10, if banks loan out all available funds. Of course, the opposite is true, too. When deposits flee the system, such as when panicked depositors prefer to keep cash under the mattress, the money supply can shrink sharply. This was one of the factors that contributed to the length and severity of the Great Depression.

† The term "discount rate" originates from the era when banks used to extend credit by buying invoices from merchants at a discount. If someone owes me $100 a month from now and the bank buys that debt obligation for $98 today, it has effectively charged me 2 percent for a one-month loan.

America's preeminent investment banks, legally converted themselves into traditional bank holding companies in part so that they would have access to emergency lending from the Fed.[7]

A central bank typically has a legal monopoly over the power to create new money, albeit electronically rather than by printing currency. This power gives an institution like the Fed the unique power to feed money into the economy or to withdraw it, thereby manipulating the "price" of money (interest rates). The authority to create new money also provides unlimited liquidity. A good lender of last resort has deep pockets, thereby convincing the financial markets that there is no need to panic. (George Bailey's honeymoon fund was big enough to persuade depositors that they would get their money back—which curtailed the demand to get their money back.) A central bank has bottomless pockets. There is no theoretical limit to the quantity of money a central bank can create to deal with economic distress. In response to the financial crisis, the Fed pumped over $4 trillion into the global economy. Who needs a spandex suit when you can do that?

And finally, a central bank can raise or lower short-term interest rates throughout the economy. Obviously Janet Yellen does not have the authority to tell Citibank what rate you ought to pay on your boat loan—but she can achieve the same thing indirectly. Central banks around the world manipulate interest rates in their respective countries by increasing or decreasing the supply of funds available to be loaned out. (How they manage to do this will be discussed in a moment.) For now, keep in mind that the interest rate is just the "price" of borrowed funds. Raising the supply of loanable funds in the economy relative to demand lowers the market interest rates. (There are more loanable funds out there, so it becomes cheaper to borrow them.) Reducing the supply of loanable funds does the opposite.

In the United States, the benchmark measure of short-term interest rates is the federal funds rate, which is the rate at which private banks loan funds to one another overnight. As noted above, the Federal Reserve cannot directly affect the interest rate at which one private bank loans money overnight to another. Instead, when the Fed decides to cut interest rates by a quarter percent, that typically means the Fed's decision makers have cut the *target federal funds* rate by a quarter percent. The Fed will do what it takes to induce private banks to lend more cheaply to one another—a quarter point more cheaply, on average. What does it take? More money in the banking system, so that the supply of loanable funds goes up and the price at which those funds are loaned out goes down. The Fed changes the supply of money in order to raise or lower the price of credit, which is a more intuitive way of describing the interest rate.

How does the Fed affect the money supply? This can be accomplished in any number of ways. Janet Yellen could put on her tight-fitting body suit and drive around the country in an armored truck passing out new money to banks. Or the folks with the fancy computers at the Fed could send new money to lucky depositors in randomly selected banks—monetary policy meets the lottery. (How much fun would that be!) As always, there is the option of dropping cash from helicopters (much of which would get deposited in banks). While each of these approaches for manipulating the money supply would be fun and exciting, they have two crucial flaws. First, the Federal Reserve would be randomly affecting the wealth of Americans, which is far beyond its mission. Second, even if Americans might tolerate random deposits when the money supply was expanding, they would be significantly less tolerant when the Fed was shrinking the money supply—Janet Yellen driving around in an armored truck randomly taking cash away from people. (Much less fun.)

Instead, central banks are much cleverer than all that. In the United States, the Fed buys and sells Treasury bonds from banks in a process called open market operations.* Banks hold bonds for the same reason individual investors do: bonds are a safe place to park funds that are

---

* In lay terms, a bond is any debt instrument with which one party loans money to another for a determined period of time at some agreed-upon rate of interest (fixed or variable). When it comes to the U.S. Treasury, the nomenclature gets more complex. Technically, a Treasury bond has a maturity of ten to thirty years. A Treasury note has a maturity of one to ten years. A Treasury bill has a maturity of less than a year. To avoid getting bogged down in jargon, I will (somewhat lazily) use the term "bond" to include all of these securities. Similarly, the term "Treasury securities" includes bills, notes, and bonds.

not needed for anything else. *Specifically, banks buy bonds with depositors' funds that are not being loaned out.* When the Fed wants to expand the money supply, the traders at the Federal Reserve Bank of New York buy government bonds from banks eager to sell them. The key is that banks are giving up government bonds, which cannot be turned into loans, for money that can. When Citibank sells $100 million in bonds for $100 million in new money, those funds can now be loaned out. (The banks with the greatest opportunities to make new loans are the most likely to sell bonds to the Fed in exchange for new money, which is another attractive feature of the process.) For reasons discussed earlier, these new funds have a cascading effect. Every new dollar the Fed injects into the banking system can support eight or nine dollars in new loans.

To shrink the money supply, the Fed sells bonds to banks, taking loanable funds out of the system. Citibank buys $100 million in bonds from the Fed and gives up $100 million that would otherwise have been loaned out. No need for Janet Yellen to ride around in an armored truck trying to take money away from banks.

The federal funds rate is the thermostat for the credit market. The FOMC sets the thermostat and then conducts open market operations until the target interest rate is achieved. You should recognize that the Fed is not creating new *wealth*, only new money. Unlike dropping money from helicopters or randomly depositing new money at banks, no one is getting richer when the Fed injects new money into the system (or poorer when the funds are withdrawn). This is all about liquidity. The Fed is exchanging money for an equivalent amount of bonds, and vice versa. As noted earlier, the Fed injected some $4 trillion in new money, or liquidity, into the economy to battle the Great Recession; over that period, the Federal Reserve System acquired $4 trillion in bonds and other assets in exchange. The financial crisis prompted the Fed to take unusual measures, which will be explained and analyzed in chapter 9. For all the fanfare and vitriol, however, these were really just new variations on the same basic plays.

At some point, presumably when the economy nears full strength, the Fed will begin to unwind this process, selling bonds into the banking system to withdraw liquidity and curtail the money supply. For years after the financial crisis, interest rates remained extremely low by historical standards and the financial news was constantly abuzz with stories about when the Fed would begin tightening the credit markets (raising interest rates).

A central bank changes the price of money. With one decision, our real-life, unembellished superhero—Woman Who Sits on a Powerful Committee—can change the price of credit and therefore the behavior of consumers and investors around the world.

What to do with this awesome power?

Manage Prices

The supply of fiat currency is essentially infinite; someone has to mind the store. A primary goal of a central bank is to maintain the value of the currency. For reasons explained in chapter 3, most central banks do not aim for zero inflation. Instead, they advertise an inflation target, or an inflation range. The U.S. Federal Reserve has a stated inflation target of 2 percent. The European Central Bank has a target of "below, but close to 2 percent."[8] New Zealand has a target range of 1 to 3 percent.[9] And so on. From there, it becomes like a carnival game: raise or lower interest rates to keep inflation near the target or in the range. (As noted above, raising interest rates is typically referred to as tightening monetary policy and lowering rates as loosening it.) Here is how it generally works.

1. Any economy has a "speed limit" in the short run—a relatively fixed capacity to produce goods and services. In the short run, we have a finite supply of the things the economy needs as it expands: land, workers, steel, yoga instructors, and so on. If the demand for goods and services exceeds our capacity to produce them, prices will rise. That is how businesses ration scarce products. A shortage of steel leads to higher steel prices. A shortage of workers leads to higher wages (which sounds like a great thing, except that the higher wages are consumed by higher prices on everything the workers want to buy). And so on.

Conversely, when there is slack in the economy, prices tend to fall (subject to the caveats discussed in chapter 3). If an auto dealer has inventory that is not moving, he marks down prices. If apartments are sitting empty, rents tend to fall.

2. The price of credit affects the demand for goods and services. You are more likely to buy a new Mercedes if you can finance it for 2 percent instead of 5 percent. The same is true for buying homes, washing machines, or anything that is typically financed. On the business side, firms find it cheaper (and therefore more profitable) to expand when interest rates fall (other things being equal). Obviously the whole process works in reverse when interest rates go up: everything that involves borrowed money becomes more expensive.*

3. Central banks manage the price of credit (interest rates) to keep an economy running as close to its speed limit as possible. If an economy "overheats"—meaning that demand exceeds what can be produced—prices across the economy will go up: inflation. On the other hand, if an economy grows more slowly than its potential, resources will sit idle. Factories close; workers are unemployed. The excess capacity causes prices to fall: deflation. There will also be significant human hardship, a point that will come up repeatedly in the second half of the book.

It is worth noting that if prices rise steadily for long enough, the process takes on a life of its own as consumers and businesses begin to anticipate inflation, so-called inflationary expectations. Workers automatically ask for higher wages to account for the inflation they

---

* Interest rates also affect the economy through two less obvious channels. First, when a central bank cuts interest rates, it tends to weaken the currency, which boosts exports, as will be explained in the next chapter. Second, an interest rate cut causes asset prices to rise, particularly housing (because low interest rates make mortgages more affordable) and stocks (because lower interest rates on bonds make stocks relatively more attractive). Rising asset prices make many households richer and therefore more inclined to spend. The key idea is that lower interest rates speed up the economy, other things held equal, and higher rates slow it down.

expect in the future; companies build regular price increases into their plans (in part because workers keep asking for more money). Once inflationary (or deflationary) expectations become anchored in the economy, it becomes very hard to reverse the trend. Prices go up or down for the same reason my mother serves oyster dressing at Thanksgiving: because that's what we did last year.*

Like most carnival games, hitting an inflation target is harder than it may first appear. Let's start with the most basic challenge when it comes to maintaining stable prices: Which prices? For all the reasons discussed in chapter 3, there is no right measure of inflation or deflation. In the United States, the Fed typically focuses on underlying inflation, which excludes food and energy prices. In contrast, "headline inflation" includes the full basket of goods in the CPI. The logic behind this decision is that food and energy prices tend to be volatile. A rapid increase in food and energy prices might reflect political tension in Venezuela or a bad harvest in Iowa more than underlying inflationary pressures across the economy. Current critics of the Fed maintain that inflation is higher than it appears because the Fed is literally looking in the wrong places. Before we can agree what time to meet, we have to synchronize our watches.

Oh, but it's much harder than that. A central bank has to fight rising or falling prices before prices begin to rise or fall. Wayne Gretzky, the greatest hockey player of all time, once described his seemingly unique talent: "I skate to where the puck is going to be, not where it has been." The same may be said for central banking. The Fed does not respond to where prices are; they respond to where they think prices are going. Just about everything related to monetary policy happens with a lag, meaning that some time elapses between cause and effect. If the corn crop is lousy in the Midwest this summer, food prices might be higher

---

* When my wife and I inherited Thanksgiving dinner about a decade ago, we successfully killed off the oyster dressing, making us the Paul Volcker of Thanksgiving dinner.

this fall, or next year, or some combination of both. An extraordinary amount of research and analysis at the Fed goes into figuring out where the puck is going. Before each FOMC meeting, Fed officials prepare a report called "Current Economic and Financial Conditions," or the "Greenbook" because of its green cover. (These people have a lot of work to do, leaving very little time for creativity.) The goal is to summarize the domestic and international economic forces relevant to Fed policy. This analysis is used to create a report called "Monetary Policy Alternatives," or the "Bluebook," which lays out the monetary policy alternatives that the FOMC could consider at the upcoming meeting.[10] (Bonus question: Why is it called the Bluebook?*)

Former Fed chairman William McChesney Martin once described the job of the Federal Reserve as taking away the punch bowl just as the party gets going. From an inflation-fighting standpoint, once people start dancing on the tables, it is too late. Although deflation has been less of a problem since the Fed was created, the metaphor still works: it's too late to spike the punch if the band has packed up and the cool people have left. In either event, the point is that when a central bank raises or lowers interest rates, the impact on the economy—and eventually on prices—also happens with a lag, particularly if inflationary or deflationary expectations have taken hold. If companies have become accustomed to raising prices 10 percent a year, and workers expect salaries to rise at that rate (or have bargained for cost-of-living adjustments that automatically raise wages to account for inflation), it is going to be hard to change those patterns. Paul Volcker recalls a labor leader telling him six months after the battle on inflation had been launched, "Well, that's all very interesting, but I'll tell you how I feel about it. I just negotiated a wage increase of 13 percent a year for the next three years for my employees, and I'm very happy about it."[11]

Higher interest rates will eventually slow the economy. But it could take months for everyone to get that memo from the Fed. How long is

---

* The Bluebook is named to honor founding Fed chairman Harry Bluebook. No, I'm just messing with you. It has a blue cover.

the lag? Well, that depends on all kinds of unique circumstances. The effect is like driving a car with a gas pedal and a brake that function with a long and unpredictable delay. Just as you push the pedal farther to the floor, the car responds to the burst of gas five minutes ago, and suddenly it's careening out of control. When you hit the brake, sometimes it works quickly, and sometimes it takes several miles.

Did I mention that Congress is also hitting the gas and the brake, often in ways that are not coordinated with the Fed's objectives? Fiscal policy—taxing and spending by the government—can also speed up or slow down the economy. Lower interest rates can promote faster growth; but so can a dollop of government spending or tax cuts under certain conditions. (Cutting government spending or raising taxes has the potential to do the opposite.) I'm sure there is a planet somewhere in the universe where Congress thoughtfully designs fiscal policy in perfect harmony with what the Federal Reserve is trying to accomplish—we just don't happen to live on it. So to stick with our driving metaphor, imagine the Federal Reserve in one of those driver's education cars and Congress and the president have their own set of pedals on the passenger side. They may be pushing on the brake or the accelerator (or both at the same time, as they have been known to do) in ways that are at odds with what the Fed is trying to accomplish.

If you still think you could win a goldfish by hitting the inflation target, we're not done yet. I've referred periodically to the speed limit of an economy—its capacity to produce goods and service without generating inflation. Here's the funny thing: *we don't really know that speed limit with any degree of certainty*. During the 1990s, Alan Greenspan and the Federal Reserve wrestled with the degree to which the Internet and information technology had increased the productivity of American workers. If workers equipped with PCs and the Internet had become significantly more productive, the economy could grow faster without inducing inflation—an increase in the speed limit. But productivity is hard to measure in real time. Nobel laureate Robert Solow famously observed in 1987, "You can see the computer age everywhere but in the productivity statistics."[12] The relationship between technology and productivity was—and still is—a crucial variable for central bankers probing the speed limit.

In the aftermath of the financial crisis, Ben Bernanke and Janet Yellen have had to evaluate whether workers who left the labor force during the economic downturn are likely to return. If so, there will be ample opportunity for the economy to grow before falling unemployment generates inflationary pressures. But if not—if the larger number of workers who stopped looking for work during the Great Recession stay out of the workforce for good—the speed limit for the American economy will be permanently lower.

Act as the Lender of Last Resort

Not every economy can count on George Bailey to give up his honeymoon savings to bail out the banking system. As described in the last chapter, one feature of a modern financial system is the need for liquidity in a crisis. The central bank is not alone in managing this vulnerability. Federal deposit insurance was created after the Great Depression to prevent bank runs. Depositors no longer race to the bank to get their money if they fear the bank is failing—because they don't care. The government will reimburse them for any losses. (Yes, this does create problems of its own, which I will come back to in a moment.) As 2008 amply demonstrated, much of the rest of the global financial system is still vulnerable to a modern variation of the same old bank run, a phenomenon that columnist and economist Tyler Cowen has described as the "age of the shadow bank run."

Cowen wrote in 2012, "The modern bank run means a rush to withdraw from money market funds, the disappearance of reliable collateral for overnight loans between banks or the sudden pulling of short-term credit to a troubled financial institution." The circumstances are new, but the behavior is familiar: when times get tough, people and institutions want their money back, which makes times tougher.[13] And for all the complexity of the Fed's response to the financial crisis, most of it looked a lot like George Bailey passing out cash in the lobby of the Building and Loan. America's central bank, in conjunction with other central banks around the world, used its full array of tools to ensure that solvent firms did not become insolvent for lack of access to credit. The danger in a financial panic is that unhealthy firms drag the rest down with them. The system was on fire, and the Fed was doing the monetary equivalent of spraying liquidity from a high-pressure hose. In the next chapter, the International Monetary Fund (IMF) will appear with a hose of its own as the lender of last resort for countries. Who do Mexico and Turkey call when they need an emergency loan? The IMF.

As you may have inferred, there is a problem with the whole lender-of-last-resort concept—namely that we would prefer not to have things catch on fire in the first place. And the better the fire department, the less the rest of us care about storing gasoline near the furnace. To understand the nature of this problem, which economists refer to as moral hazard, we will take a brief detour to understand how my brother-in-law used to buy certificates of deposit, or CDs. A certificate of deposit pays a fixed rate of interest, like a checking or savings account, but the money is locked up for a specified length of time, say six months or a year. Like demand deposits, the federal government insures CDs for up to $250,000 per depositor.

My brother-in-law used to scour the newspaper for the highest possible CD rate at any bank in the country. Sure enough, he'd find some obscure bank paying a quarter or half point more than the competitors; that's where he would send his money. If the newspaper happened to mention that the president of this obscure bank had been arrested for selling crack and that all six of the bank's branches had burned down in an accident that was "still under investigation"—no worries. Best case, the bank president is found not guilty and my brother continues to earn a higher rate than he would anywhere else; worst case, the bank goes down in flames (literally or figuratively) and the government gives him his money back. In other words, heads he wins, tails the government loses. This is a problem at the heart of all efforts to backstop the financial system—and in any other situation where protecting us from our own risky behavior is prone to cause more risky behavior. The challenge is to provide a fire department that keeps crises from spreading unnecessarily, but also to do our best to keep people from smoking in bed.

Regulate

The government ultimately shut my brother-in-law down. (To be clear, he was never doing anything wrong; he was merely responding rationally to the bad incentives created by government insurance for certificates of deposit. If I had been more industrious, I would have done the same thing.) In any event, the government changed the incentives in 2009. Regulators now prohibit banks from offering excessively high rates on CDs (relative to the national average) because they found—shockingly!—that banks with the least healthy balance sheets were the most likely to offer these attractive rates.[14]

In the United States, the Fed shares regulatory responsibility for the financial system with other government agencies. In roughly half the countries around the world, however, the central bank is the nation's sole financial regulator.[15] There is logic to having the lender of last resort play an important regulatory role. If you are the one expected to show up with bags of money when things go wrong, you would like to minimize the chances of things going wrong. One does not have to plunge into thousands of pages of federal regulations to understand the basic nature of financial regulation, whether the Fed is taking the lead role or not. Once again, the nature of regulation follows naturally from the fact that financial institutions that get in trouble impose costs that spill over to the rest of the system. The most defensible impetus for regulation is not to protect individuals or firms from making bad decisions or doing stupid things, but rather to insulate the rest of us from those poor choices (or bad luck). If you were to peruse tens of thousands of pages of financial regulation, before or after the financial crisis, they would typically fall in one of the following buckets.

Prevent behavior likely to cause a problem. (*Make it illegal to smoke in bed.*) If firms are prohibited from engaging in certain kinds of risky activities, dangerously bad outcomes are less likely. After the stock market crash of 1929, the Glass-Steagall Act restricted the kinds of activities that commercial banks could undertake, as it was believed that stock market speculation by banks had contributed to the market crash and the subsequent Depression.[16] After the 2008 financial crisis, the Dodd-Frank Wall Street Reform and Consumer Protection Act (over 3,000 pages) was passed; it includes the Volcker Rule (based on a recommendation from former Fed chairman Paul Volcker), which forbids banks from using their own capital to make speculative investments. The idea is that if firms make risky investments for their clients, only the clients lose money. In fact, firms typically earn a commission whether their clients make money or not. But if firms use their own money for such investments (if, for example, Goldman Sachs itself makes a large bet on the future of Chinese stock prices), the firms themselves stand to lose money, with all the attendant systemic problems that can cause.

Provide shock absorbers to protect institutions when bad things do happen. (*Okay, someone was smoking in bed and now there is a fire, but the sprinklers can put it out.*) Myriad regulations require that financial institutions have sufficient insulation to prevent adverse events—a market downturn or an abrupt change in interest rates—from causing a liquidity crisis or insolvency. For example, the Basel Accords—Basel I, Basel II, and Basel III—are a set of voluntary international standards related to the amount of capital that banks should hold to protect against bad loans. (The agreements are named for the Swiss city where the Basel Committee on Banking Supervision meets to make the recommendations.) Under Basel III, banks with a significant role in the global financial system should hold capital equal to 7 percent of their assets (as of 2010). This capital is their own money that can be used to make up for losses, if necessary. The Basel recommendations do not have the force of law, but they tend to be the basis for regulations imposed by national governments.

After the financial crisis, the Fed introduced stress tests to evaluate the degree to which the nation's largest banks could withstand future economic shocks—kind of like earthquake testing, only for banks. In 2015, for the first time, all thirty-one banks tested had enough of a capital cushion to stay healthy even during the financial equivalent of an earthquake. As the *Wall Street Journal* reported, "The Fed's annual 'stress test' of banks' financial health found all 31 of the biggest U.S. banks tested had enough capital to continue lending during a hypothetical economic shock where corporate debt markets deteriorate, unemployment hits 10% and housing and stock prices plunge. The exams are designed to ensure large banks can withstand severe losses during times of market turmoil without a taxpayer bailout."[17]

Protect the rest of the system. (*Darn, looks like the house is going to burn down, but we can still save the neighborhood.*) Some prospective reforms are focused on letting institutions fail without disrupting the broader system. Dodd-Frank requires institutions to create a "living will," which is a hypothetical bankruptcy plan showing that the institution can collapse without bringing down the rest of the financial system.

Designate systemically important institutions. (*If this skyscraper were to catch on fire, it would be a disaster for the whole city—so let's pay special attention to this skyscraper.*) This is the "too big to fail" problem. Some institutions are so large and have such deep and complex interconnections with the rest of the financial system that the global implications would be dire if they were to fail, or suffer serious distress. The Dodd-Frank reforms created a fifteen-member Financial Stability Oversight Council (FSOC) with responsibility for "identifying risks and responding to threats to financial stability."[18] The chair of the Fed is automatically one of the ten voting members of the council. FSOC has the authority to deem a financial institution as "systemically important." Those institutions designated as such are subject to regulatory supervision by the Fed and other "enhanced prudential standards." For 2014, that list contains some household names—JP Morgan Chase, Goldman Sachs, Citigroup—but also some less familiar global players, such as the Agricultural Bank of China.[19]

I will leave it to another author to determine which regulations actually have their intended effect. History suggests that *changing* reckless behavior is much harder than *trying to change* reckless behavior.

Fine-Tune the Economy

Unlike many other central banks around the world, the Federal Reserve is charged by statute with maintaining full employment in addition to maintaining the value of the currency. (Most other central banks are responsible solely for price stability.) This is sometimes referred to as the "dual mandate."* It is always easier to have a single governing objective rather than two or more. In the long run, stable prices promote consistent growth and maximum employment. In the short run, things are more interesting. When Paul Volcker was fighting inflation, he deliberately engineered a recession to wring inflationary expectations from the system. Businesses folded; workers were laid off. The whole point was to convince both business and labor not to anticipate 13 percent raises. Volcker recalls, "I didn't worry about the dual mandate. We were fighting inflation, pure and simple."[20]

A central bank needs to make decisions that are politically difficult. Sometimes the central bank needs to take actions to slow the economy deliberately, as Paul Volcker had to do in the late 1970s. (The public tends to be far happier with Inflation Fighter Man when his work is done than while he is doing it.) At other times, the Fed is perceived as not doing enough to speed up the economy (usually because of a fear of future inflation). Nobody likes having the punch bowl snatched away just when the band starts playing "The Twist." If the economy is running near capacity, firms are earning higher profits, and wages are going up—why not just another song or two? Politicians can exploit the gap between the wild dancing and the inevitable hangover—particularly if there is an election that falls in between the two. Arthur Burns, Fed chair from 1970 to 1978, has often been accused of spiking the punch to ensure Richard Nixon's reelection in 1974. Burns wrote in his diary, "I was looking after

---

* The Federal Reserve Reform Act of 1977 established the current objectives. This act says the Fed is to "promote effectively the goals of maximum employment, stable prices, and moderate long-term interest rates." The last injunction is typically ignored as redundant, since the best way to ensure moderate long-term nominal interest rates is via stable prices.

monetary policy and [Nixon] did not need to be concerned about the possibility that the Federal Reserve would starve the economy."[21]

I'm not sure that's enough to convict Burns of malfeasance. It does, however, reinforce the larger point that central banks tend to function best without excessive political meddling so as to shield monetary decision makers from short-term pressures that might be inimical to the nation's long-term interests. Paul Volcker recalls his meeting with President Jimmy Carter before being appointed chair of the Fed in 1979: "He invited me down to see him. We had a very short conversation. [I said,] If I'm going to be chairman of the Federal Reserve, I'm going to take a more restrictive policy than [Treasury Secretary William] Miller. I consider the Federal Reserve as independent. I feel very strongly about the independence."[22] Volcker took the independence of the Fed so seriously that when President Ronald Reagan suggested that he might drop by the Federal Reserve for a visit, Volcker told him to skip it. Years later, when Volcker was teaching at Princeton and I was his graduate assistant, we happened to have dinner shortly after one of President Bill Clinton's State of the Union addresses. Hillary Clinton had been seated next to then Fed chairman Alan Greenspan. Volcker commented that it was totally inappropriate for the Fed chairman to be seated next to the president's wife.

Across the Atlantic, the European Central Bank (ECB) is completely institutionally independent from any national governing body. While ECB officials may meet with European Union ministers of finance or the European Parliament, the ECB treaty explicitly states that they may not seek or take instructions from any other governing body. Empirical evidence demonstrates that over time and across many countries, central banks with greater independence have lower average rates of inflation and less volatility in prices. As the *Economist* explains, "Societies give unelected technocrats power over monetary policy because they think they will do a better job than politicians with an eye on the next election."[23]

Nothing in this chapter should suggest that the Fed, or any other central bank, is without flaws. Chapter 9 will examine the Fed's response to the

2008 financial crisis; chapter 14 is all about doing central banking better. (That's why the chapter is called "Doing Central Banking Better.") In fact, we know an economy can function without a central bank at all. Industrious people throughout history have found ways to engage in commerce with whatever money facilitates transactions, from bags of salt to bitcoin. The United States did not have a central bank until the Federal Reserve System was created in 1913. Two earlier central banks, the First and Second Banks of the United States, lapsed after their charters were not renewed by Congress.

Yet a properly functioning central bank makes a modern economy function more smoothly. The *Economist* wrote in 2011, when the worst of the financial crisis had passed, "Central bankers have become the most powerful and daring players in the global economy. By providing massive liquidity to the financial system, they saved the world from economic collapse in 2008. They have propped up the recovery since, not least by buying boatloads of government bonds; and they have rewritten the rules of global banking. All this has brought rock-star status."[24]

Okay, so maybe they're not superheroes. But rock star is pretty good, too.

CHAPTER 6

Exchange Rates and the Global Financial System

Devaluing a currency is like peeing in bed. It feels good at first, but pretty soon it becomes a real mess.

—Anonymous Federal Reserve official[1]

n 2013, fear swept through Iran's Manoucheri Square. Business was slowing appreciably for vendors in the square, unlike the old days when business was so good that money was literally stacked in piles all around. What had gone wrong? What had brought business to a near halt?

Peace and prosperity. Or at least the threat of it.

Manoucheri Square in Tehran is the gathering place for Iran's illegal (but generally tolerated) moneychangers. The currency bazaar evolved to trade—literally—on the fears of ordinary Iranians eager to dump Iranian currency, the rial, in exchange for dollars. The more desperate the situation for the Iranian economy and the rial, the better the business for the moneychangers. As 2013 drew to a close, the prospects for a nuclear deal with the United States were improving, which might lead to the loosening of sanctions and a jolt of energy for the sickly Iranian economy. The *New York Times* reported at the time, "The fortunes of the long-suffering Iranian currency are looking up."[2] That meant smaller profits and slower days for moneychangers whose businesses thrive on wild swings in the value of the local currency.

Nothing had been as good for business as Mahmoud Ahmadinejad, the Iranian president from 2005 to 2013 whose combative international positions and questionable domestic policies isolated the nation and sent the economy into a tailspin. "Those were fantastic days," one trader recalled for the *Times*. Ahmadinejad was denying the Holocaust, threatening to wipe out Israel, and building a nuclear program that led to steadily tightening international sanctions. As bad news bred economic decline, worried middle-class Iranians dumped rials for dollars to protect their savings. During one week in 2012, the Iranian rial fell by 40 percent against the dollar.[3]

The situation in Manoucheri Square can tell you most of what you need to know about exchange rates. The rest is detail—albeit crucially important, conflict-inducing, economically essential detail. Different countries have different currencies, each of which can be exchanged for goods and services wherever the currency typically circulates. A $10 bill will get you a taxi ride in Manhattan; a Tokyo taxi driver will not accept American currency. Conversely, a thousand yen will get you a comparable taxi ride in Tokyo while getting you nothing but scorn and contempt from a New York taxi driver.

Pieces of paper that have enormous value in one place have no immediate use somewhere else. I experienced this firsthand while staying at a cheap hostel in Australia in the late 1980s. When my traveling companion and I were out of the room, a thief or thieves broke in and stole money that was locked in our packs. The criminals took all the Australian dollars but left our American currency behind. What kind of criminal doesn't take American dollars? A lazy criminal. Because one currency can always be swapped for another, legally in most places and illegally everywhere else (even North Korea). But why and how? That is the point of this chapter. Given that no modern currency has any intrinsic value, how can we calculate at what rate one piece of paper (or bytes in an electronic ledger) should be exchanged for a different piece of paper (or different bytes)?

At the most basic level, the answer can be told with the simple example of the Iranian currency traders. One currency can be swapped for another at whatever rate two parties are willing to make a voluntary trade. How much is my 2001 Volvo worth? Whatever someone is willing to pay for it. Currencies are no different, paper or not. The traders in Manoucheri Square are just middlemen, like banks and currency exchanges. They sell dollars for rials to middle-class Iranian citizens who are worried their savings will get eroded by inflation. They then sell the rials to government officials or companies that have earned dollars abroad and would like to convert them to Iranian currency for local purchases. The currency traders are just market makers, finding the price at which the market for rials and dollars will clear—meaning that the number of buyers and sellers for each currency is roughly the same (while taking a healthy commission for doing so). We can add layers of complexity to this process, but the most important insight is that currency transactions are voluntary trades. The exchange rate between two currencies will reflect the price at which reasonable people find it advantageous to swap one currency for the other.

Governments get in the way of those transactions all the time. (The Iranian currency stalls are technically illegal, though enforcement is episodic.) Governments can also make it more or less attractive to hold a particular currency. Mahmoud Ahmadinejad did it by accident; economic distress caused Iranians to dump currency out of fear for the future. Central banks are typically more deliberate. Raising interest rates (other things being equal) attracts capital from the rest of the world, as investors seek the highest possible return. This inflow of new capital causes the currency to appreciate (e.g., foreigners have to buy dollars in order to take advantage of higher interest rates in the United States). Lowering rates has the opposite effect, causing a currency to depreciate.

Either way, our understanding of exchange rates has to begin with the simple fact that most currency transactions are trades, and all trades—from kids trading snacks in a school lunchroom to hedge fund managers buying real estate in the Hamptons—are rooted in the fact that both parties feel they will benefit from the transaction.

In the aggregate, the exchange rate between two currencies—the price at which one currency can be exchanged for another—will reflect supply and demand. If a huge number of Americans (holding dollars) suddenly want more Mexican pesos, the demand for pesos relative to dollars will go up, meaning that the "price" of pesos in dollars will climb. An economist would say that the peso has appreciated relative to the dollar, but really the price of that currency has gone up for the same reason roses are more expensive on Valentine's Day: people are willing to give up more dollars to get them. If you want to sound fancy about it, you can say roses have appreciated relative to dollars.

That brings us back to the New York and Tokyo taxi drivers. The second core principle related to exchange rates is that swapping one currency for another ought to enable you to buy more or less the same stuff, albeit in a different country. If $10 will get you a short taxi ride in New York, it's likely that converting $10 into yen at the market rate will get you roughly enough yen—somewhere in the ballpark—to take a short taxi ride in Tokyo. This is by no means a precise relationship for reasons that will be discussed for the balance of the chapter. But it is extremely unlikely that you could take $10 to the currency exchange at the Tokyo airport and get enough yen to buy a big screen television or a Honda Civic. To understand why that cannot happen, let's instead imagine that it can. In that case, you might have a conversation with your roommate that goes something like this:

YOU: Hey, what are you going to do this weekend?

ROOMMATE: I'm not sure. I found $10.53 under the cushions in the couch, so I was thinking of seeing a movie.

YOU: Have you thought about flying to Japan? The exchange rate is so crazy right now that you can convert $10 to enough yen to buy two big screen TVs. If you sell one when you get back, it will pay for your flight.

ROOMMATE: Really?

YOU: Oh yeah. There are opportunities like that all over the world. Last week I skipped lunch and used the $8 to buy a ski condo in Canada.

ROOMMATE: Cool.

If these kinds of crazy opportunities were possible—or even less extreme price imbalances—Americans would rush to take advantage of them. When people like your roommate (and hedge fund managers with far deeper pockets) aggressively sold dollars and bought yen, the yen would appreciate relative to the dollar. Meanwhile, the price of televisions and other goods would climb in Japan (as American consumers snapped them up) and fall in the United States (as entrepreneurs began reselling Japanese goods in the United States). The combination of currency rate changes and price changes would move the market toward a point where the exchange rate no longer offered spectacular bargains in either country—right back to the point where some quantity of dollars could be exchanged for enough yen to buy a comparable bundle of stuff.

This intuitive idea is known as purchasing power parity, or PPP. If $100 buys a certain basket of goods in the United States, we ought to be willing to swap $100 for whatever quantity of yen, euros, or pesos will purchase a comparable basket of goods in Japan, France, or Mexico. Obviously not every item in the basket will conform to the theory of purchasing power parity. Anyone who has traveled abroad will recognize that some things seem cheap in other countries (haircuts in India, for instance) while others seem expensive (hotel rooms in Tokyo). But the broad theory should be intuitive. If the exchange rate becomes wildly out of line with what PPP predicts, rational individuals could exploit the gap, as in the silly example above.

In fact, one thing you may have noticed is that the two items mentioned above—haircuts in India and hotel rooms in Tokyo—are not the kinds of goods that can be bought in one market and sold in another. In economic lingo, both are known as nontradable goods. Consider the practical difference between haircuts and televisions: televisions can be produced in one place and sold in another; haircuts cannot. Televisions are tradable goods—like cars, shoes, cell phones, golf balls, and the like. If there is a significant price disparity for televisions between India and the United States, an entrepreneur could make easy money by buying hundreds, thousands, or even millions of televisions with rupees in Mumbai and then importing them for sale in dollars in America (subject to transportation costs, trade restrictions, and such). In contrast, no one has yet figured out how to buy cheap haircuts in Mumbai and sell them in Miami. In fact, because of immigration restrictions, one cannot even hire cheap barbers from Mumbai and move them to Miami. Nor can a clever entrepreneur buy cheap hotel rooms in Peoria, Illinois, and sell them for a profit in Tokyo. Hotel rooms are expensive in Tokyo because land is scarce, making all goods and services that require real estate expensive relative to the rest of the world. (Dartmouth economist Doug Irwin points out a clever rule of thumb: with tradables, goods move to the people; with nontradables, the people must move to the services.)

Official exchange rates often deviate from what purchasing power parity would suggest for many reasons, including the importance of the nontradable sector. Still, PPP is an extremely useful benchmark for evaluating the relative value of currencies. Currencies that are worth more than PPP would suggest are typically described as overvalued. Suppose a cup of coffee costs three Swiss francs in Zurich and three dollars in Chicago. Purchasing power parity suggests that the exchange rate should be roughly one Swiss franc for one American dollar—parity. But what if at the official exchange rate one Swiss franc can be traded for two dollars, meaning the number of francs necessary to buy a cup of coffee in Zurich can be traded for enough dollars to buy *two* cups of coffee in Chicago. Economists would say that the Swiss franc is overvalued relative to the dollar, or conversely that the dollar is undervalued relative to the Swiss franc. (The number of dollars that will buy a cup of coffee in Chicago will buy only half a cup in Zurich.)*

---

* As with interest rates, economists make a distinction between the nominal exchange rate, the rate at which one currency can be exchanged for another (the numbers posted at the airport currency exchange) and the real exchange rate, which takes changing prices into account in both countries (inflation or deflation) and is therefore a better indicator of changes in the purchasing power of one currency relative to another. For example, assume that the U.S. dollar can be exchanged for 10 Argentine pesos, and that prices are stable in the United States but rising by 10 percent a year in Argentina. A year later, the currency exchange will swap $1 for 11 Argentine pesos. The dollar has appreciated by 10 percent relative to the Argentine peso (each dollar now buys 10 percent more pesos) but each peso buys 10 percent fewer goods in Argentina. The nominal exchange rate has changed (the numbers on the currency exchange window) but because of inflation in Argentina over the course of the year, the real exchange rate (what you can buy when you swap one currency for another) has not changed at all. Any reference to exchange rates in the balance of the chapter refers to real exchange rates.

Many years ago, the *Economist* came up with a clever, back-of-the-envelope method for using PPP to determine which of the world's currencies are over- and undervalued: the Big Mac Index (a "bun-loving guide to currencies"). This handy if somewhat tongue-in-cheek indicator is predicated on three premises. First, Big Macs are sold in lots of different countries around the world. Second, each Big Mac represents a basket of tradable and nontradable inputs: The beef and the wheat in the bun are tradable commodities; the rent for the building and the labor for the McDonald's workers are nontradable. Third, to the extent that the Big Mac represents a comparable basket of goods and services wherever it is sold, the price of a Big Mac in local currencies is a simple measure of what PPP suggests exchange rates ought to be.* If the average Big Mac costs $4.79 in the United States and £2.50 in British pounds, the exchange rate between the United States and Britain ought to be somewhere in the vicinity of $4.79 = £2.50, or $1 = £.52. Deviations from this relationship will show which currencies are sharply over- or undervalued. At this moment, $1 buys £.66 on the foreign exchange market, more than the Big Mac Index would suggest. In other words, if you took the money necessary to buy a Big Mac in the United States and converted it to pounds, you could buy a Big Mac in London and still have money left over, suggesting that the U.S. dollar is overvalued relative to the pound (or that the pound is undervalued relative to the dollar).

When economic indicators are compared across countries, they are often converted into dollars using PPP rather than market exchange rates. Suppose you were trying to evaluate economic well-being in a relatively poor country like Rwanda. At official exchange rates, per capita income in Rwanda is roughly $700 per year, meaning that if you took the annual income for a typical Rwandan and converted it to dollars at the Kigali airport, you would get $700. But that may not be the most accurate measure of the standard of living in Rwanda. Many nontradable goods tend to be cheaper in poor countries, particularly rent and food. Even though the official exchange rate says $1 equals 746 Rwandan

---

* Except India, where the Maharaja Mac is made from chicken.

francs, the economic reality is that a poor person could buy more basic goods in Rwanda with 746 francs than in the United States with $1. To compensate for this—to get a more accurate measure of how people are really living in countries like Rwanda—organizations like the World Bank and the CIA (a great source for international statistics) use PPP to convert statistics in local currencies into dollars. Using that metric, Rwanda's per capita income is $1,630, or more than twice what the official exchange rate would suggest.[4]

This chapter began with a quotation about peeing in bed. So far, we have not broached anything nearly that exciting. We have established that currencies have some logical anchor to one another based on purchasing power parity, though market exchange rates may deviate from that for assorted reasons. Anyone who plans to travel the world eating Big Macs will care deeply about all this. The rest of us might find it kind of a snooze. In fact, exchange rates have profound economic and political consequences. Governments and central banks have the capacity to manipulate their exchange rates, which in turn creates economic winners and losers—both within countries and across the global economy. One of the most significant ongoing disputes between the United States and China concerns the exchange rate between the U.S. dollar and the Chinese yuan.* East Asian countries are as likely to engage in bitter disputes over currency values as they are about islands in the South China Sea. In the aftermath of the 2008 financial crisis, commentators warned ominously of a "currency war."[5]

Nobody has peed in bed yet, but we're getting there. The political tension related to currency values stems from a single economic truism: all other things being equal, a weak currency is good for exports and bad for imports. A strong currency does the opposite: exports become more expensive and imports cheaper. This concept is so crucial to inter-

---

* China's official currency is the renminbi, often abbreviated RMB. The basic unit of that currency is the yuan. For that reason, you will see Chinese money referred to as renminbi or yuan.

national economics, and therefore to global politics, that it deserves a simple numerical example. Consider a company like Ford that builds cars in the United States for export to Canada. For the purposes of simplicity, we'll assume that Ford's key inputs—labor and parts—are priced in American dollars; the cars and trucks are sold in Canada for Canadian dollars. Suppose the exchange rate between the Canadian dollar (called the loonie for the loon on the back of the dollar coins) and the U.S. dollar is parity: one Canadian dollar can be exchanged on currency markets for one U.S. dollar. Further suppose that Ford can manufacture a car for $18,000 (in U.S. dollars) and sell it in Canada for $20,000 (Canadian dollars). That's a comfortable $2,000 profit margin after the loonies are converted back into U.S. dollars.

But now suppose that for reasons that have nothing to do with automobiles, the U.S. dollar appreciates by 15 percent relative to the Canadian dollar. Every U.S. dollar now buys $1.15 Canadian; conversely, each loonie buys only $.87 U.S. Two quick notes: First, there is nothing crazy about this kind of swing in the exchange rate. As I sit here working in the spring of 2015, the Canadian dollar has depreciated roughly 17 percent relative to the U.S. dollar over the past year. Second, firms with an exclusively domestic focus do not care about any of this. A Canadian delicatessen that pays workers and suppliers in Canadian dollars and sells sandwiches exclusively in Canada does not give a hill of beans about the exchange rate with the U.S. dollar. (A "hill of beans" is a technical term used by some currency experts to gauge the level of interest in exchange rate movements.)

Back in Michigan, Ford cares a lot. The cost of making cars in America has not changed—same parts, same union agreements, same number of U.S. dollars on all the contracts. Nor has the price at which Ford can sell cars in Canada. The typical Canadian car buyer thinks about prices in terms of loonies—because they are paid in loonies and they buy their goods in loonies. (When you walk into an appliance store, do you evaluate how much you are willing to pay for a TV based on the dollar-yen exchange rate?) If the competitive price for an entry-level Ford pickup was $20,000 Canadian before the loonie began losing value, the competitive price for the same truck after the currency loses value will be unchanged. In fact, nothing changes about selling American cars and trucks in Canada—until Ford converts that revenue back into U.S. dollars. Now $20,000 Canadian is worth only $17,400 U.S., which is less than the cost of producing that truck in America.

This is why exchange rates have such a profound effect on international firms. Nothing has changed about how Ford makes or sells cars—not the production costs, the sale price, or the relative attractiveness of Ford's vehicles. Yet Ford has gone from making money on each sale to losing money—all because of a swing in the currency market. This admittedly oversimplified example would leave executives with a dilemma: They could raise prices in the Canadian market to make up for the unfavorable exchange rate and risk losing sales. Or they could hold Canadian prices firm and accept short-term losses in the hope that the exchange rate drift will reverse itself. Or some combination of the two. Overall, it's not a great set of choices, and none of it has anything to do with building better cars and trucks.*

As a point of comparison, let's suppose Honda Motors operates a plant in Toronto, where it builds cars and trucks for the Canadian market using exclusively Canadian inputs. Neither Honda's production costs nor its sale price are affected by the change in the exchange rate with the United States. In the Canadian market, Honda is no different from the aforementioned delicatessen; it is entirely insulated from swings in the exchange rate (which is one reason firms like Honda have built plants in America and in other countries with large markets). If Honda exports cars to the United States from its Toronto factory, things get even better. Assume that prior to the Canadian currency depreciation Honda could build pickups in Canada for $18,000 Canadian and sell them south of the border for $20,000 U.S. When the two currencies

---

* International corporations subject to this kind of exchange risk will often use financial tools, such as the futures market, to protect against currency losses. This does not obviate the basic point here, which is that fluctuating currency values have a significant impact on importers and exporters. The cost of hedging against that risk becomes an additional cost of doing international business; the bigger the expected swings in exchange rates, the higher the cost of protecting against such swings.

were at parity, this was a nice $2,000 profit per vehicle. After the Canadian dollar depreciates, those exports get sweeter still. The cost structure in Canada is unchanged—each car still costs $18,000 Canadian to produce. But now the $20,000 earned from every U.S. sale is worth 15 percent more when repatriated into Canadian dollars—$23,000, to be exact. That gives Honda executives an attractive set of choices: keep prices the same and earn a higher profit, or cut prices in the U.S. market and gain market share from its American competitors. Honda could sell its cars as cheaply as $17,500 in the United States and still make $20,125 when the revenues are converted into Canadian dollars. Honda could conceivably steal business away from its American competitors, earn a slightly higher profit per vehicle, and still give consumers a better deal than before the currency depreciation.

The example above is hypothetical; the situation is not. After the 2008 financial crisis, the Japanese yen became a refuge currency as panicked investors looked for safe harbor. By 2010, the yen hit a fifteen-year high against the dollar and a similar peak against the euro. Toyota, which produces a high proportion of its cars in Japan and depends heavily on Japanese suppliers, was being buffeted by the strong yen. Other Japanese automakers, such as Nissan and Honda, have been more aggressive in moving production elsewhere in the world, leaving them less vulnerable to a rising yen. The *New York Times* ran a headline in 2010, "Japan Counted on a Cheap Yen. Oops." The story went on to explain how expensive that "oops" had become: "For every yen to the dollar that the Japanese currency gains beyond the value that Toyota assumes in its planning—90 yen to the dollar—the company says it loses 30 billion yen ($355 million) in operating profit." In contrast, Nissan was losing only half as much per yen of appreciation against the dollar because of the company's overseas production.[6]

Let us not forget that while exporters are struggling from a stronger currency, importers are giving out cake and balloons in the corporate cafeteria. Starbucks buys coffee beans from around the world. When the dollar appreciates 20 percent, all of those coffee beans become 20 percent cheaper. Maybe that means cheaper lattes for all of us or just higher profits for shareholders. Either way, it's good. Many companies are both exporters and importers, meaning that a change in the exchange rate cuts both ways. Boeing assembles 787s in Seattle for export around the globe using parts imported from Japan, Canada, Italy, France, Sweden, and other nations.[7] A weaker dollar boosts profits from jets sold abroad, but it also raises the cost of imported components. Even at Starbucks, the cafeteria party would be dampened by the fact that sales from overseas stores would be worth less in U.S. dollars.

So which is better: a strong currency or a weak one? Any currency that is wildly out of sync with PPP will unfairly reward one group of citizens at the expense of another. I cavalierly declared that the Canadian delicatessen did not give a hill of beans about the exchange rate with the dollar, as all of its sales and production costs are denominated in loonies. That's true. But the delicatessen employees likely buy some imported American goods. If the Canadian currency becomes artificially weak, imported goods become more expensive. Yes, Canadian exporters are enjoying a global advantage—but at the expense of consumers who buy imported goods. A government that deliberately keeps its exchange rate undervalued is essentially taxing consumers of imports and subsidizing producers of exports. Would you support a tax on every imported good you bought so that the government could mail checks to firms producing exports?

Obviously if we knew with exactitude what the right exchange rate for two countries ought to be, we could just make that the target. Unfortunately we do not. Purchasing power parity is a rough long-run approximation; exchange rates often deviate widely and for long periods from what PPP would predict. Alternatively, economists sometimes describe an "equilibrium exchange rate," a rate at which the economy is at full employment, inflation is low, and the flow of trade and capital in and out of the country is sustainable. This makes sense, except that we do not have a complete grasp of what is sustainable (e.g., what about America's huge and growing debt to the rest of the world?). A more practical approach is to analyze the factors that have determined exchange rates in the past and use those factors to predict what exchange rates should be now. That works great—unless the present is appreciably different from the past. The investment bank Morgan Stanley has at least thirteen different models for determining the underlying value of currencies.[8] A 2007 paper from the Office of International Affairs at the Treasury Department confirmed what you have probably been thinking: there is a lot of groping in the dark going on here. The authors write, "There is no 'fail-safe' method in estimating the proper value of an economy's foreign exchange rate or in establishing a precise measure of over- or under-valuation."[9]

As with other policies related to money, the right exchange rate is therefore as much about politics as it is about economics. Where you stand on the strength of the currency depends on where you sit. Are you selling American cars in Europe? Or importing wine from France? Within countries, different parties often advocate for a cheaper or dearer currency. What's best for the country overall? Bob McTeer, former president of the Federal Reserve Bank of Dallas, has written, "A strong dollar usually serves us well, but occasionally and temporarily, a weaker dollar serves us better." In other words, that depends, too.

A strong currency does not necessarily reflect a strong economy. The dollar was strong in the 1990s when the economy was robust and capital from around the world was rushing to Silicon Valley. The dollar was also strong in the 1980s when capital was flowing to the United States because high government deficits forced us to borrow from the rest of the world. Christina Romer, a former chair of the Council of Economic Advisers, explains, "Both developments—brilliant American innovation and troublesome American budget deficits—caused the dollar to strengthen. Yet one is clearly positive for the American economy, the other a negative. The point is that there is no universal good or bad direction for the dollar to move. The desirability of any shift in the exchange rate depends on why the dollar is moving."[10]

When the economy is running at capacity—full employment and so on—a strong dollar is a nice thing. Prosperous Americans can buy goods cheaply from the rest of the world. I remember a professor once making a statement that is obvious only after the fact: exports are the price we pay for imports. All else being equal, we would like to give up less to get more. When factories are running at capacity and everyone has a good job, what's not to like about cheaper French wine and Japanese cars? A strong dollar is like getting a discount coupon for the rest of the world's goods while selling your own stuff at full price.

When an economy is weak, however, things get more complicated. This is when countries start peeing in bed, figuratively speaking. A cheaper currency stimulates exports, and exports put people back to work. In 2010, when the U.S. economy was still staggering back from the financial crisis, a *New York Times* business article offered a tantalizing economic magic wand: "Say there was a way to create a half million American jobs over the next two years without adding a dime to the debt or deficit. And say it would also revive moribund Rust Belt factories, reduce the country's gaping trade deficit and help stabilize the international economic system." What was this job-creating elixir? A cheaper dollar relative to the Chinese yuan.

Like most elixirs, this one was probably oversold. Still, the basic idea holds: exports are good for a struggling economy; a weak currency promotes exports. Of course, there is no free lunch. A weak currency means that a nation gets less in return for what it produces. Suppose an American autoworker can use four hours' worth of earnings to buy a television set made in China. If the dollar depreciates relative to the yuan, it may take five hours of wages to buy the same television. This is effectively a wage cut—a fact that will loom large in our discussion of the eurozone in chapter 11. The situation resembles a struggling department store: yes, it would be wonderful to sell everything at full price, but if there is a lot of unsold merchandise hanging on the racks, the next best option is to hold a sale. A cheaper currency is like putting your whole country on sale for the rest of the world. As the *Economist* observed, "Once upon a time, nations took pride in their strong currencies, seeing them as symbols of economic and political power. Nowadays it seems as if the foreign-exchange markets are home to a bunch of Charles Atlas's 97-pound weaklings, all of them eager to have sand kicked in their faces."*[11]

---

* Charles Atlas developed and marketed a special bodybuilding regimen in the early twentieth century that promised to turn "97-pound weaklings" into muscular tough guys. Atlas said he was inspired to develop his special program by a bully who kicked sand in his face when he was young.

In the years after 2008, just about every economy in the world had unsold merchandise hanging on the racks. Central banks were lowering interest rates to stimulate their domestic economies and depreciate their currencies. Other things being equal, lower interest rates make a country a less attractive place to invest. When investors sell the local currency to take advantage of more attractive investments elsewhere in the world, the exchange rate weakens. Which brings us to 2010, when the *Wall Street Journal* reported, "At least half a dozen countries are actively trying to push down the value of their currencies, the most high profile of which is Japan, which is attempting to halt the rise of the yen after a 14 percent rise since May."[12] (Yes, that was the rise in the yen that was killing Toyota.) A weaker currency is a logical reaction to a global recession.

It feels good at first, but pretty soon it becomes a real mess. Yes, we have finally reached that point. The strength of a currency is relative. If one currency gets weaker, another currency has to get stronger. The head of the International Monetary Fund warned at the time, "Today, there is a risk that the single chorus that tamed the financial crisis will dissolve into a cacophony of discordant voices, as countries increasingly go it alone. This will surely make everybody worse off." It's mathematically impossible for all currencies to get weaker at the same time. It's like standing up at a football game to get a better view—a great strategy until everyone else does same thing. As the *Economist* has described (in the context of British football matches and currency depreciations), "No one's view has improved but everyone is a lot less comfortable."[13]

The irony of currency manipulation is that many nations looking exclusively after their own interests can end up in a wet, cold bed. A currency war can lead to higher inflation in the affected countries (as they all increase their money supplies) without changing relative exchange rates; worst case, trade patterns are disrupted in a way that does significant economic harm. The current situation may not be as bad as all that. It's true that from a trade standpoint, the affected countries are all standing up at the same time; no one is getting a better view. However, monetary experts like University of California–Berkeley economist Barry Eichengreen, who has also studied the competitive devaluations of the 1930s, argue that the looser monetary policy (lower interest rates) associated with weaker currencies is an important antidote for global recovery, particularly with deflation looming as a more serious problem than inflation.

Eichengreen writes about the Great Depression, "No country succeeded in exporting its way out of the depression, since there was no one to sell additional exports to. But this was not what mattered. What mattered was that one country after another moved to loosen monetary policy because it no longer had to worry about the exchange rate. And this monetary stimulus, felt worldwide, was probably the single most important factor initiating and sustaining economic recovery."[14] Eichengreen is essentially describing a situation in which a group of department stores all throw a massive sale. None succeeds in stealing customers from its competitors, since they are all offering the same basic discounts. *But the lower prices are an important stimulus to get people shopping again, which is good for the stores overall.*

Eichengreen's argument has two important implicit footnotes. First, competitive devaluations during the Great Depression were a way for countries to slip out of the economic handcuffs imposed by the gold standard. The next chapter will argue that gold does not glitter as a monetary instrument and that policymakers did extraordinary economic damage as they clung tightly to gold during the 1930s. Second, even if the post-2008 devaluations do not leave all parties wet and cold, the current process is uncoordinated and disruptive. Eichengreen writes, "Better, of course, would be for the major countries to agree to coordinate their monetary policy actions. Then exchange rates will not move by large amounts in one direction today and the opposite direction tomorrow. There will not be further disruptions to the global trading system. There will not be international recriminations over beggar-thy-neighbor policy."

This question—how the world's major economies coordinate their exchange rate policies—will come up in greater detail in the second half of the book. For now, it raises a more basic question: What is the mechanism used to value one currency against another? The answer is that different countries have different exchange rate regimes, ranging from the United States (let the market decide) to China (let's manipulate the market) to North Korea (the exchange rate is what the Great Leader says it is). More formally, the world has an array of mechanisms that can be used to value currencies relative to one another.

Floating Exchange Rates

Most of the world's largest economies have exchange rates that are determined like everything else in a market economy: by supply and demand. (China is a major exception that will get a chapter of its own.) Different currencies are traded for one another on foreign exchange markets around the world. Hence, the exchange rates are said to "float" as market conditions change, like a raft that rises and falls with the tides. This morning one Canadian dollar buys .91 American dollars; by lunch it will be slightly different. The foreign exchange market is just a bigger version of Iran's Manoucheri Square. There are individuals, firms, and governments looking to swap Canadian dollars for American dollars, and there are individuals, firms, and governments looking to sell American dollars and acquire Canadian dollars. The exchange rate at any given moment is just the price at which those two groups are willing to make a voluntary exchange.

In the long run, we would expect the exchange rate to move toward what purchasing power parity predicts, especially between rich countries where there is no appreciable difference in the cost of nontradables. In the short run, assorted global forces affect the relative demand for currencies. As noted earlier, higher interest rates make a currency more attractive (other things being equal). If the real return on government bonds is 3 percent in Canada and 3.5 percent in the United States, Canadian investors will seek the higher return in the United States. To do so, they will sell loonies and buy U.S. dollars, causing the American dollar to appreciate relative to the Canadian dollar. Strong growth opportunities will also attract global capital and strengthen the currency (e.g., Silicon Valley in the 1990s); a flagging economy or political instability will do the opposite (e.g., Iran in the Ahmadinejad era).

Fear and panic are powerful motivators when it comes to international capital flows. The Swiss franc appreciated 3 percent relative to the U.S. dollar in the first three hours after the first plane hit the World

Trade Center on September 11, 2001. A decade later, investors fearing economic disruption in the eurozone fled to the relative stability of Switzerland. In just eighteen months—between the beginning of 2010 and August 2011—the Swiss franc appreciated 43 percent relative to the euro. (This helps to explain why the Swiss franc was so overvalued according to the Big Mac Index.) Investors weren't moving capital to Zurich to buy watches and chocolate; they were avoiding the consequences of a euro meltdown that might have been precipitated by a Greek debt crisis.

Governments and central banks can always buy and sell their own currencies, affecting supply and demand directly. However, the foreign exchange market is so huge—trillions of dollars changing hands daily—that most countries do not have deep enough pockets to move the market significantly. A currency intervention is often like trying to warm a cold bathtub with spoonfuls of hot water—especially while other market participants are dumping in buckets of cold water at the same time.

The primary benefit of a floating exchange rate is that currencies can fluctuate as economic conditions dictate. The government is not responsible for conducting economic policy to maintain a particular exchange rate, leaving it free to manage interest rates and other policy tools in a way that best suits the domestic economy. As we will see shortly, any system that fixes currencies against one another, such as the gold standard, limits a government's options in this regard.

The drawback of floating exchange rates is, well, they float. More to the point, they can float a lot, often in unpredictable ways. Australia is a good example of how swings in the exchange rate can disrupt the economy. Beginning around 2009, the Australian dollar soared as China bought up its natural resources—iron, coal, and other commodities. By 2013, the Australian dollar hit its highest level in twenty-eight years, as measured against a basket of currencies weighted by their share of Australia's trade, or "trade-weighted."* Other exporters have found it

---

* For example, if two thirds of U.S. trade were with Canada and one third with China, a trade-weighted measure of the dollar's value would weight exchange rate changes with Canada twice as heavily as changes relative to the Chinese yuan.

difficult to stay globally competitive with such a dear Australian dollar. Mitsubishi closed a plant; other car companies laid off workers. Wine exports fell.[15] This phenomenon, when natural resource exports cause the exchange rate to appreciate to the point that it chokes the competitiveness of manufactured goods, is known as "Dutch disease." Dutch gas exports in the 1970s had such an effect, as have oil exports in many countries ever since.[16]

The Gold Standard

One way to avoid the vagaries associated with floating exchange rates is to fix the rate at which currencies can be exchanged against one another. No major economy uses a gold standard anymore, but it remains an important and intuitive example of how the world's currencies can be fixed against one another. Prior to World War I, the world's major trading nations fixed their currencies relative to gold. Of course, with the world's currencies linked to gold, they were also explicitly linked to one another. If $35 can be exchanged in the United States for an ounce of gold, and 350 francs can be exchanged in France for an ounce of gold, then the exchange rate has to be $35 for 350 francs. The era prior to World War I was hailed for its internationalism, in part because of the global stability facilitated by the gold standard.

The gold standard also has an elegant mechanism for sorting out trade imbalances. Suppose one country begins to suffer a major trade deficit, meaning that it is buying more from the rest of the world than the world is buying in return. For the sake of simplicity, we can do the analysis with just two countries, France and the United States, back in the day when France still had the franc and both countries were on the gold standard. Assume that France begins running a trade surplus with the United States (which means the United States must be running a trade deficit with France). French exporters are accumulating dollars, which can be redeemed for gold in the United States and repatriated to France. Gold will flow out of the United States and into France.

The flow of gold from the United States to France will affect monetary policy in both countries. With the supply of gold shrinking in the

United States, the money supply will shrink, since under a gold standard all currency must be backed by gold reserves. Conversely, the money supply will expand in France (just as it did when gold and silver were discovered in the New World). The result will be twofold: First, prices will rise in France and fall in the United States. Remember, more money chasing the same quantity of goods (France) causes prices to rise; a shrinking money supply does the opposite (the United States). These changing prices make American goods relatively more attractive, helping to reverse the trade deficit and stop the flow of gold out of the United States.

At the same time, interest rates will rise in the United States relative to France for a related reason. As the shrinking money supply in the United States makes capital scarcer, the cost of renting it rises. (The opposite happens in France as the money supply expands.) International investors, scouring the globe for the best return on investment as always, withdraw their capital (gold) from France and send it to the United States to take advantage of higher interest rates. The key point is that the gold standard has a mechanism by which global imbalances fix themselves—as one country accumulates gold, it naturally sets in motion responses (rising prices and falling interest rates) that cause the imbalance to reverse itself.*

In fact, the gold standard is awesome—until it wrecks the global economy and imperils humanity. The major drawback of the gold standard follows naturally from the simple analysis in the last paragraph: gold flows around the globe in response to economic circumstances. What can be so bad about that? A gold standard can turn a recession into a depression, as it arguably did in the 1930s. When an economy is weak (as in the United States in 1929), the best policy response is to lower interest rates to stimulate demand. But lower interest rates will cause foreigners to demand gold for their dollars so they can invest elsewhere

---

* In the run-up to the Great Depression, France (and to a lesser extent the United States) took policy measures to prevent its growing gold hoard from setting in motion the usual adjustments. My Dartmouth colleague Doug Irwin has written an intriguing article titled "Did France Cause the Great Depression?" that will be discussed in the next chapter.
http://www.nber.org/papers/w16350.

in the world; gold will flow out of the country. The result is a dilemma: to defend the nation's gold reserves, a central bank must raise interest rates—even though a weak economy needs the opposite. Economist Paul Krugman, who won the Nobel Prize in 2008 for his work on international trade, has explained how "the sacred importance of maintaining the gold value of one's currency" exacerbated the economic carnage of the Great Depression. He writes, "In the early 1930s this mentality led governments to raise interest rates and slash spending, despite mass unemployment, in an attempt to defend their gold reserves."[17] The gold standard, or any regime of rigidly fixed exchange rates, forces a nation to subvert its domestic economic interests to maintain the exchange rate.

Pegs and Bands

Nations can also fix their exchange rates against one another without gold to back up the deal. Countries can pledge to "peg" their exchange rates at some rate with another country, or a group of countries. Since 1983, the Hong Kong dollar has been pegged to the U.S. dollar at a rate of 7.8 to 1. In this system, the dollar plays the same role as gold; the Hong Kong government has pledged to take all steps necessary to maintain that exchange rate, regardless of the implications for the domestic economy. Argentina tried a similar plan in 1991; every Argentine peso was fully convertible to American dollars at a fixed rate, as with a gold standard. (Like most things related to Argentine monetary policy, this did not end well.) Prior to the adoption of the euro, many European countries were members of the European Exchange Rate Mechanism (ERM), which sought to keep the participating European currencies trading within defined "bands" relative to one another. For example, the British government pegged the pound to 2.95 German marks, with an allowable trading range of 6 percent in either direction.

The primary problem with pegs and bands is that governments must defend them, even when it means doing nasty things to the domestic economy. Global investors recognize that politicians don't always have the resolve to do that. When a currency begins to look weak, as the British pound did in 1992, speculators pounce, hoping to make huge sums when the government gives up on the peg and currency is devalued. Of course, as speculators begin aggressively selling the currency, devaluation becomes all the more likely. This is why financier George Soros is so much richer than you are. In 1992, Soros made nearly $1 billion *in a single day* by betting that the British government would not maintain its commitment to the European Exchange Rate Mechanism. As part of the ERM, the British government pledged not to let the pound fall below a floor of 2.778 marks. At the time, Britain was in the midst of a recession; the weak economy was one reason global investors were taking their money out of the UK

Despite this downward pressure, the government of Prime Minister John Major vowed to defend the pound. As noted throughout the chapter, the Bank of England had two tools for doing that: intervening directly in currency markets to buy the pound and prop up its value, and raising interest rates to draw capital back into the country. Neither option was attractive. The Bank of England had a finite amount of foreign currency with which to buy pounds; earlier efforts had been ineffectual as private investors fled pounds. Meanwhile, raising interest rates in the midst of a recession would have caused further economic damage, which is not something any elected politician is keen to do. (Norman Tebbit, who had been a cabinet minister in Margaret Thatcher's government, had taken to calling the ERM the "eternal recession mechanism.")[18] Still, Major reiterated his commitment to keeping Britain in the ERM.

George Soros called the government's bluff. In September 1992, Soros borrowed a huge quantity of British pounds and immediately sold them for other European currencies, such as the German mark (thereby further contributing to downward market pressure on the pound). John Major's government did not have what it took to maintain the pound's peg in the ERM. On September 16, Britain withdrew from the ERM and allowed the pound to depreciate against the major European currencies by roughly 10 percent. Therefore, when Soros swapped his European currencies back into pounds at the new exchange rate, he got roughly 10 percent more than he had borrowed, enabling him to pay off his loans (and interest) and keep the rest—roughly $1 billion. Not bad for a day's work. The bigger point is that fixed exchange rates are only as credible as the governments defending them. Even a hint of weakness in government resolve can bring things crashing down.

Dollarization

How much local currency can you get for $100 when you land at the airport in Quito, Ecuador? Hah, it's a trick question! No need to exchange anything. The official currency of Ecuador is the U.S. dollar. In 2000, Ecuador went through a process of "dollarization" in which the local currency, the sucre, was replaced by the American dollar. Serious inflation and a banking crisis had caused a loss of confidence in the local currency. "The decision to dollarize was taken in desperation," said Stanley Fischer, a senior official at the International Monetary Fund at the time who is now vice chair of the Federal Reserve.[19]

El Salvador dollarized in 2001, albeit for different reasons. The economy was stable; adopting the dollar was a strategy for harmonizing El Salvador's economy with the United States'. At the time, two thirds of Salvadoran exports were going to the United States, and $2 billion in remittances from Salvadoran workers in the United States were flowing the other direction (an amount equivalent to roughly 15 percent of GDP).[20] Panama adopted the dollar as its official currency at independence, way back in 1904.

So why doesn't everybody adopt the dollar? The primary drawback is that these countries lose their ability to conduct independent monetary policy. Monetary policy in El Salvador is determined by the U.S. Federal Reserve. With all due respect, the Fed does not care much about economic conditions in El Salvador (or Ecuador or Panama) when making interest rate decisions.

Currency Union

An alternative to fixed exchange rates is for a group of countries to share the same currency. The obvious example is the euro, which is now the official currency for nineteen countries in the European Union and seven countries that are not part of the EU.[21] (Other countries and territories peg their currencies to the euro.) Unlike El Salvador, the eurozone countries have their own central bank (the European Central Bank) whose mission is to oversee monetary policy for the member nations. The euro might reasonably be described as the ultimate fixed exchange rate. The member states' currencies do not fluctuate against one another—*because they are the same currency*. Currency unions offer the stability and predictability of fixed exchange rates, making it easier to conduct trade across international boundaries. One might say that the fifty American states have a currency union: they all share the dollar, with the Fed looking after the whole lot of them.

The big drawback to a currency union is that the participating countries lose the capacity to set their own monetary policy. As Harvard economist Gregory Mankiw explains, "The European Central Bank sets interest rates for Europe as a whole. But if the situation in one country—Greece, for example—differs from that in the rest of Europe, that country no longer has its own monetary policy to address national problems."[22] Chapter 11 delves into the euro, and this challenge in particular. (For now, let's just say that the Greeks and the Germans are having some issues.)

Just Make Up a Number

What's the official exchange rate between the North Korean won and the U.S. dollar? Whatever North Korean dictator Kim Jong-un says it is. Governments often create an official exchange rate that is completely untethered from economic reality (or in some cases partially untethered). The government can require companies and individuals moving money in and out of the country to exchange currency at the official rate. In 2013, when eccentric former Chicago Bulls star Dennis Rodman made a trip to North Korea to meet with the Great Leader (a big fan of the NBA, apparently), Reuters pointed out that a Chinese-made basketball selling in a Pyongyang toyshop cost $500 at the official exchange rate. Needless to say, few North Koreans were spending their entire annual salary to buy a basketball *because it doesn't really cost $500*. At the black market rate—the rate at which sane people will voluntarily trade won for dollars—the basketball cost a little less than $6.[23]

Like many things North Korean, this is kind of funny until one recognizes the human consequences. A ridiculously overvalued exchange rate is yet one more way a rotten government can enrich itself at the expense of its people. If a hypothetical North Korean firm earned $500 by selling swanky designer clothes in New York, the Pyongyang government could force the company to exchange that $500 for just enough won to buy a cheap basketball—*because that is the official exchange rate.* Here's the trick: Government officials can then use the expropriated foreign currency to load up on extravagant imports. Meanwhile, the overvalued currency makes it difficult for exporters to compete in international markets. (If North Korea were trying to export basketballs to the United States, they would sell for $500 at the official exchange rate.) North Korea is probably a bad example because its insular economy has so few export industries. Still, history is replete with official exchange rates that deviate significantly from what supply and demand would dictate. These countries invariably have black markets where the currency trades at a rate that more closely approximates purchasing power parity (e.g., the North Korean basketball should cost $6, not $500).

All of this raises two fundamental policy questions: What is the best exchange rate regime for an individual country? And how can currency values around the world be coordinated in a way that best promotes global stability and economic success?

Not easy questions, but let's start with the first. As you have probably inferred, there is no perfect exchange rate regime (though we can safely say that having Kim Jong-un arbitrarily set an exchange rate is not ideal). There are tradeoffs associated with all of the systems described above. More specifically, economists have identified what is known as the "trilemma" of international finance: no country can simultaneously allow free flow of international capital flow; use monetary policy to serve domestic economic needs; and maintain a fixed exchange rate. The term "trilemma" is a clever play on the policy dilemma here—policymakers can control any two of these two policy levers, but that requires letting go of the third.

Greg Mankiw, who is a former chair of the Council of Economic Advisers, has described each of these logical policy goals:

1. *Make the country's economy open to international flows of capital.* Capital mobility lets a nation's citizens diversify their holdings by investing abroad. It also encourages foreign investors to bring their resources and expertise into the country.

2. *Use monetary policy as a tool to help stabilize the economy.* The central bank can then increase the money supply and reduce interest rates when the economy is depressed, and reduce money growth and raise interest rates when it is overheated.

3. *Maintain stability in the currency exchange rate.* A volatile exchange rate, at times driven by speculation, can be a source of broader economic volatility. Moreover, a stable rate makes it easier for households and businesses to engage in the world economy and plan for the future.

Those sound like really great things to do! Alas, as Mankiw explains, "Here's the rub: You can't get all three. If you pick two of these goals, the inexorable logic of economics forces you to forgo the third." The best way to illustrate the trilemma is to point out the choices different countries have made—and the inevitable tradeoffs.

The United States uses monetary policy to achieve domestic policy objectives. The goal of the Federal Reserve is to maintain price stability and full employment. We also have free flow of capital in and out of the country. And our exchange rate? To quote my teenage daughter, "It is what it is."

China has chosen to manage the money supply and the exchange rate. The government uses monetary policy to promote domestic economic goals while managing the exchange rate to promote export-oriented industries. To do so, the government controls the flow of capital in and out of the country—both how much money Chinese citizens can take out of the country and how much foreign firms can invest in China.

Much of Europe is different still. The nations bound together by one currency, the euro, have controlled the exchange rate. (French companies doing business in Germany face no exchange rate risk.) There is free flow of capital throughout the eurozone. But the participating nations have given up the ability to conduct their own independent monetary policy. The fact that countries like Italy, Spain, and Greece have different economic needs than Germany is one of the stress points of the single currency.[24]

Countries, like teenagers, choose what works best for them. How is that working out for the rest of us? There are two global concerns related to exchange rates. The first is that international capital flows can sometimes turn into what looks a lot like a bank run. Capital finds its way to whatever corner of the globe promises attractive returns. But when investors run for the exits, they ditch the local currency, exacerbating the crisis and prompting more investors to get out before the currency falls further. (This is exactly why the Iranian currency traders liked the bad old days of Ahmadinejad.) The local central bank is stuck with a dilemma: raise interest rates to stop currency hemorrhaging from the country (and make the economy worse), or lower interest rates to ameliorate whatever economic problem caused the crisis in the first place (and make the currency plunge worse). Numerous countries have been through this drill just in recent decades: Mexico, Argentina, Turkey, Russia, Iceland, South Korea, Thailand. The International Monetary Fund acts as the lender of last resort for countries, just as the Fed does for U.S. banks. (Yes, this creates the same basic moral hazard problem that was broached in the last chapter.)

Such crises are destabilizing for the global financial system; obviously it would be better to prevent them in the first place. There is a consensus that floating rates are less prone to crisis, as they provide a buffer for economic shocks and do not invite attack by speculators trying to anticipate the collapse of a peg (as George Soros did). The IMF has also broached the topic of capital controls—placing limits on how quickly investors can move capital in or out of a country, or taxing such flows. This concept was previously anathema to economists, as the whole point of markets is to allow capital to flow freely to wherever it is valued most. However, the destabilizing effects of "hot money" may outweigh the benefits.

The second concern relates to whether exchange rates and capital flows are coordinated in a way that maximizes global efficiency. In 2014, Raghuram Rajan, head of India's central bank and the former chief economist at the International Monetary Fund, lamented, "International monetary cooperation has broken down." Unanticipated and uncoordinated monetary policies cause all kinds of global economic complications. By 2014, a strengthening U.S. dollar was threatening foreign firms that had borrowed heavily in dollars during the stretch of low U.S. interest rates. (These firms had to make debt repayments in dollars that were getting steadily more expensive relative to their local currencies.) The preceding years had caused a different problem: low interest rates and slow growth in the developed world sent money flooding into the developing world in search of higher yields, a phenomenon one IMF official described as an "international monetary tsunami." The result was often asset bubbles and overvalued exchange rates.[25] Raghuram Rajan told a group of schoolchildren in Mumbai (knowing full well that lots of other people were listening, including the world's central banks), "We would like to live in a world where countries take into account the effect of their policies on other countries and do what is right, broadly, rather than what is just right given the circumstances of that country."[26]

Oh, Raghu (he was a colleague at the University of Chicago, so I can call him that), we have not lived in that world for a long time. We did manage to create a system of coordinated exchange rates for a few decades in the twentieth century. Near the end of World War II, the Allies gathered in Bretton Woods, New Hampshire, to plan a global monetary system to replace the gold standard for the postwar period. This was the last successful effort to coordinate the world's major currencies. Bretton Woods produced a quasi–gold standard with the U.S. dollar pegged to gold and the other participating currencies pegged to the dollar.* (The Bretton Woods Conference also produced both the World Bank and the International Monetary Fund.) Thus, gold was the anchor of the postwar international financial system. Even then, other countries, particularly France, were upset by the dollar's outsized role in the Bretton Woods system. The system eventually broke down in 1971, when America's fiscal imbalances made it increasingly hard for the United States to redeem dollars presented by foreign nations in exchange for gold.

On August 15, 1971, after huddling with his advisers for the weekend at Camp David, Richard Nixon terminated the right of foreign governments to exchange dollars for gold, closing what had become known as the "gold window." The Bretton Woods Agreement was terminated, severing any remaining tie between the dollar and gold. From that point on, a nation holding a surplus of U.S. dollars was just holding lots of dollars. As the *Economist* noted on the fortieth anniversary of that fateful weekend, "The era of paper money and floating exchange rates had arrived."[27]

There have been bursts of global currency teamwork since. In 1985, representatives of France, West Germany, the United States, the UK, and Japan met in New York to discuss global imbalances caused by an overly strong dollar. Per the Plaza Accord, named for the hotel where it was negotiated, the participants agreed to act together to depreciate the dollar. Over the next two years, the dollar fell by 50 percent against both the yen and the German mark. The Plaza Accord has been hailed as "a high-water mark of international cooperation."[28] But here's the thing: When the world's major economies hit that high-water mark there was still an East and West Germany. Barack Obama hadn't started law school. Chapter 14 will ask if it might be time for Bretton Woods II. Is there some way to harness the flexibility of floating exchange rates without the destabilizing volatility?

The traders in Iran's Manoucheri Square hope not. Volatility is what

---

* Individuals were not able to present dollars for gold. Franklin Roosevelt severed the dollar's connection with gold in 1933. However, until 1971, foreign governments had the right to exchange dollars for gold.

makes for good business—even as the opposite is true for most firms doing business across international boundaries. There is something inherently strange about paper currencies. However, once one accepts that money is merely a claim on things of value, paper currency makes sense. Swapping one kind of paper for another begins to make sense, too. The irony is that mainstream economists are now unanimous in the belief that gold no longer has a place in international finance. As the next chapter will argue, all that is gold does not glitter.

CHAPTER 7

Gold

Had the price of gold been raised in the late 1920s, or, alternatively, had the major central banks pursued policies of price stability instead of adhering to the gold standard, there would have been no Great Depression, no Nazi revolution, and no World War II.

Robert Mundell, Nobel Prize lecture, 1999[1]

Let's stipulate that Winston Churchill was one of history's bravest, most forward-looking leaders. His unique fortitude as prime minister inspired Britain during the depths of World War II; his strategic mind was essential to winning the war. But even Churchill made some monumental mistakes. As First Lord of the Admiralty during World War I, Churchill was the chief advocate for the disastrous British attack on the Gallipoli Peninsula (in modern-day Turkey), where some 46,000 Allied troops were killed before the campaign was aborted.[2] As Chancellor of the Exchequer between the wars, Churchill was responsible for what might be described as his economic Gallipoli. Britain suspended gold convertibility during World War I (as it had during previous wars), meaning that the pound was no longer convertible to gold. With the pound untethered from gold during and after the war, prices rose steadily. By one reckoning, the British price level in 1925 was twice what it had been in 1914.[3] With the legislation suspending gold convertibility set to expire in 1925, Churchill made the decision that

Britain should return to the gold standard with the pound pegged at its prewar price relative to gold (and the U.S. dollar).

Churchill's view, shared by nearly all economic experts at the time, was that a pound sterling backed by gold was an essential feature of the British Empire. The pound had been fixed to a specific quantity of gold for two hundred years, a source of both pride and monetary stability. During the European wars of the nineteenth century, gold convertibility was temporarily suspended, but it had always been restored at the prewar exchange rate, as Churchill was attempting to do in the twentieth century. A strong pound, like the queen, was an essential feature of the British Empire. As one observer noted, "From the end of the seventeenth century to the beginning of the twentieth, the British defended the gold standard with an almost religious zeal."[4] (Note: the phrase "religious zeal" will come up again in this chapter.)

Due to British wartime inflation, postwar pounds bought fewer goods in 1925 than they had in 1914. As a result, the pound had weakened significantly relative to both gold and the U.S. dollar. (Anyone swapping gold or dollars for pounds after the war demanded extra pounds to compensate for the fact that each pound bought less than it used to.) If Britain were going to return to the gold standard at its prewar level, the pound would have to regain its lost value. The only way that could happen was if British prices fell significantly. (Lower prices in Britain would strengthen the pound by inducing those trading gold and dollars to accept fewer pounds in return, as each pound would have more purchasing power.) In other words, Churchill would have to engineer a deflation. As I've noted in earlier chapters, prices and wages do not go down without a fight. The eminent British economist John Maynard Keynes recognized this at the time. In a series of articles and essays, Keynes argued that strengthening the pound to its prewar value "would be far more difficult and painful than the Treasury supposed." Foreshadowing: he was right. If this were an economic horror movie, we would cue the scary music.

Keynes urged British policymakers to make stable domestic prices a priority rather than a fixed exchange rate with gold and the dollar. In the lingo of the last chapter, Keynes was advocating floating exchange rates so that the Treasury could focus on the domestic economy. Gold enters the economy at a rate independent of the supply of goods and services, meaning that prices will inevitably fluctuate based on gold's relative scarcity. Keynes, a fierce critic of the gold standard in general, eloquently stated the logical result: "Gold is liable to be either too dear or too cheap. In either case, it is too much to expect that a succession of accidents will keep the metal steady."[5] With regard to Churchill's plan to restore the pound to gold at its prewar value, Keynes observed—again correctly—that prices and wages are "sticky." Exporters, in particular, would need lower costs in order to stay competitive with American firms once the pound appreciated relative to the dollar. (As discussed in the previous chapter, once the pound appreciated, each dollar in export revenue would generate fewer pounds when repatriated back to the UK; that lost revenue would have to be made up somehow.) Keynes predicted that unions would fight wage cuts; the result would be higher unemployment. Churchill would be intentionally throttling the economy, just as Paul Volcker did in the United States in the early 1980s. The difference is that Volcker was trying to stabilize prices while Churchill was forcing them to fall. In Keynes's view, the economic damage was unnecessary. He famously lambasted the gold standard as a "barbarous relic"—but if Britain must return to gold, then it ought to be at a level consistent with postwar prices rather than forcing deflation.

Churchill went ahead with his plan, Keynes's objections notwithstanding. The result was significant economic disruption. With a stronger pound, export industries struggled. British coal mines were losing a million pounds a month; they responded by asking miners to take a pay cut. As Keynes had predicted, the unions balked, leading to a lockout and eventually a general strike as other unions walked off the job in sympathy with the miners. In 1925, Keynes published "The Economic Consequences of Mr. Churchill," a critical essay riffing on his earlier prescient criticism of the Versailles Treaty ending World War I ("The Economic Consequences of the Peace"). British economic problems merged with the global disruption caused by the nascent Depression. By 1931, the situation in the UK and elsewhere was eerily similar to the bust in our hypothetical rice farming village: "Bank lending had been clamped shut, forcing commodity prices to collapse, which led in turn to bankruptcies and bank failures." And so on and so forth. In the fall of that year, Britain left the gold standard, a mere six years after restoring convertibility. Churchill would describe this chapter as perhaps the worst blunder of his career. That's saying a lot, given that nearly fifty thousand British soldiers died at Gallipoli.

Gold is an element that has captivated humans across cultures since the dawn of civilization. Gold is lustrous, dense, nonreactive, noncorrosive, and uniquely malleable, so that it can be fashioned into jewelry with relative ease. Less obvious, gold is imperishable. As Peter Bernstein describes in his book *The Power of Gold*, "You can do anything you want with it and to it, but you cannot make it disappear. Iron ore, cow's milk, sand, and even computer blips are all convertible into something so different from their original state as to be unrecognizable. This is not the case with gold."[6] Most important for the balance of this chapter, gold is scarce. All the gold ever produced would fit in a single supertanker.[7] As money evolved over the ages, gold coins were a logical development. The shiny stuff was prized across different societies, so it was suitable for trade. The density and scarcity made it possible to pack a large amount of value in a small coin or bar. The malleability made minting coins possible; the indestructibility meant they lasted, or could be melted down and made into new coins or jewelry.

Having said all that, what makes for good jewelry, or for effective money in sixteenth-century Europe, does not make for good money in a twenty-first-century global economy. Churchill's experience—and Keynes's prescient objections—encapsulate the appeal and the drawbacks of a system in which money is defined as a fixed quantity of gold (or any other precious metal). No modern nation fixes its currency against gold. Paul Volcker (a man who is keenly aware of the inflation risk associated with fiat currencies), has written, "Yes, gold will be with us, valued not only for its intrinsic qualities but as a last refuge and store of value in turbulent times. Yet its days as money, as a means of payment and a fixed unit of account, are over."[8]

Still, the fascination remains, including calls in some political quarters for a return to the gold standard (among the so-called gold bugs). To economists, this is the equivalent of calling for a commission to study whether the world is flat. True, a gold standard has two important strengths:

1. It precludes hyperinflation, as the quantity of money is constrained by the quantity of gold.
2. If adopted across countries, a gold standard fixes exchange rates in a predictable way.*

Alas, the disadvantages of a gold standard follow directly from those same properties. The supply of gold is not meaningfully related to the growth rate of our global economy, as Keynes pointed out, meaning that prices will rise in periods of rapid gold production and fall when the supply of gold lags behind growth in the rest of the economy. The latter, as Churchill learned, can be especially pernicious. The rigidity of fixed exchange rates has a downside, too, as the last chapter discussed. When nations are tethered to one another via a gold standard, they must subvert their domestic economic interests to defending the exchange rate. This was Britain's undoing between the wars; it would soon become a global problem as other nations made similar mistakes, broadening and deepening the Great Depression. Hence the breathtaking assertion by Nobel Prize winner Robert Mundell that a bungled international monetary system "brought on Hitler, the Great Depression, and World War II."[9]

Mundell is not some kook. Milton Friedman also has written extensively on how a severe contraction in the supply of money turned the

---

* Even the benefits of a gold standard may be overblown. The period prior to World War I under the gold standard was a time of unique economic stability and global integration. British Prime Minister Benjamin Disraeli and others have argued that this period of economic calm caused the gold standard, rather than the other way around. Long before the gold standard collapsed, Disraeli told a group of Glasgow merchants, "Our gold standard is not the cause, but the consequence of our commercial prosperity."
Peter L. Bernstein, *The Power of Gold: History of an Obsession* (Hoboken, NJ: John Wiley & Sons, 2012), 258.

stock market crash of 1929—a relatively "minor" economic disruption, in his view—into the economic catastrophe that it became.[10] (Friedman argues that the Federal Reserve could have pursued more expansionary money policy while still maintaining the gold standard, a distinction that will be explored in chapter 9.) For now, I won't pull my punches: money backed by gold makes no sense whatsoever in a modern economy. At best, gold is a siren call, a simple fix for a complex challenge. (As such, it conforms neatly to my favorite public policy aphorism: Every public policy problem has a simple solution—and it's usually wrong.) At worst, policymakers cling tenaciously to gold like some kind of religious text; as with other kinds of fundamentalism, supporters cling most tightly during times of confusion and rapid change—exactly when new thinking is essential.

As noted earlier, the Initiative on Global Markets at the University of Chicago's Booth School of Business periodically polls an ideologically diverse group of highly respected economists on issues of the day. In 2012, Booth's IGM panel was asked to agree or disagree with the following statement: "If the U.S. replaced its discretionary monetary policy regime with a gold standard, defining a 'dollar' as a specific number of ounces of gold, the price-stability and employment outcomes would be better for the average American." Every single respondent answered "disagree" or "strongly disagree." There was not even a single "uncertain."[11]

To mainstream economists, returning the United States to the gold standard is the economic equivalent of restoring control of America to the British monarchy—such a wacky idea that it barely merits discussion. During the Reagan administration, after a decade in which the United States had been buffeted by historically high inflation, Congress did create a sixteen-person commission to examine the role of gold in domestic and international monetary affairs. In 1982, the commission concluded, "Under present circumstances, restoring a gold standard does not appear to be a fruitful method for dealing with the continuing problem of inflation."[12]

The gold standard is an idea whose time has gone. Why? Because a competent central bank managing a fiat currency has all the advantages of a gold standard without the drawbacks. The belief that the world would be better with a "hard currency" neglects a core understanding of money, banking, and central banking.

And yet . . .

There are still those who believe with great fervor that a return to gold would be economically beneficial—that gold would liberate the money supply from the hands of bureaucrats and facilitate healthier and more stable economies. Former congressman and presidential candidate Ron Paul has attracted significant support for his call to bring back gold.* He recounts a speech he gave at the University of Michigan that helped to inspire his most recent book on the subject, *End the Fed*: "When I mentioned monetary policy, the kids started cheering. Then a small group chanted, 'End the Fed! End the Fed!' The whole crowd took up the call. Many held up burning dollar bills, as if to say to the central bank, you have done enough damage to the American people, our future, and to the world: your time is up."[13] The 2012 Republican platform included a proposal for a reprise of the 1980 Gold Commission "to investigate possible ways to set a fixed value for the dollar."[14] Across the Atlantic in 2014, Swiss activists gathered the 100,000 signatures necessary to put a referendum onto the national ballot that would have forced the Swiss National Bank to hold 20 percent of its reserves in gold. The *Economist* reported at the time, "Bigger reserves, activists argue, will make the Swiss economy more stable and prosperous. In fact the opposite is true."[15] The referendum failed, though more than 20 percent voted yes.

Money backed by gold has intuitive appeal. In times of economic distress, why not return to something as "good as gold"? Isn't money with some intrinsic value better than money with none? And isn't the system more stable if money is fixed in supply rather than limitless? No, no, no. Gold is utterly impractical for a twenty-first century economy. We are better served by a more flexible, if less beautiful, form of money. Let us count the reasons.

---

* Congressman Paul was a member of the Gold Commission. He and fellow commission member Lewis Lehrman coauthored a dissenting report: "The Case for Gold: A Minority Report of the U.S. Gold Commission."

Gold is not immune from inflation. Prices under a gold standard rise and fall with the supply of gold, as they do with the supply of any other kind of money. Remember those discoveries of gold and silver in the New World? European prices went up. The same thing happened in the nineteenth and early twentieth centuries after major gold discoveries in California, Australia, and South Africa. We should not confuse two important concepts. Yes, gold exists in finite supply, but that in no way guarantees stable prices. If the quantity of gold coming out of the ground grows faster than the rest of the economy, prices (in gold) will typically rise. If growth in the supply of gold lags behind the rest of the economy, gold will become relatively more valuable and prices will fall. This was Keynes's critique—though really it is just basic supply and demand.

Deflation, in particular, can be crushing. A gold standard is prone to stretches of falling prices, and falling prices create a heap of trouble, as Mr. Churchill learned. The deflation parade of horribles includes unemployment, high real interest rates, falling asset prices, and the stress on the banking system that comes from all of those things. (More foreshadowing: the Great Depression is coming at the end of the chapter.) When William Jennings Bryan gave his famous "Cross of Gold" speech at the 1896 Democratic National Convention, America was on the gold standard. Bryan was advocating for "free coinage of silver" to supplement the money supply. (Silver money had been eliminated by the Coinage Act of 1873.) Shiny metals aside, what Bryan was really advocating for was an end to the deflation and high real interest rates that were crushing western farmers. As prices fell, farmers sold their crops for less and less while their debts remained fixed. Bryan wanted inflation (or at least less deflation) to ease the burden. Adding silver to the money supply—looser monetary policy in today's parlance—would literally have created more dollars, raising prices and lowering real interest rates, both of which were good for indebted farmers.

Bryan did not win the election, nor was the gold standard tossed aside in 1896. But there is an ironic end to the story. The discovery and exploitation of large South African gold reserves at about the same time led to a 4 percentage point per year shift in the worldwide rate of inflation—from roughly 2 percent annual deflation before 1896 to 2 percent inflation thereafter. The inflow of South African gold accomplished Bryan's objectives without any change in U.S. coinage.[16]

China, Russia, and South Africa should not be in charge of U.S. monetary policy. The money supply under a gold standard is a function of gold production. As the South Africa example above illustrates, higher gold production (other things being equal) will lead to higher prices; lower gold production has the opposite effect. Right now the world's largest gold producer is . . . China. The fourth largest producer is Russia, a real stalwart ally; South Africa is sixth. The United States is home to less than 6 percent of the world's known gold reserves. (Russia and South Africa have over 20 percent between them.)[17]

Why would any nation cede control of its money supply to foreign powers? Anything that interrupted the pace of gold mining—deliberate or otherwise—could have a serious adverse economic impact. As the United States learned during the Arab oil embargos of the 1970s, other countries can and will strategically manipulate the supply of commodities in ways that are harmful to the U.S. economy. Conversely, a major gold discovery (under the melting Arctic?) could be inflationary. In any event, the price level is determined by the amount of gold taken out of the ground rather than by policy of the government or central bank.

But wait a minute: *Isn't that exactly the point?* Obviously the people of Zimbabwe would have been better off if their money supply had been determined by global gold production rather than by the whims of an autocratic government with a special talent for printing money. Prices under a gold standard may fluctuate arbitrarily, but at least there are constraints on the degree to which money can be devalued. True enough. But let me ask this question: Was Zimbabwe a successful, thriving nation except for its monetary system? Of course not. Robert Mugabe, Zimbabwe's only leader since its independence in 1980, has a poor human rights record. He has stolen at least one election. One of his major economic policies was a land reform program that confiscated farms from white farmers. And so on and so forth. The place was an economic disaster, one symptom of which was the government printing money with reckless abandon. Which brings us to the next point.

Bad governments cause bad money, not the other way around. In *End the Fed*, Ron Paul writes, "Tyranny always goes hand in hand with government's wrecking of the money system."[18] I will concede that despoiling the currency is an important tool for any really lousy government—but there is a causality problem here.* Bad governments cause worthless money, not the other way around. Having a fiat currency is not going to turn the United States into Zimbabwe. In fact, bad governments throughout history have proved perfectly capable of stealing from their subjects by manipulating money, whether it was with the printing press or by debasing gold and silver coins. It's always for the same basic reason: they've run out of other options for paying the bills.

If the king cannot pay his obligations in gold coins, and no one is willing to loan him more, the cleverest thing to do is make the existing gold go farther. Yes, every soldier will get fifty-seven gold coins for fighting the Huns, as promised—*but each coin will have less gold than it used to.* This is really just an ancient version of turning on the printing presses.

Peter Bernstein tells the impressive story of Dionysius of Syracuse (430–367 BC) who was heavily indebted to his citizens and had insufficient income to pay them back. "[Dionysius] ordered all coins in the city brought to him, under penalty of death. He restamped the coins so that each drachma coin now read two drachmas. After that, paying off his debts was easy." You won't read that in any public finance textbook.

The Romans were impressive debasers. Silver coins had 60 percent less silver in AD 260 than they did when Augustus became emperor in 27 BC. King Jean II of France, known as Jean le Bon, financed his taste for luxury (and wars with the English) by altering the currency eighteen times *in the first year of his reign*, with seventy more debasements over the next decade. Across the Channel, England's Henry VIII may be most

---

* For a more comprehensive discussion of the difference between correlation and causation, please read my earlier book *Naked Statistics* (Norton, 2013).

famous for beheading his wives and feuding with the pope, yet he still found time to aggressively substitute copper for silver in the coinage. His efforts in this regard (and those of his successor Edward VI) are officially recognized in British history as the Great Debasement. The point is that paper currency does not cause bad monetary policy, nor does gold (or silver) protect against it.

For that matter, governments on the gold standard can always just go off, or change the price of gold. The United States has done both. Shortly after Franklin Roosevelt took office in 1933, Congress granted him the power to change the gold content of the dollar. One day every dollar was fixed to a specific amount of gold; the next day it was fixed to slightly less gold. (The director of the budget at the time predicted, "This is the end of Western civilization.") Secretary of the Treasury Henry Morgenthau described in his diary how he would meet with FDR every morning in the president's bedroom to discuss economic policy, part of which was setting the price of gold for the day. (The higher the price of gold, the less each dollar would be worth.) On one morning, Roosevelt chose 21 cents for a particular quantity of gold because it was a lucky number.

In 1934, the price of gold was fixed at $35 an ounce, up from its legal price of $20.67 in 1900. In other words, the gold value of each dollar had been reduced roughly 40 percent.[19] Of course, private citizens could no longer redeem dollars for gold anyway; Congress had ended the convertibility of dollars into gold by U.S. citizens in 1933. Only foreign governments could present dollars for payment in gold after that. In 1971, Richard Nixon abruptly ended that practice, too.[20] Key lesson: a currency is as good as gold—*until the government says it is not.*

To be fair, some advocates of gold, including Ron Paul, would remove the government altogether. Let the market dictate what individuals and firms choose as a medium of exchange. Perhaps that will be bitcoin some-day. (Ironically, bitcoin has even less intrinsic value than U.S. dollars—there is not even any paper!) Money has operated without government involvement throughout history, such as macks in federal prisons. The U.S. government currently forbids any competing legal tender other than the dollar, which seems a curious and unnecessary regulation. (If a bunch of nutjobs want to pay each other in gold, why not let them?)

The prohibition has become a cause célèbre for gold bugs, who argue that if gold were given a fair chance, it would prove to be a superior currency to fiat money like the dollar, the yen, and the euro. In a *Wall Street Journal* op-ed that embodies this view, Peter Schiff, president of Euro Pacific Capital, wrote, "Gold is money because people make it money. Paper money is money because governments make it money."[21] Gold is the libertarian people power!

The reality is that no sane person would write a long-term contract denominated in gold. The purchasing power of gold is far more volatile than any currency under the control of a reasonably competent central bank.

The CPI measures the purchasing power of the dollar over time. The price of gold measures the purchasing power of gold. Remember, the purpose of money is to facilitate transactions. Which of those two forms of money—gold or the dollar—seems like a more predictable unit of exchange? For all the criticism of the Federal Reserve's actions after 2008 (particularly from the gold bugs), the purchasing power of the currency has remained strikingly stable. As *The Atlantic* magazine pointed out in 2012, "There's been 23 times less variance in prices since the Fed started quantitative easing than there was under the gold standard."[22]

For all that, there is no reason to be hypothetical on this point. There are groups that can choose whatever money they like, regardless of the law: drug dealers and arms merchants and the like. These people not constrained by silly laws forbidding gold as legal tender; their businesses are predicated on ignoring laws in general (or else they wouldn't be dealing weapons and drugs). What is the currency of choice for arms merchants, drug dealers, dictators, and other thugs who have little interest in what the government has to say? The dollar.* When was the last time you turned on the television news and a major drug bust had confiscated two kilos of gold? The dollar circulates broadly outside of the United States on a purely voluntary basis. Presumably drug dealers and arms merchants choose the dollar for the same reason as everyone

---

* Though as chapter 13 will point out, bitcoin is making inroads on this front.

else: relative to the other options, it has strikingly consistent purchasing power over time.

Given all the grief the Fed has taken in recent years, perhaps there is even room for some kind of promotional campaign, like those American Express commercials. "Hi, people call me El Jefe. I can't give you my real name, because I lead one of Mexico's major drug cartels and I'm wanted on both sides of the border. I kill people, I take bribes, and I distribute drugs around the world. When I get paid, I like the American dollar. It's easy, dependable, and accepted everywhere." Then there would be a voiceover with the tag line: "The American $100 dollar bill: Don't leave home without a suitcase full of them."

I suspect the unimaginative folks at the Fed will reject this public relations campaign. Still, the data support my point. According to the Federal Reserve, there are twenty-three $100 bills in circulation for every American.[23] I currently have two of them, which my mother-in-law sent me for my birthday. I usually have none. Most people I know aren't carrying a wad of $100s. Where are all these big bills? According to Edgar Feige, a University of Wisconsin economist who researches this kind of thing, no one is quite sure, in part because many of them are likely being used for illicit purposes or in the underground economy. Feige explained in an e-mail, "All we know is that some fraction of U.S. cash supply is held abroad and that per capita domestic holdings far exceed the amounts of cash that U.S. firms and households admit to holding."[24]

Does gold really have intrinsic value? This is a trickier question than one might think. I've stipulated that gold has universal appeal for jewelry and ornamentation. That's not likely to change. However, people around the world also acquire gold to hoard—as a store of value that can be sold to other people who like gold if necessary. However, the price at which that gold can be sold is hard to determine. Gold has very limited industrial uses (in large part because it is scarce and expensive). Thus, the value of gold at any given time—compared to, say, wheat or snow tires—is largely driven by human emotion. There is an irony here: gold is valuable in part because other people believe gold is valuable, which is not entirely different from the reason that a $100 bill is valuable. As Peter Bernstein points out, "Gold would never have attained its position as supreme monarch of monetary systems without its unique physical attributes, yet the demand for gold became so insatiable over time because it was used as money."

Unlike the purchasing power of a $100 bill, which the Federal Reserve works hard to manage, the value of gold in terms of other goods bounces all over the place. There is no empirical way of determining how valuable gold ought to be relative to bread, milk, real estate, or other goods. As *Wall Street Journal* personal finance writer Jason Zweig points out, "With no measures like price/earnings ratios or bond yields as benchmarks of value, figuring out whether the precious metal is cheap or dear is like trying to solve a Rubik's cube while blindfolded."[25]

For personal investors, this brings up an important point: gold is a dead asset, meaning that unlike bonds or real estate or certificates of deposit, gold does not earn a return. Burying gold in the basement makes sense if you fear extreme inflation, or that society will come unraveled. (Though it seems like goats and shotguns would be a better hedge against the latter; do we really think that people would be wearing lots of jewelry in a postapocalyptic world?) Acquiring gold is a logical way to save in nations with underdeveloped banking systems, such as India, where a family's wealth may be held in the form of jewelry and bangles. Such wealth is prone to theft or loss; perhaps more important, it cannot be rented out for productive purposes. As Bernstein writes, "Hoarding is similar to buying an insurance policy. Like an insurance policy, hoarding gold has a cost, for the idle metal earns nothing." There are other ways to hedge against inflation that still earn a return on capital. Land appreciates with inflation; it can also be cultivated, generating regular income. Apartments rise in value when other prices are going up; they provide rental income at the same time. The U.S. Treasury's Inflation-Protected Securities (TIPS) pay a fixed yield plus an additional amount to compensate for inflation over the relevant period.

Hoarding a dead asset has a cost for society, too. Whatever wealth is buried in the basement or dangling from a bride's wrist is capital that cannot be loaned to an entrepreneur starting a business, or to a student attending medical school. The whole point of a financial system is to match savers and borrowers, making both parties better off in the process. Gold does not work that way. India considers this a serious enough problem that the government has floated a policy that would create gold banks that would allow Indians to deposit gold in exchange for certificates; the long-run goal is to loan out the gold on deposit in some manner.

Much of the world's gold lies in vaults deep beneath the Federal Reserve of New York. Warren Buffett, one of the most successful investors of all time, has pointed out how curious it is that something ostensibly so valuable lies idly in a vault: "[Gold] gets dug out of the ground in Africa, or someplace. Then we melt it down, dig another hole, bury it again and pay people to stand around guarding it. It has no utility. Anyone watching from Mars would be scratching their head."[26]

For all that, the most compelling argument against the gold standard may be the most prosaic. It's the one that could have made this chapter only a paragraph long. The one that made me feel chagrined when Paul Volcker pointed it out to me in his office several years ago . . .

There is not enough gold. As Volcker pointed out, "The volume of gold in the world is way, way short of all the international currencies that are around." Remember, all the gold that has ever been produced would fit on a single supertanker. It's like we started a regular poker game many years ago with five players and fifty chips. Now we have hundreds of tables playing poker—but still only fifty chips. It can't work. Or, more accurately, it cannot work in any practical way. Yes, we could set the price of gold so high that it could technically support all the currencies in circulation—say every ounce of gold was worth $10,000. But that defeats the purpose of having a gold standard. No sane person would give up $10,000 in current purchasing power for an ounce of gold. *We don't like jewelry that much.* The dollar would still effectively be backed by nothing.

The proponents of gold typically offer a litany of complaints about our current monetary system. Most of these points are entirely valid. Fiat currency can be abused in ways that lead to inflation. The Fed should be more transparent. A central bank that acts as a lender of last resort does create moral hazard. The international monetary system needs more predictability and stability. The fallacy is that gold is an effective remedy for any of these challenges. The remedy is better central banking.

For a modern economy, gold fails all three of the basic tests for effective money:

1. There is not enough of it to serve as a medium of exchange.
2. Its value fluctuates too much to be an effective unit of account.
3. It earns no return when used as a store of value.

And yet in many ways, gold is a far more intuitive form of money than paper. Reverting to gold during a time of economic distress feels like the right thing to do—then again, so did burning witches after a bad harvest. Centuries of evidence suggest that neither is likely to fix the underlying problem. So let's finish where we began, with the enormous human cost of clinging to a system that does not make economic sense, however intuitive it may feel.

Economist Barry Eichengreen has written an entire book making the case that the gold standard is the "key to understanding the Great Depression." This idea will be explored in greater depth in chapter 9. For now, it is important to recognize just how dangerous the false allure of gold can be, especially in times of economic disruption. Eichengreen writes:

> The gold standard of the 1920s set the stage for the Depression of the 1930s by heightening the fragility of the international financial system. The gold standard was the mechanism transmitting the destabilizing impulse from the United States to the rest of the world. The gold standard magnified that initial destabilizing shock. It was the principal obstacle to offsetting action. It was the binding constraint preventing policymakers from averting the failure of banks and containing the spread of financial panic. For all these reasons, the international gold standard was a central factor in the worldwide Depression. Recovery proved possible, for these same reasons, only after abandoning the gold standard.[27]

Bad ideas have consequences, then and now. There is no serious risk that the United States will return to a gold standard. Still, the same misperceptions that make gold attractive tend to complicate current monetary policy. *Financial Times* columnist Martin Wolf has described serving on a panel with a U.S. politician who asserted that the Federal Reserve's response to the 2008 financial crisis would lead to hyperinflation. Wolf writes, "Like many others, he failed to understand how the monetary system works. Unfortunately ignorance is not bliss. It has made it more difficult for central banks to act effectively."[28]

This stuff matters. Monetary policy may seem esoteric. Then again, so did some of those weird derivatives Wall Street was peddling in the early 2000s. How did that work out? When monetary policy works well, we barely notice. We go about our daily lives using money that we take for granted, making use of a financial system that is not imploding, casting aspersions on regulators who seem to make everything more complicated.

But it does not always work that smoothly. As the second half of the book will elucidate, getting money wrong can wreck economies and ruin lives.

PART II

why it matters

CHAPTER 8

A Quick Tour of American Monetary History

*You come to us and tell us that the great cities are in favor of the gold standard.
I tell you that the great cities rest upon these broad and fertile prairies. Burn
down your cities and leave our farms, and your cities will spring up again as
if by magic. But destroy our farms and the grass will grow in the streets of
every city in the country . . .*

*If they dare to come out in the open field and defend the gold standard as
a good thing, we shall fight them to the uttermost, having behind us the producing masses of the nation and the world. Having behind us the commercial
interests and the laboring interests and all the toiling masses, we shall answer
their demands for a gold standard by saying to them, you shall not press down
upon the brow of labor this crown of thorns. You shall not crucify mankind
upon a cross of gold.*

—William Jennings Bryan, "Cross of Gold" speech,
Democratic National Convention, 1896[1]

Did the Dutch really buy Manhattan from the Indians for $24
worth of beads, as we were all taught in elementary school?
And if so, was it really such a crazy bad deal for the local
Lenape Indians? To begin with, Manhattan was just a relatively uninhabited patch of land. It's not like the Dutch got Fifth Avenue,
Central Park, or anything with Donald Trump's name on it. There was
a lot of open land back in those days. The bead story may be apocryphal
anyway. A letter from a liaison for the Dutch East India Company to the

Dutch government makes reference to purchasing "the Island Manhattes from the savages for the value of 60 guilders."[2] This sum was later reckoned to be worth about $24 using a nineteenth-century exchange rate; historians point out that it's difficult to know the real value of guilders at the time for either the Dutch settlers or the Indians. Presumably guilders were only valuable to the Indians for other trades with the Dutch.

Meanwhile, it's not clear that the Indians even owned the island, let alone used it. One strand of thinking points out that "ownership" of land and water were alien concepts in Native American culture, so the sum could be interpreted as more of a fee for sharing.[3] One law professor has described the transaction as "not relinquishing the island, but simply welcoming the Dutch as additional occupants." A more insidious (and amusing) theory is that the Indians selling the land were just a band passing through from Long Island; they sold the Dutch an island they never had claim to and went home with whatever they could extract from the naïve buyers. We can debate about whether you are a fool to sell a used Mercedes for $5,000. But if you manage to sell a used Mercedes *that is not yours* for $5,000, that makes you a commercial genius.[4] It would be a wonderful irony if the real naïfs in the transaction were the Dutch. But suppose there were beads involved, rather than Dutch guilders. Who says those beads were such a bad trade? Was it silly to give up an island for a handful of shiny objects? Just about anyone reading this book would gladly part with their home, car, and other valuables in exchange for a bag of diamonds or a suitcase of gold bars—different shiny objects with little practical value.

In any event, the Manhattan story overlooks some of the more interesting things that we do know about the role money played when European settlers encountered Native Americans. The Dutch were perplexed by the value that the Native Americans assigned to wampum, the decorative beads made from clamshells and string that functioned as money. In 1650, Dominie Johannes Megapolensis, pastor of the Church of New Amsterdam, wrote, "The Indians value these little bones so highly as many Christians do gold, silver and pearls, but they do not like our money."[5] The Dutch adapted, just as American tourists do when they show up in Paris or Hong Kong. Wampum became a widespread medium of exchange among the settlers throughout the Northeast. This precipitated a challenge with commodity money that I've glossed over to this point. In theory, the benefit of a commodity-based currency is that it has a standard and widely appreciated value: tobacco is tobacco; cows are cows. In fact, some tobacco is better quality than other; some cows are fat and healthy while others are thin and sick. Wampum seemed more stable—it was always strung and the typical denomination was the length of a man's arm. Yet the Dutch observed an interesting trend: when the Indians came to receive a quantity of wampum, they would bring a towering man; when it came time for them to pay, it seemed the Indians would always bring a dwarf.[6]

In addition to smallpox and liquor, the European settlers introduced another scourge: wampum inflation. The Narragansett Indians traditionally held a near monopoly on wampum production. Supply was relatively low and steady due to the laborious production process: gather the shells, break into the hard, thick center, grind each shell to a uniform size, cut a hole through the middle, and string the shells. The Dutch brought steel tools to the process, which was the equivalent of giving more printing presses to the Zimbabwean government. The colonists generated a hundredfold increase in the supply of wampum, causing an inevitable inflation.[7] As Milton Friedman observed, "Wampum inflation is everywhere and always a monetary phenomenon." Okay, he never really said that, but he might have if he had spent more time studying Dutch colonists. Ironically (though not surprisingly) the machine-made wampum eventually rendered it obsolete as a medium of exchange.

Money has played a crucial role at every juncture in American history. And by money, I do not mean wealth (chickens, factories, and apartments)—I mean the stuff we have used as a medium of exchange to buy chickens, factories, and apartments: wampum, Spanish doubloons, continentals, gold, paper, computer bytes. American history is also the history of money. We've used commodities and gold and paper. We've had inflation. We've had deflation. We've even had stagflation. Some of the most pitched political battles in America have revolved around the nation's money, whether it was Alexander Hamilton arguing for a national bank or Andrew Jackson trying to kill that bank. William Jennings Bryan was looking after the interests of western farmers when he campaigned to expand the money supply with silver coinage; New York bankers were protecting their interests by creating the Federal Reserve to mitigate the banking panics that had characterized the nineteenth and early twentieth centuries. As the last chapter argued, America's attachment to the gold standard deepened and prolonged the Great Depression. To the extent that the Depression (which was most severe in the United States and Germany) brought about World War II, this may be the worst public policy disaster in history.

Every chapter of American history that we're familiar with—colonial times, the Revolution, the Civil War, the settling of the West, the Depression, and so on—has a corresponding monetary tale. Sometimes these tales are amusing side notes. In other cases, they have changed the nation's trajectory. Jimmy Carter lost the presidency in part because of the stagflation of the 1970s. Ronald Reagan won reelection in 1984 using the theme "It's morning in America" in part because Paul Volcker had beaten inflation. As I write, some critics are lambasting the Fed for its overly aggressive response to the 2008 financial crisis; others argue that America's central bank has not done enough to lower unemployment. Time will shed more light on this debate.

Economic historians have written volumes on each of these subjects. I have already made liberal use of Barry Eichengreen's work on the Great Depression. One of Milton Friedman's towering achievements, written with coauthor Anna Schwartz, was the tome *A Monetary History of the United States, 1867–1960*. My purpose is simpler (in large part because I know so much less about this topic than the people just referenced). The point of this chapter is to reinforce the idea that money and its related institutions matter. Money, banking, and central banking have affected the course of American history. They will continue to do so. Here is a tour of familiar chapters in American history with the less familiar monetary details attached to them—a sampling, if you will.

The Colonists: What Did Paul Revere Have in His Wallet?

The early American colonists did not have enough money. By that, I do not mean that they lacked wealth (though that was probably true for many of them). I mean they lacked a consistent form of money that could be used as a medium of exchange. Who should we blame for this? Obviously the perfidious British—the same people who brought us taxation without representation. The English sought exclusive trading relationships with each of the colonies while discouraging the colonies from trading among themselves. The English accomplished this in part by limiting the quantity of pounds sent to the colonies and by attempting to ban the colonies from minting their own currencies. The money shortage was filled by whatever else might work: the scarce pounds; Spanish dollars accumulated by traders and merchants; coins and bills issued by private banks (often suspect); and myriad commodities.[8]

Trade using "cash crops" such as livestock and tobacco was common. Many of the colonies even accepted tax payments in the form of commodities. (Just try sending a goat and three sacks of flour to the IRS these days.) Commodity tax payments presented several problems. The first was logistical. Not only did the tax collector have to chase down payment—sometimes literally—but he also had to calculate the bill as measured in cows or tobacco or bushels of corn (and then find something to do with those different goods). Meanwhile, the colonists sought to offload the worst of any commodity that was accepted for taxes. What better tax payment than a skinny bull on the brink of death? Rhode Island officials reported that they were having a very hard time keeping out the "lean" cattle. The same was true with tobacco in Virginia. In the 1680s, the auditor-general of Virginia reported "the quantity of unmerchantable leaf" paid to collectors had grown so large that "revenue from this source had dwindled almost to nothing."[9]

Not surprisingly, the colonists sought a more reliable form of money. In 1690, the Massachusetts Bay Colony became the first government in the Americas to issue paper money. Massachusetts issued paper notes to pay soldiers with the promise that the notes could eventually be redeemed for gold or silver. The notes were deemed "legal tender," meaning they could be used to settle private debts and to pay taxes.[10] Other colonies jumped into the money-making business; the colonial governments typically issued paper money to defray war costs or to avoid raising taxes. Of course, printing money is like eating one handful of popcorn; there is an enormous temptation to keep going. With the exception of Virginia, the colonies produced excessive quantities of paper money (especially Rhode Island) and experienced the inevitable inflation.[11] As experiments with paper money continued through the mid eighteenth century, a fiery debate emerged over the merits and evils of paper money. On one side were those motivated by a fear of inflation, as illustrated by a letter published in the *Virginia Gazette* on "The Manifold Evils of Paper Money."[12] On the other side were those who supported paper money as a solution to the lack of circulating currency. Benjamin Franklin wrote in 1729 that issuing paper money might bring about "the establishment of peace, love and unity."[13] We have had variations on this debate for 250 years, whether it was William Jennings Bryan and "free silver" in the nineteenth century, the gold standard in the twentieth, or quantitative easing in the twenty-first. How much money is too much?

In 1764, the perfidious British rendered the paper money debate temporarily moot by passing the Currency Act, which outlawed all of the paper money issued by the colonies. (Previously, the British had imposed limits on colonial money, but never in such a sweeping manner across all the colonies.)[14] Earlier inflation problems notwithstanding, the paper money ban imposed an economic cost. With increasing populations and expanding trade, the colonies needed a growing money supply; the British were deliberately shrinking it.[15] The Currency Act reinforced the growing sentiment that the economic interests of the colonies would always be subverted by those of the British.[16] We know where this story is going.

The Revolution: Why Ron Paul Would Not Like George Washington

Once the Revolutionary War began, the Americans were once again free to fire up the printing presses. Individual colonies issued new bills to pay for military expenditures, delighting in the opportunity to come up with new, topical bill designs. There are entire books devoted to America's early paper money. Maryland issued a series of bills with an image of "George III trampling on the Magna Charta [sic] while setting fire to an American city."[17] Alongside the state currencies, the newly formed Continental Congress began printing paper money denominated in dollars. (Spanish dollars had always circulated in the colonies, making the dollar a logical unit of account to replace the reviled pound.)[18] These continentals allowed the Continental Congress to finance the early revolution in the absence of a national tax system.[19] (Yes, there is an irony—almost certainly lost on the modern Tea Party—in the fact that the Republic was launched with deficit spending using paper money.) George Washington may be famous for his wooden teeth; his paper money is more relevant to the course of American history.

The value of the continentals declined rapidly for the usual reason—more and more continentals relative to the available goods and services.[20] The British, well versed in the economics of wartime finance, tried to do to the revolutionaries exactly what the Nazis would later try to do to them: strategic counterfeiting. In January 1776, the British controlled New York City, allowing British ships to anchor in New York Harbor. One of those ships, the HMS *Phoenix*, had forty-four guns on deck and a more potent weapon in its hull: a printing press.[21] The British were engaged in a campaign to spread counterfeit continentals through the colonies; the plan was that massive inflation would render the revolutionaries' war-financing mechanism worthless. To facilitate the circulation of the fake bills, the British even placed advertisements in New York newspapers offering travelers headed to the colonies an unlimited quantity of counterfeited continentals, as long as they paid for the paper on which they were printed.*[22] All this printing of money—by the British and the colonists—had the predictable effect. George Washington

---

* This gives me an inspired idea for fighting the periodic deflation threats in the eurozone: the European Central Bank should give unlimited free euros to anyone (me) willing to spend them on a European vacation (provided we pay for the paper on which the euros are printed).

would eventually complain to John Jay, "A wagon-load of money will scarcely purchase a wagon-load of provisions."[23]

The Continental Army managed to beg, borrow, and steal long enough to defeat the British.[24] (I mean that literally: they pleaded for money from foreign governments, borrowed domestically, and seized private property.) When the delegates gathered in Philadelphia in 1787 to draft a constitution, the monetary chaos of the colonial period was still top of mind. The Constitution specifically forbids the states from coining money or issuing bills of credit. Article One vests Congress with the authority "to coin money, regulate the value thereof, and of foreign coin, and fix the standard of weights and measures."[25] How Congress ought to exercise that authority would be a source of debate for the next 250 years (and probably beyond).

First Bank of the United States

Congress soon took advantage of its monetary prerogative, passing the Coinage Act of 1792.[26] The law sanctioned the construction of the first federal building, a United States Mint in Philadelphia.[27] Alexander Hamilton, the secretary of the Treasury, determined that the mint would make both gold and silver coins, again denominated in dollars. Any person could bring their gold or silver bullion to the mint and have it coined for free. The metallic content of the dollar was fixed in terms of both gold and silver.[28] A $10 gold coin contained 17.5 grams of gold; a $1 silver coin contained 27 grams of silver. Of course, this "bimetal" standard also fixed the value of gold and silver to each other (at a ratio of 15 to 1). The United States would operate on this bimetallic regime for the better part of a century.*

_____

* Any bimetallic regime is prone to instability, as the two metals (e.g., gold and silver) are likely to fluctuate in supply independent of each other. For example, a large new discovery of silver will diminish the scarcity of silver relative to gold—even though the law fixes their relative values. Any citizen can take gold or silver to the mint to get dollars. When silver becomes more plentiful (and therefore less valuable in the market), citizens will increasingly choose to turn silver into dollars while holding on

Meanwhile, Treasury Secretary Hamilton believed that the young country lacked adequate financial infrastructure. The money supply was not sufficient to meet the currency needs of a growing economy.[29] The government also needed a place to borrow. Hamilton proposed the establishment of a national bank that would be chartered (granted the license to operate) by the federal government but largely privately owned (though the government would own a fifth of the shares). The bank would facilitate the major financial needs of the day: making loans to (and accepting deposits from) the government; providing credit for merchants and farmers; and issuing bank notes to expand the money supply.[30] The Bank of England had been founded on a similar model in 1694.

Hamilton's bank met immediate resistance from Thomas Jefferson and James Madison as an unconstitutional expansion of federal power. The constitutional issues have obviously been resolved over time, but the pushback against central banking as an unhealthy accumulation of centralized power endures to the present. Ron Paul—no Thomas Jefferson, to be sure, but still a person who commands a large following—writes in *End the Fed*, "No single institution in society should have power this immense."[31] Jefferson and his antifederalist colleagues also believed the bank would serve rich merchants at the expense of regular folk, primarily farmers. This broad theme—the interests of bankers versus the interests of everyday Americans—has also been an enduring part of the political dialogue. If we update the language, it is "Wall Street versus Main Street" in the aftermath of the 2008 financial crisis. Sadly, even

---

to gold, or to trade gold for silver at the market rate and then use that silver to get more dollars than if the gold had been taken directly to the mint. An example with different commodities will help make the point. Suppose Congress fixed the value of the dollar in 1990 at either one mountain bike or one DVD player. At that time, the two items had roughly similar values. By 2015, a mountain bike is much more valuable than a DVD player, even if Congress says they should have the same value in terms of dollars. Anyone seeking new money will bring a DVD player to the mint, not a mountain bike. In fact, a clever person could trade a mountain bike for multiple DVD players and take those DVD players to the mint to get more dollars than if he had just "minted" the mountain bike. For this reason, most bimetal standards eventually evolved into a single metal currency, either implicitly or by law.

the political behavior is recognizable. At one point, Jefferson referred to Hamilton as a "foreign bastard."[32] (In Jefferson's defense, he was technically correct. Hamilton was born in the West Indies to an unmarried woman. Still it seems churlish.)

Hamilton arguably won the battle and lost the war, at least as the nineteenth century would play out. The First Bank of the United States was chartered in 1791 for twenty years. Over the course of the charter, the bank's $5 million in paper currency would grow to account for roughly 20 percent of the nation's money supply.*[33] By the time the bank's shareholders asked for the charter to be renewed in 1808, however, the political landscape had changed. After several years of political machinations, the bank's opponents ultimately prevailed. Vice President George Clinton broke a 50–50 tie in the Senate and voted against renewing the charter. The First Bank of the United States closed its doors in 1811.[34]

There was a sequel, as you may recall from your American history class, and the script was broadly similar to the original. Four years later, the nation was once again desperate for credit, in part because of the costs of the War of 1812. Treasury Secretary Alexander Dallas argued that "a national bank would be the best and perhaps the only adequate resource to relieve the country and the government from the present embarrassments." President James Madison (an opponent of the First Bank) was eventually persuaded that a national bank was necessary for the nation's success; in 1816, he signed a twenty-year charter for the Second Bank of the United States.[35] As in the first film, the political winds would shift by the time the Second Bank's charter was up for consideration. This time President Andrew Jackson was perfectly cast as the bank's archenemy. Jackson, a backwoods populist who founded the modern Democratic Party, reviled all that the bank represented: the

---

* The First and Second Banks of the United States also practiced a rudimentary form of monetary policy. By acquiring state bank notes, the bank provided additional reserves that state banks could use to make loans, thereby expanding the money supply. Conversely, the bank could redeem state notes for gold or silver, thereby shrinking state bank reserves against which they could lend and lowering the money supply.

financial elite, credit, centralized power, and anything with a whiff of paper money. (The fact that Jackson's image is on the $20 bill—redeemable for nothing—is another of history's delicious ironies.)

Jackson's attempt to kill the Second Bank, including his fight with the bank's "vain and arrogant" president, Nicholas Biddle, was one of America's epic political battles. Biddle deliberately restricted bank credit, hoping the subsequent economic contraction would punish Jackson and demonstrate the economic importance of the bank. Biddle declared, "This worthy President thinks that because he has scalped Indians and imprisoned judges he is to have his way with the bank. He is mistaken."[36] Jackson, no political patsy himself, wrote to Martin Van Buren, "The Bank, Mr. Van Buren, is trying to kill me, but I will kill it." In the end, Jackson prevailed. The charter of the Second Bank was not renewed. The United States would be without any semblance of a central bank until the early 1900s.[37]

The Wild West: Robberies Were Not the Biggest Banking Problem

Jackson's victory left the states responsible for chartering banks—which they did aggressively. State banks issued private bank notes backed by gold and silver, not unlike our hypothetical rice bank from a few chapters back. As with the rice bank, things did not always end happily. The quality of banks, and therefore of bank notes, varied enormously. As long as economic times were good, bankers and borrowers square danced to the music. In 1830, there were 329 banks in the country that had issued $61 million in bank notes. Just seven years later, after the closing of the Second Bank, there were 788 banks circulating $149 million.[38] (Since I wrote a statistics book, I'll do the math for you.* In less than a decade, both the number of banks and the dollars in circulation grew by roughly 140 percent.) There was no central bank to take away the punch bowl as

---

* *Naked Statistics: Stripping the Dread from the Data*, which the *New York Times* described as "sparkling and intensely readable," in case you were wondering.

the credit-induced party grew out of control. Ultimately it was the English, worried about the quality of America's credit binge, who turned on the lights and broke up the party. English lenders curtailed the flow of credit across the Atlantic. This, compounded by other factors, induced the Panic of 1837.[39] The public rushed to redeem bank notes for gold (fearing they would otherwise become worthless), which precipitated bank failures and an economic depression that lasted at least four years.[40] Economic data from the time are crude. However, medical records offer a chilling snapshot of how bad things must have become: children born in the early 1840s were, on average, nearly two inches shorter than children born the decade before.[41]

Boom, bust, repeat. Call me a lazy historian, but that pretty much characterizes the second half of the nineteenth century. When gold was discovered at Sutter's Mill in California in 1848, it helped propel the country to a decade of rapid monetary expansion and rapid growth. It was, in the words of economic historian Glyn Davies, "one of the clearest examples in history of the stimulative power of good-quality money."[42] Of course, that party ended badly, too. Yet another bank panic in the fall of 1857 caused more than 5,000 business failures over the next year.[43] At this point, there was good news and bad news. The good news was that the crisis would prove to be serious but short. As the *Economist* wrote at the time, "There was never a more severe crisis nor a more rapid recovery."[44] The bad news was that the Civil War was coming.

The Civil War (Read This Section, Even If You Already Know Who Wins)

We know who started it: the South. By "it," I mean the inevitable printing of money and inflation. The Confederacy had the weaker economy and resorted almost immediately to printing money to pay war expenses. The price level in the South increased nearly thirtyfold between 1861 and 1865.[45] The Union was able to keep the printing presses idle for a while by raising taxes and borrowing, but eventually that would not be enough. In 1862, Treasury Secretary Salmon P. Chase proposed issuing Treasury notes that would be declared legal tender but were not redeemable for gold or silver. Massachusetts senator Charles Sumner summarized the skepticism of the Congress toward such a scheme: "Surely we must all be against paper money." But even Sumner bowed to the exigencies of the situation, telling the Senate, "Your soldiers in the field must be paid and fed. . . . Reluctantly, painfully, I consent."[46]

The Union began printing "greenbacks"—a double entendre inspired by the green ink on one side of the currency and the fact that the notes were not backed by gold or silver—only by the green ink. Compared to the massive inflation in the South, the new currency fared reasonably well and helped the North solidify its economic advantage. As historian H. W. Brands argues, "The greenback underwrote the Union victory in the Civil War and accelerated America's industrial revolution."[47] In the midst of the Civil War, the North had created America's first successful fiat currency—money with no value other than the fact that the government declared it had value.

As the end of the Civil War approached, the nation's currency stock was a hodgepodge of greenbacks and notes issued by different state-chartered banks. Before accepting any bank note as payment, one would have to verify that the bank actually existed; that the note was not a counterfeit; and that the bank was financially healthy and could be trusted to redeem the note for gold or silver. All of this became more difficult as the geographic distances involved in commerce increased.[48] When a New York merchant traveled to New Hampshire with $5 bills from his local bank, he may have found someone to accept them, but typically at a price discounted from the $5 face value. Ironically, some counterfeits of notes issued by large, reputable banks were more highly valued than legitimate notes issued by lesser-known banks.

A National Currency: What Does an Albanian 1,000 Lek Note Look Like?

Imagine running a business today if your customers could pay with currency issued by any country around the world. Not only would you have to recognize an Albanian 1,000 lek note, you would have to distinguish a real one from a counterfeit. If anything, this example understates the challenge. In the 1860s, there were more state-chartered banks issuing bank notes than there are countries issuing their own currency at present. There were even publications with descriptions of different bank notes to help individuals and businesses distinguish those bills that should be accepted from those that should be turned away.[49] Congress passed the National Banking Acts of 1863 and 1864 to bring order to the monetary chaos.[50] The legislation created a process for chartering and regulating national banks. To receive a national charter, banks were required to buy Treasury bonds and keep them on account with the newly created Office of Comptroller of the Currency (which was responsible for examining and regulating nationally chartered banks). In return for this collateral, the government provided the banks with the corresponding amount of national bank notes. The new national notes were uniform in appearance but also customized with the name of the issuing bank. All national banks were required to accept the notes of other national banks at face value (no discounting), but only the issuing bank was required to redeem them for gold or silver. If the issuing bank did not have sufficient gold or silver to redeem the notes, the government would sell the bank's Treasury bills and pay off the note holders.[51] This arrangement gave the public a uniform currency while bolstering confidence in the banks and their bank notes.* Meanwhile, Congress placed a 10 percent tax on all state bank notes, which led to their eventual disappearance. The state-chartered banks remained in business, albeit as banks, not issuers of currency. This was the origin of the American dual banking system (both state and federally chartered banks) that still exists.[52] (Here is a statement of the obvious: banks with "state" in the name are chartered by the state; those with "national" in their name are chartered by the feds.)

Even with the advantage of a more uniform national currency, the nation's banking system was still unstable, for many of the reasons dis-

---

* There was an ancillary benefit of this arrangement for the Union in the final stages of the Civil War. The requirement that national banks buy Treasury bonds and deposit them with the comptroller of the currency created a bigger market for these government bonds, and therefore made it easier and cheaper for the North to raise war funds.

cussed in previous chapters. There was no mechanism to stop bank runs, for example. The government had no capacity to moderate the economic booms and busts that frequently led to manias and panics.[53] The most explosive policy issue became the role of silver and gold—or more accurately, the lack of a role for silver.[54] With the Coinage Act of 1873, Congress ended the unlimited coinage of silver and effectively put the United States on a gold standard.[55] Over the next twenty years, silver producers and their political allies argued that there was insufficient gold to meet the nation's currency needs. By and large, it was a losing battle. In 1893, however, the country sank into another deep economic slump. As agricultural prices fell, pro-silver sentiment spread across the nation, culminating in the last and best chance for the "silverites" to secure a permanent return to bimetallism: the candidacy of William Jennings Bryan in the presidential election of 1896.[56]

Bryan, a former Democratic congressman from Nebraska, focused his entire campaign on one proposal: free coinage of silver at a ratio of 16 to 1. As noted earlier, free coinage meant that the U.S. Mint would accept raw silver and provide silver coins in return. The 16 to 1 ratio represented Bryan's proposal for the value of silver compared to gold: 16 ounces of silver to 1 ounce of gold. This ratio was based on the relative market prices of the two metals in the 1830s—but it was no longer the 1830s. Since then, the value of silver had fallen dramatically. In fact, at market prices in 1896, an ounce of gold was worth roughly 32 ounces of silver—double what Bryan was proposing.[57] The whole point of Bryan's proposal was to inflate the value of silver relative to gold. If one man brought 32 ounces of silver to the mint and another man brought 1 ounce of gold, the man carrying silver would receive twice as many dollar coins, even though the market value of the underlying metals was the same. (Of course, if the guy with the ounce of gold were smarter, he would swap it for silver first and then take the silver to the mint, where he would get twice as many dollars as if he took the gold straight to the mint.) In any event, Bryan believed that the free coinage of silver would encourage people to bring silver to the mint, thereby expanding the nation's money supply and promoting inflation (to help indebted farmers) and faster economic growth.

An unmatched orator, Bryan quickly became a populist hero. His 1896 convention speech, cited at the beginning of this chapter, has been hailed as one of the greatest political speeches of all time. Bryan's ideas strongly appealed to farmers and other rural voters, many of whom were indebted. Bryan's eventual opponent in the general election was Republican William McKinley, who enjoyed strong support from bankers and other Eastern elites. (Inflation is the friend of debtors and the bane of bankers.) Bryan did not shrink from what we might now call class warfare. Audio exists of Bryan's electrifying speech at the Democratic National Convention, in which he bellows, "Burn down your cities and leave our farms and your cities will spring up again as if by magic; but destroy our farms and the grass will grow in the streets of every city in the country."*[58] In his dramatic conclusion, Bryan once again attacked the gold standard: "You shall not press down upon the brow of labor this crown of thorns. You shall not crucify mankind upon a cross of gold." He stretched his arms out to the sides, simulating a crucifixion, and then walked off the stage.[59]

William Jennings Bryan lost. Combined with a series of gold discoveries in the late 1890s that expanded the money supply and brought about an economic surge, the election of 1896 ended the debate over bimetallism.[60] Four years later, President McKinley signed into law the Gold Standard Act of 1900, which made America's de facto gold standard official and set the value of the dollar at 25.8 grains of gold, or $20.67 per troy ounce.[61]

Creation of the Federal Reserve: Take That, Andrew Jackson

In 1907, the nation faced another banking crisis. (No, you haven't read this section before; they just keep happening.) For a variety of reasons, the public lost confidence in several New York City banks and customers

---

* Bryan recorded the speech later in Gennett Studios on July 3, 1923. You can listen to it through the Authentic History Center at http://www.authentichistory.com/1865-1897/4-1896election/19230703_Cross_of_Gold_Speech_Recording-WBJ.html.

rushed to pull out their money.[62] The police were called to keep order at Knickerbocker Trust, a Manhattan bank. The *New York Times* reported, "As fast as a depositor went out of the place ten people and more came asking for their money."[63] As the panic spread throughout the city, the bankers quickly realized that there was only one man who could possibly rescue them: J. P. Morgan. With no central bank, it was Morgan, the titan of finance and industry, who would have to serve as the lender of last resort. Morgan gathered an influential group of bankers in his home; he pledged large sums of his own money to backstop the banks and cajoled others into doing so as well. In their book *The Panic of 1907*, Robert Bruner and Sean Carr describe the scene: "[Morgan] said simply that unless they raised $25 million within the next 10 to 12 minutes, at least 50 Stock Exchange houses would fail." The group raised sufficient funds to keep the system afloat.

Morgan managed the public as well as he managed his fellow bankers. He sent one group of his banking associates to the media to announce the financial details of the rescue efforts and another to the clergy, encouraging them to affirm the good health of the banks in their Sunday sermons.[64] (Remember, if people are persuaded the panic is over, the panic is over.)

A crisis had been averted—but only because of an ad hoc intervention by two of the nation's richest men. (John D. Rockefeller had also given large sums; at one point he pledged half his wealth to ensure America's credit).[65] There was an emerging consensus that America should establish a central bank, as England had done in 1694 and France in 1800.[66] In 1913, after a lengthy study, Congress and President Woodrow Wilson passed the Federal Reserve Act, which created the Federal Reserve System to act as the nation's central bank. As noted in chapter 5, strong opposition to centralized power (which had doomed the First and Second Banks of the United States) led to the Fed's decentralized structure: twelve regional banks, spread across the country, with a board in Washington to provide coordination and oversight.[67] The act also created Federal Reserve Notes, which would be legal tender convertible to gold on demand.[68] This is the paper money in our wallets today (though it is no longer redeemable for gold).

The explicit role of the Federal Reserve was to promote financial stability and end the chronic bank panics.[69] The Fed would be the lender of last resort, providing temporary loans to any healthy bank facing a run on its deposits. The Fed's other responsibilities would evolve over time. As former Fed vice chair Roger Ferguson has noted, "The original Federal Reserve Act contained almost no explicit goals for the System to follow."*[70] The first major test of the new system would come with the stock market crash of 1929 and the attendant economic disruption. Suffice it to say that the Fed failed this test abysmally.[71] The next chapter will describe this failure in excruciating detail, so we get to skip the Depression and World War II for now. Here is a preview: nearly ten thousand banks failed in the 1930s.[72] As economic historian Glyn Davies concludes, "The Fed which had been set up to provide an elastic currency strangled its patient."[73]

Bretton Woods: More Than Just a Beautiful Holiday Destination

The Mount Washington Hotel is nestled at the base of Mount Washington, the highest peak in the Northeast, in the town of Bretton Woods, New Hampshire. It is a great ski destination (particularly cross-country) and a lovely spot in the summer and fall. (Mention this book and you might be eligible for a 5 percent discount.†) Economics nerds can also visit the room in the hotel where the Bretton Woods Agreement was signed—the international agreement that created the international financial architecture for the postwar period. In the summer of 1944,

---

* The Fed was only granted the power to set interest rates independent of the Treasury in 1951. Congress amended the Federal Reserve Act in 1977 to give the Fed explicit goals: "maximum employment, stable prices, and moderate long-term interest rates." That would become known as the dual mandate despite the fact that three goals were explicitly identified.
https://www.richmondfed.org/publications/research/special_reports/treasury_fed_accord/background/; and Ferguson, "The Evolution of Central Banking in the United States."

† Probably not, but it's worth asking.

representatives from forty-four nations convened in Bretton Woods to create a system that would guard against the monetary debacles of the 1930s. The system that came out of the conference was based primarily on the ideas of two men: British economist John Maynard Keynes and Harry Dexter White, an American economist at the Treasury Department.[74] (Keynes would suffer a mild heart attack near the end of the negotiations.[75]) It was clear that the United States would emerge from World War II as the dominant military and economic power in the West, supplanting Britain in both roles. The system that was devised reflected America's preeminence: a U.S. gold standard with the world's other major currencies pegged to the dollar. As H. W. Brands hypothesized, "Perhaps it wasn't the rigorous schedule that provoked Keynes's heart attack; perhaps it was his knowledge that Bretton Woods marked the definitive eclipse of Britain and the pound sterling by America and the dollar."[76]

The United States reaffirmed the value of the dollar, pegging it at a rate of $35 per ounce (the same price Roosevelt had set ten years earlier). The United States further pledged that any nation could redeem dollars for gold at that rate. This was the anchor of the system, with the value of other participating currencies defined in terms of dollars. Countries pledged to maintain their assigned peg—the exchange rate—within a small margin.[77] For example, if the pound were appreciating (going up in value) relative to the dollar to an extent that put the peg at risk, the Bank of England would be obligated to sell pounds on the international market and buy dollars, thereby driving down the value of the pound relative to the dollar and bringing the two currencies back in line with their peg. To bolster the system, the delegates established the International Monetary Fund, an international organization that would lend currency to any country struggling to maintain its peg.[78]

Bretton Woods established the dollar as the world's reserve currency—the new gold. Central banks around the world would hold dollars to help stabilize their exchange rates and to settle international payments. Unlike gold, however, the American government can print dollars cheaply and in unlimited quantities. Even after the Bretton Woods Agreement broke down (as will be described in a moment), the dollar has retained its international supremacy. In the 1960s, a French finance minister would describe this lopsided arrangement as an "exorbitant privilege." As Barry Eichengreen explains (in his book appropriately titled *Exorbitant Privilege*), "It costs only a few cents for the Bureau of Engraving and Printing to produce a $100 bill, but other countries had to pony up $100 of actual goods in order to obtain one."[79]

By establishing the dollar as the world's reserve currency, Bretton Woods formalized America's economic dominance in the postwar order. The new monetary system, combined with Marshall Plan spending (the U.S. program to rebuild Europe after World War II), promoted spectacular economic growth in the 1950s and 1960s, in the United States and abroad. Japan and Germany, two of the countries most devastated by war, would grow into economic powerhouses.[80] By 1965, however, dollar hegemony was coming under increasing attack. French president Charles de Gaulle announced that the French would be reclaiming $400 million of their gold from its storage vault deep under Manhattan at the Federal Reserve Bank of New York.[81] De Gaulle declared, "American imperialism . . . takes all shapes, but the most insidious is that of the dollar."[82] De Gaulle's action focused attention on a different and unsettling reality: if the world's central banks demanded gold in exchange for their dollar reserves, America would not have sufficient gold to honor their demands.[83] It was the bank run problem again—only with the currency at the heart of the international financial system.

By the time Richard Nixon took office in 1969, the situation had grown steadily worse. America was importing much more than it was exporting, and this balance-of-payments deficit was rapidly draining gold from the Federal Reserve's vault.[84] (When countries sold more to the United States than they bought, they accumulated dollars, which could then be presented for payment in gold.) John Connally, Nixon's Treasury secretary, eloquently described the way that the Nixon White House viewed this looming problem: "Foreigners are out to screw us. Our job is to screw them first."[85] In August 1971, Nixon did successfully screw them first. On Friday the 13th, Nixon retreated to Camp David with his top economic advisers. Over the course of the weekend, the decision was made to close the "gold window," meaning that other nations would no longer be able to convert dollars to gold. On Sunday evening, Nixon addressed the nation (and the world) to announce that the dollar would no longer be pegged to gold. (He also announced wage and price controls in a futile attempt to deal with America's rising inflation.)[86] Franklin Roosevelt had eliminated the right of individual Americans to redeem dollars for gold in 1933; central banks had now lost that right, too.[87] Over the next two years, the major financial powers would attempt to salvage the Bretton Woods system, but it was too late.[88] The world's currencies were no longer tethered in any way to any commodity.

Stagflation: The Food Here Is Terrible and the Portions Are Too Small

The 1970s brought a handful of historical anomalies: disco, leisure suits, bad hair, and stagflation. Although I feel strongly about the first three (especially having been sent to middle school dance classes where I was forced to do line dances to the soundtrack from *Saturday Night Fever*), I shall be addressing only stagflation, the curious combination of high inflation and high unemployment. As the book to this point has sought to explain, high inflation and high unemployment should not coexist under normal circumstances. Inflation is typically what happens when an economy bumps up against its speed limit: Companies raise prices when demand for their goods exceeds supply, which usually happens when most everyone has a paycheck. Similarly, wages start to shoot up when the economy is near full employment; firms have to pay more to attract new workers.

When unemployment is high—lots of people without paychecks—prices and wages usually fall, or at least stop rising. (A department store with racks of unsold merchandise does not usually raise prices.) To paraphrase Woody Allen, unemployment and inflation are like small portions and bad food: usually only one of them is a problem. Except in the 1970s.

Economists are still sorting through what went wrong. As with leisure suits and disco, we may never know exactly who to blame. Still, there is a strong argument to be made that the Federal Reserve mismanaged the money supply, holding interest rates too low for too long. Allan

Meltzer, a Carnegie Mellon economist and author of a comprehensive history of the Federal Reserve, criticized the Fed during the 1970s as having only two speeds: too fast and too slow.[89] One problem lay in a theory embraced by many macroeconomists at the time that higher inflation would bring lower long-term unemployment, the so-called Phillips curve (named for the New Zealand–born economist William Phillips who first posited this relationship). By this way of thinking, higher inflation was *necessary* to bring unemployment down. This view of the economy has since been discarded. (Milton Friedman presciently argued against it in the 1960s.[90]) Most mainstream economists still believe that the Phillips curve can hold true in the short run, if the inflation is unexpected. Consumers are fooled into believing they are getting richer, so they spend more. Firms respond to higher spending by expanding production. (Remember Bert's Big Beef in chapter 2?) Eventually this effect wears off, as consumers and firms realize that everyone has more money but prices are higher by roughly the same amount. As Ben Bernanke has explained, "The analogy might be to a candy bar: if you eat a candy bar, in the short run it gives you a burst of energy, but after a while, it just makes you fat."[91]

Monetary policy was also complicated by an OPEC (Organization of Petroleum Exporting States) oil embargo against the United States in 1973 to protest American policies in the Middle East. Oil prices quadrupled, creating what economists refer to as a "supply shock," a disruption that causes both a rise in the price level *and* a reduction in economic output. During the 1970s, economist Arthur Okun created an indicator called the "misery index," which is the inflation rate added to the unemployment rate. During Jimmy Carter's presidency, the misery index averaged over 16 percent, the highest for any president in the postwar period. (At the end of Carter's term in 1980, it was nearly 20 percent—helping to explain why there was no second term.)[92]

Economists Alex Nikolsko-Rzhevskyy and David Papell have revisited data from the period, including reasonable assumptions about the full employment speed limit of the economy. They conclude that the federal funds rate (the short-term interest rate targeted by the Fed) was consistently too low if the Fed was aiming for 2 percent inflation.[93] Meanwhile, the public had come to accept rising prices as a fact of life, whether the economy was strong or weak. This, of course, helped to ensure rising prices whether the economy was strong or weak and complicated the Fed's inflation-fighting task. Allan Meltzer has argued that the Fed simply lost its nerve in battling inflation. He writes, "When their anti-inflationary moves caused the unemployment rate to rise to 6.5 percent or 7 percent, they forgot their promises and again began expanding the money supply and reducing interest rates."[94] The more firmly embedded inflationary expectations became in the public mind, the more painful the process would be to halt. As Ben Bernanke has pointed out, loose monetary policy was compounded by other policy mistakes. The government was running deficits to pay for the Vietnam War ("guns") and other social expenditures ("butter"), which further stoked demand. Remember that model of the economy as a driver's education car with two sets of pedals—monetary policy and fiscal policy? By the early 1970s, both the Fed and Congress were pushing the pedal to the floor. Then, with the economy running over the speed limit, the Nixon administration tried to fight inflation by imposing government wage and price controls, a policy that Milton Friedman compared to trying to fix an overheating furnace by breaking the thermostat. Prices were artificially suppressed for a while, until the policy collapsed and "prices surged, like a spring that was released," as Bernanke has described. Combined with the badly timed OPEC oil embargo, this mélange of bad policies created a seemingly unsolvable economic problem.[95]

Stagflation may in fact have been unsolvable if someone other than Paul Volcker had been appointed chairman of the Federal Reserve in August 1979. Volcker (aka Inflation Fighter Man) took the job with a determination to end inflation. The courage of this battle was described in chapter 5. Three months into Volcker's term, the Federal Open Market Committee (over which he presided) raised interest rates sharply. Volcker knew that a sustained tightening of the money supply was necessary to rid the country of inflationary expectations, despite the inevitable short-term economic costs. The Fed chair faced immense criticism from the public and from politicians over rising unemployment, which peaked at over 10 percent. Volcker's steadfastness paid off: inflation fell from twelve percent in 1980 to 3 percent by the middle of 1983.[96] In 1987, Volcker retired and was succeeded by Alan Greenspan, who would lead the Fed until 2006.

The Great Moderation: Thank You, Inflation Fighter Man

By the 1980s, disco, leisure suits, and chronic inflation were all on the wane. The next two decades were a unique period of prolonged low inflation and low variability in GDP growth. Even disruptions like the stock market crash of 1987, the first Gulf War, and the popping of the dot-com bubble caused only minor economic ripples. It is arguable that Chairman Greenspan held interest rates too low for too long, helping to set in motion the real estate bubble that precipitated the 2008 financial crisis. We'll leave that debate for the next chapter. For now, the crucial point is that the twenty-five year stretch from 1983 to 2008 was singular in American history. As Ben Bernanke has said, "One of Greenspan's important accomplishments for most of his tenure was achieving greater economic stability . . . There was so much improvement in the stability of the economy that the period has come to be known as the Great Moderation, as opposed to the Great Stagflation of the 1970s or the Great Depression of the 1930s. The Great Moderation was a very real and striking phenomenon."[97]

On the international front, things were less copacetic. The collapse of the Bretton Woods system left the world's major economic powers scrambling to coordinate exchange rates and global capital flows. Even the successful efforts in this regard, such as the Plaza Accord, were ad hoc. As described in chapter 6, the world's major powers met in New York in 1985 to coordinate policy so as to engineer a depreciation of the dollar. (America's major trading partners were persuaded to facilitate a weaker dollar—which worked primarily to the benefit of U.S. exporters—because U.S. trade deficits had grown large enough that they were perceived to be a threat to global stability.) The dollar fell 40 percent over the next two years—too far, in fact. The same players met in Paris in 1987 (the Louvre Accord) to stabilize the dollar. But that's about it. The world is currently without a formal process or institution for coordinating economic policies across nations in a way that stabilizes the system and promotes prosperity for all.

2008: It Was Bad. Very Bad. Worse Than You Know.

The Great Moderation came to an immoderate end. In the early 2000s, the real estate market was "frothy," as economists like to say. As prices climbed steadily, more and more people jumped into the market. Banks were lending eagerly. No job? No assets? No problem. True story: in about 2005, my dog Buster, a lovable but otherwise unexceptional Labrador retriever, was preapproved for a Visa card. He probably could have qualified for a mortgage, too. And why not? Housing prices were climbing so steadily that Buster could always sell his fancy doghouse at a profit if he struggled to make the payments. Almost no one—neither lenders nor borrowers—were thinking about what might happen if housing prices stalled, let alone plunged.

We know how this ends.

The next chapter will provide more gory details, including the crucial differences between the policy responses in 1929 and 2008. For now, let me just offer this tidbit of how bad things could have been. Former New Hampshire senator Judd Gregg, a point person on budget and finance issues for the Republicans, recalls being summoned to the Capitol from a black tie dinner shortly after the failure of Lehman Brothers in September 2008. The Bush administration was trying to put together a legislative backstop for the financial system (what would ultimately become TARP, the Troubled Asset Relief Program). Gregg recounts:

> I received a call around nine o'clock at night from Mitch McConnell, who had asked me to coordinate the Senate Republicans' efforts on the financial crisis. Mitch said he needed me up at the Capitol immediately. Could I get there in fifteen or twenty minutes? I said, "Sure." I went up to the Capitol, to room S-219, which is just off the Senate floor. In the room were myself, Chris Dodd, Chuck Schumer, Kent Conrad. Barney Frank and Spencer Bachus were there from the House Banking Committee.

Harry Reid came into the room, and I believe Mitch was with him. He said, "In about 10 minutes Chairman Bernanke is going to be here, along with Treasury Secretary Paulson. I want you to listen to them. It's very important what they have to say." And then they left.

So about 4 or 5 minutes later Chairman Bernanke came in with Secretary Paulson and a couple of staff, not many. They sat down, and without any sort of opening remarks, Chairman Bernanke simply said, "If Secretary Paulson doesn't get what he's asking for, and he doesn't get it within seventy-two hours, the entire banking system of the United States will fail, and it will bring the world banking system down with it."[98]

CHAPTER 9

1929 and 2008

It will become apparent that the economic policymakers of the 1920s and early 1930s were like the eighteenth-century doctors who treated Mozart with mercury. Not only were they singularly ineffective in curing the economic disease, they also killed the patient.

—MIT economic historian Peter Temin[1]

A small compensation for the enormous tragedy of the Great Depression is that we learned some valuable lessons about central banking. It would be a shame if those lessons were to be forgotten.

—Ben Bernanke, six years before the onset of the 2008 financial crisis[2]

n the summer of 2007, two hedge funds at Bear Stearns declared bankruptcy. Both were highly leveraged and had significant real estate exposure. Real estate prices had started to cool, so it was no great surprise that some hedge funds holding the most exotic mortgage-backed securities* had begun to stumble. The Bear Stearns hedge fund

---

* Mortgage-backed securities are an asset backed by a bundle of mortgages. For example, an investment bank can buy a bundle of one thousand mortgages (from the banks that made the loans), package them into a single security, and then sell that security to an investor (earning a fee in the process). The investor who owns the mortgage-backed security receives the payments from the underlying mortgages as they are

news was quickly lost in the cacophony of other stories. In hindsight, of course, it was the beginning of the end for Bear Stearns and one of the first indications of how much damage falling real estate prices could do to the broader financial system.

Roughly nine months later, on Sunday, March 16, I vividly recall working at my desk when shocking news hit the Internet: JPMorgan Chase was offering to buy Bear Stearns for $2 a share. Less than a year earlier, Bear Stearns shares had traded as high as $169. Two dollars was an unimaginably low price for one of Wall Street's venerable firms. My father had retired from Bear Stearns several years earlier, having spent the last half of his career there. I used to visit him on the frenetic trading floor, where everyone referred to him as "Wheels." He still owned a big chunk of Bear Stearns stock in his retirement portfolio.

When I saw the Bear Stearns news (which was really a collapse of the firm), I called my parents in Florida. I can't remember who answered. I vaguely recall that my wife and kids had already flown down to visit for spring break. At any rate, I said, "Tell Dad that JPMorgan is buying Bear Stearns for $2 a share." The price was so low that my parents thought I was joking. I had a habit of calling and saying implausible things ("I got on the wrong flight and I'm now in Albania"). Remarkably, they often believed me, at least for a while. On this Sunday evening, they figured a takeover at $2 a share was another practical joke. It was not. JPMorgan Chase ultimately raised the price of the deal to $10 a share, but that was small consolation. One of Wall Street's preeminent firms had been essentially wiped out by large bets using arcane real estate–related financial products.[3]

The Bear Stearns collapse was perceived for a while as an isolated event. In fact, it was the first major ripple of what would become the

---

paid; of course the investor also inherits the risk of missed payments or default. As more households have trouble paying their mortgages, the value of mortgage-backed securities can drop precipitously. Asset-backed securities can also be created using bundles of car loans, credit card debt, or other forms of debt that produce a steady stream of future payments.

2008 financial crisis.* Lehman Brothers would fail six months later, on September 15, 2008. By then, the ripple had become a tidal wave. The ensuing crisis would destroy jobs, toss Americans out of their homes, and spread similar misery around the world. Unemployment as a result of the financial crisis peaked at 10 percent. Nearly twelve million properties went into foreclosure between 2008 and 2012. The economy shrank over 4 percent in real terms before hitting bottom. And yet, as the vignette at the end of the last chapter suggests, it could have been worse—much worse. We were careening toward financial disaster, yet we managed to steer the economy away from total implosion. By comparison, the unemployment rate climbed to over 25 percent during the Great Depression; the economy shrank by about the same.

This chapter will argue that the Great Depression and the financial crisis were strikingly similar in many respects. Both had their roots in the popping of a bubble—stocks in 1929 and real estate in 2008. Both were exacerbated by the inherent vulnerabilities of the financial system, particularly bank runs (broadly construed) during a panic. Both crises fed on themselves, as people who lost savings, homes, and businesses cut back on spending (causing others to lose savings, homes, and businesses). But there is one crucial difference. During the Great Depression, the Federal Reserve—the institution created explicitly to prevent crises and smooth economic fluctuations—failed in its mission. As MIT economic historian Peter Temin asserted, the doctors killed the patient. Policymakers responded to events in 1929 and the early 1930s in ways that, with the benefit of hindsight, were wholly counterproductive.

In 2008, we saved the patient. We did so primarily because of lessons learned from the 1930s. Yes, there was still pain. Human folly and greed were on display from beginning to end. Policymakers made mistakes, some of which will become apparent only as more time passes. The regulatory changes made in response to the financial crisis may or may not avert the next major crisis. None of this should obscure the fundamental

---

* The economy went into recession at the end of 2007, but the events that we now associate with the beginning of the financial crisis did not start until 2008.

point: we were not doomed to repeat history, in large part because we learned from it.

In a fortuitous coincidence, Ben Bernanke, who served as chairman of the Federal Reserve from 2006 to 2014, is a scholar of the Great Depression. He wrote in 2000, when he was still an economics professor at Princeton, "I guess I am a Great Depression buff, the way some people are Civil War buffs."[4] That is not why he was appointed by President George W. Bush to be chair of the Council of Economic Advisers, and later to succeed Alan Greenspan as Fed chair, but it would turn out to be highly relevant. Bernanke gave a prescient speech in 2002 in Chicago at a conference to honor Milton Friedman on his ninetieth birthday. Friedman (as you will read shortly) spent much of his career expounding on the Fed's calamitous incompetence during the 1930s. Bernanke spoke that evening about the seminal work done by Friedman and his frequent coauthor Anna Jacobson Schwartz on the role of monetary policy and the Great Depression. He finished the birthday tribute with a remarkable statement, given what would happen to Bernanke, the Federal Reserve, and the United States over the ensuing decade: "Let me end my talk by abusing slightly my status as an official representative of the Federal Reserve. I would like to say to Milton and Anna: Regarding the Great Depression. You're right, we did it. We're very sorry. But thanks to you, we won't do it again."[5]

The Fed did not do it again. The policy responses in 2008, both in Congress and at the Federal Reserve, were improvised, unpopular, and often poorly explained. The long-term ramifications of those policies are still not fully known. The crisis is over, but as I write, we are not back to normal. Short-term interest rates are still near zero. The Fed is holding $4.5 trillion in assets on its books—roughly five times what it had in 2007.*[6] Bernanke's legacy will depend on the long-term implications of the Fed's extraordinary actions during the crisis. Paul Volcker's stature

---

* These are the assets that the Fed accumulated during the crisis as it injected new money into the financial system in exchange for government bonds and other securities.

has grown over time because of the durability of his victory over inflation; Alan Greenspan's has been diminished because of regulatory lapses on his watch that set the stage for the mortgage debacle. For now, there is a compelling case that the Bernanke Fed did not repeat the mistakes of the 1930s. Milton Friedman died in 2006. As best I can tell, Ben Bernanke honored his promise to him.

The Great Depression

The stock market crash of 1929 was part of a series of events that would become the Great Depression. The market crash did not cause the Great Depression—this is a key point. As Ben Bernanke has written, "The crash of 1929 was only the first step in what was a much more serious decline."[7] The plunge in share prices was almost certainly exacerbated by inept policy at the Federal Reserve and elsewhere in the government. This kind of history is admittedly tricky, as we can never know for certain what would have happened if policymakers had responded differently—the so-called counterfactual. As a point of comparison, we do know that on October 19, 1987, the stock market fell 22.6 percent in one day—a percentage drop not wildly different from Black Monday and Black Tuesday in 1929 (24.5 percent).[8] Yet the broader economic effects of the 1987 stock market crash were relatively benign. So how did the 1929 crash turn into the Great Depression—especially since the vast majority of Americans at that time, some 90 percent, did not own any stocks?[9]

The precipitous fall in share prices spread to Main Street via two accelerants discussed at length earlier in the book: leverage and the inherent frailties of the banking system. As stocks climbed vertiginously in the 1920s, investors and speculators could purchase shares on margin, meaning that buyers could pay as little as 25 percent of the purchase price and borrow the rest. (Yes, this section should remind you of real estate in the 2000s.) When prices are going up, leverage amplifies the gains. If an investor pays cash for a $100 stock and the share price doubles to $200, it is a 100 percent gain. Pretty darn good. *But it can be so much better with borrowed money.* By buying on margin (putting only 25 percent down), the purchaser can use the same $100 to buy $400 worth of shares (borrowing $300 to pay for the rest). When the shares double in price to $800, the purchaser pays back the $300 loan (plus interest paid on the borrowed funds) and pockets nearly $400—*a 400 percent gain on the initial $100 in capital.*

As with any bubble, public perception was that stock prices could go only one direction: up. Irving Fisher made what may be the worst economic prediction of all time when he pronounced on October 17, 1929, just days before the crash, "Stock prices have reached what looks like a permanently high plateau."[10] Banks and brokerage houses eagerly made margin loans, often at very profitable rates. Unfortunately, when the music stops, leverage tends to blow things up. Let's revisit the same example that made us so much money in the previous paragraph, only now let's assume the market falls by just 25 percent. If you paid cash for a $100 stock, it's now worth $75. That's not a good day, but it doesn't destroy you. You've still got 75 percent of what you started with.

But the same 25 percent drop will wipe out a highly leveraged investor. The $400 worth of shares drop in value to $300, which is how much the purchaser borrowed to buy the shares. The investor's original $100 in capital is entirely gone. Leverage has turned a 25 percent market drop into a 100 percent loss. Debt is an equal opportunity amplifier: bigger gains and bigger losses. (This theme, too, will return during the 2000s.) When investors get wiped out, rather than merely losing money, it's not long before their Wall Street bankruptcies cause pain on Main Street, even when most folks on Main Street don't own stocks.

In 1929, the music stopped with the October market crash (though the Fed had taken the punch bowl away earlier in the year by raising interest rates sharply in an effort to curb speculation). While the Fed was raising rates to rein in Wall Street, the economy was already in recession (beginning in August 1929), as Milton Friedman and Anna Jacobson Schwartz have pointed out. The Fed's first policy mistake may well have been raising interest rates when the broader economy needed more alcohol in the punch, not less. (The topic of using monetary policy to curb speculative bubbles will be discussed more generally in chapter 14.) At any rate, plummeting share prices caused more economic damage, particularly to the banking system. Shareholders and brokerage firms defaulted on their margin loans, leaving some banks insolvent. As always, the whiff of insolvency prompted bank runs. Depositors with no exposure to the market crash rushed to withdraw their savings, prompting more bank failures (and more panicked depositors). In November 1930, 256 banks failed; another 352 failed the next month.

Several mechanisms spread the crisis across the Atlantic, beginning with higher U.S. interest rates in 1928. One feature of the gold standard was that other nations were forced to match tight U.S. monetary policy (high interest rates) or risk the flight of gold to America. As noted earlier, if other countries did not respond to tight monetary policy in the United States, higher American interest rates would attract global capital, causing gold to flow to America. Countries that lost significant quantities of gold would no longer have sufficient reserves to exchange their currencies for gold at the promised rate, thereby forcing them off the gold standard. Peter Temin (quoted at the beginning of the chapter) has written, "It was the attempt to preserve the gold standard that produced the Great Depression. These attempts imposed deflationary forces on the world economy that were unprecedented in their strength and worldwide consistency."

France played a curious role in gold hoarding. Dartmouth economist Doug Irwin has written a provocative paper pointing out this unique role that France played in the monetary contraction of the 1930s. (His not-so-subtle title: "Did France Cause the Great Depression?") French economic policies placed a priority on the accumulation of gold beginning in the 1920s. As Irwin has documented, France increased its share of global gold reserves from 7 percent in 1927 to 27 percent in 1932 while short-circuiting the economic processes that would normally have rectified this imbalance.* The whole point of a gold standard is that gold

---

* France was "sterilizing" its growing gold reserves, meaning that the rising stock of gold was not used to support a concomitant rise in the stock of money, as is the usual process. Normally this process is self-correcting. Rising prices in France would have made imports cheaper and exports more expensive, which would have affected France's trade balance in a way that caused gold to start flowing out of the country again. Instead, the French government would take measures such as selling government bonds to "sop up" the extra money that would have been created by the large gold inflows.

exists in fixed quantity. If France has more, everyone else must have less—and therefore less money supported by gold. As Irwin explains, "This 'gold hoarding' created an artificial shortage of reserves and put other countries under enormous deflationary pressure."[11] (There is a bizarre historical postscript here: Osama bin Laden had a copy of Irwin's seemingly esoteric paper in his compound when it was raided by U.S. Navy SEALs.)[12]

In 1931, Kreditanstalt, Austria's largest bank, failed for reasons only tenuously related to the problems brewing in the United States. Several large German banks failed the following month. At that point, the banking systems on both sides of the Atlantic were under stress. As Milton Friedman noted, "Financial panic is no respecter of international boundaries."[13] The economic damage fed on itself. Businesses and consumers reacted to lower incomes and punishingly high real interest rates by buying and investing less (thereby lowering other people's income). America's Smoot-Hawley Tariff, passed in 1930, imposed punitive tariffs on imported goods; other nations responded in kind, leading to a trade war that left all exporters worse off.

In the six months from August 1931 through January 1932, another 1,860 banks suspended operations. According to Friedman and Schwartz, the total money stock was falling during this stretch at an annual rate of 31 percent—the largest rate of decline in the fifty-three years they studied.[14] Bank failures curtail the money supply in three ways. Obviously there are fewer banks making loans. At the same time, fearful consumers decide to keep more of their wealth in currency; cash stashed under the mattress is money that cannot be loaned out via the banking system. Finally, the banks that remain solvent tend to hold higher reserves and lend more cautiously. All of these mechanisms starve the economy of credit and do damage to businesses and households that might otherwise be healthy.

Given falling prices and failing banks, Americans were keen to hold cash—but often there just wasn't enough of it. One feature of the Great Depression was a chronic shortage of currency. The cash shortage was made worse when Roosevelt declared a bank holiday on March 6, 1933, only thirty-six hours after taking office.[15] All banks were ordered closed for four days, which would later be extended to a week.[16] In the absence of currency, governments, companies, and wealthy individuals issued an estimated $1 billion of scrip, which were just fancy IOUs: on paper, leather, metal, wood, and even old tires. When the *New York Daily News* sponsored a boxing match at Madison Square Garden in 1933, the cash crunch was bad enough that promoters offered tickets in exchange for anything worth roughly 50 cents, including spark plugs, nightgowns, frankfurters, Bibles, jigsaw puzzles, and "golf knickers."[17]

By any metric, the Great Depression was bad. There is probably a more descriptive adjective, but let's let the numbers speak. Prices fell nearly 10 percent in both 1931 and 1932 and another 5 percent in 1933. Deflation was crippling for those Americans, such as farmers, who were trying to pay fixed debts by selling a product plummeting in price. The economy shrunk by roughly a quarter between 1929 and 1933 (and 15 percent globally). Unemployment reached 25 percent in the United States. Roughly 9,000 American banks failed during the 1930s—some 4,000 in 1933 alone.[18]

Simply put, the Fed botched the job.* Just as runaway inflation must be blamed on an irresponsible central bank, the same is true for deflation.[19] One of the major contributions by Milton Friedman and Anna Jacobson Schwartz was to demonstrate compellingly that a shrinking money supply caused the massive economic disruption of the early 1930s, not the other way around. (Friedman deliberately referred to the period as the Great Contraction, not the Great Depression.) Anna Jacobson Schwartz summarized their findings: "The Federal Reserve System, by failing to act as a lender of last resort during a series of banking panics, permitted a massive contraction of the money supply that was responsible for the compression of aggregate demand, national income, and employment."[20]

---

* Doug Irwin offers a reasonable defense of the Fed, which is that it had no congressional mandate at the time. There was no clearly articulated description of what the Fed was supposed to be doing or how its performance should be measured. If the goal was to stay on the gold standard, the Fed achieved that until Roosevelt and Congress changed the policy.

The United States rebounded only when the Roosevelt administration ended the deflation by taking the country off the gold standard (depreciating the dollar significantly) and introducing deposit insurance to stop the bank panics. As Ben Bernanke has pointed out, "The two most successful things that Roosevelt did were essentially offsetting the problems that the Fed created or at least exacerbated by not fulfilling its responsibilities."[21] But why the ineptitude? What caused the Fed to kill the patient? Crop failures and drought caused some economic damage in the 1930s, but for the most part the crisis was man-made—a complete policy debacle.

Some historians blame poor leadership at the Federal Reserve. The system was young and highly decentralized. American economist John Kenneth Galbraith has described America's central bank at the time as "a body of startling incompetence."[22] Because the Federal Reserve System was made up of twelve regional banks, the Fed's actual tools for implementing monetary policy were decentralized as well. This structure caused confusion, inaction, and frequent power struggles. The Roosevelt administration eventually restructured the Federal Reserve, giving complete authority over monetary policy to the Fed's Open Market Committee in Washington, DC.*

The bigger problem, however, was ideological. Prominent leaders, inside the Fed and out, were wedded to ideas that compounded the economic problems of the Depression rather than ameliorating them. (Hence Peter Temin's comparison to treating Mozart with mercury.) Many influential thinkers at the time subscribed to a "liquidationist theory" of the economy. They argued that the economy had grown too fast in the 1920s and that a period of deflation was necessary to restore balance. As imprudent families, farms, and firms were wiped out by bankruptcy—with any remaining assets liquidated to pay off debts—it would purge the rottenness and excesses from the system and create an

---

* As was described in chapter 5, the Federal Open Market Committee (FOMC) comprises the seven presidentially appointed governors of the Federal Reserve Board, the president of the Federal Reserve Bank of New York, and four of the other eleven Reserve Bank presidents on a rotating basis.

opportunity for a fresh start. As Ben Bernanke has explained, "This theory held that the Depression was unfortunate but necessary."[23]

But the mother of all problems was the Fed's strict adherence to the gold standard, which limited its ability to save the banks and counteract falling prices. The Fed could not create new money to act as the lender of last resort for failing banks, as new money had to be backed by gold. The Fed could not lower interest rates dramatically to counteract the shrinking economy, as that would have caused outflows of gold. Other struggling nations faced the same constraint. In the United States and around the world, policymakers protected their gold supplies by keeping interest rates high—the opposite of what was necessary to promote recovery. As Peter Temin concludes in his book *Lessons from the Great Depression*, "Holding the industrial economies to the gold standard was about the worst thing that could have been done."[24]

The countries that did not adhere to the gold standard managed to avoid the Depression almost entirely (China, for instance). The countries that were first to leave the gold standard (such as Britain) were the first to recover. The countries that stayed on gold longest had the deepest and longest depressions (the United States and Germany). In fact, as Temin has pointed out, not a single country was able to sustain a meaningful recovery while still on the gold standard.

I suppose one could argue that clinging to a faulty cure is really just a different form of incompetence. Semantics aside, we can agree that the Fed failed in its core mission: delivering macroeconomic stability by keeping the value of the currency consistent and protecting against financial panics. As Ben Bernanke has written in his assessment of the Great Depression, "[The Fed] did not use monetary policy aggressively to prevent deflation and the collapse in the economy, so it failed in its economic stability function. And it did not adequately perform its function as lender of last resort, allowing many bank failures and a resulting contraction in credit and also in the money supply. So the Fed did not fulfill its mission in that respect. These are key lessons, and we want to keep these in mind as we consider how the Fed responded to the 2008–2009 financial crisis."

The point is not to heap scorn on dead policymakers. The point is to avoid making the same mistakes. With that in mind, let's take a look at the financial crisis. In particular, what did Ben Bernanke—one of the world's preeminent scholars of the Great Depression—do differently?

The 2008 Financial Crisis

At one of the worst points of the financial crisis, a college friend of mine who had gone on to become a successful CEO went to the bank, withdrew $10,000, and hid the money in his cowboy boots. When I later heard the story, I was shocked by two things: that he owned cowboy boots—and the panic this implied. Another friend of mine, who was at the epicenter of the crisis on the trading floor of one of America's biggest financial institutions, set out to buy a gun (before his wife stopped him). The system was unraveling. The closer people were to the crisis, the more terrified they were during the darkest days. As Ben Bernanke's warning to congressional leaders at the end of the last chapter suggests, we were staring into the financial abyss.

It all started in a much happier place. Rising real estate prices made lots of people richer, at least on paper. Every time a neighbor's house sold for some surprisingly high amount, my wife and I mentally recalculated the value of our own home, and therefore of our net worth. The house down the street—not as nice as ours!—just sold for $500,000? Looks like we're a hundred thousand dollars richer than we were last week. All of America was doing the same. There was a sense that real estate prices would continue to rise at a rapid pace (contrary to all historical data) and that it might become too late to buy in some markets. If Irving Fisher were alive, I suspect he may have written about why and how housing prices had reached a new high plateau (as many supposed experts did). Interest rates were low by historical standards, which made mortgages more affordable. Both political parties—in a rare bit of agreement—were promoting home ownership. House prices climbed 152 percent between 1997 and the market peak in 2006.[25] And people thought they would just keep going up. According to *The Financial Crisis Inquiry Report*, by 2005 "more than one out of every ten home sales was to an investor, speculator, or someone buying a second home."[26]

And then the music stopped. *The Financial Crisis Inquiry Report* includes poignant testimony from Warren Peterson, a Bakersfield, California, homebuilder who lived the boom and the bust. For twenty-five years, Peterson had built between three and ten custom homes a year. During the boom, however, he was building thirty a year—until demand just disappeared. Home prices began to tumble everywhere, often most sharply in the markets that had been the hottest. In 2008 alone, $11 trillion of wealth was destroyed, or about 18 percent of Americans' net worth—the largest annual drop ever recorded.[27] "I have built exactly one new home since late 2005," Peterson told the commission in 2010.

How did the party get so out of control in the first place? Why did the music stop? And when the party ended, what put the entire global financial system at risk?

There is a long answer and a short answer. A number of very good books have outlined the long answer. For all my grousing a few chapters back about *The Financial Crisis Inquiry Report* (545 pages, small print), I must concede that it is a fascinating document that draws on testimony from all the major participants. It's worth wading into, if you are stranded at an airport for several days. For a more readable account that comes to the same basic conclusions, I would recommend Princeton economist Alan Blinder's book *After the Music Stopped*. Blinder, who was vice chair of the Fed before the crisis, was close enough to the action to have a front row seat, but unlike some of the participants (Paulson or Bernanke or Geithner), he was not so close that he has to defend his actions. All accounts of the crisis document a chain of events in which rising real estate prices led to reckless borrowing and ultimately the equivalent of a modern bank run. But these were not actions by stupid people (for the most part). One of the unique features of the 2008 crisis was how many different parties, each responding to rational incentives, made money by doing financially foolish things and then quickly passing the risk along to another party, like a giant game of mortgage hot potato.

Let me see if I can squeeze all the bad actors into several pages. (This will be a major accomplishment, as there were a lot of bad actors). Let's start at the bottom: too many people borrowed too much money to buy real estate. We prefer to heap scorn on bankers and mortgage brokers.

(That will come very soon.) The reality is that the real estate bubble inspired people and businesses to borrow heavily to buy properties they erroneously believed would not fall significantly in value. Without that fundamental error in judgment, the rest of the crisis could not have happened. The typical real estate purchase was far more leveraged than the stocks purchased on margin in the run up to the 1929 crash. Putting 5 percent down on a house means the other 95 percent is borrowed. (And by the time the party was really going, 5 percent down was old-fashioned.)

Plenty of villains encouraged this reckless borrowing, largely because they were not on the hook for the outcome. Mortgage brokers were paid commissions based on the size and quantity of the mortgages they originated, regardless of whether they were ever paid off. Some of the highest fees could be earned by originating subprime mortgages for buyers whose credit was somehow impaired. Of course, it was not the mortgage brokers' capital at risk; they were literally getting paid to make loans with someone else's money (the banks). It is no wonder that the most nefarious of the mortgage brokers had little regard for the quality of the mortgages they were peddling. Bigger mortgage, bigger commission.

The banks, too, cared surprisingly little. Yes, it was their capital being loaned out, but this was no longer George Bailey's Building and Loan, where a bank would write thirty-year mortgages and then hold those loans on their books as they were paid off. Banks could quickly sell off their loans in a process called securitization. Other financial firms, notably the investment banks, bought and bundled packages of mortgages into securities that had the basic attributes of a bond—the so-called mortgage-backed securities. Your condo loan might be packaged with 999 other mortgages and sold off to an investor who wanted to receive the steady stream of income as those mortgages were (hopefully) paid off.

That was just the beginning. Not only were mortgages bundled together; those bundles were often sliced and diced in various ways. A bundle of one thousand mortgages might be carved up into five different securities: the owners of the safest security would get the first mortgage repayments; the owners of the second safest security would get the next payments; and on down to the bottom, where the riskiest security would be the one punished severely if property owners began missing mortgage payments. Some of these fancy securities were engineered even further (with firms earning healthy fees for doing the engineering). The effect was to obfuscate the risk embedded in these increasingly complex mortgage bundles. Suppose you took ten days of newspapers and ran them through a paper shredder. Then imagine that someone asks you about the details of a baseball game that was described in last Wednesday's sports section. There is very little hope of piecing together the details, literally in the newspaper case and figuratively with the assorted and exotic mortgage-backed securities. As *The Financial Crisis Inquiry Report* describes, "By the time the process was complete, a mortgage on a home in south Florida might become part of dozens of securities owned by hundreds of investors—or parts of bets being made by hundreds more."[28]

The ratings agencies come next in our chain of avarice and incompetence: Moody's, Standard & Poor's, and Fitch. If this whole crisis were a massive car wreck, the ratings agencies would be the ones who gave the keys to the drunk driver and helped ease him into the driver's seat. There is nothing inherently wrong with securitizing mortgages as long as investors understand the quality of the assets that have been bundled into the security. The ratings agencies were supposed to be the ones who made sense of this process by evaluating individual securities and assigning them a rating based on their relative risk: AAA, AA, BBB, and so on. Safer securities get higher ratings (AAA); riskier securities get lower ratings (BB). Buyer beware. If a film critic gives the new Adam Sandler film half a star, you can't really demand your money back when it turns out to be a stupid movie. But what if the film critics start giving bad movies four stars—*because the film producers are paying for the ratings?*

Once again the incentives were broken. The ratings agencies, believe it or not, are paid by the firms issuing the securities, which really is just like having film producers pay to have their own movies rated. Obviously, taking a check from Adam Sandler and then telling the world that his movie stinks is not good for repeat business, whereas giving four stars to *Grown Ups 2* makes it more likely that you'll be hired to rate *Grown Ups 3* and *4*. (For the record, and to make this analogy crystal clear, *Grown*

Ups 2 was a horrible, horrible film. Also for the record: Adam Sandler does not pay for film reviews.) Through some combination of greed, incompetency, and dishonesty, the ratings agencies awarded a AAA rating—the very safest form of debt—to a shockingly high proportion of mortgage-related securities, despite clear evidence that the trend in real estate prices during the 2000s was historically anomalous; and that mortgage underwriting processes across the country were growing steadily sloppier, and in many cases overtly fraudulent.

Two major quasi-government entities, Fannie Mae and Freddie Mac, arrived at the dance just as the band was playing "Twist and Shout."* Fannie Mae was created as a government agency during the Great Depression to buy mortgages from lenders, thereby freeing up capital that can be used for new loans. Whenever a bank sells off a mortgage, it can use the capital to make new home loans. In normal times, this is a good thing. Congress created Freddie Mac in 1970 for the same basic purpose. Both "Fannie" and "Freddie" have historically played an important role in securitizing conventional mortgages.[29] Here's the quirky thing: Fannie and Freddie were both spun off by the government as publicly traded companies. Their unique history—private companies originally created by the government to serve a public function—created the belief that the government would bail them out if they got into trouble (which is ultimately what happened).

The two firms, known as government-sponsored enterprises, or GSEs, combined the worst of both worlds: the private sector hunt for profits with an implicit government guarantee if things went wrong. In 2005, Fannie and Freddie began buying and holding bundles of subprime mortgages—almost exactly at the peak of the real estate market. Suffice it to say, this turned out badly. In September 2008, the federal government took over both Fannie Mae and Freddie Mac after huge losses threatened to bankrupt them.

Last but not least, the firm AIG (American International Group) put the frosting on this poop cake by insuring some of the most exotic

---

* Their full names are Federal National Mortgage Association (Fannie Mae) and Federal Home Loan Mortgage Corporation (Freddie Mac).

mortgage-related securities. Technically, AIG offered "credit default swaps," which are promises to pay compensation in the event the issuer of a security defaults or misses a payment. Unlike regular forms of insurance, however, AIG was not required to set aside reserves against potential losses. When real estate prices were rising steadily, this was a great business—like writing hurricane insurance in Florida when it's not hurricane season. What's not to like about the steady flow of checks? But when the hurricane season arrived—the collapse of the real estate market—AIG was not able to make good on its promises. This, too, ended badly. In September 2008, the federal government seized control of AIG, providing $85 billion in new capital to keep it afloat.*[30]

The chain of broken incentives was encapsulated by what one witness, a corporate educator who trained loan officers, told the Financial Crisis Inquiry Commission: "I knew that the risk was being shunted off. I knew that we could be writing crap. But in the end it was like a game of musical chairs. Volume might go down but we were not going to be hurt."[31]

Except that in the end, we were all hurt.

By the time 2007 rolled around, investors around the world had borrowed heavily to load up on extremely complex mortgage-backed securities in the belief that they were safe investments. As with overvalued stocks in the 1920s, the bursting of the real estate bubble was just the beginning of the problem. As Ben Bernanke has pointed out,

> If you put together all the subprime mortgages in the United States and assumed they were all worthless, the total losses to the financial system would be about equivalent to one bad day in the stock market: they were not very big. The problem was that they were distributed throughout different securities and different places and nobody really knew where they were and who was going to bear the losses.[32]

---

* The capital was an $85 billion loan from the Federal Reserve. As part of the deal, the federal government took a 79.9 percent ownership stake in AIG.

Now that real estate prices were collapsing, who owed what to whom? What exactly was embedded in those complex securities that financial firms had been selling for the past five years (and holding on their balance sheets)? Sophisticated investors were staring at a pile of shredded newspaper, suddenly interested in reading the stories.

That brings us to the short answer for what happened during the crisis: the popping of the housing bubble created a modern-day bank run. This was not customers standing outside the Bailey Building and Loan trying to get their deposits back; FDIC insurance protected regular depositors. Instead, the leverage and lack of transparency embedded in the complex mortgage-related securities coursing through the financial system created a different kind of panic. In the decades after the Great Depression, a shadow banking system evolved to provide different ways for corporations to store cash or to borrow. One of these innovations was the creation of sale and repurchase agreements, or "repos." These were very short loans, often overnight, made to creditworthy firms that typically posted securities as collateral.

For all intents and purposes, the repo market functioned as a bank for large firms. Remember, FDIC deposit insurance typically only insures an account up to $250,000. As Gary Gorton has pointed out, "There is no checking account insured by the FDIC if you want to deposit $100 million."[33] Instead, firms need a relatively safe, liquid place to park large amounts of cash while earning a reasonable return. The repo market was just that.

For example, a mutual fund company like Vanguard, which buys stocks and bonds on behalf of its account holders, might have several hundred million dollars in cash on hand that it is preparing to invest in the stock or bond markets. Rather than leaving this money in a file cabinet, or depositing it in a conventional bank, Vanguard can loan the excess funds *overnight* for a small fee to a firm that needs short-term capital. Many companies, particularly Wall Street firms, use the repo market to finance their activities, rolling over the short-term loans as needed. If you need to borrow $100 million, you can borrow that sum for ten years, or you can borrow it over and over every day for ten years. The latter is more flexible (though potentially more cumbersome), but during normal times, there is not much difference.* Firms borrowing in the repo market posted collateral for the full amount of the loan; asset-backed securities, such as the mortgage-related bonds we have been discussing, were a typical form of collateral.

Maybe you can now see where this is going. As I've noted earlier, if it lends like a bank, and it borrows like a bank, it's a bank. It just might not be insured like a bank. By the 2000s, the whole shadow banking system had the fundamental vulnerabilities of any banking system without the protections put in place after the Great Depression. In fact, many of these institutions had been designed explicitly to avoid those protections and their associated costs. (For example, banks pay a fee on their deposits to be eligible for FDIC insurance.)

The repo market was essentially a bank. Firms lending into the repo market are like depositors. They can get their money whenever they want it. But rather than rushing to the bank to make a withdrawal, they just stop renewing the overnight loans (or they demand much more collateral). This is when borrowing $100 million for ten years starts to feel very different than borrowing $100 million every day over and over again. Firms like Bear Stearns and Lehman Brothers were borrowing short-term in the repo market to finance long-term operations. It would be like paying off your house by refinancing the mortgage every evening; if the value of the property drops, that refinancing gets a lot harder.

When lenders became skittish about the value of the mortgage-related securities being posted as collateral, bad things began to happen. Some lenders refused to renew repo loans. Others demanded more collateral (e.g., posting $120 million in securities for a $100 million loan). Bear Stearns and others began to find themselves short of capital. To raise funds, they were forced to sell assets (such as mortgage-backed securities), driving down the price of those assets and causing more financial distress throughout the system. It was impossible to gauge the exposure of different firms to this

---

* In theory, the interest rate on a ten-year loan should be the same as the expected average rate on a series of ten consecutive one-year loans. Each one-year loan is the expected average rate on 365 overnight loans.

financial distress because of the way mortgage debt, particularly subprime debt, had been packaged, sliced, and diced. Gary Gorton compares the role that bad mortgage debt played in the crisis to the discovery of ground beef contaminated by *E. coli*. He explained in his testimony before the Financial Crisis Inquiry Commission, "Millions of pounds of ground beef might be recalled because the location of a small amount of *E. coli* is not known for sure. If the government did not know which ground beef possibly contained the *E. coli*, there would be a panic: people would stop eating ground beef. If we all stopped eating hamburgers for a month, or a year, it would be a big problem for McDonald's, Burger King, Wendy's, and so on. They would go bankrupt. That's what happened."[34]

Nobody wanted to be holding the contaminated ground beef, or lending to anyone holding contaminated ground beef, or entering into trades with firms that might have exposure to contaminated ground beef. Former Fed governor Kevin Warsh has said that the "Panic of 2008" is the most apt description of what happened. Yes, a real estate bubble set it in motion. Yes, irresponsible lending and the securitization of bad loans amplified and spread the problem. But at the end of the day, this was an old-fashioned financial panic. Customers were not lined up outside of banks; instead firms and institutional investors were demanding their cash back from financial firms like Bear Stearns, Lehman Brothers, Citibank, and the other names you've seen in the news. As one witness told the Financial Crisis Inquiry Commission, "The repo market, I mean it functioned fine up until one day it just didn't function."[35]

The Financial Crisis Inquiry Commission spread the blame widely: shoddy mortgage lending; too many fancy derivatives; irresponsible ratings agencies; massive failures in corporate governance and risk management; a breakdown of ethics; widespread regulatory failures; and a toxic combination of "excessive borrowing and risky investments."

But the most powerful statement in the whole report is the commission's first finding: "We conclude this financial crisis was avoidable."*[36]

---

* The FCIC concluded that Fannie Mae and Freddy Mac contributed to the crisis but were not a primary cause. Also, the commission concluded that the Community Reinvestment Act, a 1977 law designed to promote bank lending in low-income neighborhoods, was "not a significant factor in subprime lending or the crisis." I

As with the Great Depression, adverse feedback loops exacerbated the economic damage. Troubled banks made fewer loans, which starved the private sector of credit. Struggling firms laid off workers and postponed capital investments. Unemployed workers had trouble paying their mortgages, compounding the damage being done by mortgage-related securities. Banks sold homes in foreclosure, driving real estate prices down further and making it harder for other households to refinance or sell their homes with some equity intact. Even healthy households and firms hoarded cash and postponed purchases, dragging down industries like autos and hospitality. More workers were laid off. And so on and so forth. You remember all this, right?

So the Fed Did What?

For all the complexity of the various programs, the nature of what the Fed was trying in response to the Panic of 2008 was relatively straightforward, albeit with some novel twists and on a scale never undertaken before. The Fed sought to carry out its fundamental responsibilities (and avoid repeating the mistakes of the 1930s):

1. Protect the financial system by acting as a lender of last resort.
2. Use monetary policy to stimulate the flagging economy and protect against deflation.
3. Fix the regulatory structure to prevent future crises.*

---

point this out because one convenient if wholly inaccurate version of the financial crisis is that bad government policy caused the private sector to go off the rails. The government certainly fell down on the regulatory front, but it is a wholly inaccurate interpretation to suggest that the financial crisis was the result of excessive government intervention or affordable housing goals gone awry. As this chapter should amply demonstrate, the private sector messed up over and over again.

* As an aside, let me say that whoever named the various Fed interventions—TALF and QE (and TARP over at Treasury)—should be imprisoned with the gold in the vaults beneath the Federal Reserve Bank of New York. The good news is that one could actually live down there. The vaults are locked every night, but one quaint tradition is that sandwiches are placed inside the vault at closing time in case anyone is inadvertently locked inside overnight.

Provide liquidity. The most important role of a central bank during a crisis is to act as lender of last resort. As Walter Bagehot first prescribed, the central bank should lend freely (and at a punitive rate) against good collateral to healthy firms that would otherwise be starved of credit by the panic. The Fed did that in all kinds of ways. Beginning in December 2007, the FOMC lowered the discount rate (the rate at which it loans to banks) from 4.75 percent to 0.5 percent and significantly lengthened the maturity of such loans. The target federal funds rate (the rate at which banks lend to one another) was lowered to near zero. The Fed made loans to other central banks around the world that might need dollars to support their banks.

As the crisis spread, the Fed had to find ways to provide liquidity to financial firms beyond traditional commercial banks, as they were at the epicenter of the crisis. Section 13(3) of the Federal Reserve Act gives the Fed authority to lend to just about any entity willing to post collateral in "unusual and exigent circumstances." If your grandmother showed up at the Fed with a set of Elvis collector plates in 2009—when there were clearly unusual circumstances—the Fed could have advanced her some cash. I choose that example only somewhat facetiously; many nonbank institutions were holding assets that were only marginally more liquid than collector plates. Fed Vice Chair Donald Kohn described a key part of the strategy as "lending to solvent institutions against illiquid collateral," so those institutions could get the liquidity they needed (Grandma now had cash) and could avoid selling assets in a fire sale (which would exacerbate the crisis). The Fed created programs for lending to money market mutual funds, securities dealers, and other "key nonbank market participants." Along with the Treasury, the Fed created a mechanism for lending against securities backed by student loans, auto loans, credit card loans, and loans guaranteed by the Small Business Administration. And so on.

The point of all these programs was to provide liquidity to firms that needed it by creating a market for assets that had become illiquid during the crisis. Once the Fed was willing to lend against Grandma's Elvis collector plates, those plates regained value. As Ben Bernanke has written, "What was different about this crisis was that the institutional structure was different. It was not banks and depositors; it was broker-dealers and repo markets, money market funds and commercial paper. But the basic idea of providing short-term liquidity in order to stem a panic was very much what Bagehot envisioned when he wrote *Lombard Street* in 1873."[37] In 2010, the Fed reported to Congress that there was not a single default among the roughly 21,000 loans made by the Federal Reserve during the crisis. In fact, we taxpayers earned interest.[38]

There is one uncomfortable wrinkle in this George Baileyesque summary of the Fed response. In the process of saving capitalism as we know it, the Fed (and Congress) was forced to rescue firms and individuals whose egregious behavior contributed to the crisis. These parties were not merely smoking in bed. As the last few pages should have made clear, they were smoking cigars in the furnace room while lounging on open canisters of gasoline. We saved those morons, too. The Fed fire department rushed in and pulled them out of the blaze, along with all the less culpable victims.

Policymakers ran smack into what is now referred to as the "too big to fail" problem. It's all well and good to yell "liquidate, liquidate, liquidate." There is great satisfaction in watching people who do stupid things suffer the consequences. *But many of the rest of us would have been taken down in that purge of rottenness.* The part of the crisis response that rankles—all the way from Main Street up to the boardrooms at the Fed and Treasury—is that the parties most responsible for the crisis benefited significantly from the rescue efforts. Some were saved by the liquidity the Fed provided; others were insolvent, or at risking of becoming so, and needed an injection of new capital, which came from Congress in the form of the Troubled Asset Relief Program (TARP). In either case, these actors behaved in ways that destabilized the entire global financial system, earned handsome sums when times were good, and then earned more handsome sums from a government rescue when things fell apart.

Bernanke and others reckoned that these firms were too big to fail. More specifically, there was no orderly process for allowing a handful of giant troubled firms to go bankrupt in a way that would not cause the rest of the system to unravel (e.g., Fannie Mae, Freddie Mac, AIG). In this respect, the fire department analogy still holds. There was just no way to save the neighborhood without also saving the perpetrators. Or, to put it slightly differently, if the furnace room cigar lounge exploded, we were all going to be caught in the blaze. Bernanke explains, "The problem we had in September 2008 was we really did not have any tool—legal tools or policy tools—that allowed us to let Bear Stearns and AIG and the other firms go bankrupt in a way that would not cause incredible damage to the rest of the system." The Fed chose the lesser of two evils.[39]

The problem with rescuing the negligent parties is not just the injustice of it. The other problem is that bailouts make bailouts more likely. This is the moral hazard problem once again. The prospect of a government rescue encourages the kinds of risks that necessitate rescues: heads I win, tails the government will fix the mess for me. Bernanke has stated emphatically of the AIG bailout, for example, "That must never happen again."[40] He will not find much disagreement on that point.

Monetary stimulus. The other mechanism for steering through the crisis was using monetary policy to encourage economic activity and ward off the adverse feedback loops that could amplify the downturn (as in the 1930s). The traditional tool for stimulating borrowing and spending is lowering the federal funds rate; by increasing the money supply, the Fed can lower short-term interest rates to stimulate business investment and consumer spending. There was a problem during the financial crisis: with short-term interest rates essentially at zero, the Fed was operating at the zero bound. The Fed had no practical way of lowering short-term nominal interest rates below zero.

The solution was to use monetary policy to lower long-term interest rates. In many ways, long-term interest rates have a more powerful effect on spending and investment, as they affect things like mortgage rates and the cost of long-term corporate borrowing. The process for lowering long-term interest rates is somewhat more complicated, though. Long-term interest rates reflect expectations about what short-term rates are likely to be over a long period of time. If short-term interest rates are low now, but investors fear they will be much higher in five years, then long-term rates will be higher. A simple math example will help. Suppose interest rates are 2 percent this year, but investors expect the Fed will raise them to 4 percent next year. A two-year bond would likely have a 3 percent interest rate—reflecting an average of the current annual rate and the expectation for next year's annual rate.

Typically the Fed cannot directly affect next year's rate, and certainly not rates twenty-nine years from now. Who knows who the Fed chair will be then—wide ties might even be back in style. To deal with this challenge (lowering the long-term interest rate, not the wide ties), the Fed did two things. First, they offered "forward guidance" about their future plans with interest rates. The FOMC declared at various junctures either that rates would stay low for some fixed amount of time (e.g., until the first quarter of 2010) or until the economy hit some benchmark (e.g., unemployment falls below 6 percent). That is saying to bond buyers, "Look, short-term rates are low now, and we are promising they will be low next year, so if you buy a two-year bond you should accept a low interest rate on that, too."

The other approach was more direct. The Fed used its power to create money to purchase long-term bonds. This was what Quantitative Easing (QE) sought to do (and the subsequent rounds, QE2 and QE3). In each case, the Fed purchased huge quantities of long-term government bonds. The effect was to drive demand up, and therefore the interest rate down. (It's a supply and demand thing: with more demand for long-term bonds, the issuers—the Treasury and federal agencies, in this case—can offer bonds with a lower interest rate.) Again, for all the hoopla, this was really a new riff on an old song. Monetary policy always involves buying and selling government securities; that's the basic tool of open market operations. And when the Fed is seeking to lower interest rates, it is always creating new money to buy those securities. Admittedly, the scale was unprecedented and the nature of the intervention was new, but no one was practicing witchcraft. As Ben Bernanke has explained, "This was really monetary policy by another name: instead of focusing on the short-term rate, we were focusing on the longer-term rates. But the basic logic of lowering rates to stimulate the economy is the same."[41]

It appears to have had its intended effect. In 2014, the *Economist* reported, "There is a consensus among researchers that QE has indeed lowered borrowing costs, and thus increased both economic output and inflation, as its advocates intended."[42]

Prevent the crisis of 2023. In a lecture after the financial crisis to students at George Washington University, Ben Bernanke noted, "The Fed made mistakes in supervision and regulation." This is certainly a nominee for understatement of the decade. *The Financial Crisis Inquiry Report* was more expansive in its criticism, pointing out that the Fed was the only government entity empowered to set prudent mortgage lending standards before the crisis, which it failed to do.[43] The Fed was not alone in dereliction of duty, of course. The Financial Crisis Inquiry Commission concluded that "widespread failures in financial regulation and supervision proved devastating to the stability of the nation's financial markets."[44] Ouch.

Ever since, politicians have been falling all over themselves to nail the barn door shut. I've already read the 500-page *Financial Crisis Inquiry Report*. I don't have the energy to read the 2,300-page Dodd-Frank Act, which was Washington's response to the crisis. To be fair, financial panics erupt with striking frequency, so nailing the barn door shut is not a bad place to start. Dodd-Frank contains provisions to protect against many of the things that went wrong in 2008: a consumer protection bureau to protect against predatory financial products; higher capital requirements to strengthen financial institutions; more transparency around financial derivatives to make it easier to gauge their risk; and so on. Perhaps most important, Dodd-Frank created the Financial Stability Oversight Council, composed of the heads of the major federal financial regulatory agencies, to look across the financial system and identify threats to its stability. The Federal Deposit Insurance Corporation (FDIC), the independent government agency that insures and monitors banks, was granted "orderly liquidation authority" for large financial institutions. This gives the FDIC the power to take over and liquidate large financial firms—including those previously thought too big to fail—in an orderly and efficient way, just as it has historically done with insolvent banks.

Broadly speaking, Dodd-Frank is a logical response to what went wrong in 2008. That said, regulation is notorious for producing unintended consequences; financial firms are clever at finding ways to avoid doing what they have been told. Whether Congress has prevented the next crisis—or perhaps even made it more likely—is an open question.

The Critics

On May 4, 2009, the *New York Times* published two opinion pieces by prominent economists: one by columnist and Princeton professor Paul Krugman and one by Carnegie Mellon economist Allan Meltzer. These are both very smart guys with a deep understanding of monetary policy. And yet their prescriptions were diametrically opposed. Krugman warned that falling wages could worsen household debt, dampen the recovery, and lead to deflation and economic stagnation. He called for more economic stimulus. The piece concluded ominously, "The risk that America will turn into Japan—that we'll face years of deflation and stagnation—seems, if anything, to be rising."[45] Anyone reading that piece would be inclined to call Ben Bernanke's personal line at the Fed and demand some Super Quantitative Easing (SQE).

But on the very same op-ed page, Meltzer had a different take on the situation. He accused the Fed of going far beyond its mandate in ways that were bound to lead to inflation. He wrote, "Independent central banks don't do what this Fed has done." In fact, he argued that inflation, if measured correctly, was already under way. The piece concluded ominously, "For the next few years, [the Federal Reserve] cannot neglect rising inflation."[46] At that point, you would call back on Bernanke's private line: "Uh, yeah, I just left a message calling for some Super Quantitative Easing. Is it too late to cancel that order?"

A 2012 piece on Ben Bernanke in *The Atlantic* noted, "The left hates him. The right hates him even more."[47] Why the rancor? It all boils down to a simple question, with profound consequences: too much, too little, or just right? The Fed gets generally high marks for its immediate response to the crisis, particularly on the liquidity front. But as time has gone on—up to the current tenure of Janet Yellen—the question on the monetary policy front has become "How much monetary stimulus is too much?"

Critics from the political left have tended to be most vociferous in calling for more aggressive monetary easing to put Americans back to work, though they are not alone. The *Economist* (typically right-leaning on economic issues) warned in late 2014 that "ending quantitative easing may be penny-wise, pound foolish." This camp has argued steadily that the global recovery is still weak and precarious. Unemployment is higher than it need be and wages are more or less stagnant. The Fed and other central banks around the world need to keep stepping on the gas until the recovery is stronger. Adam Posen, American member of the Monetary Policy Committee for the Bank of England, wrote in 2011, long after the worst of the crisis was over, "Throughout modern economic history, whether in Western Europe in the 1920s, in the United States in the 1930s, or in Japan in the 1990s, every major financial crisis has been followed by premature abandonment—if not reversal—of the stimulus policies that are necessary for sustained recovery. Sadly, the world appears to be repeating this mistake."[48]

On the other hand, a number of conservative economists and investors wrote an open letter to Ben Bernanke in 2010 with the following admonition: "We believe the Federal Reserve's large-scale asset purchase plan (so-called "quantitative easing") should be reconsidered and discontinued. We do not believe such a plan is necessary or advisable under current circumstances. The planned asset purchases risk currency debasement and inflation, and we do not think they will achieve the Fed's objective of promoting employment."[49]

And Now?

So far, the inflation fears have been unfounded. Still, it's too early to declare victory. The outcome will all hinge on one thing: reserves. American banks are sitting on a staggering $2.7 trillion in reserves kept on account at the Fed.[50] In other words, a large portion of the money the Fed has been pumping into the economy is sitting idle in the equivalent of bank vaults. Critics of quantitative easing, particularly the later rounds, fear that if banks begin suddenly loaning out these reserves, the money supply will explode and prices will shoot up. Fed officials insist that there are many tools for managing the reserves and "unwinding" the Fed balance sheet (selling off all the securities the Fed accumulated during the crisis). Time will tell whether in fighting this crisis the Fed has laid the groundwork for another. For now, one can say unequivocally that Ben Bernanke did not make the mistakes of the Great Depression.

Will an excessively slow recovery turn America into Japan, as Paul Krugman has warned? I don't know. But that does raise a great question: What the heck has been happening in Japan for the last two decades?

CHAPTER 10

Japan

Yes, nobody wants to be Japan, the fallen angel that went from one of the fastest growing economies in the world for more than three decades to one that has slowed to a crawl for the past 18 years. No one wants to live with the trauma of the deflation (falling prices) that Japan has repeatedly experienced.

—Kenneth Rogoff, Harvard economist and former chief economist for the International Monetary Fund, 2010[1]

Japan in the 1990s wrote the book on how policy stumbles can tip a modern economy into deflation. Now it is adding a chapter on how to pull out.

—Jacob Schlesinger, *Wall Street Journal*, 2014[2]

Suppose you run into a friend who has just returned from the doctor's office. Your friend reports that the doctor has told him repeatedly to gain more weight, yet he keeps failing. Each appointment they set a target together—another five pounds. And each appointment he disappoints, often losing a pound or two. He just can't seem to pull off the weight gain that the doctor recommends. At times, your friend questions whether it is even possible, as he has developed all kinds of habits that seem to preclude weight gain (running uncomfortably long distances, eating nasty bran muffins, wearing spandex). You explain that gaining weight is remarkably easy—and fun, too. In fact, you have excelled at it for most of your adult life. Pizza helps. Ice cream is really good. And popcorn—don't skimp on the butter. Never drink light beer. Fry things. Always have a snack before bed. In general, if it tastes good, eat it.

Your friend commits to gaining weight and then misses the goal once again. Finally, in exasperation (having recently gained twelve pounds yourself), you exclaim, "It's not hard to gain weight! Look around, most of the country has the opposite problem. Every diet book that's ever been written is about losing weight. Every food that tastes good has lots of calories. This should not be a problem!" Your belly jiggles slightly as you yell this last bit. The stress of the situation makes you crave a chocolate donut.

Ben Bernanke gave this speech in 2002. Okay, not exactly this speech. But if one recognizes that losing weight is a metaphor for deflation, he gave this speech. In the history of fiat currencies—the era in which governments could make more money at will—the scourge has always been inflation. Irresponsible governments can pay their bills by creating more money. The resulting inflation devalues the existing government debt. In the process, of course, the rising prices make the citizens using the currency worse off. The ability to print extra money is the sundae bar of monetary policy—hard to resist.

If Zimbabwe is the poster child for this irresponsible temptation—heaping caramel on top of hot fudge—Japan is the curious exception. For over two decades, Japan has struggled with deflation and its attendant economic costs. When prices are falling, real interest rates can be relatively high, even when nominal rates look cheap. Consumers postpone purchases to wait for lower prices (which forces retailers to cut prices). Debts grow in real value. Assets like real estate fall in price, making households less wealthy and harming banks holding those assets as collateral. An International Monetary Fund report concluded in 2003, "Japan's ongoing experience is a warning to policy-makers elsewhere about the costs of even mild deflation and the need to prevent it from manifesting rather than face the challenge of curing it. For Japan, the lesson is clear: deflation, however mild, continues to impose significant costs on the economy. Policies to revive inflation expectations are therefore critically needed."[3]

For years, economists have admonished Japan to induce inflation, or at least stop prices from falling. Like gaining weight, it should be really, really easy. Just do the things that would be irresponsible under other circumstances. Print more money and find a way to put it in the hands of consumers. This is the monetary policy equivalent of making a third trip to the buffet. As you push an old lady out of the way to take the last eggs Benedict, you can say apologetically, "Sorry, my doctor says I need the hollandaise sauce."

When Ben Bernanke addressed the National Economists Club (yes, such a group really exists) in 2002, his major theme was why Japanese-type deflation could never afflict the United States. He spoke like a central banker: "Under a fiat (that is, paper) money system, a government (in practice, the central bank in cooperation with other agencies) should always be able to generate increased nominal spending and inflation, even when the short-term interest rate is at zero." Stilted language notwithstanding, Bernanke's speech may be one of the most consequential talks ever delivered by a Federal Reserve official. He pointed out that the Fed can always combat falling prices by increasing the supply of dollars (or threatening to do so). For example, the government could cut taxes, with the Fed buying up the equivalent amount of government debt, thereby financing the tax cut with "new money." Bernanke told his audience, "A money-financed tax cut is essentially equivalent to Milton Friedman's famous 'helicopter drop' of money."[4] It was at that moment that Bernanke earned the nickname Helicopter Ben.

Bernanke went on to explain that a central bank would not "run out of ammunition" even when short-term interest rates hit zero—the zero bound that has been mentioned previously. He described a series of nontraditional tools for stimulating the economy: buying longer-term government bonds; committing to hold short-term rates low for a specified amount of time; lending to banks against a wide range of private assets deemed eligible as collateral, including mortgages; and so on. He asserted, "A principal message of my talk today is that a central bank whose accustomed policy rate has been forced down to zero has most definitely *not* run out of ammunition." The tools he described were the playbook the Fed used to combat the financial crisis several years later. *It's all in that speech.*

Bernanke left one crucial question unanswered: What was happening in Japan? This has become one of the great macroeconomic puzzles of our time. Japan's economic stagnation, beginning with the popping of a massive real estate and stock bubble in 1989, has dragged on for more than two decades. (What was originally described as the "lost decade" has now become the lost decades.) In 2011, the *Wall Street Journal* commented, "Japan has been a puzzle to economists for years, like a patient with a low-grade fever that doesn't get worse, doesn't get better and won't go away."[5]

The causes of the economic malaise are complex, and Japan is still one of the world's richest countries, but nearly any analysis of Japan's travails has concluded that deflation has compounded the economic malaise. Rising prices might not cure all that ails the Japanese economy, but ending the deflation would help, perhaps significantly so. If creating inflation is so easy in an era of fiat money, why can't (or won't) the Japanese central bank engineer higher prices? *Just order a milkshake with that piece of pie.*

Then again, perhaps conventional economics has it wrong. The former head of the Bank of Japan (the central bank) insisted that trying to create inflation given Japan's unique demographics was like "punching air."[6] (His critics countered that expectations matter; if the central bank chief does not believe that prices will rise, no one else will either.) Japan is a rich country with a shrinking and aging population, a high level of public debt, and organized political groups whose interests do not necessarily align with the health of the overall economy. (Deflation tends to be good for savers and old people on fixed incomes.) Given that much of the developed world will eventually resemble Japan (slow growth, lots of old people), we ought to look carefully at the lost decades and the role that monetary policy and the banking system have played in losing them.

First, the Crisis

If you are going to have a full-blown financial crisis, it helps to begin with a bubble. Maybe stocks. Maybe land. Or in the case of Japan, both. Even by bubble standards, this was a doozy. Beginning in 1986, real estate and land prices began to rise sharply relative to past trends. Commercial property prices rose more than 75 percent between 1986 and their peak five years later. Stock prices rose even more. The Nikkei 225, an index based on the share prices of Japan's largest public companies, rose from roughly 13,000 in 1986 to 39,000 in 1989.[7] As with all bubbles, there was a euphoria accompanying (and ostensibly explaining) these dizzying price gains. One of the best-selling books in Japan during the 1980s was *Japan as Number One: Lessons for America*.[8] I graduated from college during this stretch, and there was a sense that Japan was on the brink of buying up America and taking over the global economy. When Mitsubishi Estate Company bought a controlling stake in Rockefeller Center in 1989, the *New York Times* breathlessly described the transaction as "only the latest instance of the Japanese buying a vital piece of the American landscape." (Sony had purchased Columbia Pictures one month earlier.)[9] I recall being told that the land under the Imperial Palace in Tokyo was more valuable than the entire state of California. I have no idea where that trivia nugget came from, but the fact that anyone could say it with a straight face gives you a sense of the times.

Predictably, banks loaned into the bubble. As discussed in chapter 4, banks are procyclical, meaning that they expand lending in the good times and curtail it when times turn bad—thereby exacerbating economic swings. One might say, less politely, that when prices are going up, bankers tend to lose their friggin' minds. Both the Japanese government and the Bank of Japan were aware that a raucous party was under way. The Bank of Japan raised interest rates in 1989 to restrain rising stock prices and nascent inflation. The following year the government made regulatory changes to curb rising land prices.[10]

Pop.

The Nikkei peaked on December 29, 1989, at 38,957. Suffice it to say that would have been a very bad time to buy Japanese stocks. Share prices fell more or less steadily for two decades, hitting bottom in 2009 at just over 7,000—*82 percent below the 1989 peak*. Land prices hit their pinnacle slightly later, in 1991, and then "declined relentlessly thereafter," in the words of University of California–Berkeley economist Maurice Obstfeld.[11] For reasons described just about everywhere in this book, plunging real estate and stock prices imposed huge capital losses on Japanese banks and other financial institutions. Households, too, saw huge amounts of wealth evaporate. For the record, Mitsubishi walked away from its investment in Rockefeller Center in 1995 when the partnership controlling the property filed for bankruptcy. The *New York Times* reported (less breathlessly this time), "Mitsubishi's sudden decision to exit Rockefeller Center is the most striking in a string of recent retreats from the trophy properties stretching from New York to Honolulu that Japanese companies acquired during a real estate binge in the 1980s."[12]

Bad things happen when bubbles burst. Growth slowed from 3.3 percent in 1991 to less than 1 percent in 1992 to 0.2 percent in 1993 to -2.4 percent in 1994.[13] The banks were in deep trouble because of their extensive real estate lending and stock market exposure. A large number of firms were struggling or bankrupt (further weakening the banks). The Japanese economy was also suffering from something mentioned back in chapter 6, the Plaza Accord. Recall that in 1985 the finance ministers from the United States, West Germany, Japan, the UK, and France convened at the Plaza Hotel in New York to coordinate efforts to bring down the value of the U.S. dollar. In a foreign currency twist on the old expression "what goes up must come down," when the dollar goes down, the yen must go up. The yen appreciated almost 75 percent between 1985 and 1988 relative to the dollar.

A strong yen made American properties like Rockefeller Center look relatively cheap in the 1980s for Japanese buyers. The flipside, of course, is that it made Japanese products more expensive for the rest of the world. Japan's economic ascendancy had been built on a competitive export sector. Part of the American economic paranoia of the 1980s was the result of the dominance of a growing number of Japanese brands: Honda, Toyota, Sony, Panasonic, Canon, Nintendo, Mitsubishi. The rapid appreciation of the yen was punishing for Japanese exporters.

Still, there was hardly mayhem in the streets. Japan was suffering a fairly standard-issue recession and banking crisis. In fact, deposit insurance insulated the general public from bank failures, creating what Charles Kindleberger, the guru on manias and panics, described as "a crash without a panic."*[14] There are standard macroeconomic tools for this kind of thing:

1. Cut interest rates to induce more spending and investment.
2. Clean up the financial system. Like spilled milk, the bad loans have already been made; somehow the failing banks need to be recapitalized. Credit is essential for a modern economy, and banks are the primary conduit for credit (especially in Japan), so fix them.
3. If necessary, spend public money and/or offer tax cuts to create a fiscal stimulus. As my teenage daughter might say, "It's a recession. Deal with it."

Yet now we get to the point where Japan's economic travails become unique. Policymakers most certainly did *not* deal with it. Instead, the "zombie firms" were born.

Zombies: Good for Horror Films, Bad for the Economy

Every so often, one of my children will spill something on the floor. Then they will stare at the broken glass and the spilled milk or water. Maybe there will be some tears. Eventually I will say (admittedly with less patience than I should), "Don't just stand there. Clean it up." Japanese policymakers spent a long time staring at the mess. Years and years. Admittedly, it was a big mess. Chicago Booth economist Anil Kashyap estimated in 2006 that cleaning up the financial system would cost 20 percent of Japan's GDP.[15] Nobody likes a bailout, but the fundamental problems in Japan were familiar: boom, bust, bad loans, failing banks. This is when Japan deviated sharply from the traditional script.

---

* That said, there was an increase in the sale of safes, so savers could stash cash at home. With prices falling, there is no penalty for hoarding currency. Money stuffed in a safe gains value over time, rather than losing purchasing power as it would when prices are rising.

"To Lose One Decade May Be Misfortune . . ." *Economist*, December 30, 2009.

Instead, the response consisted largely of pretending there was not a problem.

Regulators pressured banks to continue making loans to insolvent borrowers. This process, known as "evergreening," postponed the firms' inevitable collapse. One study estimated that in the early 2000s a shocking 30 percent of Japanese firms in manufacturing, construction, real estate, retail, wholesale, and service sectors were on "life support" from the banks. These were the so-called zombie firms—dead in an economic sense but still going through the motions of life.

Zombie firms served a lot of short-term economic needs. The government was eager to prop up failing firms to ward off bankruptcies and job losses. The banks complied because evergreening prevented defaults and hid the depths of their own balance sheet problems. Depositors were insured against losses, so they were not rushing to get their funds, regardless of the bad loans their banks were making. Everybody pretended things were fine, like some kind of dysfunctional Thanksgiving dinner. *Just don't ask why Cousin Joanie has a bulge in her stomach.* Obviously, pretending that Cousin Joanie is not pregnant does not make the problem go away. She's going to be even bigger at Christmas.

To be fair, by global standards things weren't that bad—which, ironically, may have been part of the problem. Tokyo remained rich and bustling. Unemployment was relatively low (though rising). Kenneth Rogoff, the former chief economist at the IMF who was quoted at the outset of this chapter, has described Japan's decades-long problems as a "slow-motion crisis."[16] Short-term relief precluded long-term reform. Propping up the zombie firms directed capital to companies that should have been buried, making it hard for more innovative and efficient firms to enter those industries. *It's hard to make money competing against a firm not making money.* The zombies used their evergreen loans, which were essentially government subsidies, to pay artificially high wages and charge unrealistic prices. As Anil Kashyap concludes, "By taking a very short-term view of the economic crisis, politicians and regulators kept everybody stuck in the wrong place."[17]

The Bank of Japan Drives (Very Slowly) to the Rescue

The Bank of Japan was administering the traditional monetary remedies—up to a point. The central bank cut its overnight rate steadily from 8 percent in 1991 to essentially zero by 1999. The zero interest rate policy even acquired its own acronym: ZIRP. For reasons described earlier in the book, nominal interest rates cannot typically go below zero. The Bank of Japan hit the zero bound yet GDP was basically flat in 2001 and 2002. More ominously, prices were falling by nearly 1 percent a year.[18]

I should note as an aside that deflation is not always such a terrible thing. There are times when rising productivity can lead to falling prices, leaving everyone better off. Imagine an agricultural nation that has a bountiful harvest. Prices fall because the supplies of corn and wheat and pigs are abnormally high. Society is better off because everyone is getting more to eat. Even farmers may be better off if a higher volume of sales offsets the lower prices. Japan was not experiencing the "good" deflation; rather, prices were falling because of diminishing demand. (To use the farm analogy, corn and wheat and hog prices were falling because consumers were buying less of all of them. Farmers were selling less *and* getting lower prices.) What was happening in Japan, as Ben Bernanke has described, was "a drop in spending so severe that producers must cut prices on an ongoing basis in order to find buyers."[19]

Japan's unemployment rate had climbed to 5.5 percent by 2003—not catastrophic, but more than twice the rate in 1993.[20] The problem was not that people were starving in the streets, but that one of the world's most robust economies was just sputtering along well below its potential. As Kenneth Kuttner, an economics professor at Williams College, and Adam Posen pointed out way back in 2001, "No other country in the OECD [Organisation for Economic Co-operation and Development] has suffered such a lengthy period of unremittingly below-potential growth, or even one half so long and steep."[21] With some modest interruptions, the Japanese consumer price index fell for fifteen years. Consumer prices fell an average of 0.3 percent from 1999 to 2012.

Along with the usual deflation-related problems, such as high real interest rates, deflation messes with labor markets, particularly if wages are relatively inflexible. When prices are falling, real wages are going up, even though the number on the paycheck stays the same. (The same paycheck buys more stuff.) *Even a wage freeze gives everyone a raise in real terms.* As a result, a worker earning 2,000 yen an hour gets steadily more expensive to the firm as the deflation grinds on. Because it is hard to cut nominal wages (due to unions, contracts, and the psychological factors discussed in the first half of the book), firms often respond with layoffs instead. Businesses are also cautious about hiring new workers, who will automatically grow more expensive (in real terms) over time. In a striking analysis, George Akerlof, winner of the 2001 Nobel Prize in Economics, and his two coauthors calculated that 1 percent deflation in the United States would increase the long-run equilibrium rate of unemployment from 5.8 percent to 10 percent.[22]

Most economists observing the Japanese stagnation prescribed inflation; rising prices would not fix the economy, but they would surely help—just like the patient who needs to gain weight at the beginning of the chapter. A 2003 IMF report concluded, "Prolonged, unanticipated deflation has impeded monetary policy efficacy, hampered financial market activities, squeezed corporate profitability, and raised the real burden of private and public debt."[23] Moreover, rising prices should in theory be easy to engineer, just like gaining weight. Remember those guys in Zimbabwe? If they could get the price of a beer to go up by $50 billion in an hour, presumably Japan could get prices to rise 2 or 3 percent a year. Zimbabwe abandoned its local currency in 2008. The central bank still had 2,000 employees, most of whom were doing nothing. I assume that the former head of Zimbabwe's central bank, Gideon Gono, was looking for a job. Hire that guy![24] Nothing says you are serious about creating inflation like hiring the people who introduced the $100 trillion bill.

Silliness aside, economists argued throughout the lost decades that more could and should be done. Kuttner and Posen offered up the equivalent of a policy "free lunch"—something that isn't supposed to be possible. The Bank of Japan should coordinate with the government to print and spend lots of new money.* *No matter the outcome, the result would be good for the country at no cost to taxpayers.* Either the spending would not cause inflation, in which case the nation would get new bridges and roads and social benefits—all without higher taxes or more government debt. Or the collaboration between the government and the central bank would cause inflation, *in which case the deflation would be cured.*

This takes us right back to the analogy at the beginning of the chapter: the guy who needs to gain weight. Of course he should order the double cheeseburger with fries and a shake. Either he gains weight, as the doctor has advised, or he doesn't gain weight but gets to eat a lot of food that tastes really, really good.

So what gives? Why did the Japanese government and central bank tolerate nearly two decades of falling prices when a treatment, if not necessarily a cure, was ostensibly as simple as printing money? What are we missing here? Is it really so easy to push prices up when the banks are broken and the economy is struggling on multiple fronts? And if so, why didn't the government and the central bank pursue such a course? Or maybe the economics are more complicated than we think.

Inflation Is Not Possible. Seriously?

There is no obvious or conclusive answer as to why the Bank of Japan did not do more. Ironically, Bank of Japan governor Masaaki Shirakawa studied at the University of Chicago, where he took a class from Milton Friedman. Shirakawa asserted during his tenure at the Bank of Japan that Friedman's proposition that prices will rise if enough money is pumped into an economy has been "disproven by the facts." Shi-

---

* From a practical standpoint, this would be accomplished by "monetizing" government debt. The government would issue bonds to pay for new spending. Rather than selling the bonds to the public, where they would add to government debt, the bonds would instead be sold to the Bank of Japan in exchange for new money. In essence, the government would be using new money to pay its bills. Normally that is a wildly irresponsible practice; in Japan, economists argued, a little more irresponsibility would be a good thing.

rakawa and many other top officials within the Bank of Japan were skeptical that monetary policy could be effective in the face of strong deflationary economic pressures, such as a declining population, slow productivity growth, and mounting competition from China and other rising Asian powers. In a 2011 interview with the *Wall Street Journal*, Shirakawa defended the Bank's post-bubble response and declined to name a single mistake.[25]

To be fair, even Paul Volcker, our inspiration for Inflation Fighter Man, was skeptical that Japan's central bank could create higher prices. In 2011, I asked Volcker what would happen if the Bank of Japan tried to do the opposite of what he had done in the United States in the early 1980s—to credibly commit to 4 percent inflation. "They couldn't do it," Volcker said. The assorted pressures pushing prices down were just too strong.[26] Economic factors aside, the Bank of Japan routinely failed on the "credibly commit" part. If prices are to stop falling, the public has to be persuaded that prices will stop falling. (In Zimbabwe, for example, the public was *totally persuaded* that prices were going up.) Senior officials in the Bank of Japan signaled on occasion that deflation might not be so bad. Kenneth Kuttner describes a 2000 speech in which then Bank of Japan governor Masaru Hayami "contended that Japan's deflation was beneficial, or at least benign, and argued strenuously against policy measures intended to combat it."[27]

Ironically, others feared that aggressive monetary policy would work too well. I recall visiting Japan in the early 2000s and asking a member of the Diet (the lower house of parliament) why the country was not more aggressive in printing money. He explained that the hyperinflation in the aftermath of World War II had left an enduring fear of irresponsible monetary policy. (The same has been true in Germany, as the next chapter will explore.) Meanwhile, some Japanese policymakers, particularly economic conservatives, worried that propping up the economy with monetary stimulus would hide the need for more structural economic reforms. The same argument was raised in the United States as the Federal Reserve held rates low for an extended stretch after the 2008 crisis. The unifying explanation for Japanese inaction may simply be that the Japanese economy never suffered a heart attack, which would have forced all kinds of action until the patient responded. It was more like arthritis, slowing and weakening the victim, but in a way that still allows him to continue his regular activities.

For all that, Japan's politicians did eventually lose patience. In 2010, a group of legislators in the ruling Democratic Party of Japan formed the Anti-Deflation League. Within a year, it grew to include nearly a quarter of all representatives in the lower house of the Diet. One leader of the group pointedly gave central bank governor Shirakawa an F for his monetary efforts.[28] By 2012, voters were fed up, too. In December of that year, Shinzo Abe was elected prime minister with a solid parliamentary majority and an explicit mandate to end the economic malaise. Abe offered three "economic arrows": more fiscal stimulus to jump-start the economy; a massive monetary boost to end the deflation; and structural reforms to improve the long-term efficiency of Japan's economy.[29]

It is called Abenomics.

Deflation Fighter Man

In what one longtime Japan observer described as a transformation "from self-induced paralysis to Rooseveltian resolve," Prime Minister Abe immediately began firing his arrows.[30] The fiscal arrow included a series of large spending packages designed to stimulate demand. The structural reform arrow was intended to raise the speed limit of the economy by "slashing business regulations, liberalizing the labor market, cutting corporate taxes, and increasing workforce diversity."[31] Our focus here is obviously the monetary policy arrow, where Prime Minister Abe promised a "regime change."

The Bank of Japan's new governor, Haruhiko Kuroda, declared that one of his goals was to "drastically change the expectations of markets and economic entities." In 2013, for the first time ever, the Bank of Japan announced an explicit inflation target of 2 percent and a willingness to do whatever it would take to get there in two years. The rhetoric was accompanied by massive efforts to expand the money supply using a variety of tools. A *Wall Street Journal* headline proclaimed, "Stagnant Japan Rolls Dice on New Era of Easy Money."[32] There was a predictable "chorus of naysayers." One senior government official told the newspaper, "It's impossible, of course. I think Mr. Kuroda knows it's not possible."[33]

The scale of intervention was unprecedented anywhere in the world. The value of the assets held by the Bank of Japan reached 57 percent of GDP in 2014—more than twice the size of the U.S. Federal Reserve's holdings in the aftermath of the financial crisis.[34] When Mr. Abe's proposed reforms ran into political trouble, he called a general election in 2014 to earn a new mandate from voters for more Abenomics. His ruling Liberal Democratic Party won a decisive victory. His government is now testing the limits of what monetary policy can achieve.

So far, Prime Minister Abe's arrows seem to be wobbly but generally heading for their targets. Japan expert Adam Posen wrote at the end of 2014, "In essence, the Japanese recovery is going right even if it is not going well."[35] There have been glimmers of inflation. Japan's consumer price index, excluding fresh food and the impact of a new, higher consumption tax, rose about 1.5 percent by the middle of 2014.[36] Inflation slipped back to zero in early 2015, in part due to falling global oil prices.[37]

The Council on Foreign Relations offered its assessment in a 2015 briefing: "So far, the success of these 'three arrows' is unclear. Despite massive government stimulus, Japan fell back into recession in the second quarter of 2014. Inflation initially inched upwards but is now falling on the back of plunging global oil prices, and the country may again face deflation in 2015. Concerns over ballooning debt remain, and many doubt that Abe can muster the political will for difficult structural reforms—some of which remain deeply unpopular among certain industries—even after his coalition's strong showing in early elections called in December 2014."[38]

What We Can Learn from Japan's Experience

Time will render judgment on Abenomics. Whatever the outcome, Japan's case is unique and instructive. The lessons from a place like Zimbabwe are pretty simple: don't let an autocrat go crazy printing money. The lessons from Japan are subtler, more complex, and arguably more relevant. Japan is an aging country with a developed economy and a somewhat ossified political structure. The world's other rich countries are headed in that direction. Here's what we can infer so far from the lost decades and Abenomics.

It's better than it looks—and worse. There is a temptation to dismiss Japan's lost decades as not so bad. Japan's shrinking population does distort the nation's economic indicators. Japan's GDP *per capita* grew faster than both the United States' and the eurozone's between 2001 and 2010 (an admittedly anomalous stretch). Still, the appropriate benchmark is how the Japanese economy has performed over the past two decades relative to its potential. As Kenneth Rogoff has written, "No one wants to go from being a world-beater to a poster child for economic stagnation." That's what Japan has done. The gap between Japan's economic performance and its potential—the so-called output gap—has been extraordinary, in both its size and its duration. When an economy underperforms, the most vulnerable citizens suffer from the lack of growth. Homelessness and suicide climbed during the malaise; the slow economy was particularly punishing for young people looking for decent jobs.[39] Japan's underperformance is made all the worse by the compelling case that it was probably unnecessary, had policymakers acted differently. As the *Economist* has argued, "If one believes that Japan would have functioned as a more or less normal economy over the last decade or two had it not been stuck at the zero lower bound, then its experience at the deflationary trap has cost the economy trillions of dollars' worth of output, and individual Japanese workers untold jobs and wage increases."[40]

Financial crises are bad. As Paul Volcker pointed out to me (while chuckling, if I recall correctly), "The first lesson is don't permit two huge bubbles to be created in the first place."[41] The real estate and stock market crashes created an economic mess that was going to be hard to clean up no matter how policymakers responded. Better to prevent those booms and busts in the first place. Ben Bernanke made the same basic point when he explained in 2002 why and how the United States could resist a Japanese-style crisis: "The Fed should and does use its regulatory and supervisory powers to ensure that the financial system will remain resilient if financial conditions change rapidly."[42] *But wait a minute: while Bernanke was giving that speech, the real estate bubble in the United States was just gaining steam.* The interesting question—based on both the Japanese and the U.S. experiences—is whether a central bank can recognize a bubble, and if so, what ought to be done about it. This is one of the major challenges in central banking and will come up again in chapter 14. In any event, if a bubble does burst, clean up the mess, particularly the banks and related institutions. As one Japan expert points out, "There is nothing worse than having a crippled financial sector hanging over your head."[43] This is a message that American policymakers took to heart during the 2008 financial crisis.

Deflation is bad enough that central banks ought to err on the side of inflation. The problem with perfect price stability—zero inflation—is twofold. First, even a tiny bump can turn it into deflation, setting in motion a cascade of other problems. Second, it gives the central bank less room to maneuver real interest rates. If inflation is 2 percent and the nominal interest rate is 1 percent, the real interest rate is negative 1 percent—providing a robust monetary stimulus. The central bank cannot generate negative real interest rates when inflation is zero or negative. For these reasons, the Fed and other central banks now typically keep a buffer zone, a target inflation rate of 1 to 3 percent, rather than aiming for zero.

Deflationary expectations are just as powerful as inflationary expectations. It's the same basic idea. Prices tend to change in the way people expect prices to change. In Japan, an entire generation of young people have never seen consistently rising prices. A Big Mac in Tokyo cost the same in 2014 as it did in 1998. One employee at a tech company in Kobe told the *New York Times*, "I've never experienced inflation. It doesn't seem real to me."[44] When Japan's largest retailer announced that it would be giving 54,000 employees pay increases in 2013, the news was so startling that Japan's public broadcaster made it the lead story on the nightly news.[45] Businesses that have raised prices are issuing apologetic notes.

The Kidoizumi Brewery wrote to its customers, "It truly pains our hearts to announce that we will soon revise our prices."[46] As the *Economist* summarizes, "Re-establishing consistently positive inflation is a confidence game. If households believe [prices will rise] they will spend, firms will hire, and prices will rise. If households doubt the government's commitment to generating more inflation then the game is lost."[47]

Monetary policy is no substitute for supply-side reform, though it can be an important complement. Monetary policy keeps the economy running at its speed limit; economic reform, such as encouraging women to enter the workforce or building productive infrastructure, raises the speed limit. Throughout the lost decades, Japan was suffering on both fronts; Abenomics has now aimed arrows in both directions. As Kenneth Rogoff has written, "Inefficiency in agriculture, retail, and government are legendary. Even at Japan's world-beating export firms, reluctance to confront the ingrained interests of the old-boy network has made it difficult to prune less profitable product lines—and the workers who make them."[48] Yes, these things need to be fixed. But structural reforms are always politically easier when an economy is growing, rather than shrinking or stagnant. A small dose of inflation can provide the grease to lubricate the process—making it easier to cut real wages, for example.

Money is supposed to make the economy work more smoothly. It is supposed to blend into the background, like the officials in a professional sporting match. If you spend a lot of time focusing on the officials, something has gone wrong. So it is with money. When currencies end up in the headlines, the stories are not typically happy ones.

Just ask the Greeks and the Germans.

CHAPTER 11

The Euro

*We argue that the gold standard and the euro share the attributes of the young
lady described by Henry Wadsworth Longfellow:*

> *"There was a little girl, who had a little curl*
> *Right in the middle of her forehead,*
> *And when she was good, she was very, very good.*
> *But when she was bad she was horrid."*

—Barry Eichengreen, University of California–Berkeley,
and Peter Temin, MIT[1]

*What is the appropriate domain of a currency area? It might seem at first
that the question is purely academic since it hardly appears within the realm of
political feasibility that national currencies would ever be abandoned in favor
of any other arrangement.*

—Robert Mundell, 1961—thirty years before the creation of the euro[2]

On January 1, 2002, the French franc went out of existence.
And the German deutsche mark. And the Italian lira. At the
stroke of midnight, twelve of the countries in the European
Union (EU) adopted a common currency, the euro. (The
official launch was three years earlier; bank deposits and electronic transfers were denominated in euros beginning in 1999.) The ATM machines
dispensed crisp new euro notes. Prices across the eurozone were posted

in the new transnational currency. A new European Central Bank, the ECB, was created to conduct monetary policy for all of the participating nations with a strict mandate to maintain price stability (defined as an inflation rate "below, but close to, 2% over the medium term").[3] The national central banks, such as the German Bundesbank, continued to operate in their regulatory capacity and as a source of support for the ECB. The launch of the euro was unprecedented in its scale and ambition. The euro replaced local currencies for more than 300 million people.[4] One news account compared the launch of the euro to the Wright Brothers, who proved that something heavier than air could fly, because the euro proved monetary union was possible without political union.[5] By 2015, nineteen countries in the European Union were members of the so-called eurozone. Several small countries outside of the EU have also adopted the euro; many other nations have pegged their currencies to it.

A Happy Beginning

The launch of a common currency for much of Europe was heralded with all the excitement of a marriage. After all, these were not just any countries. One could say, literally and figuratively, that the twentieth century had been a bloody disaster for many of them: Germany, France, Italy, Belgium. (Nor were many of the previous centuries marked by peace and cooperation.) The nations that had faced one another from the trenches of World War I, and then again as Hitler terrorized the world, were now linked in a bold economic endeavor. This marriage was an act of reconciliation designed to move Europe aggressively toward the vision of Jean Monnet, the French diplomat who envisioned a unified Europe in the years after the calamity of World War II.

The euro was a significant step in an ongoing journey of European integration. Less than a decade after the end of World War II, a handful of European states, including France and West Germany, created the European Coal and Steel Community to share natural resources among participating nations. One explicit goal was minimizing future armed conflict. Other supranational organizations would follow, each expanding economic and political cooperation across the continent. The

European Economic Community (1958) established a free trade zone among the member nations and imposed a common tariff for goods imported to the zone. The European Rate Mechanism (1979) created a set of pegged exchange rates with narrow bands to minimize exchange rate volatility among member nations. In 1992, the Maastricht Treaty created the European Union (EU), an organization of twenty-eight states that share a set of common laws (regarding labor, food safety, and so on); free movement of people, goods, services, and capital throughout the member states; and assorted supranational political institutions, such as the European Parliament.

In other words, these countries had been dating for a long time. A common currency would consummate the relationship. As Paul Krugman has written, "The creation of the euro was proclaimed the logical next step in this process. Once again, economic growth would be fostered with actions that also reinforced European unity."[6] A single currency would facilitate European trade and promote transparency in pricing. (It's much easier to spot price differences across international boundaries when comparable goods are priced in the same currency.) In the eyes of some participants, the euro would lead naturally to even closer political cooperation. In particular, it would anchor a bigger (postreunification), powerful Germany firmly within a strong Europe. For their part, the Germans were assured that the new European Central Bank would have the same passion for fighting inflation—even the barest hint of it—that had characterized Germany's central bank, the Bundesbank.

As with any marriage, especially when the families have a history of bad blood, there were some misgivings. Milton Friedman argued that the creation of the euro would cause political tensions, rather than ameliorate them. To Friedman, the nations proposing union did not have enough in common to share the euro. He wrote two years before the euro's launch, "As of today, a subgroup of the European Union—perhaps Germany, the Benelux countries, and Austria—come closer to satisfying the conditions favorable to a common currency than does the EU as a whole." A single currency would "exacerbate political tensions by converting divergent shocks that could have been readily accommodated by exchange rate changes into divisive political issues."[7]

That's pretty much what happened. For some time now, Greece and Germany have been hurling insults at each other. The group of southern European nations struggling under the constraints of the euro—Portugal, Italy, Greece, and Spain—has been branded the PIGS, which is never a good sign.* (This is an insulting play on investor shorthand for Brazil, Russia, India, China, and South Africa: the BRICS.) There is risk that the euro will collapse, perhaps at great cost to the global economy. Whatever the outcome, the honeymoon is clearly over. Long over. Greece and Germany have grown so rancorous that Greek politicians have demanded reparations for the Nazi occupation of Greece during World War II.[8] The possibility of Greece exiting the euro has even acquired its own name: "Grexit." As when any relationship goes sour, people are now wondering, "Why didn't we listen?"

But I am getting ahead of myself. The launch of the euro was a time of excitement and economic promise. There was no prenuptial agreement. None of the treaties creating the European Union and the euro made any contingency for dissolving the common currency. This was a deliberate act. Money and finance are built on confidence. Negotiating the dissolution of the euro at the beginning of the endeavor would have suggested a lack of commitment to its success (which is the same reason some people do not like prenuptial agreements). Sure enough, in the early years, it was a happy union. The family grew as additional countries joined: Greece, Cyprus, Estonia, Latvia, Slovenia, and others. The euro fell in value initially but then climbed steadily, making it a candidate to replace, or at least supplement, the dollar as the world's reserve currency.

But Wait—Why Not One World Currency?

There is a more basic question lurking here, one that my daughter's friend/boyfriend† recently asked, innocently enough: Wouldn't the

---

* Ireland, another country on the periphery of Europe that eventually needed a bailout, is sometimes included, making it PIIGS.

† They were definitely dating at one point and went to a dance together. But then

world be better off if we all shared the same currency? Many prominent thinkers, including the philosopher and political economist John Stuart Mill and Walter Bagehot (whose writings on central banking were mentioned earlier), have asked variations on the same question. Why can't we all use the dollar, or the euro, or the "worldo"? Just pick one. Having multiple global currencies seems like the economic equivalent of the fallout from the Tower of Babel. If currencies are like languages, then having fewer would presumably promote cooperation and integration. The dollar seems to work well for the United States, in places as distant and diverse as Vermont and Texas. Why would the euro not work for France and Italy? What is possibly to be gained by having to swap francs for lira to undertake trade between two neighboring countries—places that are geographically closer than California and Illinois? Remember, these are just pieces of paper anyway. The point of trade is to promote the "real economy," swapping French wine for Italian shoes, so that everyone is better off. How could using one kind of paper currency to do that bring Europe to the point of economic collapse?

Here's a clue: A common currency is like the gold standard. It fixes the value of currencies across countries, making international transactions easier and more predictable. If you've read the rest of the book, you will recognize that the phrase "gold standard" has some baggage, namely that it limits countries' abilities to use monetary policy to manage their domestic economies. That is at the heart of what has gone wrong between Germany and Greece. It is also the fundamental tradeoff between sharing a currency and having your own. Economist Robert Mundell won the Nobel Prize in 1999 for his analysis of why the world should not have just one currency. Mundell's insight was that the benefits and drawbacks of sharing a currency derive from the concept of an optimal currency zone. A region can be too small to have its own currency, too big, or just right. (I suppose Robert Southey, author of "Goldilocks and the Three

---

they supposedly broke up, though they still go hiking together and he parks at our house before school almost every day. I really have no idea what is going on. In any event, he is a very nice and intelligent guy who asks good questions about monetary policy.

Bears," also deserves some credit for this intellectual insight, though he died in 1843 and therefore was not eligible to share the Nobel Prize.)

The advantage of sharing a currency over any particular area is that it lowers transaction costs—no need to change money when trading with a neighboring state, country, or region. Imagine the counterfactual: the United States with fifty different currencies. Every transaction across a state border would require foreign exchange; there would also be additional uncertainty around the movement of exchange rates. A California wine producer would have expenses denominated in California dollars while earning revenues denominated in forty-nine other currencies, each of which would be fluctuating relative to the California dollar. A single currency, or at least as few as possible, would make global transactions easier, more transparent, and more predictable.

For all the joys of sharing a common currency, there are two countervailing considerations. First, countries that share a common currency must also share a common monetary policy. The European Central Bank sets interest rates for the whole eurozone, just as the Fed's interest rate decisions apply to all fifty states. When France gave up the franc, it also gave up the ability of the French central bank to set interest rates separately from Germany. If one country in the eurozone is in recession and another is booming, what should the ECB do with regard to monetary policy? Robert Mundell asked presciently in 1961, "A system of flexible exchange rates was originally propounded as an alternative to the gold-standard mechanism which many economists blamed for the world-wide spread of depression after 1929. But if the arguments against the gold standard were correct, then why should a similar argument not apply against a common currency system in a multiregional country?"[9]

Second, sharing a currency eliminates a country's ability to use the exchange rate for influencing patterns of trade with the rest of the world. Remember, a weak currency is like throwing a sale for consumers in other countries. It makes goods cheaper when exported to countries whose currencies have grown relatively stronger. Of course, there is an economic downside to devaluing a currency, as noted in chapter 6. Imports become more expensive and residents of the nation with the weakening currency get less in return for what they sell abroad—a reduction in real income. Still, a weak currency is often the best way to stimulate the economy or remedy a trade imbalance.

In particular, a weakening currency is often the easiest way for a nation to stay competitive with other countries that are getting relatively more productive. Let's take two random countries with their own currencies, say Germany and Greece before the advent of the euro. (Okay, not so random.) Both countries make and export manufactured goods. Suppose German firms grow 5 percent more productive than Greek firms, meaning they can produce the same quantity of goods at 5 percent lower cost. Whatever can be produced in Greece for $100 can now be produced in Germany for $95. This gives German firms a nice set of choices. One option is to pay workers more. This would make German workers better off than their Greek counterparts (because of the productivity growth); it would also make the price differential between Greek and German products go away because the pay raise for German workers restores the cost of the German goods to $100. German and Greek goods would once again be competitive on global markets because the rising German productivity has been offset by higher German wages. The Germans have grown richer than their Greek counterparts, but the Greeks are still employed at their old wages. All good.

Another option would be for German firms to take advantage of their increased productivity by cutting the price of their products on world markets; they could lower the price of the goods to $95 and still earn the same profits as before.* This puts the Greeks in a tough position. To stay competitive with the Germans, they have to reduce their cost of production by 5 percent. Typically that involves cutting wages. If we've learned anything so far, it's that wages are hard to cut. There is a psychological aversion to getting a smaller paycheck; there are also institutional constraints that make it difficult to reduce labor costs in the short run (e.g., unions). Economists say that wages (and the prices of other inputs) are typically "sticky," meaning that they often do not

---

* Obviously, there is a range of options in between.

adjust as quickly as economic circumstances might warrant. In our not-so-hypothetical example, cutting costs by 5 percent for the Greeks is a tough thing to do.

But wait! Before the advent of the euro, there was a more politically and economically expedient way for the Greeks to stay competitive with the Germans. The Greek government and central bank could allow the Greek currency, previously the drachma, to depreciate by 5 percent relative to the German mark. The Greeks have not grown more productive, nor have they successfully reduced manufacturing costs; *instead they have marked down the price of all exports 5 percent by devaluing the currency.* There is no free gyro platter here; the Greeks pay a price for the depreciation—literally. The weaker currency makes all imports 5 percent more expensive. The Greeks are worse off relative to the rest of the world, just as they would be if wages were cut. This, too, is a reduction in real income. The difference is that devaluing the currency is much easier to accomplish. The central bank can do it via monetary policy. No union negotiations, no broken contracts, and in most cases, no politicians involved. As Milton Friedman cogently explained, "It is far simpler to allow one price to change, namely the price of foreign exchange, than to rely upon changes in the multitude of prices that together constitute the internal price structure."[10]

This happens to be an example of money illusion. Workers typically object less when their real wages are diminished by a change in the exchange rate than they do when the number on the paycheck changes. As is the case with inflation, imperfectly rational humans tend to focus on nominal wages (the number on the check) rather than real wages (what the check buys). Paul Krugman has offered a striking example in this regard. During the euro crisis, Ireland had to endure two years of severe unemployment to push prices down roughly 5 percent. Less than a decade earlier, when Ireland still had its own currency (the punt), a devaluation of the punt brought down wages 10 percent relative to Germany far more quickly and painlessly.[11]

But wait again! If having one's own monetary policy is so important, why is this not a problem across the diverse states in America, all served by the Federal Reserve? What if Maine is in recession while Oklahoma is in the midst of a boom because there is so much fracking going on?* Or what if workers in South Carolina are growing steadily more productive than workers in Michigan? How is this any different from Germany and Greece? Robert Mundell's insight was that the optimal currency zone depends on the degree to which the area is economically integrated (for instance, when workers can move easily from one place to another) and the quality of the supporting institutions (as when there is a government that can transfer money from thriving areas to struggling ones).

The American states do not merely share a currency and a central bank; they share a language and a central government. South Carolina and Michigan are two states in the same federal system. This is not an incidental observation. When the economy weakens in Michigan, the federal government automatically redistributes income from areas of the country that are doing better. Income taxes are proportionate to income, so regions that are growing faster will pay more and regions in distress will pay less—an automatic tax cut. Similarly, government spending tends to rise in areas that are undergoing a slump: federal welfare benefits, food stamps, unemployment insurance, crop insurance, and so on. Some federal programs may target struggling areas explicitly, such as infrastructure spending. Labor mobility helps, too. Detroit and Charleston share a common language. There are no legal or significant cultural barriers to prevent workers from leaving Michigan to find work in areas where the economy is doing better. Finally, there is logic to having regions that share a currency also share a common financial regulator, given the role that banks and financial institutions play in causing economic booms and busts.

To summarize, having many different currencies helps promote faster economic adjustment but at a significant cost in terms of trade, particularly as the number of currencies rises. Mundell articulated that sharing a currency across some area or "zone" makes sense when certain conditions are met: labor mobility across the currency zone; a common

---

* Note to anyone with a filthy mind: fracking is a process of horizontal drilling used to release natural gas.

financial regulator; a political apparatus that covers the whole currency zone; and a willingness to tolerate unemployment or inflation in the event of regional imbalances. That's an extensive set of preconditions. As Mundell observed in 1961, "In the real world, of course, currencies are mainly an expression of national sovereignty, so that actual currency reorganization would be feasible only if it were accompanied by profound political changes."

So There Were Some Issues from the Beginning . . .

Let's evaluate the optimal currency area checklist for the United States:

Labor mobility: Yes.

A common financial regulator: Yes.

A political structure that covers the whole dollar zone: Yes.

A willingness to tolerate regional inflation and/or unemployment in the face of economic imbalances: Yes.

Congratulations. You have been approved to share a currency.

Now let's evaluate Europe back in 1990, as the excited eurozone nations were picking out bridesmaids' dresses while preparing to tie the currency knot.

Labor mobility: Not so much. Most of the nations in Europe do not share a common language; the cultural gaps are significant. While the laws of the European Union allow citizens to move and work anywhere among the member nations, it is difficult in practice for a Greek bricklayer to move to Munich to find a job.

A common financial regulator: No. The European Central Bank was created to manage monetary policy for the eurozone, but national governments (and the national central banks, which were not dissolved) remained responsible for financial regulation within their respective countries.[*]

A political structure that covers the whole eurozone: Kind of. The

---

[*] In 2011, the European Banking Authority was established with the authority to overrule national regulators if necessary to protect the broader EU banking system.

European Union has myriad supranational political institutions. However, at the time the euro was launched, the EU lacked crucial powers, such as the capacity to redistribute funds on a large scale across the eurozone or to lend to member nations in a crisis.

Willingness to tolerate inflation and/or unemployment in the face of regional imbalances: No. I have not yet mentioned that the Germans, who have played a dominant role in the design and operation of the European Central Bank, have a phobia of inflation. *Nein rising prices or wages!* The fear of inflation was born of the German experience after World War I, when the currency was devalued to the point that people were pushing around wheelbarrows of cash to make purchases, or burning it to heat their homes. The postwar response among German policymakers was to focus relentlessly on maintaining a strong, stable currency, the deutsche mark. When the euro was launched, German chancellor Helmut Kohl told French president François Mitterrand, "The D-mark is our flag. It is the foundation of our post-war reconstruction. It is the essential part of our national pride; we don't have much else."[12]

Also, just to make things worse, the Germans are huge savers. That is often a virtue—but not when other areas of the continent are suffering a recession and need German consumers to buy more of their goods to promote recovery.

The above checklist for the euro is the currency union equivalent of seeing the groom making out with one of the bridesmaids on the night before the wedding. It's not a great sign for the impending marriage. At the time of the launch, even the optimists suggested that the euro would be like an arranged marriage. Things might not be perfect at first, but the partners would grow in the union and work things out over time.

Many observers predicted economic convergence across the continent as the relatively poorer southern euro nations caught up to the richer nations in the north. This was not an unreasonable expectation. After the Civil War, the American South was the poorest region in the country; it grew the fastest over the next hundred years and converged steadily with the north.[13] Countries like Greece and Italy could borrow more cheaply after they joined the euro because global investors no longer had to fear that the value of the bonds would be eroded by a steadily depreciating currency. And perhaps some of Germany's fiscal and monetary responsibility would rub off on her more slovenly neighbors. As a prerequisite for joining the euro, the participating nations were required to meet "convergence criteria" with limits on inflation, budget deficits, and long-term interest rates.[14] This was like having the smart, studious college students share dorm rooms with the slackers! (One point worth noting is that Greece was a slacker from the beginning: the country failed to meet the euro admission criteria but was admitted anyway.)

There were some happy times. By the middle 2000s, German bonds and PIGS bonds traded at similar prices, suggesting that the Teutonic sense of responsibility had indeed rubbed off.[15] Analysis showed that trade across the eurozone was higher than it would have been without a shared currency.[16] Like the gold standard in the pre–World War I era, the euro promoted exchange rate stability (because there were no exchange rates). Wait, the gold standard? Haven't we been hating on that? As Eichengreen and Temin have written, "Fixed exchange rates facilitate business and communication in good times but intensify problems when times are bad."[17]

The euro is the ultimate fixed exchange rate. And times got bad.

2008: A Marriage in Crisis

Relationships are stressed when things go bad: death in the family, unemployment, money trouble. For the eurozone, the 2008 financial crisis was all of those things rolled into one—after which the Germans and Greeks started running over each other's family pets. The popping of the American real estate bubble (and some others around the world) set in motion three overlapping European crises, each of which made the others worse. The first (in no particular order) was a banking crisis. European banks were big purchasers of American toxic assets (with their ridiculous AAA ratings). Spain and Ireland had real estate bubbles of their own, leaving the banks with a mess. As we've learned, when banks are in trouble, they tend to drag the rest of the economy down with them.

The second problem was sovereign debt—borrowing by governments. Greece and other countries had used their new opportunity to borrow at low rates to engorge themselves with debt. (There was arguably moral hazard on the lending side because of the belief that Germany and/or the European Central Bank would come to the rescue of fiscal miscreants like Greece.) In the aftermath of the financial crisis, skittish investors took a more jaundiced view of heavily indebted governments like Greece and Italy. Interest rates shot up, making it more expensive for the affected countries to finance their borrowing. The sovereign debt problem also exacerbated the banking problem, since European banks, including German banks, were big lenders to the indebted governments.

The third problem was slow growth in countries like Greece, Spain, and Italy, as they struggled to stay competitive with Germany and the more productive European bloc. This is where the euro has arguably done the most damage. The euro nations lost the ability to make their own monetary policy or to devalue their currencies, both of which would have stimulated their economies. The ECB (under heavy German influence) was unwilling to tolerate a level of inflation elsewhere in Europe that might have helped the struggling southern European nations adjust.* Instead, inflation was near zero, and even flirting with negative territory, forcing firms to cut wages and prices to stay competitive. As I have noted over and over again, that is a hard thing to do. The result in places like Greece was wage cuts and unemployment, which fed back in adverse ways to the first two problems. A weak economy does more damage to the banks and also makes it harder for governments to repay their debts. The result, according to a 2011 analysis, was "a spiral of falling bond prices, weakening banks and slowing growth."[18]

The mounting crisis focused attention on the many institutional weaknesses surrounding the euro. A single regulator might have stopped the bubbles that emerged in places like Spain and Ireland, or at least minimized the banking problems that spread across the eurozone. It was

---

* For example, if inflation were 4 percent across the eurozone, and Greek firms held nominal wages constant, that would amount to a 4 percent real pay cut—which would help firms stay competitive. Inflation also lessens the real value of outstanding government debt by allowing countries to pay back their debts with money that is worth less—the equivalent of reducing the outstanding balance in real terms.

clear that a number of European countries were in trouble, but there was disagreement over the role that the European Central Bank ought to play in dealing with the crisis. Unlike the Fed, the ECB's sole mandate was price stability, not promoting employment or even acting as a lender of last resort. The European Union had no mechanism for dealing with an insolvent member or for lending to governments in need of liquidity to get through a panic. One news account summarized the dire state of affairs in 2010: "The real problems are the absence of a credible plan to deal with errant countries (as the Germans have recognized), the structural imbalances between Germany and the less competitive southern members and, most of all, the miserable growth prospects for those poorer, weaker southerners, made worse by their fiscal retrenchment. Denied the possibility of devaluation, slow-growing countries like Portugal and now Spain should be looking for structural reforms that can reduce their labor costs, enhance enterprise, stimulate competition and regain competitiveness."[19]

Bailouts: Can the Relationship Be Saved?

In April 2010, Standard & Poor's downgraded the rating on Greek bonds to "junk" status.[20] (Technically, the rating is "below investment grade.") Greek debt was over 100 percent of GDP (meaning it would take the entire country's income for more than a year to pay back its creditors). The budget deficit* was nearly 14 percent of GDP—suggesting to global investors that the government debt would continue to balloon uncontrollably. By any reasonable metric, Greece was insolvent.[21]

But that was not the worst of it. A Greek default could take down not just the rest of the eurozone, but the entire global economy. The whole point of the euro was to bind the economies of Europe more closely together, like mountain climbers tethered to a single line (a metaphor I've used before). If one falls, they all fall—unless there is some way to

---

* The annual difference between what the government was spending and what it was collecting in revenues.

sever the cord without making the situation worse. A financial disaster in Greece would make investors look more closely at Italy, a far bigger economy that is nonetheless vulnerable in many of the same ways. And that would be the beginning of the end. As the *Economist* observed in 2011, "When the world's third-largest bond market [Italy] begins to buckle, catastrophe looms. At stake is not just the Italian economy but Spain, Portugal, Ireland, the euro, the European Union's single market, the global banking system, the world economy, and pretty much anything else you can think of."[22]

So it was bad. And remember, there was no prenuptial agreement for separating what the Eurocrats had joined together.

The result was a series of interrelated responses that have continued to the present. First, there were bailouts, as various European institutions sought to prop up the weaklings and stop the contagion. The European Commission, the International Monetary Fund, and the European Central Bank cobbled together multibillion-dollar rescue packages for Greece.[23] (Yes, that was plural. When one bailout was insufficient, they did it again.) By 2012, Ireland, Portugal, and Spain had all come to the European trough for bailouts. In 2013, Cyprus, whose banks were big holders of Greek bonds, needed a rescue package, too.

Second, each bailout came with strings attached, some deeply onerous for the nations seeking help. There was logic to this. The bailout packages sought to fix the underlying economic weaknesses that got Europe's periphery nations in trouble in the first place: excessive government deficits and inefficient private sectors. (At the time it sought help, Spain was ranked by the World Bank 133rd in the world in ease of starting a business, right behind Kenya.[24]) Greece was forced to freeze government salaries, raise taxes, cut spending, curb early retirement, and so on. When the next package came along, they had to do more. The sacrifices, in Greece and elsewhere, were known generically (and accurately) as "austerity."

Third, the euro nations were trying to build this boat as they sailed it. New institutions were created, such as the European Banking Authority, established to coordinate the work of national regulators. Older institutions, such as the European Central Bank (ECB), did new things.

In 2012, Mario Draghi, president of the ECB, famously pledged to do "whatever it takes" to protect the euro, including massive purchases of bonds issued by struggling euro nations.[25] This was a significant departure for a central bank whose original mission was narrowly defined as price stability.

Not surprisingly, voters across the continent hated the bailouts—*both the voters paying for them and the voters getting them.* For the more fiscally responsible European nations, particularly Germany, bailing out profligate neighbors was not supposed to be part of the euro bargain. The Germans were not terribly sympathetic to the costs imposed on other nations by austerity, in part because they had been through their own. In the aftermath of reunification, Germany undertook grueling reforms to stay globally competitive—holding down wages, making labor markets more flexible, and curtailing government programs.[26] Labor costs ultimately fell 20 percent relative to the rest of the EU—but not before unemployment peaked at 12 percent.[27] Why couldn't Greece, Spain, and Portugal do the same?

If anything, those being helped were even angrier. Austerity is unpleasant. That's why they call it austerity. The *New York Times* reported, "The spending cuts have produced what many Greeks consider to be a humanitarian crisis. Twenty-five percent of the country's population is unemployed; Greece's gross domestic product has shrunk by a quarter; suicides and homelessness have increased; hospitals, woefully underfunded, scrounge for medicines."[28] By the end of 2014, youth unemployment in Italy and Spain was over 40 percent.[29] One of the few books that sold better in Portugal than *Fifty Shades of Grey* was *Why We Should Leave the Euro.*[30]

There is a cruel irony to all the economic pain: it didn't accomplish much. When countries cut their budgets, their pensions, and their wages, the economy shrinks, making it harder for the government to pay down its debts. As Paul Krugman explained in 2011 (in an article appropriately titled "Can Europe Be Saved?"), "Even when countries successfully drive down wages, which is now happening in all the euro-crisis countries, they run into another problem: incomes are falling, but debt is not."[31] True, government spending has been cut drastically—but revenues have fallen almost as fast. Greek indebtedness as a percentage of GDP actually climbed, not because the numerator (debt) was getting bigger, but because the denominator (GDP) was shrinking. (I'll give you a moment to think about that . . .)

Meanwhile, countries outside the euro were saying, "I told you so." Iceland is a good example. The country suffered a devastating banking collapse in 2008. But it bounced back, in large part because of a massive devaluation of the currency, the Icelandic krona. Prices fell 40 percent relative to its trading partners, restoring Iceland's competitiveness and reinvigorating the economy. Iceland was free to set its own monetary policy to meet its needs.[32] By comparison, the euro was feeling a lot like the gold standard. To paraphrase the quote at the outset of the chapter, when it was bad it was horrid.

The Love Is Gone

In 2015, Greece elected a coalition of leftist parties known as Syriza in a backlash against austerity. The Greek attitude toward euro bullying was embodied in the new Greek finance minister, Yanis Varoufakis, with his shaved head, flamboyant shirts (no tie!), leather jackets, and (gasp) motorcycle. This is not what finance ministers are supposed to look like. (Elsewhere in Europe, Varoufakis was described as a "nightclub bouncer" and a "used-car salesman.") He did not act much like a finance minister either. After meeting with German Finance Minister Wolfgang Schäuble, they had the following exchange at a press conference:

> SCHÄUBLE: "We have agreed to disagree."
> VAROUFAKIS: "We didn't even agree to disagree, from where I'm standing."[33]

This was not a relationship born to thrive. Greece, unable to make a forthcoming debt payment at the time, was also unwilling to make the additional compromises demanded by the usual gang of creditors looking to bail them out once again. Officials at the IMF privately described Greece as "the most unhelpful country the organization has dealt with in its 70-year history."[34] There was more angry posturing and then eventually another bailout deal in the summer of 2015, ending the worst of the crisis and contagion risk. Still, the fundamental questions were not resolved: Can countries as dissimilar as Greece and Germany coexist in a currency union? If so, how does Greece make its economy more competitive within the straitjacket imposed by the euro?

In the coming years, or perhaps even months, the fate of the euro will be resolved, with huge global economic implications. The participating nations may fix and strengthen the union, using this crisis as an opportunity to make changes to the structure of the relationship. (A number of reforms have already been undertaken.) Or there may be a "Grexit," in which Greece (and perhaps other struggling nations) leave the euro, with all the attendant disruption that would entail. Euros in Greece would be exchanged for a new currency, presumably the drachma. The Greeks would default on some portion of their euro debts and start anew with a currency that would depreciate sharply against the euro. (Given a choice, would you rather hold Greek currency or German currency?)

Alternatively, some subset of northern European nations (France, Germany, etc.) could leave the euro and start a currency of their own. That would cause the same basic sort of mess, albeit with a different party leaving the house. There would still be the same fighting over the children and the vacation home, figuratively speaking. In many ways, it is a distinction without a difference, as either split would leave one strong European currency and one that is much weaker. Therein lies the fundamental challenge of a breakup. Even the hint of a euro divorce would cause massive capital flight—a different kind of a bank panic—as anyone with euro deposits in Greece or Portugal rushed to move them to Germany to get the more valuable currency in the divorce. To prevent that, policymakers would have to impose capital controls (which limit the movement of capital in or out of a country) and perhaps even short-term limits on bank account holders' access to their cash. Meanwhile, everybody would be suing everybody else, as this would all be virgin legal terrain. The *Economist* remarked during the depths of the crisis, "Like Victor Frankenstein, they defied nature and created a monster. Part of the horror story is that the cost of returning to national currencies is greater than keeping the euro."[35]

Paul Krugman accurately summarizes the two tragedies of how things have turned out. First, the euro has, so far, been a case of good intentions gone bad. And second, many of the signs of trouble—basic economics, really—were there at the beginning. He writes, "The tragedy of the Euromess is that the creation of the euro was supposed to be the finest moment in a grand and noble undertaking: the generations-long effort to bring peace, democracy and shared prosperity to a once and frequently war-torn continent. But the architects of the euro, caught up in their project's sweep and romance, chose to ignore the mundane difficulties a shared currency would predictably encounter—to ignore warnings, which were issued right from the beginning, that Europe lacked the institutions needed to make a common currency workable."[36]

Yes, time will tell whether the euro is a bold step forward in monetary policy or a failed experiment. So far, it has been both. Sharing a currency is a hard thing to do. But here is the weird thing: *not sharing a currency is hard, too.* That is one of the major sources of friction between the United States and China at the moment.

CHAPTER 12

The United States and China

The Chinese are subsidizing the American way of life. Are we playing them for suckers—or are they playing us?

—James Fallows, *The Atlantic*, 2008

The U.S. and Chinese economies—the world's largest and the fastest-growing major economy, respectively—have become inextricably intertwined, locked in a kind of co-dependency that neither side thinks is particularly healthy, but which for the moment neither will move to break."

—*Washington Post*, on the eve of President Obama's
first official visit to China, 2009[1]

In November 2009, President Obama made his first visit to China. In the months prior to that meeting, the *New York Times* reported that Chinese officials were asking their American counterparts extensive and detailed questions about the health care legislation that would eventually become the Affordable Care Act, or "Obamacare." Obviously Obamacare does not affect health care delivery in China, so why were Chinese bureaucrats so interested in the arcane details of the legislation making its way through Congress? There are numerous potential explanations.

One explanation is that the Chinese officials were studying health care reform in order to better make small talk with President Obama when he arrived in Beijing. Any good host finds out what his guest's interests are and then steers the conversation in that direction. During a lull in the conversation at the diplomatic banquet, for example, a Chinese official might say something like, "I was impressed with the incentives for community health organizations to economize on their use of mammography machines, as was described in the footnote on page 731 of your health care legislation." How could the president not be impressed and engaged by such attention to his legislative priorities? So that is one possibility.

Another explanation is that the Chinese officials had a deep intellectual interest in health care. How would a private, insurance-based system with a personal mandate compare in terms of access and cost to a single-payer system like Canada and Britain? These are the kinds of things that my economics colleagues discuss (voluntarily and with enthusiasm) over lunch. Health care is a remarkably difficult public policy challenge, in the United States and around the world. The legislation that would become the Affordable Care Act was complex, unique, and transformative. How could any policy wonk *not* be interested in the details? So maybe the Chinese were fascinated by the policy nuances of health care, like my work colleagues.

No. It turns out neither of these explanations is anywhere near correct. Chinese officials were interested in American health care reform for the same reason that the bank holding the mortgages on your home, vacation home, and two cars would be interested in the new forty-seven-foot boat you plan to buy. It has nothing to do with boating or fishing or the cool captain's hat you bought to wear when taking the helm. *The bank wants to know whether you can pay back your loans, especially now that you are laying out more cash on a very expensive boat.* The *New York Times* article describing the health care briefing in Beijing went on to explain, "Chinese officials expect that they will help finance whatever Congress and the White House settle on, mostly through buying Treasury debt, and like any banker, they wanted evidence that the United States had a plan to pay them back."[2]

At that time, China owned roughly $800 billion in U.S. Treasury debt. Now it is closer to $1.3 trillion. China is the American government's largest foreign creditor.[3] There are drawbacks to being dependent on a large lender. (Ask the Greek government about this.) Someone who regularly lends you funds can use that financing as a source of leverage. Might American dependence on Chinese lending be used as a diplomatic weapon in areas of disagreement, such as human rights or Taiwan or control of the South China Sea? On the other hand, as John Maynard Keynes once pointed out, "If you owe your bank manager a thousand pounds, you are at his mercy. If you owe him a million pounds, he is at your mercy." And if you owe him $1.3 trillion, he is practically a prisoner, as some Chinese officials have asserted.[4] America may be dependent on China for new lending, but China is dependent on America *to pay back more than a trillion dollars.** In 2013, when Congress reached a budget impasse and the Republicans were threatening not to raise the debt ceiling—which technically could have led to a default on some U.S. government debt—the response by the Chinese government was shrill. The official Xinhua news agency issued a statement that read like it had been drafted by a hysterical teenager. It called for a replacement of the dollar as the world's reserve currency (not necessarily by the yuan—but by something!) and a "de-Americanized world." A *New York Times* headline captured the bigger picture: "Seeing Its Own Money at Risk, China Rails at U.S."[5]

The two nations are locked in a curious embrace, the unhealthy codependency described in the quote at the outset of the chapter. China has been running vast trade surpluses—selling more to the rest of the world than it buys. The United States is China's largest market for those exports, causing Chinese firms to accumulate huge stocks of American dollars.[6] If those dollars were routinely spent on American goods and services, the rest of this chapter would be unnecessary. In that case, Chinese exports to the United States would be broadly equivalent to U.S.

---

* Technically speaking, this debt may not have to be paid back. There are many reasons the Chinese government may choose to hold large quantities of interest-bearing U.S. securities, which can be paid off at maturity by issuing new securities. The larger point still holds: the Chinese government does not want the value of its U.S. bonds significantly devalued by default, threat of default, or inflation.

exports to China. That's generally how trade works: you swap things of roughly equivalent value. Both sides are left better off because they prefer what they are getting to what they are giving up. Just watch little kids in a school lunchroom—potato chips for a chocolate chip cookie, and everyone leaves smiling.*

The U.S.–China trade relationship is more imbalanced; Chinese exports to America are not offset by exports crossing the Pacific in the other direction. In fact, the usual mechanism for ameliorating trade imbalances has been short-circuited. What would normally happen is that Chinese firms that have accumulated surplus dollars would convert those dollars into yuan to spend at home. If China is running a chronic trade surplus—selling more stuff to America than America sells to China—there will be more firms looking to sell dollars for yuan on the foreign exchange market than the other way around. What happens when the butcher has more pork chops than customers want to buy? He lowers the price until consumers are induced to buy all the chops in the cooler. In the U.S.–China case, the surplus dollars are the product that needs to be moved; the firms selling dollars for yuan lower their price until they can move all the merchandise. Of course, the price is the exchange rate with the yuan. That is the self-correcting mechanism. As the dollar depreciates relative to the yuan, American exports to China get cheaper; Chinese exports to the United States become more expensive; and the changing relative prices work to fix the original trade imbalance. Floating exchange rates have the potential to naturally ameliorate trade imbalances.

Alas, the last paragraph used phrases like "under normal circumstances" and "floating exchange rates." The U.S.–China relationship is not normal; the Chinese yuan does not float. Over the last several decades, China has consistently run large current account surpluses with the United States. (The current account consists of the trade bal-

---

* Yes, I realize that the child with a serious nut allergy may not end up smiling, but rather in anaphylactic shock from the nut residue in the chocolate chip cookie. Still, as an example, let's just go with it.

ance plus some other flows of funds between the countries, such as remittances and income from foreign investments.) Despite the perennially lopsided trade relationship, the yuan has not appreciated relative to the dollar as sharply as some observers feel it ought to. (I'll come back to those observers—including some very angry members of Congress—in a moment.) Instead, the policy of the Chinese government for the past twenty years has been to "recycle" the accumulated dollars back to the United States by buying Treasury securities—in effect, loaning the dollars back to America. One explicit purpose of this policy is to prevent the yuan from appreciating as quickly as it otherwise would—because the dollars earned in America are not converted back into yuan. U.S. Treasury bonds are also a relatively safe place to park huge quantities of accumulated capital. (The Chinese government may rail at U.S. policymakers for their profligacy, but if you've read the last two chapters, you will recognize that neither the yen nor the euro is a great substitute.)

There is a lot to like about this arrangement for both countries—*in the short run.* For China, the cheap yuan has helped facilitate a robust export-led growth strategy. For a relatively poor country like China, one proven method of becoming less poor is to take advantage of cheap labor by producing things for export to richer countries around the globe. This is the path that Japan pursued after World War II. It also explains the economic success of the "Asian tigers": Singapore, South Korea, Taiwan, and Hong Kong. One way to bulk up the export sector is to keep the currency undervalued (or at least keep it from appreciating significantly). Remember, a cheap currency is like a discount coupon for the rest of the world looking to buy your stuff. The cheaper the currency, the bigger the discount.

Meanwhile, American consumers are getting that discount. If it says "Made in China" and you bought it with dollars, the weak yuan (and relatively strong dollar) has made your paycheck go farther. *But that's not all!* China's huge purchases of U.S. Treasury debt has pushed down interest rates in the United States. Like everything else in life, bonds respond to the law of supply and demand. When there is great demand—e.g., China purchasing billions of dollars of them every month—the Treasury can offer a lower rate of interest. So the U.S. government can borrow more cheaply and consumers get lower interest rates, too. Nothing says "America!" better than cheap goods and easy credit for buying them.

What's the problem? The relationship is not sustainable over the long run. China is supporting its export market by loaning huge quantities of funds to its customers. Not only does that lead to the steadily mounting American debt that Chinese officials are now monitoring anxiously, but the artificially cheap yuan creates distortions within the Chinese economy. The dollars that are recycled to the United States might be better invested at home—in infrastructure, schools, and public health. An economy built on export-led growth must eventually transition to producing goods for the domestic market, a process discouraged by the implicit subsidy that an undervalued currency provides to exporters. Policymakers around the world often exhort China to pursue "more balanced growth."

For its part, the United States has literally been living beyond its means—buying more from the rest of the world than we sell in return and paying for the difference with borrowed funds. That's not a sustainable situation; at some point the lenders stop lending if they begin to fear they won't get paid back. As many commentators have noted, China is living less well than it could, and America is living better than it should. Nicholas Lardy, a China expert at the Peterson Institute for International Economics, compares it to the relationship between an addict and a drug dealer: "Americans became hooked on cheap goods and cheap money, and China came to depend on the income from selling those goods."[7]

So here we are: America's and China's imbalances come together in one glorious dysfunctional relationship, symbiotic in the short run and unsustainable in the long run, thereby inviting economist Herbert Stein's famous observation, "If something cannot go on forever, it will stop." James Fallows, a correspondent for *The Atlantic* and longtime China observer, channels Herb Stein in his assessment: "Like so many imbalances in economics, this one can't go on indefinitely, and therefore won't. But the way it ends—suddenly versus gradually, for predictable reasons versus during a panic—will make an enormous difference to the

U.S. and Chinese economies over the next few years, to say nothing of bystanders in Europe and elsewhere."[8]

This Is So Weird

Let's step back for a moment to examine in greater depth just how curious the U.S.–China economic relationship has become. To begin with, poor, fast-growing countries do not typically loan huge sums to rich, mature countries. As economist and former Harvard president Larry Summers has pointed out, "From a distance, this, to say the least, is strange."[9] *Both theory and history suggest the capital should flow the other direction*—accumulated in rich countries and loaned to developing countries, where the marginal return on investment is likely to be higher. Building a new road or port or factory should have more impact—and therefore produce higher potential profits—in places with relatively few roads, ports, and factories than it would in a developed nation like the United States. This is why capital flowed from the rest of the world to the United States in the nineteenth century. *But from China to the United States in the twenty-first century?* Fallows points out that for all the ink devoted to glittering Chinese investments, there are plenty of places, particularly outside of the cities, where improvements in basic infrastructure could have a significant impact on the quality of life and future productivity of citizens. He writes, "Better schools, more abundant parks, better health care, better sewers in the cities—you name it, and if it isn't in some way connected to the factory-export economy, China hasn't got it, or not enough."[10]

In a similar vein, China has a bizarrely high national savings rate—on the order of 50 percent. The act of saving implies that a dollar spent in the future (including the interest earned) will produce more value (or satisfaction or happiness) than a dollar spent today. That's a curious determination to make when so many households are still relatively poor. Yes, China has been growing rapidly, but from a very low base. GDP per capita (measured using an exchange rate based on purchasing power parity) is still only around $13,000. And that's just an average, meaning that hundreds of millions of people are much poorer. In the absence of a well-developed social safety net (no Social Security or Medicare, for example), it makes sense for poor households to tuck away significant sums for a rainy day (that washes away the house). Still, saving 50 cents for every dollar earned is a significant act of self-denial in a country where many basic needs are not being met.

Just as curiously, the savings rate in the United States is bizarrely low, necessitating large net borrowing from abroad. Personal saving fell from an average of 7 percent of GDP in the 1960s, 1970s, and 1980s to 4.5 percent in the 1990s to 1.1 percent in the 2000s. Government saving has been negative in the 2000s (due to chronic deficits).[11] America, a country with a GDP per capita of $55,000,[12] does not have the cash on hand to finance all of its consumption and investment.* Thus, it's not a complete caricature to say that China (a poor country) is denying itself some basic needs so that America (a very rich country) can buy a handbag *that it cannot afford but must have today* (figuratively speaking).

Now, I have not meant to imply that individual Chinese firms and households are responsible for this saving decision. One defining feature of China's nondemocratic, managed economy is that the government maintains a heavy hand in allocating capital. Specifically, firms that accumulate dollar earnings from export sales must ultimately surrender those earnings to the central bank, the People's Bank of China, at a rate stipulated by the government. Unlike in the United States or other open economies, firms do not have the option of spending or investing the dollars; they go to the People's Bank. The process is more circuitous than I've described, but the operative point is that Chinese export earnings are "recycled" into dollar-denominated Treasury securities via explicit government policy, not because many economic actors independently decide to invest surplus dollars in America. As one commentator has noted, "At no point did an ordinary Chinese person decide to send so much money to America."[13]

To be fair, Chinese government policy has built an export juggernaut

---

* National saving consists of saving (or dissaving) by the government, households, and businesses. Net national saving takes that figure and subtracts depreciation of the existing capital stock (e.g., buildings and computers that are less valuable this year than last).

that has lifted an unprecedented number of people out of poverty in the span of a single generation. Chinese policymakers maintain that Japan was bullied into allowing the yen to appreciate sharply as a result of the Plaza Accord in 1985, thereby contributing to the subsequent bubble and economic stagnation.[14] (The IMF has gone to great lengths to rebut this argument, to no apparent avail.[15]) The 2008 financial crisis only deepened Chinese skepticism that free-flowing capital and floating exchange rates work swimmingly in a modern economy. In 2010, then Chinese premier Wen Jiabao defended his country's exchange rate policy: "If the yuan is not stable, it will bring disaster to China and the world. If we increase the yuan by 20 percent or 40 percent, as some people are calling for, many of our factories will shut down and society will be in turmoil."[16] Okay, that would be bad.

Nobody Likes a Manipulator

The Chinese yuan does not float. When the Chinese government buys huge quantities of U.S. Treasury securities, one explicit purpose of accumulating a stockpile of dollar assets is to manage the exchange rate of the yuan vis-à-vis the dollar, so that the yuan neither appreciates nor depreciates significantly against the dollar. This rough peg to the dollar is essential for a robust export sector, which in turn is the key to rising prosperity. As Arthur Kroeber, a China expert at the Brookings Institute, explains, "Chinese leaders observe that all countries that have raised themselves from poverty to wealth in the industrial era, without exception, have done so through export-led growth. Thus, they manage the exchange rate to broadly favor exports, just as they manage other markets and prices in the domestic economy in order to meet development objectives such as the creation of basic industries and infrastructure."[17] So far, the strategy is working—just as it did for Britain in the nineteenth century and the United States in the twentieth, two countries, as Kroeber points out, that became advocates for free trade *after* "their firms were secure in global technological leadership and the need for protection waned." The exchange rate is one tool in a broader development strategy.[18] Wild swings in the exchange rate would endanger this development strategy, which in turn could easily cause political instability. Remember, there are not a lot of real elections going on. The legitimacy of the Chinese government depends on delivering steady growth and a rising standard of living.

Meanwhile, across the Pacific (where there are real elections), American politicians have been railing against China's "unfair" trade practices. Senator Debbie Stabenow, a Michigan Democrat, said on the Senate floor, "The No. 1 trade barrier used by Asian countries is currency manipulation." In 2015, she and Senator Rob Portman, an Ohio Republican, cosponsored an amendment to legislation associated with the Trans-Pacific Partnership (a twelve-nation trade pact*) that would have pressured trade negotiators to include rules against currency manipulation in such agreements. The amendment failed in a close vote (48–51). The Obama White House opposed the amendment, as did Republican Majority Leader Mitch McConnell, on the grounds that the currency manipulation rules would make it harder to negotiate successful trade agreements. Still, forty-eight votes in the Senate is tough talk on currency manipulation. The cheap yuan (or any other undervalued currency) is the equivalent of a subsidy paid to exporters, as if a foreign government is picking up part of the tab for every toaster oven an American buys at Wal-Mart. This is perceived as stealing profits from American firms, taking jobs from American workers, and contributing to America's chronic current account deficit. It's no coincidence that Senators Stabenow and Portman hail from Michigan and Ohio, two states where manufacturing has been under siege from Asian competition.[19]

Free trade, in the eyes of China's critics, depends on fair trade, and fair trade means a currency that is not artificially suppressed below its true value. China's trade partners are not the only ones taking issue with the undervalued yuan. The International Monetary Fund has expressed concern about the "imbalances" generated by the U.S.–China relationship as a potential source of instability for the global financial system. The IMF Articles of Agreement forbid currency manipulation to gain

---

* China is not included in the Trans-Pacific Partnership trade agreement.

"unfair competitive advantage," though the IMF has never ruled a member nation guilty of such misdeeds and has no meaningful enforcement power even if it did. Rules aside, the whole point of prices in a market economy is to convey information; when prices are "wrong," they send bad signals and distort decisions, both within China and globally.

Of course, it's one thing to say a currency is undervalued and another to declare China a currency manipulator. Yes, for the bulk of the past two decades, the circumstantial case has been strong. China's monetary policy has been the equivalent of a guy standing near a crime scene holding a stolen purse. It doesn't look good: constant intervention in foreign exchange markets; a steady accumulation of dollars; a currency that looks cheap based on benchmarks like purchasing power parity. In 2010, the *Economist* proclaimed as part of its annual Big Mac Index that an undervalued currency is no free lunch, but in China "it can provide a cheap one." Based on the dollar-yuan exchange rate at the time, a Big Mac cost the equivalent of $2.18 in Beijing, compared to an average of $3.71 in the U.S.[20]

However, as you will remember from chapter 6, there is no precisely correct exchange rate from an economic perspective. In 2005, IMF economists sampled a broad range of studies in the hope of establishing if China's trade prowess could be attributed to an artificially cheap yuan. They were not able to answer that basic question. Different studies at different times with different methodologies have arrived at different assessments of the degree to which the yuan was undervalued, ranging from zero to 50 percent.[21] That's not good enough to convict.

During his confirmation hearing as Treasury secretary, Tim Geithner submitted written answers to questions posed by senators. An answer to a question from New York senator Charles Schumer, a strenuous critic of China's currency policy, used the m-word: "President Obama—backed by the conclusions of a broad range of economists—believes that China is manipulating its currency." But the administration quickly walked the statement back, declaring that the testimony had been written by a mid-level staffer and did not reflect the opinions of Mr. Geithner.[22]

More recently, the Initiative on Global Markets Forum at the Booth School of Business asked an ideologically diverse panel of prominent economists to evaluate the following statement: "Economic analysis can identify whether countries are using their exchange rates to benefit their own people at the expense of their trading partners' welfare." The most common answer was "uncertain" (37 percent), with the balance of the experts almost evenly divided between "agree" (30 percent) and "disagree" (34 percent). Not a single expert answered "strongly agree" or "strongly disagree."[23] The IGM panel was asked a follow-up question that may be more important from a policy standpoint: Are Americans really made worse off by foreign currency shenanigans? Specifically, the experts were asked to agree or disagree with the statement "Bank of Japan monetary policies that result in a weaker yen make Americans generally worse off." Yes, it's the yen, not the yuan, but the basic idea is the same. Most experts disagreed with the assertion that the weaker yen harms Americans (54 percent); another 36 percent were uncertain. Only 9 percent agreed that a cheaper yen comes at the expense of Americans (overall).[24]

When asked in 2012 if trade with China "makes most Americans better off"—the cheap yuan presumably implicit in the question—100 percent of the economists answered "agree" or "strongly agree."[25] Sure, Ford may lose some customers to Toyota . . . but then again, every American walking into a Toyota dealership is going to get a better deal.

Is It as Bad as All That?

A few paragraphs back, I mentioned that the cheap yuan is like giving Wal-Mart shoppers a discount on all the Chinese merchandise. On the continuum of financially nefarious activities, that doesn't seem so awful. In fact, if Americans can buy Chinese imports more cheaply because the dollar is relatively strong, that leaves money to be spent elsewhere. And money spent elsewhere creates jobs! While an undervalued Chinese currency is unequivocally bad for American firms competing with Chinese exports (or trying to export goods to China), it is less obvious what the effect of the undervalued currency might be on the American economy overall. Let's stipulate for a while that the yuan is substantially weaker than economic fundamentals suggest it ought to be. So what? Again, the

258 · naked money

academic literature is divided. A 2012 report by the Peterson Institute for International Economics estimated that the United States has lost between one and five million jobs due to foreign currency manipulation, with China as one of the "largest manipulators." Not surprisingly, the authors call on the United States to take aggressive action against the currency cheaters, such as levying tariffs on imports from the relevant nations.[26]

Conversely, an analysis done by economists for the Federal Reserve Bank of New York of data from the 1980s and 1990s concluded that "exchange rate movements do not have large effects on numbers of jobs or on hours worked." However, the authors do find an impact on wages in certain industries, with bigger effects in industries with low margins (such as textiles and lumber) than in industries with large markups (such as jet engines).[27] Edward Lazear, a Stanford economist and former chair of the Council of Economic Advisers for President George W. Bush, has pointed out that the U.S.–China exchange rate does a lousy job of explaining trade flows over the past several decades. The dollar-yuan exchange rate was pegged tightly from 1995 to 2005 (at just over 8 yuan to the dollar). During that stretch, Chinese exports to the United States grew at an annual rate of roughly 20 percent a year. In 2005, the Chinese currency appreciated sharply—making Chinese goods roughly 21 percent more expensive—and yet exports to the United States continued to grow at roughly the same pace.

Similarly, the yuan depreciated relative to the euro over a period when it was pegged to the dollar (2000–2004), yet the growth in Chinese exports to the two regions was roughly the same. To Lazear, Chinese currency manipulation is a scapegoat for weak U.S. economic performance that is better explained by American economic policies than by wily Chinese central bankers.[28]

Yet there is that issue of the imbalances, namely the $1.3 trillion of U.S. Treasury debt China has accumulated. This creates a risk for America that feels more James Bond than Tim Geithner: *financial blackmail*. Has the United States made itself vulnerable by becoming so indebted to a strategic rival? Suppose the United States and China come to disagreement over some geopolitical issue, such as the future of Tibet or control of the South China Sea or pirated Taylor Swift CDs being sold on the streets of Shanghai? Can Beijing get what it wants by threatening to sell American bonds and wreck our economy? If the Chinese government were to dump American bonds (or even make a credible threat of doing so), the price of those bonds would plunge, sending the U.S. financial system into a tailspin. Interest rates would shoot up and the economy would be shocked into a deep recession, if not worse. Economist and former Treasury secretary Larry Summers has called it "the balance of financial terror."

Maybe the Pentagon should do a war game around such financial blackmail, but it is an extremely unlikely scenario, primarily because of the damage China would have to inflict on itself in the process of punishing America. As David Leonhardt describes, "Were China to cut back sharply on its purchase of Treasury bonds, it would send the value of the bonds plummeting, hurting the Chinese, who already own hundreds of billions of dollars' worth."[29] In fact, experts have adopted the Cold War language of nuclear deterrence to explain away the danger. During the Cold War, game theorists argued that peace between the United States and the Soviet Union would be maintained as long as each nation had second-strike capability—meaning that each country could strike a massive nuclear blow *even after being attacked first.* The logic was that neither the Americans nor the Soviets would launch an attack if they knew for certain that they would be destroyed in the counterattack—hence the name "mutually assured destruction," or MAD. (By this logic, ironically, anything that can protect against a nuclear strike, such as a missile defense shield, is particularly destabilizing to the balance, and therefore peace, between nuclear powers.) As James Fallows has written, "China can't afford to stop feeding dollars to Americans, because China's own dollar holdings would be devastated if it did. As long as that logic holds, the system works. As soon as it doesn't, we have a big problem."[30]

The good news is that neither the United States nor the Soviets ever fired a nuclear missile during the Cold War. The bad news is that mutually assured destruction does not preclude a crisis set in motion by accident or misunderstanding. Just as the Americans might have wrongly perceived a blip on the radar over Alaska as an incoming Soviet missile—and responded in kind—the bond markets could easily get spooked by rumors or intemperate Chinese comments. (Neither the Chinese government nor the People's Bank are known for their transparency.) Any hint of China unloading Treasury bonds would create the same kind of panic as a bank run: sell your bonds now; ask questions later. To state the obvious: any system that is safe because the alternative is total destruction should give us pause.

How Does This End?

Things are getting better. There are not many good things to come out of the financial crisis, but a narrowing of the imbalances between China and the United States is one of them. As the American economy slowly gained strength in the years after the financial crisis, the Chinese economy began to struggle (relative to past performance). While the Fed began discussing interest rate hikes, the People's Bank was injecting stimulus. The yuan no longer looks so undervalued. China ended its formal peg to the dollar in 2005; the yuan has appreciated by a third relative to the dollar since then (and even more so against other currencies, given the recent strength of the dollar).[31] That said, one response to China's stock market crash in the summer of 2015 was an abrupt 2 percent depreciation of the yuan relative to the dollar—not huge, but big enough to scrape the scab off the old disputes.

In 2015, the IMF declared the yuan to be fairly valued, though not without giving the Chinese an earful of policy advice. First Deputy Managing Director David Lipton urged China to address economic imbalances, promote consumption as a source of future growth, and move toward a more flexible exchange rate.[32] (The U.S. Treasury responded by describing the yuan as "severely undervalued" but stopped short, once again, of using the m-word.)[33] Lipton said China should aim for a floating currency within two or three years as a tool for managing China's large and growing economy.

Just because the United States and China are getting along better than Germany and Greece does not mean the monetary challenges are over. In simple terms, the United States needs to save more and consume less; China needs to do the opposite. In the short run, the transition will be difficult on both sides of the Pacific. In the long run, both countries will end up better off. Former Treasury secretaries Hank Paulson and Robert Rubin, a Republican and a Democrat respectively, coauthored a 2015 essay urging both countries to "act on each other's economic critiques."[34] In other words, both countries are right in their prescription for the other. The United States needs to get its fiscal house in order—and not just because the Chinese government is worried about the cost of Obamacare. America's large and growing debt is arguably unsustainable given the projected costs of future entitlement spending (Social Security and Medicare for an aging population), unfair to future generations, and potentially destabilizing should investors ever begin to doubt U.S. creditworthiness.

China needs to rebalance its economy away from such a heavy dependence on exports in favor of more production for domestic consumption. Chinese officials have visions of the yuan as a global reserve currency, partially or fully supplanting the dollar as the reserve currency of choice. That is part of the overheated rhetoric around a "de-Americanized world." To make the yuan more attractive, Chinese monetary policy—and the economy overall—will have to be more transparent, more open to international capital flows, and less subject to government manipulation. Ironically, these are all things that would be good for the economic relationship with America and the broader global financial system.

Both countries benefit from robust trade across the Pacific. (One argument for resolving the U.S.–China dispute over the value of the yuan—economics aside—is that bad blood over currency manipulation might prompt Congress to pass protectionist legislation.) Meanwhile, all of the world's developed economies need to examine whether the current global financial architecture—or rather lack thereof, after the collapse of the Bretton Woods Agreement—is up to the task of managing twenty-first-century capital flows in a way that does not lead to dangerous imbalances. As the dominant economic powers for the foreseeable future, the United States and China will have to be the anchors of that system. Tim Geithner declared during his time as Treasury secretary that managing a system of exchange rates that does not favor one country over another is "the central existential challenge of cooperation internationally."[35]

Hank Paulson and Robert Rubin write, "The greatest American threat to China's economic future is the possibility that America's economic success could come to an end; the greatest economic danger China poses to the U.S. is the chance that China's economy fails to grow. By contrast, if each country gets its own house in order and thus succeeds economically, that should diminish economic insecurity, which generates friction, and increase confidence about the future, which fosters a constructive relationship."[36]

Both governments have work to do. But amid all the debate over governments and currencies, something curious has been happening: entrepreneurs have created new kinds of money that cut governments out of the loop entirely. Is that the answer to all this conflict?

Is bitcoin the future?

CHAPTER 13

The Future of Money

Who knows what will be the future incarnations of money? Computer bytes?

—Milton Friedman, 1994[1]

There are lots of ways to make money: You can earn it, find it, counterfeit it, steal it. Or, if you're Satoshi Nakamoto, a preternaturally talented computer coder, you can invent it. That's what he did on January 3, 2009, when he pressed a button on his keyboard and created a new currency called bitcoin. It was all bit and no coin. There was no paper, copper, or silver—just thirty-one thousand lines of code and an announcement on the Internet.

—Joshua Davis, *The New Yorker*, 2011[2]

Is bitcoin money?

To answer that future-oriented question, ironically, we need to begin by looking back in time. In the nineteenth century, the Pacific island of Yap gained notoriety when European explorers discovered its giant stone money. There was nothing unique about the inhabitants of Yap developing their own medium of exchange; that is the basic story of all civilizations. One would expect a relatively isolated society to find money that works for it, just like mackerel in prison or wampum in colonial America. But Yap's money is, well, really big. Specifically, the islanders use large discs of limestone with holes carved in the middle known as rai to conduct important transactions. The largest and most valuable circular stones can reach more than ten feet in diameter and weigh thousands of pounds. These giant rai are moved, if necessary, by groups of men who carry the stone on a pole slid through the hole in the center.*

The stone used to make rai is not indigenous to Yap. Rather, the limestone was mined on the islands of Palau—some 250 miles away—and carried back to the island by canoe or raft (and later ships). The costs of producing the stones—mining, carving, and transporting—helped to create the scarcity essential for any commodity that serves as money. We have heard variations on this story over and over again. To express amazement that people on a Pacific island use large round stones as currency, when we eagerly acquire pieces of paper with Ben Franklin's likeness on them, would be culturally arrogant, to say the least. (True, it doesn't take six people and a pole to carry a $100 bill; on the other hand, the rai are harder to counterfeit.) For all that, one curious incident involving a single rai offers striking insights into the future of money.

More than one hundred years ago, a boat carrying a large rai back to Yap sailed into a storm. In the turbulent seas, the valuable stone was lost to the depths of the ocean. Yet that particular rai continued to function on Yap as money. At first, this seems crazy. If your wallet falls into a sewer grate, you can't walk into Starbucks and buy coffee with the dollars lost in the bowels of the water treatment system, no matter how persuasive you might be. But the more one thinks about how rai function to facilitate commerce, the more sense it makes that a stone on the bottom of the ocean can work just fine. In fact, it makes perfect sense—though it takes a short intellectual journey to get to that understanding.

Let's begin our intellectual journey with the fact that rai were used primarily for large transactions and as a store of value—more like jewelry than a $100 bill. Because the rai were different sizes, and therefore had different values, they did not function well as a unit of account. Prices were typically quoted in baskets of common food crops, such as taro.

---

* The U.S. dollar is now legal tender on Yap and other island states in Micronesia, but the rai are still used for some purposes.

Michael F. Bryan, "Island Money," Federal Reserve Bank of Cleveland Commentary, February 1, 2004.

(There is some disagreement among scholars about whether rai were really money in the technical sense of the term.) For now, imagine keeping a giant rai on your front lawn until one of the kids goes to college, at which point you would give your rai to the University of Yap. (I don't know if there is a University of Yap, but it would make a great sweatshirt for monetary policy geeks.) At any rate, the university takes possession of the rai, and when the U of Yap (just known as the U on the island) hires a superstar monetary policy expert, he or she might get the rai. Here is the curious part: *the rai would still be in your front yard.* When ownership of rai changed, the stones did not typically move, which makes sense when you have a currency that can weigh up to ten thousand pounds. "Those involved in the exchange need only communicate that purchasing power has been transferred," explains Michael Bryan, an economist at the Federal Reserve who has studied the island currency.[3] The process is like transferring the title to a car. The ownership change is clear, regardless of where the car happens to be parked.

Yap and its stone currency are typically introduced as some wondrous curiosity. In fact, everything I have just described makes perfect sense if one takes a broader view of the role of money. Some cultures like big, round stones; others like gold and silver. Each of these minerals is scarce and serves well as a store of value. The fact that rai change ownership without being physically moved should not be puzzling; this turns out to be a feature of any modern banking system. As Bryan points out, "Most dollar transactions in the course of an ordinary business day occur without the transfer of anything physical. Electronic payments, which represent the overwhelming share of the value of all dollar transactions, require only balance sheet adjustments between banks." Under the gold standard, people were not hauling around bars of gold. The precious metal sat in a bank vault, with paper certificates circulating to keep track of who had the right to come claim it (even if they never did). At the international level, countries settled debts by transferring gold to one another. Even then, a high proportion of the world's gold was stored in a giant vault deep beneath the Federal Reserve Bank of New York. (To this day, the vault still holds gold on behalf of many other countries. The exact number of countries storing gold at the Fed is secret, and despite my best efforts, the New York Fed would not even give me a hint.) When countries settled up, gold was wheeled from one room in the Fed's vault to another. The gold really served as an accounting tool—no more or less practical than a large, round stone in your front yard.

You may recall the comment from chapter 7 commonly attributed to Warren Buffett, "[Gold] gets dug out of the ground in Africa, or someplace. Then we melt it down, dig another hole, bury it again and pay people to stand around guarding it. It has no utility. Anyone watching from Mars would be scratching their head."[4] Buffett's insight brings us to the end of our short intellectual journey, with a question: If the gold never comes out of the Fed vault but still serves to facilitate commerce via transfers of ownership, how is it different than a rai sitting at the bottom of the ocean?

It's not.

When the rai was lost to the depths, there was agreement on its size, value, and ownership. When that is known, and all parties agree, what difference does it make whether the rai is in your front yard or on the bottom of the Pacific, or in a vault beneath the New York Fed? The whole purpose of the stone is just to sit someplace—anyplace—and keep track of the credits and debits as people on Yap exchange things of value, like a bank ledger or chips in a casino. The information is what matters, not the stone or the ledger or the chips. As Michael Bryan explains, "Yap stones serve as a memory of one's contributions on the island." If we focus too narrowly on the curious commodities used as money, we can miss the larger purpose, which is to keep track of who has provided a good or service to someone else.

Imagine some kind of commune in which the basic tasks are shared: raking leaves, babysitting kids, making bootleg liquor. If an hour of labor has consistent value—babysitting for an hour is just as valuable as making moonshine for an hour—then money is not theoretically necessary. The hours worked could be tracked on a giant Excel spreadsheet; the laggards could be reminded periodically that they owe some work to the group. However, the spreadsheet would become a real mess when the community grows larger or when different tasks are accorded different values. (I raked your lawn for an hour. You spent thirty minutes doing couples counseling with Fred and Angela, but couples counseling is 1.75 times more valuable than leaf raking—and so on and so forth.) Money enables us to decentralize this accounting process. Rather than trying to reconcile what we all owe each other in a giant spreadsheet, we pass tokens among ourselves as the transactions take place. As an added bonus, we no longer need to remind the laggards that they are getting more from the group than they are giving; they just run out of tokens at some point. *The movement of money through the community is an implicit record of the transfer of value—a more convenient version of changing names on the stone rai or updating the ledger.* Bryan writes, "Some have argued, at least as far back as the seventeenth-century philosopher John Locke, that money is merely a communication device that serves as a societal memory of someone's production and consumption."

Money is memory.

As cool as that phrase sounds, I didn't come up with it. In 1996, Narayana Kocherlakota wrote a staff report for the Federal Reserve Bank of Minneapolis with the title "Money Is Memory." Kocherlakota made the case that anything that can be accomplished with money, in terms of efficient economic transactions, could in theory be accomplished with memory—or to be less poetic about it, with really good record keeping. Kocherlakota wrote his thought piece long before the creation of bit-coin, but he anticipated its essence. Kocherlakota pointed out that credit card use was rising at the time—not because of changes in the laws or practices around short-term debt, but because the costs of storing and accessing information were plunging. He explained, "Like money itself, credit cards are primarily mnemonic devices."[5] Of course, so is the rai at the bottom of the ocean. Kocherlakota offers his own version of Milton Friedman's famous dictum: *"Money is always and everywhere a mnemonic phenomenon."*[6]

This is the point where the past converges with the future. If money is accounting, or "memory," then bitcoin, an electronic currency generated by computer code, is not appreciably different than the stone rai. Each is a record-keeping device. (It is an ironic coincidence that both rai and bitcoins are "mined," one in stone quarries and the other using complex computer algorithms.) There is a reason that an economist at the Federal Reserve was writing about stone money on Yap. Way back in 2004 (still several years before the advent of bitcoin), Michael Bryan connected the dots between commodity money, fiat money (issued by governments and having no intrinsic value), and future money. He reasoned, "Fiat money can keep track of transactions as effectively as a commodity, while saving on production and storage costs. In fact, from this perspective, we might foresee a future in which all transactions are costlessly and instantaneously recorded for all to see, making the idea of money, at least as a physical construct, obsolete."

That future has arrived. Narayana Kocherlakota wrote in his money-is-memory thought piece, "If the function performed by money can be superseded by a perfect historical record of transactions, then money's only technological role must be to provide that record." *Bitcoin does that.* It is a decentralized ledger that allows participants to transfer bitcoins electronically anywhere in the world—like Western Union, only faster, cheaper, anonymously, and using a new unit of account, bitcoins, rather than dollars. It is a historical record of transactions made possible by the Internet, clever programming, powerful cryptography, and the willingness of entrepreneurs, speculators, libertarians, and others to trade money that has the legal backing of a government for electronic currency that does not.

If bitcoin is science fiction, its creation is more befitting of a mystery. A programmer who called himself Satoshi Nakamoto introduced bitcoin to the world in 2008. This may or may not have been his (or her) real name.* Nakamoto occasionally communicated with other programmers on message boards. Maybe "Nakamoto" was a pseudonym for a group. No one has ever stepped forward to take credit. At any rate, the guy (or woman or group) called Nakamoto wrote a computer program that enabled anyone who logged in via the Internet to earn bitcoins by solving complex mathematical problems. These are the bitcoin miners. As with real mining, the more resources one throws at the task, the more produc-

---

* I can neither confirm nor deny that I am Satoshi Nakamoto.

tive it is likely to be. Bitcoin miners are rewarded for solving complex factoring problems. At the risk of oversimplification, it's as if the bitcoin program has selected random winning numbers between one and infinity. Miners use their computers to search for those numbers. The faster the computer, and the more sophisticated the search process, the more numbers a computer can sift through at a time, increasing the chances of finding a match.

When a computer does solve a problem, it is the electronic equivalent of striking gold; the reward is 25 bitcoins. The original program was written so that 50 bitcoins would be discovered on average every ten minutes, with the discovery rate to fall by half every four years.[7] As I write, there are roughly twelve million bitcoins in circulation with the expectation that only nine million more will ever be given out. This promise of a fixed supply—beyond the reach of governments and central bankers—is part of the appeal. This is electronic gold.

The bitcoin network is entirely decentralized. Bitcoin miners can be normal people who decide to devote time and computer processing power to running the bitcoin program—just like the Americans who headed west during the California gold rush. I once met several students at a very prestigious prep school who spoke all through dinner about their mining efforts. Of course, as with gold or diamonds, the prospect of riches tends to attract bigger firms with deeper pockets and more sophisticated tools. As the *Wall Street Journal* explained in 2013, "Mining costs, industry parlance for the investments in sophisticated technology required to create bitcoin, are soaring as companies and people race to build ever-more-powerful computers to jump into the market."[8] I suspect the prep school students—the bitcoin equivalent of guys with a donkey, a pick, and a shovel—are no longer having much luck. One recent news account described a mining operation in Iceland "with more than 100 whirring silver computers, each in a locked cabinet and each cooled by blasts of Arctic air shot up from vents in the floor." The costs of ever more powerful computers (and the electricity to run them), combined with the deliberate release of bitcoins at a declining rate, will produce diminishing returns—again like real mining. The bitcoin mine described above was located in Iceland to take advantage of relatively cheap geothermal and hydroelectric electricity.[9] For anyone without supercomputers and cheap electricity, the easiest way to acquire bitcoins is to buy them on an exchange for dollars, like getting euros at the bank before a vacation in France.

The most important facet of this whole operation is that any computer running the bitcoin program also becomes part of the peer-to-peer network that maintains the constantly updating log of who owns which bitcoins. This is the price one pays for being a miner. The decentralized record of bitcoin ownership is known as the "block chain"—this is the electronic ledger that economists previously contemplated only in theory. When one party wants to send bitcoins to someone else, the network computers check their logs to verify that the person offering up the bitcoins actually owns them. Meanwhile, the person transferring bitcoins to another party must provide a private key that proves consent to the transaction. Joshua Davis summarized the process in *The New Yorker*: "The bitcoin software encrypts each transaction—the sender and receiver are identified only by a string of numbers—but a public record of every coin's movement is published across the entire network. Buyers and sellers remain anonymous, but everyone can see that a coin has moved from A to B, and Nakamoto's code can prevent A from spending a coin a second time."[10]

Thus, every transaction requires both the public key—verification by the network that the person really owns the bitcoins—and a private key—verification by the individual that he or she approves the transaction. The process is the electronic equivalent of opening a bank safety deposit box, which typically requires the simultaneous use of two keys: one kept by the bank and one kept by the owner of the box. (With bitcoins, the private key is a string of numbers, akin to a password.) After a bitcoin transaction takes place, every computer in the system automatically updates its log to reflect the change in ownership. In this way, a decentralized network of random people provides all the computational power needed for the payment system to work. As economist François Velde wrote in a bitcoin primer published by the Federal Reserve Bank of Chicago, "What, in the end, is this new currency? It is a list of authorized transactions, beginning with the creation of the unit by a miner and ending with the current owner. The currency can be exchanged because all potential recipients have the means to verify past transactions and validate new ones, and one's ownership rests on the consensus of the nodes."[11] Even bitcoin's detractors, who include just about every serious person I've ever spoken to on the subject, see value in this technology.

But wait—why would anyone want bitcoins? Or any of the knockoffs, including alphacoin, fastcoin, peercoin, namecoin, worldcoin, flycoin, zeuscoin, and even bbqcoin.[12] I can create Charlie Coins that I give out to people who run laps around my house. That doesn't mean anyone will want to accumulate them, let alone accept them for goods that have real value, like a pizza or a car. Bitcoins are just strings of numbers earned by solving relatively pointless math problems. At least with paper currency, you can burn it or use it as toilet paper if it loses all other value.

The short answer is that bitcoins have acquired value because bitcoins have acquired value. Early entrepreneurs, such as Netscape cofounder Marc Andreessen and Cameron and Tyler Winklevoss,* made investments—both in the technology and in bitcoins themselves—that persuaded others that bitcoin might become a viable electronic currency, or at least gain value over some period of time. Every time the value of bitcoins rose, others were persuaded that there might be some gain in owning bitcoins, which drove up the value. One of the most notorious bitcoin transactions took place in 2010, when a pioneering bitcoin enthusiast, Laszlo Hanyecz, made a post on a bitcoin message board offering 10,000 bitcoins to anyone who delivered him two pizzas. Another bitcoin nerd accepted the deal and had two Papa John's pizzas delivered to Hanyecz. By 2015, those 10,000 bitcoins were worth $2.3 million. Cryptocurrency enthusiasts now celebrate the anniversary of that seminal transaction, May 22, as Bitcoin Pizza Day.[13]

Along the way, some mainstream merchants, such as OkCupid (online dating) and WordPress (blogging), have begun to accept bitcoins. The

---

* The twins famous for their early involvement in Facebook, and then even more famous for their amusing portrayal in the film *The Social Network*.

LA Clippers basketball team accepts bitcoin for tickets.[14] So far, this feels more like a marketing gimmick than a mechanism for improving the ease of commerce. Retailers typically convert their bitcoin revenues into dollars immediately via third-party payment firms.[15] In 2014, the *Wall Street Journal* reported that a Lake Tahoe property was sold for 2,739 bitcoins.[16] Again, this feels like the exception that proves the skepticism. Is it news when a house is sold for dollars or euros?

The fact that someone could end up paying the equivalent of $2.3 million for a couple of pizzas is one of several things that make bitcoin lousy money, despite the whiz-bang technology. An asset that is rising and falling unpredictably in value makes for a miserable currency, electronic or otherwise. *Money works best when it maintains relatively constant purchasing power.* As Steve Forbes has lamented, "Money is most optimal when it is fixed in value just as commerce is facilitated when we have fixed weights and measures. When you buy a pound of hamburger you expect to get 16 ounces of meat. An hour has 60 minutes. A mile has 5,280 feet. These measurements don't 'float.'"[17] Forbes's column was aptly titled, "Bitcoin: Whatever It Is, It's Not Money!" I'm going to toss my lot with Steve Forbes on this one. To circle all the way back to chapter 1, money has three basic functions: as a unit of account, a store of value, and a medium of exchange. Bitcoin fails two of these measures, and perhaps even the third.

Bitcoin is not a meaningful *unit of account*. Let's go back to that Lake Tahoe property purchased for 2,739 bitcoins. Is that a big lot or a small lot? You have no idea. But when I tell you that the property was worth $1.6 million at the time of the transaction,[18] you immediately know it is a very nice piece of property (or perhaps a modest lot in a really swanky area). For most people on the planet, $1.6 million means something and 2,739 bitcoins does not. (To my point, the *Wall Street Journal* article trumpeting this groundbreaking real estate transaction in bitcoin quoted the price in dollars in the first paragraph and the price in bitcoins in the second.) Sure, people can figure out the value of a bitcoin at any given point in time, just as they do when visiting a new country and learning to think in the local currency. But bitcoin has been bouncing all over the place. *The value of a single bitcoin grew 5,000 percent between January 2013 and January 2014.*[19] The climb was not steady. Bitcoin began the year at $15, climbed to $230 in April, fell to $70 in July, then climbed vertiginously above $1,000 in November.[20] (This is how someone ends up spending the equivalent of $2.3 million on pizza.) In August 2014, bitcoin fell 12 percent in a single day. The owner of a bitcoin investment fund explained at the time, "This is just how bitcoin trades, for better or worse."[21] Let's put that in perspective: if the domestic purchasing power of the dollar fluctuates by more than 3 or 4 percent *in a year* that is considered to be lousy work on the part of the Fed. Twelve percent in a day?

Let's go back to our old financial friends, euphoria and panic. For most people, the most attractive thing about bitcoin has been its steadily rising value. If you buy an asset primarily in the hope that it will rise in value, you are speculating. And if you are speculating on an asset that has no underlying value (profits or rents or some other stream of income), watch out for a bubble. The greater fool theory—buying something today in the belief that someone else will pay more for it tomorrow—has had a seat at the table for every bubble in the history of human civilization. If people are induced to buy bitcoins by rising values, there is no reason they won't dump them when things look like they are going in the other direction. Bitcoin, like the euro, dollar, and yen, has no intrinsic value. The difference is that no government or central bank is responsible for maintaining the value of bitcoin, nor does any government stipulate that they must be accepted as legal tender. As the *Economist* noted, "All currencies involve some measure of consensual hallucination, but bitcoin, a virtual monetary system, involves more than most."[22]

Even if the bubble does not burst, the whole point of a unit of account is to have predictable purchasing power, especially over the long run. The dollar is an effective form of money not merely because you can buy coffee with it right now but also because you can buy a house in dollars with a thirty-year mortgage. Both you and the bank have a reasonable idea of what the dollar will be worth over those decades. The future value of the dollar is not perfectly predictable, but its purchasing power is a heck of a lot more stable than a bitcoin. Proponents of bitcoin get excited when the e-currency's value rises relative to the dollar (and therefore relative to most goods and services). What's not to like when the 30 bitcoins you bought from the hipster at the bike store buy seven times more marijuana than they did last year? (This drug reference is not entirely gratuitous, as I will illustrate in a moment.) *But any currency with such wild swings in value is miserable for longer-term transactions.* Imagine the financial danger of taking out a mortgage, or entering into any other contract, in which you commit to making payments that could end up being ten or twenty or fifty times what you expected in real terms. And obviously if bitcoins fall sharply in value, the party on the receiving end of the payment stream suffers the loss instead.

Consider this: even the Bitcoin Foundation doesn't really pay its people in bitcoin. Instead, the organization quotes salaries in dollars and then makes payments in bitcoin at whatever the exchange rate happens to be on payday.[23]

For similar reasons, bitcoin is not a good *store of value*, the second key function of money. The quantity of bitcoins that will ever be mined is ostensibly fixed, unlike fiat money, which can be produced at will by a central bank. No meddling by bureaucrats with printing presses (or the electronic equivalent). Fair enough. But given that we cannot identify who wrote the bitcoin program, one might reasonably ask how we can be certain that the fixed quantity is credible. (Electronic money is potentially even less scarce than paper.) If we are going to put "no government oversight" in the bitcoin benefit column, we might want to put it in the drawback column as well.

One of the most significant limitations of electronic money as a store of value—bitcoin and its competitors—may be the most prosaic: it can easily be lost or stolen. Each bitcoin has a personal key—a string of numbers—that can be stored electronically in an electronic wallet. Or you can just write the numbers down and stick them in a drawer with all your passwords. Neither is failsafe. Two software security researchers discovered 120 different kinds of malware designed to steal bitcoin wallet files from personal computers. Those experts recommend "cold storage" offline, like storing "cash in a physical safe."[24] Either way, if the personal key is lost, so are the bitcoins, forever. Have you ever forgotten or lost a password? Now imagine looking for a yellow Post-it note frantically, because if you don't find it your retirement savings will be gone forever. Or was it a blue Post-it?

This is a good place for an intriguing aside. One potential benefit of electronic money of any kind is that it may have a salutary effect on crime. Street crime is often predatory and opportunistic; fewer (real) wallets bulging with cash means fewer opportunities. A group of researchers associated with the National Bureau of Economic Research asked the question, "If cash motivates crime, could the absence of cash reduce crime?" The answer appears to be yes, based on a clever study in Missouri, where the state transferred its welfare and food stamp benefits from checks (which are cashed) to an electronic system with cards that can be swiped at retailers. The transition was phased, with different counties going electronic at different times. Going digital led to a significant decrease in crimes like burglary and assault (with no corresponding decrease, unfortunately, in crimes like rape, prostitution, or drug offenses).[25]

But let's not get too excited. Jesse James said he robbed banks because that's where the money was. Well, he would rob different places in the twenty-first century. In an era when hackers can steal personnel info for eighteen million federal employees, it is naïve to think digital currency is immune, particularly with no institution responsible for its safekeeping. After all, the ultimate robbery is one where you can steal a huge amount of money using a computer in your living room while watching a football game. *That's already happened.* In February 2014, the largest bitcoin exchange, Mt. Gox in Tokyo, reported that 744,400 bitcoins were missing, presumably stolen by cyberthieves.*[26] (By then, that was more than enough to buy a pizza—on the order of half a billion dollars.) About a week later, a Canadian "bitcoin bank" closed down when hackers stole all the bitcoins in its "hot wallet" (online storage for bitcoins). And so on.[27] The cost of these cyber-robberies is more than just the money

---

* Okay, since the thieves were never caught, we don't know if they pulled the heist from a living room while watching football. But we do know that they didn't have to storm into a bank wearing masks.

heisted electronically; there is typically a fall in the value of bitcoin, which spreads losses to everyone else holding the currency. That was never the case when Jesse James robbed dollars from banks.

This brings us to the last core function of money, as *a medium of exchange*. In this respect, bitcoin has enormous value—for some people. Bitcoin has the potential to play an important role in countries like Argentina and Venezuela, where there is a history of hyperinflation, the banks are a mess, and currency controls have made it hard to move money in or out of the country. The *New York Times* reported in 2015, "Argentina has been quietly gaining renown in technology circles as the first, and almost only, place where bitcoins are being regularly used by ordinary people for real commercial transactions."[28] Throughout history, individuals have resorted to using gold and gems when the traditional financial system has broken down. E-gold might serve the same function.

Digital money combines many of the benefits of cash with the reach and convenience of electronic payment systems. Anyone who wants to make an international purchase with a credit card typically incurs a large fee and leaves a trail of personal information. No one likes the fee. Bitcoin's unique technology has the potential to lower significantly the cost of moving money around the globe, particularly for groups like foreign workers sending remittances back to their home country. Other parties really don't like the paper trail. Anyone looking to buy weapons in Kazakhstan—without leaving lots of electronic evidence for law enforcement authorities—has to find a way to get suitcases of cash into the country. Cryptocurrencies combine the relative anonymity of cash with the convenience of a wire transfer. Bitcoin makes it possible to ship suitcases of cash around the world electronically—and is therefore particularly attractive to people who like to do large anonymous deals.

Now, I'm sure there are a lot of honest, upstanding people who do not want the Internal Revenue Service, the Drug Enforcement Agency, and the Federal Bureau of Investigation all up in their business. I also know that there are a lot of drug dealers, tax cheats, and arms merchants who would prefer not to share their receipts with the IRS, DEA, or FBI. From inception, bitcoin has provided a very attractive medium of exchange for some very unattractive characters. For example, Silk Road was the first website where one could buy and sell illicit goods, mostly drugs, with ease and impunity using bitcoin and another new technology, Tor, that allows a party to host a website without revealing its physical location.[29] One news outlet described the site as "Amazon for illegal drugs."[30] The FBI closed Silk Road down in 2013, but not before the site had facilitated more than 1.6 million bitcoin in sales. (To my earlier point, that probably means nothing to you; it's about $365 million at the current exchange rate.)

More surprisingly, Charles Shrem, a Bitcoin Foundation board member and CEO of a prominent website where bitcoins can be purchased using dollars, was arrested in January 2014 for alleged involvement in Silk Road. There are layers of irony in these bitcoin-related busts. Shrem was arrested at Kennedy Airport on his way to speak at the North American Bitcoin Conference.[31] The FBI shut down Silk Road and seized 144,000 bitcoins from the company, making the U.S. government the largest owner of bitcoins at the time.[32] The bigger point is that law enforcement and regulators are going to do whatever they can to keep up with the technology. As Ben Bernanke observes, "It's hard to become a globally useful currency if regulators keep cracking down on it, which they will do if they see it primarily as a vehicle for illicit activities."[33] Meanwhile, one has to expect that the luster will rub off digital currencies—even for libertarians—if some of the major beneficiaries are drug lords and terrorists.

For most of us, however, the primary problem with new forms of electronic money is that they are not very good at what they purport to do—act as money. As a professor (and not a particularly hard grader), here is my assessment:

Cryptocurrencies as unit of account: F.

Cryptocurrencies as a store of value: D.

Cryptocurrencies as a medium of exchange: C for most people; B+ if you are in a country where the government is falling apart; A+ if you are a terrorist, weapons merchant, drug dealer, or kidnapper.

But let's not throw out the awesome technology with the cryptocurrencies. Bitcoin and related technologies have the potential to transform how we pay for things and move money around, even if it is in dollars rather than bitcoins. Traditionally we have had two basic options for any transaction that moves a token of value from one party to another. The most straightforward process is using physical currency. The elegance of cash is that when I give you a dollar, you have it and I don't. It's hard to have much confusion or dispute around that. All other payment mechanisms have traditionally relied on an intermediary to verify a transaction. If I write a check or use a debit card, my bank verifies that I have funds in the account and then transfers those funds to someone else's account. Visa, MasterCard, Western Union, and PayPal are all doing variations on the same basic thing. They verify that recipients are getting money from me that really exists and that I'm not simultaneously spending it in six other places. (In the case of credit cards, they may also loan me the money that I'm spending.) These parties take a significant fee for playing intermediary, which is not unreasonable given the importance of electronic payments in a modern economy.

Historically, any electronic form of payment without an intermediary has been doomed by the very nature of digital information: it can be copied over and over again. Suppose I have a digital file of some sort that represents $50 of value. It's the opposite of cash. After I e-mail it to you, I still have it. In fact, I can e-mail it to the rest of my contact list, too. Now we all have a file worth $50. That cannot work as a payment system. The genius of bitcoin is that the decentralized peer-to-peer network verifies the transaction, not an intermediary like Visa. As the Chicago Fed's François Velde explains, "The bitcoin protocol provides an elegant solution to the problem of creating a digital currency—i.e., how to regulate its issue, defeat counterfeiting and double-spending, and ensure that it can be conveyed safely—without relying on a single authority."[34] That innovation has the capacity to transform commerce and capital flows— making them faster, easier, and cheaper. *Which is what money is supposed to do.* Even the *Economist* (whose editorial views on cryptocurrencies tend to include terms like "bitconned") draws a parallel to Napster, the peer-to-peer file music sharing service that was shut down for copyright infringement but still managed to transform the music industry.[35]

This is a good place to make explicit one theme of the whole chapter. *There is a fundamental difference between electronic payment systems—mechanisms for making electronic transactions using traditional currencies—and a whole new form of digital money.* For all the reasons I've explained, the latter faces huge barriers. But the former—cheaper and easier ways of doing commerce electronically—will inevitably march forward. For example, M-Pesa is a popular mobile payment system in Kenya that allows users to transfer money using mobile phones. Users can buy goods using their phones, or even withdraw cash at stores and stands. M-Pesa lessens the need to keep cash around, which minimizes theft. As the *Wall Street Journal* describes, "[Transactions] come from cow herders in the country's dusty Rift Valley villages, pedicab drivers in the bustling port of Mombasa and technology entrepreneurs in traffic-clogged Nairobi."[36] According to one study released by the Kenya Bankers Association, some 60 percent of Kenyans use their phones to carry out financial transactions, while only 30 percent go to the bank and 8 percent use ATMs.[37] But do not lose sight of a crucial detail: *all those transactions are in Kenyan shillings.*

People may reasonably assert that cash will die out; at a minimum, paper money will become less common as we increasingly swipe cards, wave phones, tap wallets, and use any other technology that makes it faster and easier to buy a bagel. We have already seen airlines and other institutions transition to accepting only electronic forms of payment. I suspect there will always be some demand for cash, because of its anonymity and ease of use for small transactions—time will tell. (It boggles the mind that we still have pennies, but that's for another book.) This is a good time to step back and remind ourselves that the purpose of money is to make the rest of the economy work better, whether we are using paper dollars, bitcoins, stone rai, or pouches of mackerel. In that respect, we can make some powerful predictions.

We will always need a stable unit of account, even if we are buying coffee at Starbucks via mental telepathy. Government-backed currencies in nations with a responsible central bank, particularly the U.S. dollar, have had remarkably consistent and predictable purchasing power over the past three decades. At the risk of replacing Irving Fisher, I'm going to say that government-backed currencies will not be supplanted anytime soon. The nature of money and transactions will change—but not the fundamental need to maintain a unit of account.

There will always be borrowers and lenders. The nature of that borrowing and lending will evolve. Traditional banking has been partially supplanted by shadow banking. Futurists have declared that the Internet will give rise to peer-to-peer lending, in which borrowers and lenders find each other online and cut out the middleman. Maybe. Yet hopefully history has taught us that any system of lending is prone to panics. Perhaps someday borrowers and lenders will rendezvous in space to consummate their deals, having arrived on cheap commercial spacecraft. Whatever. Unless human nature changes, there will be circumstances in which lenders want their money back immediately and borrowers will not have it. Space travel will not help, unless it gets Jimmy Stewart to the scene and he starts passing out his honeymoon cash to calm the panic. The situation requires a lender of last resort.

The global economy is inherently prone to disruption, whether by natural disaster, technological change, war, financial panic, or any of the other phenomena that man and nature can throw at us. One proven tool for managing that disruption is lowering or raising the price of borrowed money—interest rates. One irony of bitcoin is that its founder Satoshi Nakamoto was motivated in part by anger over the financial crisis. Bitcoin was meant to be a currency that could stand apart from bankers and politicians and central bankers. Writing in the *New Yorker*, Joshua Davis surmises, "If Nakamoto ran the world, he would have just fired Ben Bernanke, closed the European Central Bank, and shut down Western Union."[38] Yet it was the Federal Reserve's capacity to inject new money into the system that prevented the crisis from growing worse. And since the crisis, the purchasing power of the dollar has been far more stable than the purchasing power of the bitcoin. Bitcoins enter the economy as the computer algorithm dictates, not because the economy needs more bitcoins to ease a downturn or to maintain stable value in terms of goods and services.

Let's recap:

The way we conduct transactions will continue to evolve—but not the need for a stable unit of account.

The nature of lending and borrowing will change—but not the nature of financial panics and the need to protect against them.

Our economy will evolve—but it will still be prone to economic fluctuations, perhaps even bigger and more destabilizing as the global economy becomes more interconnected.

What institution has responsibility for managing all of those things? A central bank. People get excited about Google glasses and self-driving cars, but in terms of innovation, one of the most important things we can do to promote growth and stability in the twenty-first century is to continue refining how we do central banking.

CHAPTER 14

Doing Central Banking Better

By the mid-2000s, it was indeed not unreasonable to think that better mac-roeconomic policy could deliver, and had indeed delivered, higher economic stability. Then the crisis came.

—Olivier Blanchard, Giovanni Dell'Ariccia, and Paolo Mauro,
IMF report, 2010[1]

I think no one can claim that every year in every circumstance in every crisis the Fed got its policies exactly right. But what is beyond debate is that this institution has served the country well.

—Paul Volcker, ceremony commemorating the centennial
of the Federal Reserve Act[2]

The Fed celebrated its 100th birthday in December 2013. The centennial celebration was subdued by American celebratory standards—nothing like the American bicentennial that I remember vividly from elementary school. No fireworks, no documentaries on television, no parades. Although the worst of the financial crisis had passed by 2013, the Fed was still under siege politi-cally from both the left and right. Conservatives were warning of ram-pant inflation as the result of the Fed's aggressive intervention in the bond markets. Progressives pilloried the Fed for the opposite, for doing too little to put more Americans back to work more quickly. Fed chair

Ben Bernanke must have been one of the few people ever to face the wrath of both Elizabeth Warren and Rick Perry. Meanwhile, Ron Paul continued to make it his mission to end the Fed and paper money. There was no cake at the Fed to celebrate the 100th birthday.*

That's too bad, because by any reasonably objective standard, the centennial should have had caviar, ice sculptures, and one of those large dance bands. For all the economic trauma of the past decade, the Fed as an institution has much to celebrate, as do other central banks around the world. Shrill criticism notwithstanding, the Federal Reserve steered the United States and the world through a crisis that might have been more catastrophic than the Great Depression had there not been an aggressive intervention. Longer term, the Fed and other responsible central banks around the world have demonstrated that it is possible to maintain low inflation with a fiat currency, thereby harnessing all the benefits of commodity money without the drawbacks. True, the Fed failed its first big test, the Great Depression. The 2008 financial crisis was a chance for a redo. This time the Fed did a heroic job. People actually use that word: heroic. Alan Blinder, the Princeton economist and former Fed vice chair who hails from the political left, gives Bernanke an A- (with points off for letting Lehman Brothers fail). Hank Paulson, the Treasury secretary appointed by George W. Bush, has described Bernanke not merely as courageous but "one of the greatest Fed chairmen of all times."[3] So let's call that an A.

The numbers support those grades. Unemployment peaked around 25 percent during the Great Depression, compared to 10 percent during the financial crisis.[4] The Great Depression stretched on, with some temporary reversals, for the better part of a decade. The financial crisis caused a recession that lasted only three years in the United States (albeit with slow growth after that). So why were there no ice sculptures at the centennial celebration? Part of the reason is that those grades for Bernanke and the Fed are provisional. The worst of the financial crisis may

---

* I checked this. A Fed official sent me the following note: "There was no cake associated with the 100th anniversary event in 2013."

be over, but the final chapters are not written. The Fed's balance sheet is still huge by historical standards; America's central bank acquired an unprecedented quantity of Treasury securities and other assets as it fed liquidity to the economy. The Fed will have to manage those assets, gradually selling them off or letting them mature. Meanwhile, banks are holding unprecedented quantities of reserves (that they acquired from the Fed). The Fed's critics in Congress have proposed a bill that would require audits of the Fed, which is really an attempt by lawmakers to involve themselves more directly in monetary policy decisions. On Main Street, many Americans are still angry about the bailouts.

I had occasion to interview Ben Bernanke during the summer of 2015. He did not have the bearing of a guy who was running around high-fiving people to celebrate the Fed's impressive performance over the past seven years, or the ninety-three before that. He looked more like a general who had been through years of combat, victorious but exhausted. The 2008 financial crisis was the central banking equivalent of a war—a huge, unexpected shock to the financial system. The Fed response employed lessons from past conflicts—the Great Depression, the United States in the 1970s, Japan in the 1990s—while also improvising as circumstances required. Central banking, like medicine or manufacturing, is a process that should get steadily better as past experiences are incorporated into present practices. As the United States emerges from the financial crisis and the Fed begins its second century as an institution, now is a good time to look back, look around, and look forward. What did we learn about central banking during the crisis, and more important, how can we use those lessons to prepare for the next crisis or panic—*because there will be one.* How can we do central banking better?

We Were Right

Many of the basic principles that undergird central banking—the stuff I was taught in grad school—were reinforced during the financial crisis. As with combat, some of the basic lessons are timeless (e.g., hold the high ground). Here are some of the classic lessons of central banking, tested once again, that future policymakers ignore at their peril.

We need a lender of last resort. A bank run is a bank run, whether it is Bailey Building and Loan or the repo market. The financial crisis, at bottom, was a financial panic. Ben Bernanke often refers to it as the Panic of 2008. He told the American Economic Association in 2014, "The crisis bore a strong family resemblance to a classic financial panic, except that it took place in the complex environment of the twenty-first-century global financial system." When panic spreads, sick institutions infect healthy ones. Individuals and firms and governments all scramble for liquidity, making the underlying crisis worse. Over time, historians and economists will critique the specifics of the Fed's performance, as they should. However, as the visceral fear associated with the crisis recedes, we should not forget how bad things might have become. As humans, we are really bad at envisioning the counterfactual—what might have happened if different choices had been made. We cannot forget how close we came to a complete financial meltdown but for the intervention of the world's major central banks.

In October 2008, the Royal Bank of Scotland, one of the biggest banks in the world, came to the brink of default before turning to the British government for assistance. Alistair Darling, British chancellor of the Exchequer at the time, has said, "I think we came within hours of a collapse of the banking system."[5]

How bad might it have been? David "Danny" Blanchflower, a member of the Bank of England rate setting committee during the crisis, recalls a conversation in which Alistair Darling described those crucial hours: "He's told me that he asked the staff, 'What happens if I don't rescue them?' And they said, 'Chancellor, we don't exactly know, but we think there is a significant probability that every credit card in the world and every cash machine will stop working tomorrow.' And he said, 'Not much of a choice you've given me then, have you?' And they said, 'No.'"[6]

A central bank with the power to loan unlimited sums to solvent but illiquid institutions is uniquely positioned to stop a financial panic. Until either human nature or the world of finance changes fundamentally, there will be panics. And as long as there are panics, we need central banks to lend when they strike.

Monetary policy matters. Money is often treated as a footnote in introductory economics courses. What matters is the exchange of goods; money is merely a tool for facilitating that process. That's true. As the book has sought to point out, pouches of mackerel can serve that function, as can large, round stones or pieces of paper. And money is neutral in the long run, meaning that we cannot make society steadily richer by adding zeroes to the currency. But in the short run, changing the price of credit—the price at which money is loaned out—is most certainly not neutral. Central bank policy affects who buys cars and washing machines this year, which in turn affects the unemployment rate among those who make cars and washing machines, which in turn affects other spending in the economy, and so on. The Fed acted boldly as the economy collapsed in 2008, taking short-term interest rates from 5.25 percent to near zero, and lowering long-term rates via quantitative easing and other interventions. We cannot directly observe the counterfactual, but the evidence is compelling that those actions cushioned the fall and hastened the recovery.

A central bank's political independence is crucial to its effectiveness. We have known for some time that central banks with a high degree of political independence are better at warding off inflation and delivering stable growth. Politicians have short-term incentives; central bankers need to play the long game. Keeping the former from meddling too much with the latter is an important part of effective monetary policy. However, the traditional danger has been politicians keen to feed money to the economy now at the expense of higher inflation later. One lesson from the financial crisis, and also from Japan's lost decades, is that central banks need protection from the anti-inflation folks, too. Some of the most virulent criticism of the Fed in the aftermath of 2008 came from the political right, where a broad range of influential persons—from academics to politicians—insisted that each Fed action was bound to generate runaway inflation, or even hyperinflation. So far, those predictions have proved to be egregiously wrong. (No one ever taught me in grad school that politicians might want too little inflation.) Had meddling politicians hampered the Fed's actions, the result almost certainly would have been less effective policy. Of course, the political left was hammering on the central bank, too, with some critics demanding inflation as high as 6 percent in the aftermath of 2008.

I am not going to tell you that the Fed response to the 2008 crisis was perfect. I will tell you that it was better than anything Congress could have produced in the moment. And yet Congress is seeking more control over monetary policy. Former member of the Fed board of governors Frederic Mishkin wrote in an op-ed, "Who says bipartisanship in Washington is dead? Although Republicans and Democrats can't agree on how to tame budget deficits, both want to weaken the Federal Reserve's independence, which bodes ill for the economy."[7] A bill is currently winding its way through Congress that seeks to audit the Fed. To be clear, the Fed's financial operations are already audited by the Government Accountability Office and by an outside auditor hired by the Office of the Inspector General. Janet Yellen cannot back a van up to the Fed and take money home to buy groceries. Rather, Congress is seeking to audit monetary policy decisions. The bill would require the Fed to adopt explicit rules for making monetary policy and then report to Congress when it deviates from those rules.

Alice Rivlin, former vice chair of the Fed and a well-respected policy expert for decades, did not mince words in testimony before a House committee exploring the possibility of more Fed oversight: "Monetary policy decisions can be politically unpopular, and the creators of the Federal Reserve were wise to insulate those decisions from political pressures. Injecting another group into the mix to second guess monetary policy decisions would undermine an independent agency which is working hard to do the job Congress created it to do."[8]

Paul Volcker needed to be protected from the political process in order to fight the inflation of the 1970s.* This is the same independence Ben Bernanke needed to fend off deflation. Either way, central bank independence is a good thing. As the *Economist* noted in a report on the

---

* Fed trivia: Paul Volcker wrote his college thesis on how the Fed ought to restore the independence that it lost during World War II.

Transcript of the Ceremony Commemorating the Centennial of the Federal Reserve Act, Washington, DC, December 16, 2013.

world's central bankers, "Politicians need to set clearer goals for central banks—then leave them alone."[9] We'll get to what those goals ought to be in a moment.

A modest inflation target is better than zero. Prior to the financial crisis, a consensus had emerged among central bankers that the ideal inflation target was not zero, but rather something in the 1 to 3 percent range. The Fed has since adopted an official target of 2 percent. This is not to say that inflation is a good thing; there is nothing particularly attractive about a currency that is steadily losing value. But a low, predictable rate of inflation gives the central bank more room to cut real interest rates during a downturn before hitting the zero bound. We've done the math before. If inflation is zero and the Fed lowers the nominal interest rate to zero, the real interest rate—the true cost of borrowing—is also zero. That can provide some important stimulus to the economy. *But if inflation is 2 percent and the Fed lowers the nominal rate to zero, the real interest rate is negative 2 percent.* When changing prices are taken into account, borrowers can pay back less (in terms of purchasing power) than they borrowed. That's even more stimulus.

The other benefit of a modest inflation target is that it keeps the economy further away from deflation and all its attendant problems. If you are worried about falling over a cliff, don't walk right on the edge. Similarly, if you are worried about deflation, don't aim for zero inflation, where even a small misstep can lead to falling prices. Better to aim for 2 percent inflation, and then if the economy is weaker than expected, the result is 1 percent inflation, not 1 percent deflation.

The central bank should regulate the institutions for which it is the lender of last resort. If I serve in the volunteer fire department that has agreed to drop everything and rush to your house if there is a fire, it is not crazy for me to ask you to move the oily rags out of your furnace room. The need for a lender of last resort is well established; so is the risk of moral hazard. The only way to reconcile these two forces—the fact that individuals or institutions that are protected from some harm are therefore more inclined to act recklessly—is to put some limits on potentially reckless behavior. In some countries, including the United States, the regulatory role is shared between the central bank and other government entities. There is a larger and more complicated discussion to be had around how firms ought to be regulated most effectively—but the operative word is *how* not *if*. Any institution that performs rescues when times are bad ought to be conducting inspections when times are good. That is the price firms pay for having ready access to liquidity during a panic.

We Learned New Things in 2008

I'll be honest: central bankers were a smug lot in the early 2000s. The United States was enjoying the Great Moderation. Inflation was defeated. We had monetary policy figured out. As the *Economist* has noted, "Before the financial crisis, central bankers were backroom technocrats: unelected, unexciting men in grey suits, who adjusted interest rates to keep prices stable on the basis of widely agreed rules."[10] Then things got more exciting. Yes, a lot of the old rules still applied (see the last section), but the Fed began to improvise like a jazz musician. The books I used in grad school became outdated. With the financial crisis (mostly) in the rearview mirror, here are some of the lessons that will be in the new textbooks.

There are plenty of effective tools after the Fed hits the zero bound. Prior to the financial crisis, it was an academic question, literally, as to what the Fed policy response could and should be if the federal funds stayed near zero for an extended stretch. At that point, the Fed would arguably run out of ammunition, as it is difficult (though not technically impossible) to make nominal interest rates negative. Keynes used the phrase "pushing on a wet noodle" as a metaphor for the futility of monetary policy when rates are near zero and the economy is still flagging. He, and later others, believed that the only remedy at that point would be fiscal policy—using tax cuts and/or government spending to stimulate demand. The Fed's response in 2008 proved that the monetary toolkit includes much more than short-term interest rates.

The Bank of Japan had experimented with quantitative easing in the

2000s (using new money to purchase longer-term bonds once short-term rates hit zero), but the effort was relatively tepid and the outcome not overly compelling. During the financial crisis, the Federal Reserve used multiple rounds of quantitative easing to more dramatic effect, along with other policies not in the textbooks (but perfectly consistent with things that *are* in the textbooks). Ben Bernanke's academic interest in the Great Depression turned out to be shockingly relevant. That's the point here: the monetary toolbox is far bigger than one might have imagined ten or fifteen years ago. And those central bankers in grey suits? A 2012 article gushed, "They saved the world from economic collapse in 2008. They have propped up the recovery since, not least by buying boatloads of government bonds; and they have rewritten the rules of global banking."[11]

We need to pay more attention to systemic risk. Before the crisis, we had a decent grasp of the risks that might swamp an individual institution. To go back to the fire analogy, we knew the most common dangers: smoking in bed; faulty electrical outlets; oily rags stored near the furnace; and so on. Unfortunately we had no idea how quickly a blaze, once started, might spread. Many experts believed that the housing market was overheating in the early 2000s. Others warned about shoddy mortgage underwriting and the curious derivatives being engineered from sliced and diced bundles of mortgages. Yet virtually no one anticipated how a drop in housing prices would set in motion a cascade of events that would bring the global economy to the brink of collapse.

The new buzz phrases are "systemic risk" and "macroprudential regulation," both of which reflect the idea that discrete events can add up to something much worse than the sum of the parts. Sure, your oily rags may be stored outside your garage, far from the furnace. And I don't smoke in bed; I smoke outside when I go for a walk. Prior to 2008, we believed we had those risks under control. What we learned in the financial crisis is that if I toss my smoldering cigarette butts near your driveway as I walk by, and your oily rags are piled outside your garage, we may have a systemic problem. Small disturbances can interact, spread, and grow in ways that policymakers had not previously anticipated.

Transparency and good communication matter at the Fed, as they do in most institutions. It is curious, bordering on bizarre, that monetary policy has often been shrouded in mystery. William Greider's 1987 bestselling book on the Federal Reserve was titled *Secrets of the Temple.* The back cover describes the Fed as a government institution "in some ways more secretive than the CIA and more powerful than the President or Congress." One review marvels at the "awkward little secret" that the "federal government deliberately induces recessions to bring down inflation and interest rates." Leaving aside that the federal government is not synonymous with the Federal Reserve, and that interest rates typically go up when inflation comes down*—this supposed "awkward little secret" is really just monetary policy.

Secrecy and suspicion are not good for central banking. One of the most important things a central bank can do is set expectations. If the public believes inflation will be 2 percent next year, inflation will most likely be 2 percent next year. That is the power of expectations. Meanwhile, we know central banks are institutions that engender distrust from both the political left and the right. The functions that they undertake—the mechanics of monetary policy—are poorly understood. The Fed is fodder for myriad conspiracy theories, some of them disturbingly hateful and anti-Semitic. The Fed ought to broadcast exactly what it is doing and why it is doing it—to set expectations for the markets; to inform the Main Street of America about what is going on; and to give the crazies less to write about on the Internet.

One of Ben Bernanke's major initiatives during his tenure was to make the Fed a more transparent institution. Bernanke began holding regular press conferences after FOMC meetings. Bernanke appeared on *60 Minutes*, spoke to university students, and held town hall meetings. The Fed now even has a Twitter feed.[12] Meanwhile, the Fed adopted its first ever formal inflation target (2 percent) and began using tools like

---

* Long-term interest rates can sometimes fall when the Fed raises short-term rates to fight inflation because bond buyers no longer expect high inflation in the future and will therefore accept lower nominal rates.

"forward guidance" that derived their power from telling the markets what to expect in the future.

These changes were not caused by the financial crisis. Bernanke took the post in 2006 with a commitment to "fostering transparency and accountability."[13] However, the communications piece became more important when Fed policy turned more unorthodox. Suddenly, the world was paying attention to central bankers—unelected leaders with extraordinary power using tools that are poorly understood by the general public. Going forward, if the Fed is going to retain the independence it needs to operate effectively, the institution cannot be "more secretive than the CIA." In 2011, a group of monetary policy experts released a report entitled "Rethinking Central Banking" with reform recommendations based on experiences during the crisis. One section of the report acknowledged the unique need by central banks to maintain both political independence and political legitimacy. Citizens in democratic nations are being asked to surrender power to institutions deliberately insulated from politicians. That's a fine line to walk. The final report noted, "Independence is politically viable only with accountability, and the best way to enhance accountability is for central banks to become more transparent and forthright about their objectives and tactics."[14]

We Are Still Learning

The financial crisis rocked the economics establishment. Lots of models were chucked out the window, without ready replacements. While the past decade may have taught us a few things, or reinforced prior beliefs, it has also raised questions that have yet to be answered conclusively. If the goal is to do central banking better—to deliver macroeconomic and financial stability—here are the questions experts are still wrestling with and arguing over.

Can the Federal Reserve unwind its balance sheet in a way that does not cause the next crisis? As we know, the Fed responded aggressively to the financial crisis by buying bonds and other securities. The purpose was to inject liquidity into the economy and lower interest rates. So far, so good.

Here's the thing: when the Fed buys assets with new money, those assets have to go somewhere—in a really big safety deposit box, in the corner of the Fed chair's office—just somewhere. It turns out that where they go from an accounting standpoint is on the Fed's balance sheet. That's the way monetary policy always works. When the Fed lowers interest rates, it buys Treasury securities in exchange for new money, putting those securities on the balance sheet as assets while entering the new money as a liability. That's just double-entry bookkeeping applied to monetary policy. To raise rates, the Fed does the opposite, selling assets from the balance sheet in exchange for bank reserves (thereby eliminating both the assets and the liabilities).

If you like the accounting stuff, great; if not, the important point is that the Fed now owns an unprecedented quantity of securities. The accounting geeks will appreciate that the asset side of the balance sheet swelled from roughly $800 million in 2005 to over $4 trillion in 2015.[15] The rest of you can imagine boxes and boxes of bonds piled in the Fed chair's office and spilling out into the corridors. Remember, the Fed bought these securities from banks, so there is a parallel development: the banking system is sitting on nearly $3 trillion of reserves—electronic money held on account at the Fed that could in theory be loaned out at any time. How does this unprecedented situation resolve itself?

The sanguine view is that as the economy recovers, the Fed can begin tightening by selling assets and drawing down bank reserves. That would be lovely. A less optimistic scenario is that banks, feeling a burst of confidence as the economy recovers, will begin loaning out these reserves, sending new money coursing through the banking system and causing the inflation that critics have been warning about for years. A related concern is that as interest rates begin to rise, the Fed will lose money on the securities in its portfolio. (Bond prices move inversely to interest rates, so as interest rates rise, the value of the Fed's huge bond portfolio will fall.) The Fed is not overly worried about either of these prospects, in large part because there are tools to manage the rate at which banks begin loaning out their reserves, such as raising the interest rate the Fed pays on excess reserves held at the Fed. (Remember, the Fed is the banker for banks; it can raise or lower the rate it pays on deposits held there by commercial banks just like those banks do for their customers.) If the Fed raises the rate it pays on excess reserves, the banks holding those reserves will be less inclined to use them to make new loans. Meanwhile, the Fed is not like a sandwich shop or an insurance company. The fact that the Fed is "losing money" because of the change in value of assets on its balance sheet is largely a meaningless concept. (When you can conjure money with taps on a keyboard, the normal rules of finance don't apply the same way.)

Still, we cannot declare the 2008 financial crisis over until it's over. Allan Meltzer, one of the monetary policy experts who anticipated significant inflation after the Fed's early interventions, still sees the huge quantity of bank reserves as a threat. He wrote in late 2014, "I have admitted publicly that I made a mistake by failing to anticipate that banks would decide to hold idle $2.5 trillion of the new reserves that the Federal Reserve supplied. Nothing to that extent had ever happened. The $2.5 trillion sits on the banks' balance sheets. There is a slight chance that the Federal Reserve will find a way to gradually remove the idle reserves without causing inflation or a recession—or both. However, Federal Reserve history does not give reason for confidence that it will succeed in this task."[16]

Meltzer compares declaring the Fed's actions a success at this point to claiming victory in a sporting event at halftime. He has a point. We may be nearly a decade past the onset of the financial crisis, but the fat lady is still in her dressing room. This unusually long period of near-zero interest rates may have planted the seeds that become the next crisis; at a minimum, there are likely to be unintended consequences. We can see light at the end of the tunnel, but we are still in the tunnel. Critics still see a train coming, as they have ever since 2008; we cannot yet prove them wrong.

What should the Federal Reserve be trying to do? This is not a trick question. There is an ongoing argument over whether America's central bank should focus exclusively on price stability—promulgating its inflation target and then hitting that target—or if the Fed should also commit to maintaining full employment, as the law currently prescribes. The focus on price stability *and* maximum employment is the so-called dual mandate created by the Federal Reserve Act of 1977.* As with any life endeavor, providing two objectives muddies the task. If I send my daughter off to college telling her, "Stay safe and have fun"—which one is it? Sometimes staying safe isn't so fun, and sometimes having fun isn't so safe. It's not always a tradeoff, but sometimes it is, and managing a tradeoff is inherently harder than focusing on a single indicator. Other central banks around the world, such as the European Central Bank, are charged exclusively with maintaining price stability.

To critics, the dual mandate is the central banking equivalent of attention deficit disorder, causing the Fed to lose focus on its primary responsibility, which should be fighting inflation. This group, which tends to hail from the political right, considers the Fed's focus on jobs to be ineffective and potentially reckless. The massive bond purchases associated with quantitative easing magnified this concern. CNN reported in 2010, "Some critics are sick and tired of the Fed prioritizing job creation at the risk of rising prices. They say the juggling act of promoting growth while staving off inflation has proven ineffective, and has led to a policy of too much cheap money with dangerous consequences for the economy."[17] Around the same time, Mike Pence, a Republican congressman from Indiana (and now governor), introduced legislation that would have limited the Fed's mission to maintaining price stability.[18] All the while, critics on the left were blasting the Fed for not acting more aggressively on the jobs front, given the absence of inflation.

Paul Volcker claims the term "dual mandate" never passed his lips during his tenure at the Fed, primarily because getting inflation under control was a prerequisite for a healthier economy. He recalls, "The most important thing we can do for a prosperous, stable growth is to maintain price stability. So we were discharging the dual mandate."[19] Yet the slow

---

* As noted in chapter 5, the Federal Reserve Act of 1977 assigns the responsibility for three objectives: price stability, full employment, and moderate long-term interest rates. Because low inflation leads naturally to moderate long-term interest rates, these two objectives have become redundant and policymakers now speak of the two remaining objectives as the dual mandate.

recovery after the financial crisis, when conditions were totally different than in the 1970s, argues that the Fed has an important role to play in boosting employment apart from its role as guardian of prices. So far, unemployment has fallen steadily without any signs of inflation (and faster than in other parts of the world where central banks acted less aggressively). Ben Bernanke offers a nuanced defense of the dual mandate that is at odds with Volcker's singular focus on inflation. Bernanke explains, "In practice, all central banks have dual mandates, at least to some extent. Lars Svensson coined the term 'flexible inflation targeting,' which basically means that you try to bring inflation to its target over a 2–3 year horizon, but in the short term you have some scope to respond to economic conditions, including developments in the labor market. If you looked at the actual behavior of the Fed and the Bank of England, say, they wouldn't look radically different, even though the Bank of England is formally an inflation-targeter while the Fed has a dual mandate. The flexible inflation-targeting approach gives that leeway; in the case of the Fed, the mandate to pay attention to employment is just more explicit."[20]

Does a central bank operate more effectively with explicit money policy rules or with the discretion to act as necessary? In other words, did all that jazz improvisation do more harm than good? Maybe the Fed should just read the sheet music. There is broad agreement on the general parameters of how the Fed ought to operate: lower interest rates when the economy is operating below potential; raise them when things are at risk of overheating. The question is whether concepts like "below potential" and "lower interest rates" can be more rigidly codified to remove what Fed critics would describe as arbitrary meddling. In other words, would the Fed function more effectively by following an explicit monetary policy rule rather than adhering to the discretion of the Fed chair and his or her fellow FOMC members? Milton Friedman proposed letting a computer govern the money supply.[21] But when it turned out that the relationship between the money supply and the economy was much less stable than he thought, he backed away from the idea. (The possibility that the relationship between variables may change over time, or under different economic circumstances, is an argument against strict policy rules.)

More recently, John Taylor, a Stanford economist who is a proponent of a more rules-based approach, described his vision in an op-ed for the *Wall Street Journal*: "A single goal of long-run price stability should be supplemented with a requirement that the Fed establish and report its strategy for setting the interest rate or the money supply to achieve that goal. If the Fed deviates from its strategy, it should provide a written explanation and testify in Congress."[22]

Not coincidentally, the most common monetary policy rule is the Taylor rule—yes, named for the aforementioned John Taylor. The Taylor rule suggests an optimal federal funds rate based on a formula that reflects where the economy is relative to its output potential and how prices are trending relative to the inflation target.* The intuition is obvious and consistent with everything discussed in the previous thirteen chapters. *The appeal is in the simplicity and the precision.* One can plug in the numbers and get the "right" answer. By this thinking, not only could my twelve-year-old son do monetary policy with the Taylor rule, good data, and a calculator, but sticking to the formula would lead to fewer mistakes than an overactive and arbitrary Fed. John Taylor has argued that the Fed held rates too low before the real estate bust, then overshot in raising them, and has now held them too low for too long. More important, he believes that a rules-based approach would have avoided these mistakes.[23]

Not surprisingly, central bankers are loath to believe that they can be replaced by a formula and a twelve-year-old with a calculator. Econo-

---

* $i = r^* + pi + 0.5 (pi\text{-}pi^*) + 0.5 (y\text{-}y^*)$

Where:

i   = nominal fed funds rate

r^* = real federal funds rate (usually 2 percent)

pi = rate of inflation

pi^* = target inflation rate

y   = logarithm of real output

y^* = logarithm of potential output

http://www.investopedia.com/articles/economics/10/taylor-rule.asp.

mists uniformly embrace the Taylor rule as a handy back-of-the-envelope tool that does a nice job of describing how monetary policy has operated over the past several decades. The policy question is whether it has *prescriptive* value going forward. That is a tougher case to make. Leave the twelve-year-old aside for the moment and just think about the data. David "Danny" Blanchflower, the Dartmouth economist who served on the rate-setting committee for the Bank of England, points out that the rule suggests a false precision. He explains, "The dispute, more than anything, about the Taylor rule is what you put in it. You have to guess on the scale of the output gap [how far the economy is from its natural speed limit]. In 2008, the biggest difference between me and the rest of the committee was basically the size of the output gap and what was happening to it."[24]

If there is disagreement over the economy's speed limit, and even sometimes over how fast we are currently traveling, no formula is going to tell us whether we are going too fast or too slow. Moreover, the economy's potential output is going to change over time, as will some of the other relationships in the model. As former Fed governor Kevin Warsh has said, "Economics, and the conduct of monetary policy, after all, is not physics."[25] And as Ben Bernanke points out, it's not like the Fed is pulling interest rates out of a hat. There are explicit goals and rule-based processes—just none that ties the hands of the Fed as tightly as critics would like.

Is a 2 percent inflation target high enough? Twenty years ago, no one could have imagined this as a serious question. Too little inflation? Seriously? Yet one lesson from the financial crisis is that a higher rate of inflation during normal times provides a central bank with more room to cut rates when times turn bad, as described earlier in the chapter. This is one of the ideas advanced in a report entitled "Rethinking Macroeconomic Policy" prepared by economists at the IMF in 2010. Olivier Blanchard, the Fund's chief economist, and his colleagues wrote, "Higher average inflation, and thus higher nominal interest rates to start with, would have made it possible to cut interest rates more [during the financial crisis], thereby probably reducing the drop in output and the deterioration of fiscal positions."[26] I made the case earlier for a modest inflation target, but if 2 percent is good, might 4 percent be better? We know the harms of inflation, but they are minimized when the target is clear and the inflation is expected. A world that has become used to 2 percent inflation could adapt to 4 percent in the same way. Expectations would be reset and central banking would become modestly easier.

Or would it? The battle against inflation was hard fought. If the public is persuaded that the inflation target needs to double, what's to stop it from doubling again? Paul Volcker (aka Inflation Fighter Man) is a critic. Inflation Fighter Man did not reset the world's inflation expectations so that policymakers could squander that accomplishment. In a *New York Times* op-ed, Volcker warned of the siren song of higher inflation, which is both "alluring and predictable." Volcker was criticizing the idea of a temporary boost in inflation, rather than a permanent change in the target, but his critique is generalizable. "The instinct will be to do a little more—a seemingly temporary and 'reasonable' 4 percent becomes 5, and then 6 and so on." Inflation Fighter Man has no desire to come out of retirement to beat back rising inflation expectations once again.[27]

There is another option that, in theory, could combine the benefits of inflation targeting with more flexibility around the appropriate rate of inflation: nominal GDP targeting. (Nominal GDP growth is real growth plus inflation—the change in the production of goods and services plus the change in the price of those goods and services.) Under this approach, the Fed would aim to hit a consistent rate of nominal GDP growth, say 5 percent. The inflation rate would then be allowed to fluctuate depending on how the economy is performing. Suppose real growth is only 1 percent—below what most economists believe is the economy's natural long-run rate of growth (around 3 percent). Nominal GDP targeting would prescribe an inflation rate of 4 percent—extra easy monetary policy until growth returns to trend. Conversely, a booming economy, say 4.5 percent real growth, would prescribe much tighter monetary policy and a lower inflation rate (just 0.5 percent). Targeting nominal growth rather than a specific inflation target gives policymakers more flexibility in dealing with economic fluctuations. As one economic blogger points out, "It is a surreptitious way of temporarily raising the inflation target without the toxic politics of doing so explicitly."[28] (Others have made the same basic point, including *New York Times* columnist Paul Krugman.) Thus, how you feel about nominal GDP targeting probably depends on how you feel about the Fed moving its inflation target around.

Ben Bernanke raises a more pragmatic concern: nominal GDP targeting requires the public to have a sophisticated understanding of what the Fed is trying to do, including the moving target for inflation. It is harder to anchor expectations around a moving target than around a single number. If the public's inflation expectations do not track with what the Fed is trying to do, the policy will not work.

The larger point here is that the Fed is always looking for better tools. When Paul Volcker took the helm as Fed chair, the Fed was primarily concerned with managing interest rates. Under Volcker's direction, the Fed switched to a policy that managed the money supply, which gave the Fed more power to fight inflation. In the 1990s, the Greenspan Fed adopted inflation targeting, albeit without a formal target. Ben Bernanke made the 2 percent inflation target explicit. What might the next formal refinement be?

Should the central bank try to pop bubbles? Asset price bubbles—our old friends euphoria and panic—are the bane of the financial system. Bubbles are to finance what car accidents are to transportation: given the inevitable forces at work, what is the best way to minimize the harm? To what extent, if at all, should the central bank use monetary policy to prevent bubbles from getting out of control, as opposed to cushioning the blow after the inevitable accidents happen? One line of thinking among economists has been that central banks should "lean against the wind" by raising interest rates when asset prices appear frothy. Higher interest rates will dampen the euphoria and make the panic either less likely or less damaging if it does happen. The Fed has been accused of contributing to the housing bubble by holding rates too low for too long in the 2000s. (The Financial Crisis Inquiry Commission rejected this explanation for the crisis, pointing out, for example, that there were housing bubbles in other countries with much tighter monetary policy.)

The opposing view is that monetary policy is a lousy tool for dealing with asset price bubbles and the Fed should instead stand ready to clean up any postbubble mess by providing liquidity and low interest rates after the fact. This approach is not as negligent as it sounds. It is hard to spot an asset bubble before it bursts. In any event, higher interest rates might be a costly tool if the rest of the economy is weak—the proverbial smashing of a gnat with a sledgehammer.

Of late, there has been some refined thinking in the "lean versus clean" debate. Economist and former Fed governor Frederic Mishkin has drawn a distinction between bubbles that seriously infect the credit markets and those that do not. In a credit-driven bubble, excessive borrowing fuels irrational exuberance, causing a credit-induced spiral and then a crash that does damage to the broader financial system. We know the basic script: borrowing causes a rise in asset values, which encourages further lending against such assets, which drives up prices, and so on. In the euphoria of rising prices, financial institutions become less concerned about lending standards because the rising value of the collateral they are lending against will protect them against losses. Does any of that sound familiar?

When the bubble bursts, it all goes in reverse: asset prices fall, loans go bad, lenders cut back on credit, asset prices fall further. Financial institutions get in trouble, further restricting credit in the broader economy. We've seen this film before: Japan in 1989, the United States in 2008, our idyllic rice-growing village in chapter 4. However, there is a less scary film—a second type of bubble in which the irrational exuberance does not interact so deeply with the financial system. For example, the Internet bubble in the late 1990s involved very little lending against rising share prices. Yes, high-tech companies had ridiculous valuations. Yes, firms that had never earned a dollar in profit were worth more on paper than companies like IBM. Yes, seventeen-year-old hipster CEOs said ridiculously stupid things. ("Technology will make government irrelevant."*) Yet for all the idiocy and craziness, the popping of the

---

* Yes, I really heard someone say that.

tech bubble had only a modest impact on the broader economy because there was no significant spillover to the financial system.

This suggests a third way in the "lean versus clean" debate. Regulators may not be able to identify a bubble before it's too late, but they can certainly spot shoddy lending practices, regardless of whether assets turn out to be overpriced. As noted earlier, my dog was offered a preapproved Visa card with a five-digit credit limit sometime around 2005. (I subscribed to *The New Yorker* in his name, W. Buster Wheelan, and some credit card issuer obviously bought the list.) This would suggest that the credit markets were out of control. The subsequent real estate bust would not have been nearly as catastrophic if financial institutions had not been lending to dogs, literally and figuratively. Ben Bernanke told the American Economics Association in 2010, "Stronger regulation and supervision aimed at problems with underwriting practices and lenders' risk management would have been a more effective and surgical approach to constraining the housing bubble than a general increase in interest rates."[29]

We have established an important point: *dogs should not be getting credit cards*. Which raises the next question.

Have we got the regulation right? In 2005, the city of Boise, Idaho, implemented a ban on full nudity in public, leaving an exception for "serious artistic" expression. Shortly thereafter, the Erotic City Gentlemen's Club in Boise began holding "art nights," during which patrons were given pencils and sketch pads as they ogled fully naked women. The police cited the club for breaking the law (because "officers concluded that patrons were not focused on art").[30] Still, you have to admire the cleverness—and as a regulator, you need to fear it. The nature of financial regulation is that it seeks to constrain certain kinds of activities conducted by certain kinds of institutions, typically with hundreds of pages of legislative language devoted to defining those activities and institutions as specifically as possible (e.g., "bank" and "lending" and "serious artistic expression").

Regulating the financial system is like playing whack-a-mole. Financiers are clever people. Like the rest of us, they don't like the government telling them what to do, or what not to do. When regulators try to fix one vulnerability in the financial system, they often open the door for some other problem (for instance, the rise of the shadow banking system). As Ben Bernanke explains, "One of the inherent problems is that all regulations have a fence. Everybody inside this category has to do 'this' and everybody outside is exempt. So naturally there are always going to be attempts to get just outside the fence. That's just the way financial markets work, and the way human beings work."[31] Congress devoted some three thousand pages to try to change the behavior that contributed to the financial crisis. Smart people will get paid a lot of money to find the loopholes. ("Hey, this isn't a strip club! It's an art school.") Then maybe we'll need another thousand pages.

Voters are prone to dislike regulators in any event. Just think about the nature of what those regulators are trying to do. If regulation averts a crisis—the real goal—the public never knows there would have been a crisis. We will just resent whatever cost and inconvenience the regulations impose, totally unaware that those precautions may have prevented a debt crisis or a real estate crash. There are no heroes for stopping a problem before it happens. Of course, that is the most successful kind of government intervention. And if something bad does happen, regulators will be blamed for not having prevented it.

There is also a less benign view of why regulation is not as effective as it might be: Wall Street firms have the clout to get what they want from Congress. Simon Johnson, former chief economist at the International Monetary Fund and author of *13 Bankers: The Wall Street Takeover and the Next Financial Meltdown*, points out that one of the many revolving doors in Washington is between high-level regulatory positions in government and extremely lucrative jobs in finance or in consulting to big financial firms. That relationship may be too cozy, at great cost to taxpayers. Johnson says, "We often discuss central banking in very dry, technocratic terms, and we forget about the power structures behind them. When we look at other countries, we see the power structures. We don't like to look at it in the United States."[32]

It's clear post-2008 that central banks must focus on financial stability. Many of the regulations passed since then make perfect sense.

For example, the creation of "living wills" for systemically important financial institutions theoretically protects the system from contagion without promoting moral hazard. The living will is a plan for the orderly dissolution of a firm in the case of insolvency to avoid spreading panic and instability to the rest of the system. Will it work? Will financial institutions reinvent themselves and their products in ways that leave them just outside the perimeter of the regulatory fence? I have no idea, but I do know that the answers will determine whether the financial crisis is a unique event in the twenty-first century or whether we will have to start numbering them, like our world wars.

Is it time for Bretton Woods II? Everybody has a complaint about the post–Bretton Woods era. The United States accuses China of manipulating the yuan. China resents the dollar's role as the world's reserve currency. Small countries with their own currencies are whipsawed by huge swings in exchange rates. Small countries without their own currencies worry about becoming the next Greece. The whole world is worried about imbalances—huge caches of international reserves accumulated by countries like China and enormous deficits run up by the United States. Capital flows across borders faster than ever, exacerbating any inherent instabilities. What's not to dislike?

The more constructive question is: What might be better? Answers do not leap off the page. One lesson from the euro is that supranational monetary arrangements do not work well without a corresponding governmental apparatus; at present, there is no international institution with the authority and enforcement power necessary to make a new international monetary system work. And what might that look like anyway? The lesson from the last several decades is that monetary policy has significant "cross-border spillovers," as the Brookings Institution's Rethinking Central Banking committee described it. When the United States engages in quantitative easing, countries from India to Brazil must worry about an appreciating currency or sudden inflows of capital seeking a higher return.[33] It would be great if the system were more orderly and predictable.

Like the gold standard? As a former senior Treasury official pointed out, the more orderly and predictable the international monetary system, the more rigid it is in a crisis. And the more rigid it is in a crisis, the more difficult the needed adjustments. We want the impossibility set: the benefits of free-flowing capital without the disruptions; the flexibility of floating exchange rates without the unpredictability; and the ability to adapt monetary policy to domestic needs without the headaches caused when other countries do the same. Simon Johnson describes a grand global deal for some kind of Bretton Woods II arrangement as "basically impossible."[34]

So we're going to have to figure that one out.

None of this should detract from what the world's central bankers, supported by lots of important economic thinking, have accomplished. Sure, the financial crisis is cause for humility. Then again, the outcomes were appreciably better than they were during the Great Depression or the many panics before that. We are getting steadily better at this.

There will always be unique challenges associated with managing a fiat currency—*the awesome power to create money where none existed. Or to take it away.* Just as neurosurgeons can manipulate a living brain— presumably for the better, but always with the risk of making things worse—a central bank has a similar awe-inspiring influence on the entire economy: our jobs, our savings, our homes. People may not literally live or die based on Fed decisions, but they are affected profoundly. At a minimum, I hope I have persuaded you that money matters, not just because you'd rather have more of it than less, but because the system that puts $20 in your pocket makes possible all the other economic activities that we care about.

Notes

Introduction

1. John Whitesides, "Senior U.S. Lawmakers Condemn 'Provocative' Currency Devaluation," Reuters, August 11, 2015.

Chapter 1: What Is Money?

1. Carl Menger, "On the Origins of Money," *Economic Journal* 2 (1892).
2. Choe Sang-Hun, "North Korea Revalues Its Currency," *New York Times*, December 2, 2009.
3. Ibid.
4. Barbara Demick, "Nothing Left," *New Yorker*, July 12 and 19, 2010.
5. See www.federalreserve.gov/monetarypolicy/bst_recenttrends.htm.
6. Justin Scheck, "Mackerel Economics in Prison Leads to Appreciation for Oily Fillets," *Wall Street Journal*, October 2, 2008.
7. "Hard to Kill," *Economist*, March 31, 2012.
8. Ibid.
9. Ibid.
10. Michael Phillips, "U.S. Money Isn't As Sound as a Dollar," *Wall Street Journal*, November 2, 2006.
11. Ibid.
12. "Airtime Is Money," *Economist*, January 19, 2013.
13. "The Nature of Wealth," *Economist*, October 10, 2009.
14. Damien Cave and Ginger Thompson, "Coupons Ease Chaos in Efforts to Feed Haitians," *New York Times*, February 3, 2010.
15. Susan Njanji, "Small Change Sparks Fights in Coin-Starved Zimbabwe," *Mail & Guardian*, August 5, 2012.
16. Steve H. Hanke and Alex K. F. Kwok, "On the Measurement of Zimbabwe's Hyperinflation," *Cato Journal* 29, no. 2 (Spring/Summer 2009).

17. "Gold Standard," IGM Forum, University of Chicago Booth School of Business, January 12, 2012, http://www.igmchicago.org/igm-economic-experts-panel/poll-results?SurveyID=SV_cw1nNUYOXSAKwrq.

Chapter 2: Inflation and Deflation

1. Merle Hazard, "Inflation or Deflation?" https://www.youtube.com/watch?v=2fq2ga4HkGY&feature=PlayList&p=5BF8673A2848C5B0&index=0&playnext=1.
2. "A Crisis It Can't Paper Over," *Los Angeles Times*, July 14, 2008.
3. "Fly Me to the Moon," *Economist*, May 2, 2002.
4. "Frequent-Flyer Economics," *Economist*, May 2, 2002.
5. William Neuman, "Price Controls Keep Venezuela Cupboards Bare," *New York Times*, April 21, 2012.
6. Milton Friedman, *Money Mischief: Episodes in Monetary History* (New York: Harcourt Brace & Company, 1994), xi.
7. Ibid., 193.
8. C.R., "When Did Globalisation Start?" Free Exchange, *Economist*, September 23, 2013, http://www.economist.com/blogs/freeexchange/2013/09/economic-history-1.
9. See http://www.boxofficemojo.com/alltime/domestic.htm.
10. See http://www.boxofficemojo.com/alltime/adjusted.htm.
11. See http://www.dol.gov/whd/minwage/chart.htm.
12. "The Perils of Panflation," *Economist*, April 7, 2012.
13. Matthew Q. Clarida and Nicholas P. Fandos, "Substantiating Fears of Grade Inflation, Dean Says Median Grade at Harvard College Is A-, Most Common Grade is A," *Harvard Crimson*, December 3, 2013.
14. "The Perils of Panflation," *Economist*.
15. See https://www.bundesbank.de/Redaktion/EN/Downloads/quotes_by_karl_otto_poehl.pdf?__blob=publicationFile.
16. Stephen G. Cecchetti, "Prices During the Great Depression: Was the Deflation of 1930–32 Really Unanticipated?" NBER Working Paper 3174, National Bureau of Economic Research, November 1989.
17. "Irving Fisher: Out of Keynes's Shadow," *Economist*, February 12, 2009.
18. Joan Sweeney and Richard James Sweeney, "Monetary Theory and the Great Capitol Hill Baby Sitting Co-op Crisis," *Journal of Money, Credit, and Banking*, February 1977.
19. Paul Krugman, "Baby-Sitting the Economy," *Slate*, August 13, 1998.
20. "The Babysitting Co-op: Crises of Confidence," *Economist*, October 11, 2011.

Chapter 3: The Science, Art, Politics, and Psychology of Prices

1. Megan Woolhouse, "A Government Agent, on the Prowl," *Boston Globe*, October 9, 2012.

2. Emily Wax-Thibodeaux, "The Government's Human Price Scanners," *Washington Post*, November 11, 2013.

3. See Consumer Price Index, Bureau of Labor Statistics, Frequently Asked Questions (FAQs), http://www.bls.gov/cpi/cpifaq.htm.

4. Wax-Thibodeaux, "The Government's Human Price Scanners."

5. Ibid.

6. Christmas Price Index, PNC Bank, https://www.pncchristmaspriceindex.com/pnc/about.

7. Consumer Price Index, FAQs, http://stats.bls.gov/cpi/cpifaq.htm#Question_3.

8. "Current Price Topics: The Experimental Consumer Price Index for Older Americans (CPI-E)," Focus on Prices and Spending, U.S. Bureau of Labor Statistics 2, no. 15 (February 2012).

9. Ibid.

10. Interview with Steve Reed, BLS economist, Consumer Price Index Program, January 9, 2015.

11. "The Experimental Consumer Price Index for Older Americans (CPI-E)," BLS.

12. Robert J. Gordon, "The Boskin Commission Report and Its Aftermath," National Bureau of Economic Research, Working Paper 7759, June 2000.

13. "And Now Prices Can be 'Virtual' Too," *Economist*, June 12, 1997.

14. Timothy Aeppel, "An Inflation Debate Brews Over Intangibles at the Mall," *Wall Street Journal*, May 9, 2005.

15. "Report on Quality Changes for 2015 Model Vehicles," Producer Price Indexes, Bureau of Labor Statistics, November 18, 2014, http://www.bls.gov/web/ppi/ppimotveh.pdf.

16. Doug Short, "Chained CPI Versus the Standard CPI: Breaking Down the Numbers," October 22, 2014, Advisory Perspectives, http://www.advisorperspectives.com/dshort/commentaries/Chained-CPI-Overview.php.

17. "Current Price Topics: A Comparison of the CPI-U and the C-CPI-U," Focus on Prices and Spending, Consumer Price Index 2, no. 11 (November 2011).

18. "In 2014, Various Tax Benefits Increase Due to Inflation Adjustments," IRS, IR-2013-87, October 31, 2013, http://www.irs.gov/uac/Newsroom/In-2014,-Various-Tax-Benefits-Increase-Due-to-Inflation-Adjustments.

19. See http://www.ssa.gov/history/reports/boskinrpt.html.

20. Gordon, "The Boskin Commission Report and Its Aftermath."

21. Kathy Ruffing, Paul N. Van de Water, and Robert Greenstein, "Chained CPI Can Be Part of a Balanced Deficit-Reduction Package, Under Certain Conditions," Center on Budget and Policy Priorities, February 12, 2012.

22. Gordon, "The Boskin Commission Report and Its Aftermath."
23. Dr. Econ, "What is 'core inflation,' and why do economists use it instead of overall or general inflation to track changes in the overall price level?" Federal Reserve Bank of San Francisco, October 2004, http://www.frbsf.org/education/publications/doctor-econ/2004/october/core-inflation-headline.
24. "Lies, Flame-Grilled Lies and Statistics," *Economist*, January 29, 2011.
25. "Motion of Censure," *Economist*, February 9, 2013.
26. "United States Government Bonds," Bloomberg Business, http://www.bloomberg.com/markets/rates-bonds/government-bonds/us/.
27. "Bryan's 'Cross of Gold' Speech: Mesmerizing the Masses," History Matters, American Social History Project, http://historymatters.gmu.edu/d/5354/.
28. Eldar Shafir, Peter Diamond, and Amos Tversky, "Money Illusion," *Quarterly Journal of Economics* CXII, no. 2 (May 1997).
29. Professor E. W. Kemmerer, as quoted in Shafir, Diamond, and Tversky, "Money Illusion."
30. Shafir, Diamond, and Tversky, "Money Illusion."
31. Binyamin Appelbaum, "In Fed and Out, Many Now Think Inflation Helps," *New York Times*, October 26, 2013.

Chapter 4: Credit and Crashes

1. Gary Gorton, "Questions and Answers about the Financial Crisis," testimony prepared for the U.S. Financial Crisis Inquiry Commission, February 20, 2010.
2. Irving Fisher, *Booms & Depressions: Some First Principles* (New York: Adelphi Company, 1932).
3. Andrew W. Lo, "Reading about the Financial Crisis: A Twenty-One-Book Review," *Journal of Economic Literature* 50, no. 1 (March 2012).
4. "The Financial Crisis Inquiry Report," FCIC at Stanford Law School, http://fcic.law.stanford.edu/.
5. Kenneth R. French et al., *The Squam Lake Report: Fixing the Financial System* (Princeton, NJ: Princeton University Press, 2010).
6. See http://www.imsdb.com/scripts/It's-a-Wonderful-Life.html.
7. The Internet Movie Script Database (IMSDb), http://www.imsdb.com/scripts/It%27s-a-Wonderful-Life.html.
8. "The Dangers of Demonology," *Economist*, January 7, 2012.
9. Ibid.
10. Tami Luhby, "Cash-Poor California Turns to IOUs," CNN Money, July 2, 2009.
11. Stephanie Simon, "Cash-Strapped California's IOUs: Just the Latest Sub for Dollars," *Wall Street Journal*, July 25, 2009.

12. Charles P. Kindleberger and Robert Aliber, *Manias, Panics, and Crashes* (Hoboken, NJ: John Wiley & Sons, 2005), 82.

13. Michiyo Nakamoto and David Wighton, "Citigroup Chief Stays Bullish on Buy-Outs," *Financial Times*, July 9, 2007.

14. As quoted in Kindleberger and Aliber, *Manias, Panics, and Crashes*, 47.

15. Robert Solow, Foreword to Kindleberger and Aliber's *Manias, Panics, and Crashes*, 2011 edition.

16. Ibid., 10.

17. Ibid., 11.

18. Securities Industry and Financial Markets Association (SIFMA), January 12, 2015, http://www.sifma.org/research/statistics.aspx.

19. Walter Bagehot, *Lombard Street: A Description of the Money Market*, 1873; reprinted by CreateSpace Independent Publishing Platform (2013), 21.

20. As quoted in Kindleberger and Aliber, *Manias, Panics, and Crashes*, 205.

21. "Rick Santelli and the 'Rant of the Year,'" https://www.youtube.com/watch?v=bEZB4taSEoA.

22. "The Chicago Fire," Chicago Historical Society, http://www.chicagohs.org/history/fire.html.

23. "The Slumps that Shaped Modern Finance," *Economist*, April 12, 2014.

Chapter 5: Central Banking

1. "The Role of Monetary Policy," *American Economic Review* 58, no. 1 (March 1968), 13.

2. William Poole, "President's Message: Volcker's Handling of the Great Inflation Taught Us Much," Federal Reserve Bank of St. Louis, January 2005, http://www.stlouisfed.org/publications/regional-economist/january-2005/volckers-handling-of-the-great-inflation-taught-us-much.

3. Poole, "President's Message."

4. "Feeling Down," *Economist*, February 21, 2015.

5. Kenneth Silber, "The Fed and Its Enemies," *Research Magazine*, February 1, 2010.

6. "Bin Ladin's Bookshelf," Office of the Director of National Ingellience, http://www.dni.gov/index.php/resources/bin-laden-bookshelf?start=3.

7. Jon Hilsenrath, Damian Paletta, and Aaron Lucchetti, "Goldman, Morgan Scrap Wall Street Model, Become Banks in Bid to Ride Out Crisis," *Wall Street Journal*, September 22, 2008.

8. "Monetary Policy," European National Bank, https://www.ecb.europa.eu/mopo/html/index.en.html.

9. "Inflation," Reserve Bank of New Zealand, http://www.rbnz.govt.nz/monetary_policy/inflation/.

10. Federal Open Market Committee (see "Greenbooks," "Bluebooks"), http://www.federalreserve.gov/monetarypolicy/fomc_historical.htm.

11. Paul Volcker, interview with author, May 2, 2011.

12. Robert M. Solow, "We'd Better Watch Out," *New York Times*, July 12, 1987.

13. Tyler Cowen, "The Age of the Shadow Bank Run," *New York Times*, March 24, 2012.

14. "Weekly National Rates and Rate Caps," FDIC, https://www.fdic.gov/regulations/resources/rates/.

15. James R. Barth, Gerard Caprio, and Ross Levine, "Bank Regulation and Supervision in 180 Countries from 1999 to 2011," Social Science Research Network, January 19, 2013, http://dx.doi.org/10.2139/ssrn.2203516.

16. Julia Maues, Federal Reserve Bank of St. Louis, "Banking Act of 1933, Commonly Called Glass-Steagall," Federal Reserve History, http://www.federalreservehistory.org/Events/DetailView/25.

17. Ryan Tracy and Victoria McGrane, "Big Banks Pass First Fed Test," *Wall Street Journal*, March 6, 2015.

18. "Financial Stability Oversight Council," U.S. Department of the Treasury, http://www.treasury.gov/initiatives/fsoc/about/Pages/default.aspx.

19. "2014 Update of List of Global Systemically Important Banks (G-SIBs)," Financial Stability Board, November 6, 2014, http://www.financialstabilityboard.org/wp-content/uploads/r_141106b.pdf.

20. Paul Volcker, interview with author, May 2, 2011.

21. Gerald P. O'Driscoll, Jr. "Debunking the Myths about Central Banks," *Wall Street Journal*, February 27, 2013.

22. Paul Volcker, interview with author, May 2, 2011.

23. "The Grey Man's Burden," *Economist*, December 1, 2012.

24. Ibid.

Chapter 6: Exchange Rates and the Global Financial System

1. Francesco Guerrera, "Currency War Has Started," *Wall Street Journal*, February 5, 2013.

2. Thomas Erdbrink, "Money Traders Fret Over Possible U.S.–Iran Pact," *New York Times*, November 20, 2013.

3. Thomas Erdbrink and Rick Gladstone, "Violence and Protest in Iran as Currency Drops in Value," *New York Times*, October 3, 2012.

4. See http://databank.worldbank.org/data/download/GNIPC.pdf.

5. David Keohane, "All Currency War, All the Time," Alphaville, *Financial Times*, February 5, 2015, http://ftalphaville.ft.com/2015/02/05/2111521/all-currency-war-all-the-time/.

6. Hiroko Tabuchi, "Japan Counted on Cheap Yen. Oops: Exchange Rate Hurts

Toyota, Giving Rivals a Chance to Leapfrog It," *New York Times*, September 3, 2010.

7. Sam Ro, "Boeing's 787 Dreamliner Is Made of Parts from All Over the World," *Business Insider*, October 10, 2013, http://www.businessinsider.com/boeing-787-dreamliner-structure-suppliers-2013-10.

8. "Misleading Misalignments," *Economist*, June 23, 2007.

9. T. Ashby McCown, Patricia Pollard, and John Weeks, "Equilibrium Exchange Rate Models and Misalignments," Occasional Paper No. 7, Office of International Affairs, Department of the Treasury, March 2007.

10. Christina Romer, "Needed: Plain Talk About the Dollar," *New York Times*, May 22, 2011.

11. "Race to the Bottom," *Economist*, March 4, 2010.

12. Tom Lauricella and John Lyons, "Currency Wars: A Fight to Be Weaker," *Wall Street Journal*, September 29, 2010.

13. "War Games," *Economist*, January 19, 2013.

14. Barry Eichengreen, "Competitive Devaluation to the Rescue," *Guardian*, March 18, 2009.

15. "Resources Boomerang," *Economist*, April 20, 2013.

16. "Too Strong for Comfort," *Economist*, September 3, 2011.

17. Paul Krugman, "Misguided Monetary Mentalities," *New York Times*, October 12, 2009.

18. Norman Tebbit, "Black Wednesday? I think of the glorious day we left the ERM as Bright Wednesday," *Telegraph*, September 13, 2012.

19. Stanley Fischer, "Ecuador and the IMF," address at the Hoover Institution Conference on Currency Unions," Palo Alto, California, May 19, 2000, https://www.imf.org/external/np/speeches/2000/051900.htm.

20. "El Salvador Learns to Love the Greenback," *Economist*, September 26, 2002.

21. "What Is the Euro Area?" Economic and Financial Affairs, European Commission, http://ec.europa.eu/economy_finance/euro/adoption/euro_area/index_en.htm.

22. N. Gregory Mankiw, "The Trilemma of International Finance," *New York Times*, July 9, 2010.

23. James Pearson, "Insight: Won for the Money: North Korea Experiments with Exchange Rates," Reuters, November 3, 2013.

24. Mankiw, "The Trilemma of International Finance."

25. "The Reformation," *Economist*, April 7, 2011.

26. Kartik Goyal, "Rajan Warns of Policy Breakdowns as Emerging Markets Fall," Bloomberg News, January 31, 2014.

27. "Forty Years On," *Economist*, August 13, 2011.

28. "Trial of Strength," *Economist*, September 25, 2010.

Chapter 7: Gold

1. Robert A. Mundell, "A Reconsideration of the Twentieth Century," Nobel Prize lecture, Stockholm University, December 8, 1999.

2. Christopher Klein, "Winston Churchill's World War Disaster, History.com, May 21, 2014, http://www.history.com/news/winston-churchills-world-war-disaster.

3. Peter L. Bernstein, *The Power of Gold: History of an Obsession* (Hoboken, NJ: John Wiley & Sons, 2012).

4. James Ashley Morrison, "The 1925 Return to Gold: Keynes and Mr Churchill's Economic Crisis," paper presented at the 2009 meeting of the American Political Science Association. Also see James Ashley Morrison, "Shocking Intellectual Austerity: The Role of Ideas in the Demise of the Gold Standard," *International Organization* 70, Winter 2016.

5. John Maynard Keynes, *Essays in Persuasion* (London: Macmillan, 1932), 201.

6. Bernstein, *The Power of Gold*.

7. Ibid.

8. Ibid.

9. Mundell, "A Reconsideration of the Twentieth Century."

10. New River Media Interview with Milton Friedman, PBS.org, http://www.pbs.org/fmc/interviews/friedman.htm.

11. "Gold Standard," IGM Forum, University of Chicago Booth School of Business, January 12, 2012, http://www.igmchicago.org/igm-economic-experts-panel/poll-results?SurveyID=SV_cw1nNUYOXSAKwrq.

12. Donald T. Regan et al., "Report to the Congress of the Commission on the Role of Gold in the Domestic and International Monetary Systems," report of the Gold Commission, vol. 1, March 1982.

13. Ron Paul, *End the Fed* (New York: Grand Central Publishing, 2009), 4.

14. "We Believe in America," 2012 Republican Platform, https://cdn.gop.com/docs/2012GOPPlatform.pdf.

15. "Full of Holes," *Economist*, November 29, 2014.

16. http://www.bradford-delong.com/why-not-the-gold-standard-talking-points-on-the-likely-consequences-of-re-establishment-of-a-gold-st.html

17. "Gold," U.S. Geological Survey, Mineral Commodity Summaries, February 2014, http://minerals.usgs.gov/minerals/pubs/commodity/gold/mcs-2014-gold.pdf.

18. Paul, *End the Fed*, 117.

19. Bernstein, *The Power of Gold*.

20. "FAQs: Gold and Silver," Federal Reserve Bank of Richmond, https://www.richmondfed.org/faqs/gold_silver/.

21. James Hookway, "Malaysian Muslims Go for Gold, But It's Hard to Make Change," *Wall Street Journal*, September 2, 2010.

22. Matthew O'Brien, "Why the Gold Standard Is the World's Worst Economic Idea, in 2 Charts," *Atlantic*, August 26, 2012.

23. Edgar L. Feige, "New Estimates of U.S. Currency Abroad, the Domestic Money Supply and the Unreported Economy," Munich Personal RePEc Archive, September 2011, https://mpra.ub.uni-muenchen.de/34778/1/MPRA_paper_34778.pdf.

24. Edgar Feige, e-mail to author, April 21, 2015.

25. Jason Zweig, "Is Gold Cheap? Who Knows? But Gold-Mining Stocks Are," *Wall Street Journal*, September 17, 2011.

26. Matt DiLlallo, "Why Warren Buffett Hates Gold," *The Motley Fool*, September 13, 2014, http://www.fool.com/investing/general/2014/09/13/why-warren-buffett-hates-gold.aspx.

27. Barry Eichengreen, *Golden Fetters: The Gold Standard and the Great Depression 1919–1939* (New York: Oxford University Press, 1992).

28. Martin Wolf, "Only the Ignorant Live in Fear of Hyperinflation," *Financial Times*, April 10, 2014.

Chapter 8: A Quick Tour of American Monetary History

1. "Bryan's 'Cross of Gold' Speech: Mesmerizing the Masses," History Matters, American Social History Project, http://historymatters.gmu.edu/d/5354/.

2. "Dutch New York," Thirteen: WNET New York Public Media, September 1, 2009, http://www.thirteen.org/dutchny/interactives/manhattan-island/.

3. https://historymyths.wordpress.com/2015/04/12/revisited-myth-45-the-dutch-bought-manhattan-for-24-worth-of-beads/.

4. Matt Soniak, "Was Manhattan Really Bought for $24," Mental Floss, October 2, 2012, http://mentalfloss.com/article/12657/was-manhattan-really-bought-24.

5. Gilbert W. Hagerty, *Wampum, War, and Trade Goods, West of the Hudson* (Interlaken, NY: Heart of the Lakes Publishing, 1985), 110.

6. Jason Goodwin, *Greenback: The Almighty Dollar and the Invention of America* (New York: Henry Holt, 2003), 25.

7. Glyn Davies, *A History of Money: From Ancient Times to the Present Day* (Cardiff: University of Wales Press, 1994), 39.

8. Ibid., 456–57.

9. Alvin Rabushka, "The Colonial Roots of American Taxation, 1607–1700," *Policy Review*, August 1, 2002, Hoover Institution, http://www.hoover.org/research/colonial-roots-american-taxation-1607-1700.

10. Ibid.

11. Davies, *A History of Money*, 461.

12. David A. Copeland, *A History of Money: From Ancient Times to the Present Day* (Cardiff: University of Wales Press, 1994), 146

13. Copeland, *A History of Money*, 149.

14. Davies, *A History of Money*, 462.

15. Ibid.

16. Jack P. Greene and Richard M. Jellison, "The Currency Act of 1764 in Imperial-Colonial Relations, 1764–1776," *William and Mary Quarterly* 18, no. 4 (October 1961), 518.

17. Eric P. Newman, *The Early Paper Money of America* (Racine, WI: Whitman Publishing Company, 1967), 12.

18. H. W. Brands, *Greenback Planet: How the Dollar Conquered the World and Threatened Civilization as We Know It* (Austin: University of Texas Press, 2011), 4.

19. Ben Baack, "Forging a Nation State: The Continental Congress and the Financing of the War of American Independence," *Economic History Review* 54, no. 4: 641.

20. Ibid., 643.

21. Kenneth Scott, *Counterfeiting in Colonial America* (New York: Oxford University Press, 1957), 253.

22. Ibid., 254.

23. Ibid., 262.

24. Baack, "Forging a Nation State," 654.

25. "Coinage Clause Law and Legal Definition," USLegal, http://definitions.uslegal.com/c/coinage-clause/.

26. Brands, *Greenback Planet*, 4.

27. "About the United States Mint," United States Mint, http://usmint.com/about_the_mint/.

28. Angela Redish, *Bimetallism: An Economic and Historical Analysis* (Cambridge, UK: Cambridge University Press, 2000), 214.

29. Brands, *Greenback Planet*, 5.

30. Ibid.

31. Ron Paul, *End the Fed* (New York: Grand Central Publishing, 2009), 11.

32. Jerry Markham, *A Financial History of the United States* (Armonk, NY: M.E. Sharpe, 2002), 90.

33. "The First Bank of the United States," American History: From Revolution to Reconstruction, University of Groningen, http://www.let.rug.nl/usa/essays/general/a-brief-history-of-central-banking/the-first-bank-of-the-united-states-%281791-1811%29.php.

34. Brands, *Greenback Planet*, 6–7.

35. "The Second Bank of the United States," Federal Reserve Bank of Philadelphia, December 2010, https://www.philadelphiafed.org/publications/economic-education/second-bank.pdf.

36. Gary May, *John Tyler* (New York: Times Books, 2008), 42–43.

37. "The Second Bank of the United States," Federal Reserve Bank of Philadelphia.

38. James Roger Sharp, *The Jacksonians Versus the Banks: Politics in the States After the Panic of 1837* (New York: Columbia University Press, 1970), 27.

39. Major L. Wilson, *The Presidency of Martin Van Buren* (Lawrence: University of Kansas Press, 1984), 47.

40. Ibid., 123.

41. Jessica M. Lepler, *The Many Panics of 1837: People, Politics, and the Creation of a Transatlantic Financial Crisis* (New York: Cambridge University Press, 2013), 232.

42. Davies, *A History of Money*, 484.

43. "The Second Bank of the United States," Federal Reserve Bank of Philadelphia.

44. Davies, *A History of Money*, 484.

45. Ibid., 487.

46. Brands, *Greenback Planet*, 12.

47. Ibid., 1.

48. Richard S. Grossman, "U.S. Banking History, Civil War to World War II," EH.net Encyclopedia, ed. Robert Whaples, March 16, 2008, http://eh.net/encyclopedia/us-banking-history-civil-war-to-world-war-ii/.

49. Ibid.

50. Ibid.

51. "The State and National Banking Eras," Federal Reserve Bank of Philadelphia, December 2011, 9, https://www.philadelphiafed.org/-/media/publications/economic-education/state-and-national-banking-eras.pdf.

52. Davies, *A History of Money*, 489.

53. "The State and National Banking Eras," Federal Reserve Bank of Philadelphia, 12.

54. Davies, *A History of Money*, 492.

55. Ibid., 494–95.

56. Hal R. Williams, *Realigning America: McKinley, Bryan, and the Remarkable Election of 1896* (Lawrence: University of Kansas Press, 2010), 36.

57. Ibid., 36–37.

58. Ibid., ix.

59. Ibid., 85.

60. Redish, *Bimetallism*, 237.

61. Andrew Glass, "President McKinley Signs Gold Standard Act, March 14, 1900," *Politico*, March 14, 2013, http://www.politico.com/story/2013/03/this-day-in-politics-88821.html; and Davies, *A History of Money*, 497.

62. Jon Moen, "Panic of 1907," EH.net Encyclopedia, ed. Robert Whaples, August 14, 2001, http://eh.net/encyclopedia/the-panic-of-1907/.

63. Robert F. Bruner and Sean D. Carr, *The Panic of 1907: Lessons Learned from the Market's Perfect Storm* (Hoboken, NJ: John Wiley & Sons, 2007), 79.

64. Ibid., 100–103.

65. Ron Chernow, *Titan: The Life of John D. Rockefeller, Sr.* (New York: Random House, 1998), 543.

66. Lawrence J. Broz, *The International Origins of the Federal Reserve System* (Ithaca, NY: Cornell University Press, 1997), xi; and Ben S. Bernanke, *The Federal Reserve and the Financial Crisis* (Princeton, NJ: Princeton University Press, 2013), 5.

67. Davies, *A History of Money*, 502.

68. Brands, *Greenback Planet*, 32–33.

69. Bernanke, *The Federal Reserve and the Financial Crisis*, 14.

70. Roger W. Ferguson, Jr., "The Evolution of Central Banking in the United States," speech, European Central Bank, Frankfurt, Germany, April 27, 2005.

71. Davies, *A History of Money*, 509.

72. Bernanke, *The Federal Reserve and the Financial Crisis*, 22.

73. Davies, *A History of Money*, 509.

74. Sandra Kollen Ghizoni, Federal Reserve Bank of Atlanta, "Establishment of the Bretton Woods System," Federal Reserve History, http://www.federalreservehistory.org/Events/DetailView/28.

75. Brands, *Greenback Planet*, 63–64.

76. Ibid., 64.

77. Ibid.

78. Ghizoni, "Establishment of the Bretton Woods System."

79. Barry Eichengreen, *Exorbitant Privilege: The Rise and Fall of the Dollar and the Future of the International Monetary System* (New York: Oxford University Press, 2011), 3.

80. Brands, *Greenback Planet*, 68–69.

81. William L. Silber, *Volcker: The Triumph of Persistence* (New York: Bloomsbury Press, 2012), 43.

82. Brands, *Greenback Planet*, 75.

83. Silber, *Volcker*, 43.

84. Brands, *Greenback Planet*, 77.

85. Ibid.

86. Sandra Kollen Ghizoni, Federal Reserve Bank of Atlanta, "Nixon Ends Convertibility of U.S. Dollars to Gold and Announces Wage/Price Controls," Federal Reserve History, November 22, 2013, http://www.federalreservehistory.org/Events/DetailView/33.

87. Silber, *Volcker*, 91.

88. Brands, *Greenback Planet*, 83.

89. Allan H. Meltzer, "Inflation Nation," *New York Times*, May 3, 2009.

90. Bernanke, *The Federal Reserve and the Financial Crisis*, 33.

91. Ibid., 32–33.

92. "Index by President," United States Misery Index, http://www.miseryindex.us/indexbyPresident.aspx.

93. Alex Nikolsko-Rzhevskyy and David H. Papell, "Taylor Rules and the Great Inflation," Journal of Macroeconomics 34, no. 4 (2012).

94. Meltzer, "Inflation Nation."

95. Bernanke, *The Federal Reserve and the Financial Crisis*, 32–34.

96. Ibid., 35.

97. Ibid., 38.

98. Judd Gregg, interview with author, April 29, 2015.

Chapter 9: 1929 and 2008

1. Peter Temin, *Lessons from the Great Depression* (Cambridge, MA: MIT Press, 1991), 12.

2. Ben S. Bernanke, "Asset Price 'Bubbles' and Monetary Policy: Remarks Before the New York Chapter of the National Association for Business Economics," New York, October 15, 2002.

3. Financial Crisis Inquiry Commission, *The Financial Crisis Inquiry Report* (New York: PublicAffairs, 2011).

4. Ben S. Bernanke, *Essays on the Great Depression* (Princeton, NJ: Princeton University Press, 2000), xi.

5. Ben S. Bernanke, "Remarks at the Conference to Honor Milton Friedman," University of Chicago, November 8, 2002.

6. "Credit and Liquidity Programs and the Balance Sheet," Federal Reserve, http://www.federalreserve.gov/monetarypolicy/bst_recenttrends.htm.

7. Ben S. Bernanke *The Federal Reserve and the Financial Crisis* (Princeton, NJ: Princeton University Press, 2013), 17.

8. "Dow Jones Industrial Averages: All Time Largest One Day Gains and Losses," Market Data Center, *Wall Street Journal*, http://online.wsj.com/mdc/public/page/2_3047-djia_alltime.html.

9. "The Great Depression: 48b. Sinking Deeper and Deeper: 1929–33," U.S. History, Independence Hall Association in Philadelphia, http://www.ushistory.org/us/48b.asp.

10. Gary Richardson, Alejandro Komai, Michael Gou, and Daniel Park, "Stock Market Crash of 1929," Federal Reserve History, http://www.federalreservehistory.org/Events/DetailView/74.

11. Douglas A. Irwin, "Did France Cause the Great Depression?" National Bureau of Economic Research, Working Paper 16350, September 2010.

12. "Bin Ladin's Bookshelf," Office of the Director of National Ingelligence, http://www.dni.gov/index.php/resources/bin-laden-bookshelf?start=3.

13. Milton Friedman and Anna Jacobson Schwartz, *The Great Contraction 1929–1933* (Princeton, NJ: Princeton University Press, 2007), 34.

14. Ibid., 40.

15. Robert Jabaily, Federal Reserve Bank of Boston, "Bank Holiday of 1933," Federal Reserve History, http://www.federalreservehistory.org/Events/DetailView/22.

16. William L. Silber, "Why Did FDR's Bank Holiday Succeed?" FRBNY Economic Policy Review, July 2009, http://www.newyorkfed.org/research/epr/09v15n1/0907silb.pdf.

17. Stephanie Simon, "Cash-Strapped California's IOUs: Just the Latest Sub for Dollars," Wall Street Journal, July 25, 2009.

18. Bill Ganzel, "Bank Failures," Farming in the 1930s, Wessels Living History Farm, 2003, http://www.livinghistoryfarm.org/farminginthe30s/money_08.html.

19. I am indebted to Doug Irwin, whom I heard make this point on the EconTalk podcast (EconTalk.org), October 11, 2010.

20. Friedman and Schwartz, The Great Contraction, ix.

21. Bernanke, The Federal Reserve and the Financial Crisis, 23.

22. John Kenneth Galbraith, as quoted in Thomas E. Hall and J. David Ferguson, The Great Depression: An International Disaster of Perverse Economic Policies (Ann Arbor: University of Michigan Press, 1998), 110.

23. Bernanke, The Federal Reserve and the Financial Crisis, 20.

24. Temin, Lessons from the Great Depression, 34.

25. Financial Crisis Inquiry Commission, The Financial Crisis Inquiry Report, 156.

26. Ibid., 5.

27. Kevin Warsh, "Remarks at the Council of Institutional Investors 2009 Spring Meeting," Washington, DC, April 6, 2009.

28. Financial Crisis Inquiry Commission, The Financial Crisis Inquiry Report, 10.

29. Kate Pickert, "A Brief History of Fannie Mae and Freddie Mac," Time, July 14, 2008.

30. Matthew Karnitschnig, Deborah Solomon, Liam Pleven, and Jon E. Hilsenrath, "U.S. to Take Over AIG in $85 Billion Bailout; Central Banks Inject Cash as Credit Dries Up," Wall Street Journal, September 16, 2008.

31. Financial Crisis Inquiry Commission, The Financial Crisis Inquiry Report, 8.

32. Bernanke, The Federal Reserve and the Financial Crisis, 71–72.

33. Gary Gorton, "Questions and Answers about the Financial Crisis," testimony prepared for the U.S. Financial Crisis Inquiry Commission, February 20, 2010.

34. Gorton, "Questions and Answers about the Financial Crisis," 12–13.

35. Financial Crisis Inquiry Commission, The Financial Crisis Inquiry Report, 136.

36. Ibid., xvii–xxv.

37. Bernanke, The Federal Reserve and the Financial Crisis, 97.

38. Ibid., 99.

39. Ibid., 86.

40. Roger Lowenstein, "The Villain," Atlantic, April 2012.

41. Bernanke, The Federal Reserve and the Financial Crisis, 104–5.

42. "Early Retirement," *Economist*, November 1, 2014.

43. Financial Crisis Inquiry Commission, *The Financial Crisis Inquiry Report*, xvii.

44. Ibid., xviii.

45. Paul Krugman, "Falling Wage Syndrome," *New York Times*, May 4, 2009.

46. Allan H. Meltzer, "Inflation Nation," *New York Times*, May 4, 2009.

47. Lowenstein, "The Villain."

48. Adam S. Posen, "Central Bankers: Stop Dithering. Do Something," *New York Times*, November 20, 2011.

49. "Open Letter to Ben Bernanke," Real Time Economics, *Wall Street Journal*, November 15, 2010, http://blogs.wsj.com/economics/2010/11/15/open-letter-to-ben-bernanke/.

50. "Reserve Balances with Federal Reserve Banks," Economic Research, Federal Reserve Bank of St. Louis, https://research.stlouisfed.org/fred2/series/WRESBAL/.

Chapter 10: Japan

1. Kenneth Rogoff, "Japan's Slow-Motion Crisis," Project Syndicate, March 2, 2010.

2. Jacob M. Schlesinger, "Bank of Japan Offers Lessons in Easing Deflation," *Wall Street Journal*, November 9, 2014.

3. Taimur Baig, "Understanding the Costs of Deflation in the Japanese Context," IMF Working Paper, WP/03/215, Asia and Pacific Department, November 2003.

4. Ben S. Bernanke, "Deflation: Making Sure 'It' Doesn't Happen Here," Remarks Before the National Economists Club, Washington, DC, November 21, 2002.

5. Jon Hilsenrath and Megumi Fujikawa, "Japan's Bernanke Hits Out at His Critics in the West," *Wall Street Journal*, March 1, 2011.

6. Phred Dvorak and Eleanor Warnock, "Stagnant Japan Rolls Dice on New Era of Easy Money," *Wall Street Journal*, March 21, 2013.

7. Maurice Obstfeld, "Time of Troubles: The Yen and Japan's Economy, 1985–2008," NBER Working Paper 14816, March 2009, 5–6.

8. Ezra F. Vogel, *Japan as Number One: Lessons for America* (Cambridge, MA: Harvard University Press, 1979).

9. Robert J. Cole, "Japanese Buy New York Cachet with Deal for Rockefeller Center," *New York Times*, October 31, 1989.

10. Obstfeld, "Time of Troubles," 7.

11. Ibid.

12. Stephanie Strom, "Japanese Scrap $2 Billion Stake in Rockefeller," *New York Times*, September 12, 1995.

13. Obstfeld, "Time of Troubles," 7.

14. Charles Kindleberger and Robert Aliber, *Manias, Panics, and Crashes: A History of Financial Crises* (Hoboken, NJ: John Wiley & Sons, 2005), 5.
15. Anil K. Kashyap, "Zombie Lending in Japan: How Bankrupt Firms Stifle Economic Reform," Capital Ideas, University of Chicago Booth School of Business, September 2006.
16. Rogoff, "Japan's Slow-Motion Crisis."
17. Kashyap, "Zombie Lending in Japan."
18. Obstfeld, "Time of Troubles," 11.
19. Bernanke, "Deflation: Making Sure 'It' Doesn't Happen Here."
20. Baig, "Understanding the Costs of Deflation in the Japanese Context," 16.
21. Kenneth N. Kuttner and Adam S. Posen, "The Great Recession: Lessons for Macroeconomic Policy from Japan," Brookings Papers on Economic Activity, 2:2001, 99–100.
22. George A. Akerlof, William T. Dickens, and George L. Perry, "The Macroeconomics of Low Inflation," Brookings Papers on Economic Activity, 1:1996.
23. Baig, "Understanding the Costs of Deflation in the Japanese Context."
24. Farai Mutsaka and Peter Wonacott, "Zimbabwe to Overhaul Its Central Bank," *Wall Street Journal*, September 18–19, 2010.
25. "Transcript: Shirakawa on Japan's Economy," *Wall Street Journal*, March 1, 2011, http://www.wsj.com/articles/SB10001424052748704615504576172300556921580.
26. Paul Volcker, interview with author, May 2, 2011.
27. Kenneth Kuttner, "Monetary Policy During Japan's Great Recession: From Self-Induced Paralysis to Rooseveltian Resolve," PIIE Briefing 14-4, Peterson Institute for International Economics, December 2014, 71.
28. Hilsenrath and Fujikawa, "Japan's Bernanke Hits Out at His Critics in the West."
29. "The Battle for Japan," *Economist*, June 28, 2014.
30. Kuttner, "Monetary Policy During Japan's Great Recession."
31. James McBride and Beina Xu, "Abenomics and the Japanese Economy," CFR Backgrounders, Council on Foreign Relations, March 10, 2015, http://www.cfr.org/japan/abenomics-japanese-economy/p30383.
32. Dvorak and Warnock, "Stagnant Japan Rolls Dice on New Era of Easy Money."
33. Phred Dvorak and Eleanor Warnock, "Japan Central Bank Plan Meets Skepticism," *Wall Street Journal*, April 3, 2013.
34. McBride and Xu, "Abenomics and the Japanese Economy."
35. Adam S. Posen, "An American's Assessment of Abenomics at Mid-Term," PIIE Briefing 14-4, Peterson Institute for International Economics, December 2014.
36. Tatsuo Ito and Jacob M. Schlesinger, "Japan's Zero Inflation a Setback for Abenomics," *Wall Street Journal*, March 27, 2015, http://www.wsj.com/articles/japan-inflation-hits-zero-1427416851.

37. Ibid.

38. McBride and Xu, "Abenomics and the Japanese Economy."

39. "To Lose One Decade May Be Misfortune . . ." *Economist*, December 30, 2009.

40. "About That Debt," Free Exchange, *Economist*, November 18, 2014.

41. Paul Volcker, interview with author, May 2, 2011.

42. Bernanke, "Deflation: Making Sure 'It' Doesn't Happen Here."

43. Kenneth Kuttner, interview with author, June 1, 2015.

44. Hiroko Tabuchi, "Yen-Pinching Undercuts Japan's Push Against Years of Deflation," *New York Times*, March 10, 2014.

45. "Waging a New War," *Economist*, March 9, 2013.

46. Tabuchi, "Yen-Pinching Undercuts Japan's Push Against Years of Deflation."

47. "About That Debt," *Economist*.

48. Rogoff, "Japan's Slow-Motion Crisis."

Chapter 11: The Euro

1. Barry Eichengreen and Peter Temin, "Fetters of Gold and Paper," National Bureau of Economic Research, Working Paper 16202, July 2010.

2. Robert A. Mundell, "A Theory of Optimum Currency Areas," *American Economic Review* 51, no. 4 (September 1961), 657.

3. "Monetary Policy," European Central Bank, https://www.ecb.europa.eu/mopo/html/index.en.html.

4. "Use of the Euro," European Central Bank, https://www.ecb.europa.eu/euro/intro/html/index.en.html.

5. "On a Wing and a Prayer," *Economist*, December 2, 2010.

6. Paul Krugman, "Can Europe Be Saved?" *New York Times Magazine*, January 12, 2011.

7. Milton Friedman, "The Euro: Monetary Unity to Political Disunity," Project Syndicate, August 18, 1997.

8. Suzy Hansen, "A Finance Minister Fit for a Greek Tragedy?" *New York Times Magazine*, May 20, 2015.

9. Mundell, "A Theory of Optimum Currency Areas," 660.

10. Milton Friedman, *Essays in Positive Economics* (1953), as quoted in "Forty Years On," *Economist*, August 13, 2011.

11. Krugman, "Can Europe Be Saved?"

12. "The Nico and Angela Show," *Economist*, November 12, 2011.

13. Robert J. Barro and Xavier Sala-I-Martin, "Convergence across States and Regions," Brookings Papers on Economic Activity, 1:1991.

14. "Who Can Join and When?" Economic and Financial Affairs, European Commission, http://ec.europa.eu/economy_finance/euro/adoption/who_can_join/index_en.htm.

15. Krugman, "Can Europe Be Saved?"
16. Ibid.
17. Eichengreen and Temin, "Fetters of Gold and Paper."
18. "A Very Short History of the Crisis," *Economist*, November 12, 2011.
19. "Saving the Euro," *Economist*, November 18, 2010.
20. "The Cracks Spread and Widen," *Economist*, April 29, 2010.
21. "Acrópolis Now," *Economist*, April 29, 2010.
22. "That's All, Folks," *Economist*, November 12, 2011.
23. "Greece Takes Bailout, but Doubts for Region Persist," DealBook, *New York Times*, May 3, 2010, http://dealbook.nytimes.com/2010/05/03/greece-takes-bailout-but-doubts-for-region-persist/?_r=0.
24. "Destructive Creation," *Economist*, November 12, 2011.
25. "Casting a Spell," *Economist*, September 15, 2012.
26. "On a Wing and a Prayer," *Economist*.
27. "The Nico and Angela Show," *Economist*.
28. Hansen, "A Finance Minister Fit for a Greek Tragedy?"
29. "The World's Biggest Economic Problem," *Economist*, October 25, 2014.
30. Patricia Kowsmann and Marcus Walker, "Idea of Euro Exit Finds Currency in Portugal," *Wall Street Journal*, May 28, 2013.
31. Krugman, "Can Europe Be Saved?"
32. Charles Forelle, "In European Crisis, Iceland Emerges as an Island of Recovery," *Wall Street Journal*, May 21, 2012.
33. Hansen, "A Finance Minister Fit for a Greek Tragedy?"
34. Karl Stagno Navarra, Ben Sills, and Marcus Bensasson, "IMF Considers Greece Its Most Unhelpful Client Ever," *Bloomberg Business*, March 18, 2015.
35. "Europe on the Rack," *Economist*, June 30, 2012.
36. Krugman, "Can Europe Be Saved?"

Chapter 12: The United States and China

1. Keith Richburg, "For U.S., China, Uneasiness about Economic Codependency," *Washington Post*, November 16, 2009.
2. Helen Cooper, Michael Wines, and David Sanger, "China's Role as Lender Alters Obama's Visit," *New York Times*, November 15, 2009.
3. "Major Foreign Holders of Treasury Securities," Department of the Treasury/Federal Reserve Board, October 16, 2015, http://www.treasury.gov/ticdata/Publish/mfh.txt.
4. Richburg, "For U.S., China, Uneasiness about Economic Codependency."
5. Mark Landler, "Seeing Its Own Money at Risk, China Rails at U.S.," *New York Times*, October 15, 2013.
6. "Distribution of Chinese Exports in 2014, by Trade Partner," Statista, http://www.statista.com/statistics/270326/main-export-partners-for-china/.

7. David Leonhardt, "The China Puzzle," *New York Times Magazine*, May 13, 2009.

8. James Fallows, "The $1.4 Trillion Question," *Atlantic*, January/February 2008.

9. Ibid.

10. Ibid.

11. Craig K. Elwell, "Saving Rates in the United States: Calculation and Comparison," Congressional Research Service, September 14, 2010.

12. "Country Comparison: GDP Per Capita (PPP)," CIA World Factbook, https://www.cia.gov/library/publications/the-world-factbook/rankorder/2004rank.html.

13. Fallows, "The $1.4 Trillion Question."

14. Arthur R. Kroeber, "The Renminbi: The Political Economy of a Currency," *Foreign Policy*, September 7, 2011.

15. "IMF to China: Plaza Accord Didn't Sink Japan," *Wall Street Journal*, April 11, 2011.

16. Damian Paletta and John W. Miller, "China, U.S. Square Off over Yuan," *Wall Street Journal*, October 7, 2010.

17. Arthur Kroeber, "China's Currency Policy Explained," Up Front, Brookings Institution, September 7, 2011.

18. Kroeber, "The Renminbi: The Political Economy of a Currency."

19. Siobhan Hughes and William Mauldin, "Senate Rejects Manipulation Rules in Trade Bill," *Wall Street Journal*, May 23–24, 2015.

20. "An Indigestible Problem," *Economist*, October 16, 2010.

21. Steven Dunaway and Xiangming Li, "Estimating China's 'Equilibrium' Real Exchange Rate," IMF Working Paper, October 2005.

22. David Leonhardt, "The China Puzzle."

23. "Currency Manipulation," IGM Forum, University of Chicago Booth School of Business, June 16, 2015, http://www.igmchicago.org/igm-economic-experts-panel/poll-results?SurveyID=SV_bCrHQToXMqPfLzD.

24. Ibid.

25. "China–US Trade," IGM Forum, University of Chicago Booth School of Business, June 19, 2012, http://www.igmchicago.org/igm-economic-experts-panel/poll-results?SurveyID=SV_003w6LBGnkOfDuI.

26. C. Fred Bergsten and Joseph E. Gagnon, "Currency Manipulation, the US Economy, and the Global Economic Order," Peterson Institute for International Economics, Policy Brief, December 2012.

27. José Manuel Campa and Linda S. Goldberg, "Employment Versus Wage Adjustment and the U.S. Dollar," *Review of Economics and Statistics* 83, no. 3 (August 2001).

28. Edward P. Lazear, "Chinese 'Currency Manipulation' Is Not the Problem," *Wall Street Journal*, January 8, 2013.

29. David Leonhardt, "The China Puzzle."

30. Fallows, "The $1.4 Trillion Question."

31. "Feeling Valued," *Economist*, May 30, 2015.

32. Mark Magnier and William Kazer, "IMF Says Yuan Is Now Fairly Valued," *Wall Street Journal*, May 27, 2015.

33. "China's Yuan Currency 'No Longer Undervalued': IMF," *Daily Mail*, May 26, 2015.

34. Henry M. Paulson, Jr., and Robert E. Rubin, "The Blame Trap," *Atlantic*, June 2015.

35. Damian Paletta and John W. Miller, "China, U.S. Square Off over Yuan," *Wall Street Journal*, October 7, 2010.

36. Paulson and Rubin, "The Blame Trap."

Chapter 13: The Future of Money

1. Milton Friedman, *Money Mischief: Episodes in Monetary History* (New York: Harcourt Brace & Company, 1994), xii.

2. Joshua Davis, "The Crypto-Currency," *New Yorker*, October 10, 2011.

3. Michael Bryan, "Island Money," Federal Reserve Bank of Cleveland Commentary, February 1, 2004.

4. "Gold Gets Dug Out of the Ground," Quote Investigator, May 25, 2013, http://quoteinvestigator.com/2013/05/25/bury-gold/.

5. Narayana R. Kocherlakota, "Money Is Memory," Federal Reserve Bank of Minneapolis, Research Department Staff Report 218, October 1996.

6. Narayana R. Kocherlakota, "The Technological Role of Fiat Money," *Quarterly Review*, Federal Reserve Bank of Minneapolis, Summer 1998.

7. Noam Cohen, "Bubble or No, This Virtual Currency Is a Lot of Coin in Any Realm," *New York Times*, April 8, 2013.

8. Robin Sidel, "Race to Mine Bitcoin Gathers Steam," *Wall Street Journal*, November 6, 2013.

9. Nathaniel Popper, "Into the Bitcoin Mines," *New York Times*, December 22, 2013.

10. Joshua Davis, "The Crypto-Currency."

11. François R. Velde, "Bitcoin: A Primer," *Chicago Fed Letter*, Number 317, December 2013.

12. Joe Light, "Bbqcoin? Virtual Money Is Smoking," *Wall Street Journal*, November 21, 2013.

13. John Biggs, "Happy Bitcoin Pizza Day," Tech Crunch, May 22, 2015, http://techcrunch.com/2015/05/22/happy-bitcoin-pizza-day/.

14. Robin Sidel, Michael J. Casey, and Christopher M. Matthews, "Bitcoin's Boosters Struggle to Shore Up Confidence," *Wall Street Journal*, April 4, 2014.

15. Sydney Ember, "Bitcoin's Price Falls 12%, to Lowest Value Since May," *New York Times*, August 18, 2014.

16. Candace Jackson, "Sold! To the Bidder with Bitcoin," *Wall Street Journal*, August 9–10, 2014.

17. Steve Forbes, "Bitcoin: Whatever It Is, It's Not Money!" *Forbes*, April 16, 2013.

18. Candace Jackson, "Sold! To the Bidder with Bitcoin."

19. Nathaniel Popper, "Bitcoin Figure Is Accused of Conspiring to Launder Money," *New York Times*, January 27, 2014.

20. "Bitcoin Under Pressure," *Economist*, November 30, 2013; and "The Bitcoin Bubble," *Economist*, November 30, 2013.

21. Sydney Ember, "Bitcoin's Price Falls 12%, to Lowest Value Since May," *New York Times*, August 18, 2014.

22. "Bitcoin Under Pressure," *Economist*.

23. Timothy B. Lee, "12 Questions about Bitcoin You Were Too Embarrassed to Ask," *Washington Post*, November 19, 2013.

24. Nicole Perlroth, "To Instill Love of Bitcoin, Backers Work to Make It Safe," *New York Times*, April 2, 2015.

25. "Less Coin to Purloin," *Economist*, April 5, 2014.

26. "Mt Gone," *Economist*, February 25, 2014.

27. "Bitconned," *Economist*, March 5, 2014.

28. Nathaniel Popper, "Can Bitcoin Conquer Argentina?" *New York Times Magazine*, April 29, 2015.

29. "Bitcoin Buccaneers," *Economist*, January 17, 2015.

30. "Tales from the Crypt," *Economist*, February 4, 2015.

31. Nathaniel Popper, "Bitcoin Figure Is Accused of Conspiring to Launder Money."

32. Sidel, Casey, and Matthews, "Bitcoin's Boosters Struggle to Shore Up Confidence"; and Nicole Perlroth, "To Instill Love of Bitcoin, Backers Work to Make It Safe."

33. Ben Bernanke, interview with author, July 6, 2015.

34. François R. Velde, "Bitcoin: A Primer."

35. "Mining Digital Gold," *Economist*, April 13, 2013.

36. Matina Stevis and Patrick McGroarty, "Africa's Top Bankers: Mobile Phones," *Wall Street Journal*, August 16–17, 2014.

37. Chad Bray and Reuben Kyama, "Tap to Pay (Not So Much in the U.S.)," *New York Times*, April 2, 2014.

38. Joshua Davis, "The Crypto-Currency."

Chapter 14: Doing Central Banking Better

1. Olivier Blanchard, Giovanni Dell'Ariccia, and Paolo Mauro, "Rethinking Macroeconomic Policy," IMF Staff Position Note, International Monetary Fund, February 12, 2010.

2. "Ceremony Commemorating the Centennial of the Federal Reserve Act," Wash-

ington, DC, December 16, 2013, http://www.federalreserve.gov/newsevents/press/other/20131216-centennial-commemoration-transcript.pdf.

3. John Ydstie, "Bernanke's Fed Legacy: A Tenure Full of Tough Decisions," NPR, January 27, 2014.

4. "The Recession of 2007–2009," BLS Spotlight on Statistics, U.S. Bureau of Labor Statistics, February 2012, http://www.bls.gov/spotlight/2012/recession/pdf/recession_bls_spotlight.pdf.

5. Alistair Darling, interview with David Blanchflower, CNBC Squawk Box, June 4, 2009.

6. David Blanchflower, interview with author, September 10, 2015.

7. Frederic S. Mishkin, "Politicians Are Threatening the Fed's Independence," *New York Times*, September 29, 2011.

8. Alice M. Rivlin, "Preserving the Independence of the Federal Reserve," testimony before the Subcommittee on Oversight and Investigations, House Committee on Financial Services, July 14, 2015.

9. "The Grey Man's Burden," *Economist*, December 1, 2012.

10. Ibid.

11. Ibid.

12. Binyamin Appelbaum, "Bernanke, As Professor, Tries to Buff Fed's Image," *New York Times*, March 21, 2012.

13. Ben S. Bernanke, "The Federal Reserve: Looking Back, Looking Forward," Remarks at the Annual Meeting of the American Economic Association, January 3, 2014.

14. Barry Eichengreen et al., "Rethinking Central Banking," Committee on International Economic Policy and Reform, Brookings Institution, September 2011.

15. "All Federal Reserve Banks – Total Assets, Eliminations from Consolidation," Economic Research, Federal Reserve Bank of St. Louis, https://research.stlouisfed.org/fred2/series/WALCL.

16. Allan H. Meltzer, "My Response to NYT Columnist Krugman," e21, Economic Policies for the 21st Century at the Manhattan Institute, September 16, 2014.

17. Annalyn Censky, "Republicans to Fed: Forget about Jobs," CNN Money, December 3, 2010.

18. Daniel Foster, "Pence: 'End the Fed's Dual Mandate,'" *National Review*, November 16, 2010.

19. Paul Volcker, interview with author, May 2, 2011.

20. Ben Bernanke, interview with author, July 6, 2015.

21. Roger Lowenstein, "Imagine: The Fed Dead," *New York Times*, May 1, 2011.

22. John B. Taylor, "The Dangers of an Interventionist Fed," *Wall Street Journal*, March 29, 2012.

23. Ibid.

24. David Blanchflower, interview with author, August 18, 2015.

25. Kevin Warsh, "The Federal Funds Rate in Extraordinary Times," Remarks at the Exchequer Club Luncheon, Washington, DC, May 21, 2008.

26. Blanchard, Dell'Ariccia, and Mauro, "Rethinking Macroeconomic Policy."

27. Paul Volcker, "A Little Inflation Can Be a Dangerous Thing," *New York Times*, September 18, 2011.

28. "NGDP Targeting Will Not Provide a Volcker Moment," Free Exchange, *Economist*, November 1, 2011.

29. Ben S. Bernanke, "Monetary Policy and the Housing Bubble," Remarks at the Annual Meeting of the American Economic Association, Atlanta, Georgia, January 3, 2010.

30. "Strip Club's 'Art Nights' Fail to Skirt Nudity Ban," *Times* wire report, April 6, 2005, http://articles.latimes.com/2005/apr/06/nation/na-briefs6.5.

31. Ben S. Bernanke, interview with author, July 6, 2015.

32. Simon Johnson, interview with author, July 27, 2015.

33. Barry Eichengreen et al., "Rethinking Central Banking."

34. Simon Johnson, interview with author, July 27, 2015.

Index

value:
aggregate, 107–8
decreases in, 17, 20–21, 24
intrinsic, 6, 11, 15, 16–17, 24, 36–38,
106, 141, 268, 271, 273
prediction of, 18, 273–74
relative, 110
store of, 11–12, 16–17, 21, 147–49, 150,
264, 265–66, 272, 274, 277
transfer of, 267
Van Buren, Martin, 165
Vanguard, 198
Varoufakis, Yanis, 243
Velde, François, 270, 278
Venezuela, 25, 276
Versailles Treaty (1919), 137
Vietnam War, 177
Virginia, 159, 160
Virginia Gazette, 160
Visa, 179, 278, 302
Volcker, Paul, xv, 82, 94n, 95, 100, 102,
103, 137, 138, 149, 158, 177–78,
184–85, 221, 282, 287, 295, 296,
299, 300
Volcker Rule, 100

wages, 11, 20, 28, 29, *30*, 31, 56, 57–58,
81, 92, 93–94, 95, 118, 136, 175, 207,
208, 218–19, 224, 225, 233–35, 237,
242, 258
Wall Street, 163, 181–86, 197, 198–99,
301–5
Wall Street Journal, 10–11, 101, 119, 146,
213, 221, 222, 269, 272, 279, 297
Wal-Mart, 255, 257
wampum, 155–57, 263
War of 1812, 164
Warren, Earl, xv
Warren, Elizabeth, 74–75, 283
Warsh, Kevin, 200, 298
Washington, George, 8, 38, 55–56, 160,
161–62
Washington Post, 246

wealth:
accumulation of, 4, 32, 91, 252–54
collective, 23, 84
definition of, xviii–xix, 7, 155–57
hoarding of, 4–5, 34, 37–38, 147–49,
188–89, 216n
loss of, 4–5, 12, 193
welfare benefits, 57, 275
Wen Jiabao, 33, 254
Western Union, 268, 278, 280
"What Did the Fed Chief Say?," 85
White, Harry Dexter, 173
White Star Line, 85n
Why We Should Leave the Euro, 242
wine exports, 123
Winklevoss, Cameron and Tyler, 271
Wolf, Martin, 151
women's lingerie, 40–41, 51
won (North Korean currency), 3–7,
128–29
World Bank, 112, 133, 241
World War I, 135, 136, 137, 139n, 228, 237
World War II, 19–20, 21, 23, 135, 139,
158, 172, 173, 174, 228, 230, 287n
Wright Brothers, 228

Xinhua news agency, 248

Yap island, 263–68
Yellen, Janet, xv, 83–84, 86, 89, 90, 91, 97,
207, 287
yen, xviii, 14, 18, 53, 106, 108–9, 113, 115,
133, 146, 215, 219, 250, 273
yuan, xvi–xvii, xix, 4n, 14, 112, 118, 248,
249–50, 251, 254–62, 304

"zero bound" rates, 36, 218, 289–90, 294
zero interest rate policy (ZIRP), 218
Zimbabwe, *12*, 14, 19, 20–21, 24, 29,
38–39, 55, 83, 86, 143–44, 157, 211,
219, 221, 223
"zombie firms," 216–17
Zweig, Jason, 148